N

| 0 | 200 Miles |
| 0 | 300 Kilometers |

AMERICAN HORTICULTURAL SOCIETY

WHAT
PLANT
WHEN

LONDON, NEW YORK, MUNICH, MELBOURNE, DELHI

Writers **Martin Page**, with Andrea Loom
New edition revised and updated by **Simon Maughan**

DK LONDON
Senior Editor **Helen Fewster**
Senior Art Editor **Elaine Hewson**
Database Manager **David Roberts**
Managing Editor **Esther Ripley**
Managing Art Editor **Alison Donovan**
Production Editor **Joanna Byrne**
Production Controller **Mandy Inness**
Associate Publisher **Liz Wheeler**
Art Director **Peter Luff**
Publisher **Jonathan Metcalf**

North American Editors **Kate Johnsen, Rebecca Warren**
AMERICAN HORTICULTURAL SOCIETY
David J. Ellis, Mary Yee, Caroline Bentley, Eileen Powell

DK INDIA
Editor **Nidhilekha Mathur**
Designer **Nitu Singh**
DTP Operator **Anurag Trivedi**
Managing Editor **Suchismita Banerjee**
Managing Art Editor **Romi Chakraborty**
DTP Manager **Sunil Sharma**

First American edition, 2003 published as *Plants for Every Season*
This American edition, 2011

Published in the United States by DK Publishing
375 Hudson Street, New York, New York 10014

12 13 14 15 16   10 9 8 7 6 5 4 3 2 1
001—180269—June/2011

Published in Great Britain by Dorling Kindersley Limited.
A catalog record for this book is available from the Library of Congress.

ISBN 978-0-7566-7558-5

Printed and bound by Star Standard Industries Pte Ltd, Singapore.

DK books are available at special discounts when purchased in bulk for sales promotions,
premiums, fund-raising, or educational use. For details, contact: DK Publishing Special Markets,
375 Hudson Street, New York, New York 10014 or SpecialSales@dk.com.

Discover more at
www.dk.com

CONTENTS

USING THE GUIDE

The aim of this book is to help you to select plants for your garden that will provide color and interest throughout the year. There are seven chapters, based on the six seasons of the gardening year, plus a final section suggesting plants that offer year-round interest. This "All Seasons" chapter will help you to choose some plants that give shape and structure to the garden, or that have evergreen foliage. They may be used to create a permanent framework into which other flowering plants can be introduced.

It will come as no surprise to learn that the largest chapters relate to late spring and to early and late summer, but you may be interested to discover how many plants are in flower at other times of year. Use this book to plan ahead so your garden has fall interest as well as color in the winter and early spring.

In each chapter the plants have been divided into color categories— white, pink, red, purple, blue, green, yellow, and orange—and then presented in alphabetical order. Some may flower over a long period or have several seasons of interest, but here they are placed in the season in which they make

the most significant impact. So a flowering cherry may have found its way into "Fall" due to its attractive foliage, while pyracanthas may be grown for their early summer flowers as well as their bright clusters of winter berries.

SYMBOLS USED

Sun/Shade Preferences/Tolerances

☼ Full sun

◑ Partial shade; either dappled shade or shade for part of the day

● Full shade

Soil Moisture Preferences/Tolerances

◊ Well-drained soil

◖ Moist soil

◆ Wet soil

NB *Where two symbols appear from the same category, the plant is suitable for a range of conditions.*

f Fragrant flowers or aromatic leaves.

USDA HARDINESS ZONE RATINGS
A plant's generally accepted cold tolerance is given as a range (for example, Z5-8), based on the system developed by the US Department of Agriculture. See the front endpaper.

AHS HEAT ZONE RATINGS
A plant's generally accepted heat tolerance is given as a range (for example, H9-1), based on the AHS Heat Zone Map. See the back endpaper.

PLANNING YOUR GARDEN

I t is a good idea to plan before you plant by making a rough drawing of your existing garden and plotting in various permanent plants and features like paths, patio, or shed. Computer programs are available to help you visualize how your garden will look, but a sheet of graph paper and a pencil can give the same results at a much lower cost. Hard landscaping, such as paths and patios, should be done before the garden is planted. It is also important to think about your garden's use, whether you need space for entertaining or areas for pets and children to play. Once your priorities are established, you can turn to the plants.

SELECT IN ORDER

Start by choosing trees and shrubs. These provide the permanent backbone of the garden. Boundary hedges or mixed shrub screens give shelter from wind, privacy, and buffer noise. Specimen shrubs and especially trees need enough room to develop unhindered. They can grow to a large size, so it is usually better to plant one or two modest specimens and allow them to grow naturally rather than spoil their appearance by heavy pruning or removing them after a few years.

Once these long-term plants are in place, you can turn your attention to the small shrubs and herbaceous perennials. Often simplicity is the key. Rather than using lots of different plants, it is better to plant groups of three or five of the same variety, which will merge together and create more impact. The final elements are the bulbs and annuals, all of which give instant color in their first year, and are invaluable for filling gaps. Hardy annuals can be sown and bulbs can be naturalized under trees and in grass.

YEAR-ROUND INTEREST

The seasons do not begin and end at set times. It depends on the climate where you live, your garden situation, and the weather. In mild years, flowers start to open one or two weeks earlier than in others; summers can be brought to an abrupt halt by severe drought or an unseasonable frost.

To achieve year-round interest in the garden, start by choosing a few plants for winter, when the choice is most limited: perhaps a tree with

Dual purpose
Bergenias are easygoing ground cover plants for sun or light shade. This one has bright pink spring flowers and the foliage colors in the winter.

interesting bark or a cluster of winter-flowering shrubs and some early bulbs. Then select for early spring and fall; some plants will double up with spring flowers and bright fall tints. Move on to make your selection for late spring before looking through the summer sections. Consider planting a few containers for each season; again there is a huge choice for the summer, but varieties of plants like pansies bloom throughout the year.

COLOR

Many people enjoy lots of color, but some of the most appealing borders, containers, or garden areas have a color theme. You might choose shades of one color, but this can be dull, or use a limited palette. White and pastel colors are cool and show up well at dusk— good near a patio or path. Blues and mauves are hazy and give a sense of distance, whereas hot reds, oranges and yellows appear closer.

ASSESSING YOUR SITE

Planting a new garden can be an exciting prospect, but before you rush to the garden center, it is wise to assess your site by testing the soil and identifying areas of sun and shade. If your site is bare, one way of finding out what grows well in your area is to look at what succeeds in neighboring gardens, or ask at the garden center. Try to select plants that suit the conditions rather than fighting against nature; this helps to prevent expensive disappointments, and the plants will be healthier and need less attention.

If you have acquired a garden that is well established, try to control your enthusiasm and observe it for a year. In doing so,

Focal points
The variegated *Yucca gloriosa* is an excellent architectural plant and provides a strong focus in a border in well-drained, sunny gardens. It may also be grown in containers.

you discover its hidden delights, such as bulbs, and see how plants perform through the seasons. Only then should you consider changes. If possible, keep established trees for the maturity they give, but smaller plants can be moved, ideally in the early spring.

TESTING THE SOIL

The soil is critical in determining which plants will grow well in your garden, and you need to establish its characteristics. Sandy soil is free draining, low in nutrients, and feels gritty as you rub it between your fingers. At the other extreme is clay soil, which is smooth and malleable when handled. It is nutrient rich, but sticky when wet, becomes rock hard when dry, and often has poor drainage. The ideal soil is moist and well-drained, retaining water, but without becoming waterlogged. Soil conditions are easy to ameliorate. Sandy soils can be improved by adding plenty of well-rotted manure or garden compost on a regular basis. Clay soil may be lightened by deep digging, adding grit and organic matter such as garden compost or leaf mold.

To test whether your soil has poor drainage, dig a hole about 3ft (1m) square and fill it with water.

If the water has not drained away within a few hours, the site drains poorly. You then have the option of growing moisture-loving plants and perhaps creating a bog garden or installing sub-surface drainage.

You should also test the pH of your soil to find out whether it is acid or alkaline. Soil-testing kits are available from most garden centers, and this simple test can save you money in the long term, since some plants, like many heathers and rhododendrons, will only thrive on acid or neutral soil.

EXPOSURE

The orientation of your house and garden is another important factor that determines which plants grow best. In a north-facing garden the area close to the house will always be shady, and it is likely to be cold and windy in the winter. This limits the choice of plants to those that are hardy and tolerate shade. South-facing gardens are more sheltered but can be hot in the summer, so unless you plant shade trees, confine your choice to sun lovers. Southwest-facing gardens are ideal because they offer full sun and some shade throughout the year. In windy situations it advisable to plant a sheltering hedge or screen.

CARING FOR PLANTS

All perennials, especially trees and shrubs, need well-prepared sites. Dig the soil, remove all traces of perennial weeds, and incorporate plenty of well-rotted organic matter. Although most plants are sold in containers throughout the year, deciduous trees and shrubs, including roses, are best planted in the dormant season between late fall and early spring, when the soil is neither frozen or sodden. Conifers and evergreens are best left until spring. Plant herbaceous perennials in the fall, while the soil is still warm, or (better for plants of borderline hardiness) in the spring.

PLANTING

Water plants in containers an hour or two before transplanting them; after planting, water again. Then cover the root area, particularly around shrubs and trees, with a thick mulch of organic matter or composted bark to conserve soil moisture and suppress weeds. Make sure they never go without water in dry periods during the first year, or two or three years for shrubs and trees. Bulbs are normally planted in the fall, but some are planted in the spring.

They need a well-drained site and, as a general rule, plant them at twice their depth.

AFTERCARE

In the spring remove winter debris, clearing away the dead growth of perennials and cutting back ornamental grasses when new shoots begin to show. Weed and prick the bare soil of beds and borders with a fork to aerate, being careful not to pierce emerging bulbs. Rake in balanced fertilizer and then, when the soil is moist and temperatures rising, mulch with organic matter. Insert supports so they will be covered by the new foliage of perennials.

Once frosts are over, bedding and tender plants, such as dahlias, gladiolus, begonias, and cannas can be put out, but be prepared to cover them with fabric in case temperatures fall at night.

Deadheading is the main job for summer: it keeps plants neat and stimulates the development of new buds and more flowers. Containers and hanging baskets will need daily watering and feeding every 10-14 days unless a slow-release fertilizer was added at the time of planting.

Water plants in borders, particularly those recently planted. Irrigate thoroughly to encourage deep roots; watering little and often results in surface roots, and exposes plants to drought and damage.

In the fall the remains of annuals can be cleared away and perennials cleaned up for the winter. Perennials with hollow stems like delphiniums and lupines should be cut down to the ground, but others including grasses and those not entirely hardy, like kniphofias, are better left intact for protection. These and shrubs of borderline hardiness benefit from a protective mulch of straw or loose leaves in all but mild areas; keep it in position throughout the winter. Move tender plants under glass for the winter, and lift dahlias, begonias, cannas, gladiolus to store in a cool frost-free place over the winter.

Repeat performance
Large herbaceous borders are glorious during the summer. Deadhead plants regularly to extend the display.

EARLY SPRING

Winter's cold grip seems to loosen as the bulbs begin to flower. Their growth initially can be quite slow, but the first warm day stirs them from their slumber. It is often very cold at night and some early flowers, like magnolias and camellias, may be damaged in exposed areas. Keep newspaper and fleece at hand to protect plants from overnight frost.

The flowers opening beneath deciduous trees and shrubs are a feature of early spring. Bulbs, hellebores, primroses and starry blue hepaticas in mixed and woodland borders take advantage of the light before the leaves on overhanging branches unfurl. In more open sites and lawns, naturalized crocuses and daffodils make drifts of mauve, white or sunny yellow. Allow the foliage of bulbs to die down naturally wherever they grow to ensure they flower well in future.

Magnolias are the monarchs of the spring garden, but not all are large or slow to flower; 'Star Wars' blooms from a very young age, and the smaller *M. stellata*, is ideal in an urban garden. Other trees and shrubs in blossom at this time are fragrant corylopsis and daphnes, early-flowering apricots and cherries (*Prunus*), and the tangled shoots of Japanese quince (*Chaenomeles*).

FOLIAGE FOUNDATIONS

Dramatic foliage is always an asset. The bright purple-red leaves of *Photinia x fraseri* 'Red Robin' stand out like beacons in spring sunshine, and it makes an unusual hedge. Many pieris, such as 'Wakehurst', also boast brilliant red leaves but they turn shades of pink and cream before maturing to green.

Hellebores have flowers in a wide range of subtle colours, but *Helleborus foetidus* also makes a valuable foliage plant, adding height and structure to the garden at the start of the year.

Anemone blanda 'White Splendour'

PERENNIAL

A spreading plant with knobby tubers and irregularly lobed leaves, the petals of the flowers are white with a pink tint underneath. It enjoys a sunny spot and well-drained soil and will quickly spread to form a large clump. Plant the tubers in the fall at a depth of about 3in (8cm) and then leave them undisturbed to root.

☼ ◊   Z4–8 H8–1

‡ to 4in (10cm) ↔ to 6in (15cm)

Erica arborea var. *alpina*

EVERGREEN SHRUB

This attractive tree heather bears masses of fragrant flowers from the end of the winter to midspring. Perfect for adding height to a rock or heather garden, this variety prefers to be grown in full sun in well-drained, slightly acidic soil but will tolerate mildly alkaline conditions. The first year after planting, prune back by about two-thirds after flowering to form a bushy plant. After that further pruning is not necessary.

☼ ◊ *f*   Z9–10 H10–9

‡ to 6ft (2m) ↔ to 34in (85cm)

Erica x *darleyensis* 'White Glow'

EVERGREEN SHRUB

The Darley Dale heath is compact and bushy with fine, lance-shaped leaves. Masses of white flowers with reddish-brown tips appear in the late winter and early spring. It benefits from a sunny location and well-drained, preferably acidic soil, although slightly alkaline soils are acceptable. Trim off the previous season's growth after it has flowered to keep the plant neat.

☼ ◊   Z7–8 H8–7

‡ to 10in (25cm) ↔ to 20in (50cm)

Helleborus x *hybridus*

PERENNIAL

These hybrid hellebores have leathery, green leaves. The nodding flowers are white, pink, green, or purple and are often covered with small red spots. Vigorous, variable plants, they prefer heavy, moist, neutral or alkaline soil that is rich in organic matter. They will tolerate full sun but are best planted in the dappled shade of a woodland border or beneath the branches of deciduous trees or shrubs. Although they regularly self-seed, the best plants are purchased from specialty nurseries.

☼ ☀ ◑   Z6–9 H9–6

‡ ↔ to 18in (45cm)

Hyacinthus orientalis 'White Pearl'

BULBOUS PERENNIAL

The large, pure white, rather waxy, bell-shaped flowers of this bulbous plant are intensely fragrant and emerge in the early spring on stiff stems among bright green leaves. Plant the bulbs at a depth of 4in (10cm), about 3in (8cm) apart, in sun or partial shade in deep, well-drained fertile soil, and group them in clumps or use in a bedding design. Bulbs planted in pots of bulb fiber can be forced into flower early to create an indoor show for the winter months.

☼ ☀ ◊ *f*　　　　　Z5–9 H9–1

‡ to 10in (25cm) ↔ to 3in (8cm)

Leucojum vernum

BULBOUS PERENNIAL

The spring snowflake is one of the earliest bulbs to bloom. Leafless stalks produce one or two green-tipped, white flowers amid clumps of strap-shaped, glossy green leaves. For the greatest impact, plant groups of bulbs in moist soil, rich in organic matter in the partial shade below deciduous trees or shrubs. Propagate by division in the spring, or sow seed in the fall.

☀ ◊　　　　　Z4–8 H9–3

‡ to 6in (15cm) ↔ to 4in (10cm)

Lysichiton camtschatcensis

PERENNIAL

The white skunk cabbage bears large, white, hooded flowerheads in the early spring. Large, dark green leaves follow shortly after, which eventually grow taller than the flowers. The thick roots require deep, permanently moist, fertile soil so it is not suitable for growing in containers, but it can be used beside a pond as a marginal plant or planted in a bog garden. Allow space for clumps to develop and the leaves to expand.

☼ ☀ ◊ ◊   Z5–9 H9–1

‡ to 30in (75cm) ↔ to 24in (60cm)

Magnolia stellata

DECIDUOUS SHRUB

The star magnolia is a vigorous and free-flowering shrub or tree, suitable for even the smallest of gardens. Left to its own devices it forms a broad-spreading shrub, covered in the winter with fat, silky-haired flower buds. The star-shaped spring flowers open on bare branches and are composed of numerous narrow, white petals. Plant this magnolia in a sheltered location in sun or light shade and moist, well-drained, fertile soil. It requires no pruning.

☼ ☀ ◊ ◊   Z5–9 H9–5

‡ to 10ft (3m) ↔ to 12ft (4m)

Magnolia stellata 'Waterlily'

DECIDUOUS TREE

The star magnolia is a fairly compact tree that is suitable for smaller gardens. Just ensure it has sufficient space to spread its branches. 'Waterlily' bears an abundance of pure white, slightly fragrant flowers in the late spring. These are made up of numerous straplike petals. This magnolia needs a sunny or partially shaded spot and moist, well-drained soil.

☼ ❂ ◊ ◗ *f*   Z5–9 H9–5

↕ to 10ft (3m) ↔ to 12ft (4m)

Narcissus 'Cheerfulness'

BULBOUS PERENNIAL

An attractive, early-flowering daffodil with white outer petals that surround clusters of smaller petals in the center. The long-lasting blooms have a strong fragrance and are good for cutting. For maximum visual impact, plant the bulbs in bold groups in the late summer to early fall in well-drained, fertile soil. The bulbs should be planted at one-and-a-half times their depth below the soil surface.

☼ ◊ *f*   Z3–9 H9–1

↕ to 16in (40cm) ↔ to 6in (15cm)

Narcissus 'Merlin'

BULBOUS PERENNIAL

The blooms of this dainty daffodil
are good for cutting and have pure
white, rounded petals and a flat,
cup-shaped, yellow trumpet with
a reddish-orange rim. It prefers a
sunny location and well-drained
soil and flowers in the middle of
the spring. The bulbs should be
planted as for 'Cheerfulness' (*see
opposite*) in an herbaceous border,
or it can be grown in grass and left
to naturalize.

☼ ◊   Z3–9 H9–1

↕ to 18in (45cm) ↔ to 6in (15cm)

Narcissus 'Thalia'

BULBOUS PERENNIAL

This vigorous daffodil will form large
clumps and is suitable for naturalizing
in the border or rock garden. Deep,
long-lasting, funnel-shaped flowers
with milky-white petals, often with
three or more blooms per stem, are
produced in the early to midspring.
They also make excellent cut flowers.
Plant the bulbs as for 'Cheerfulness'
(*see opposite*) in a sunny location and
well-drained, fertile soil.

☼ ◊   Z3–9 H9–1

↕ to 14in (35cm) ↔ to 6in (15cm)

Narcissus triandrus
BULBOUS PERENNIAL

Angel's tears is a dwarf narcissus that bears nodding, pale cream flowers with reflexed petals and rounded cups. The leaves are green and strap-shaped. A small-growing plant, it performs well in containers and will naturalize, if the conditions are right, in a sunny rock garden or raised bed in well-drained soil. There is also a white-flowered variety, *albus*. Plant the bulbs as for 'Cheerfulness' (*see p.18*).

☼ ◊　　　　　　　　　　Z3–9 H9–1

‡ to 10in (25cm) ↔ to 3in (8cm)

Prunus 'Snow Goose'
DECIDUOUS TREE

This small, flowering cherry tree bears white to very pale pink blossoms from early to mid-spring. The rest of the year it is a narrow, upright deciduous tree. This type of cherry is not grown for its fruit, but the fall leaf color can be spectacular when the leaves turn from green to orange and yellow before they fall. Its compact size and narrow style make it good for small gardens. It is suitable for most soil types, including clay and limestone and does best in full sun.

☼ ◊ ◖　　　　　　　　　Z6–8 H8–5

‡ to 20ft (6m) ↔ to 10ft (3m)

Prunus spinosa

DECIDUOUS TREE

Blackthorn is nature's answer to the barbed wire fence. A vigorous shrub or small tree, it has star-shaped, white flowers that open on bare branches in the early and midspring. The branches are armed with sharp thorns, and it makes a superb, impenetrable hedge. It bears purple fruit, or sloes, in the fall, which can be used to make a tasty liqueur. It grows well in full sun on moist, well-drained soils and can be cut back hard in the early spring. Hedges can be pruned at any time.

☼ ◊ ◐   Z5–9 H9–5

‡ to 15ft (5m) ↔ to 12ft (4m)

Pulmonaria **'Sissinghurst White'**

PERENNIAL

The leaves of this lungwort are elliptic and covered with small white spots. The flowers are pale pink when in bud and open in the spring to form pure white, funnel-shaped blooms. It makes good ground cover and is ideal for planting beneath deciduous trees in organic, moist but well-drained soil. Cut back after it has flowered to encourage fresh foliage. To keep the plant vigorous, it is a good idea to divide and replant it every few years.

☼ ☼ ◊ ◐   Z6–8 H8–6

‡ to 12in (30cm) ↔ to 24in (60cm)

Sanguinaria canadensis 'Plena'

PERENNIAL

Bloodroot is aptly named because its fleshy roots exude a red sap when cut. The white spring flowers, often tinted pink on the reverse, are succeeded by waxy, heart- or kidney-shaped, grayish-green leaves that provide excellent ground cover in damp, shaded spots. Divide large clumps after flowering.

☀ ☀ ◐   Z3–9 H9–1

‡ to 6in (15cm) ↔ to 12in (30cm)

Tulipa biflora

BULBOUS PERENNIAL

Well suited to a sunny site in a rock garden, the fragrant, star-shaped flowers of this dwarf tulip are creamy-white or ivory with bright yellow centers. The blooms are produced from the late winter and last through the early spring. Plant the bulbs in groups in the late fall in a light, fertile, well-drained soil, and leave undisturbed so clumps can develop. The bulbs like to be dry in the summer, so do not plant near plants that may need watering.

☼ ◊ *f*   Z4–7 H7–1

‡ to 4in (10cm) ↔ to 5in (13cm)

Bergenia 'Sunningdale'

EVERGREEN PERENNIAL

An early flowering plant, its deep pink spring blooms are borne on stiff red stems. The rounded, leathery leaves become bronze-colored in the fall. It should be grown in full sun or partial shade and is suitable for planting beneath bushes and deciduous trees. Propagate it by division in the spring after the flowers have finished, and remove tattered leaves at this time too.

☼ ◐ ◊ ◊   Z3–8 H8–1

‡ to 18in (45cm) ↔ to 24in (60cm)

Camellia x *williamsii* 'Donation'

EVERGREEN SHRUB

This camellia is valued for its deep pink, double flowers that appear in the late winter and persist through the spring. A vigorous, free-flowering bush, it also boasts glossy, dark green foliage. Plant it in partial shade, away from the early morning sun, in moist but well-drained, neutral or acidic soil mixed with plenty of organic matter, or grow it in containers of acidic soil mix. For perfect blooms, stand pots in an unheated greenhouse or sunroom.

◐ ◊ ◊   Z7–8 H8–7

‡ to 15ft (5m) ↔ to 8ft (2.5m)

Chaenomeles speciosa 'Moerloosei'
DECIDUOUS SHRUB

This flowering quince can be used as a free-standing bush or trained along a wall. It produces a tangle of spiny stems, covered with glossy, dark green leaves, while clusters of saucer-shaped, white and pink flowers appear in the early spring. The blooms are followed in the fall by edible, greenish-yellow fruits that can be made into jelly. Cut back after flowering if grown against a wall.

☀ ◑ ◊   Z5–9 H9–1
↕ to 8ft (2.5m) ↔ to 15ft (5m)

Chionodoxa 'Pink Giant'
BULBOUS PERENNIAL

This medium-sized, bulbous perennial produces soft pink, star-shaped flowers with white centers in the early spring. It is ideal for a rock garden or for planting beneath shrubs where the bulbs can be left to naturalize. It prefers a sunny spot and well-drained soil. Plant bulbs in the fall in groups, and propagate by dividing established clumps or by seed.

☀ ◊   Z3–9 H9–1
↕ to 10in (25cm) ↔ to 2in (5cm)

Clematis 'Apple Blossom'

CLIMBER

The glossy, dark, evergreen leaves of
this vigorous climber are accompanied
in the spring by large clusters of pink-
tinged, scented, white flowers with
deeper pink undersides that pale to
pinkish-white. It is fairly hardy but
should be planted in a sunny location
against a south- or west-facing wall in
a well-drained soil. Purchase plants
from a reputable source since there
are a lot of inferior seedlings available.
It can be pruned back after flowering
but not into old dark wood.

☼ ◊ *f*   Z7–11 H9–7
‡ to 15ft (5m)

Daphne cneorum 'Eximia'

EVERGREEN SHRUB

A low-lying shrub with small oval, dark
green leaves. The rose pink flowers are
highly fragrant and borne in clusters at
the end of the branches. To grow well, it
needs a rich soil, which should be mixed
with well-rotted garden compost or leaf
mold when planting. All parts of the
plant are harmful if ingested, and the
sap can irritate the skin on contact.

☼ ◊ *f*   Z5–7 H7–5
‡ to 4in (10cm) ↔ to 20in (50cm)

Erica x darleyensis 'Kramer's Rote'
EVERGREEN SHRUB

Bronze-tinted green foliage and bright magenta spring flowers are features of this bushy heather. It should be grown in moist but well-drained, organic or peaty soil. It prefers acidic conditions but tolerates slightly alkaline soil and is a useful ground cover plant. Trim off the previous season's growth after flowering to keep the plant neat. 'Archie Graham' is similar heather, but with mauve-pink flowers.

☼ ◊ ◑   Z7–8 H8–7
‡ to 12in (30cm) ↔ to 24in (60cm)

Hyacinthus orientalis 'Queen of the Pinks'
BULBOUS PERENNIAL

This is one of the best pink hyacinths with bright green leaves and highly fragrant flowers borne on robust stems in the spring. Plant the bulbs outside in the fall where they should flower the following year in fertile, well-drained soil at a depth of 4in (10cm) and about 3in (8cm) apart. They can be grown in informal clumps, used in a bedding plan, or grown in pots. Feed after flowering to help the bulbs build up their strength.

☼ ☀ ◊ *f*   Z5–9 H9–1
‡ to 12in (30cm) ↔ to 3in (8cm)

Magnolia x *loebneri* 'Leonard Messel'
DECIDUOUS SHRUB

A substantial bush or small tree with large, rounded leaves, in the spring it bears fragrant flowers that have a dozen lilac-pink, strap-shaped petals, the color of which is most intense during warm springs. It grows well in most soils and tolerates alkaline conditions. Plant where it has adequate space to spread since magnolias do not like to be moved. It needs no pruning.

☼ ☀ ◊ ◑ *f*   Z5–9 H9–5
‡ to 25ft (8m) ↔ to 20ft (6m)

Magnolia 'Star Wars'
DECIDUOUS TREE

This recently introduced magnolia bears massive, deep pink blooms at a very early age. It was named after the shape of the flowers, which can measure up to 12in (30cm) across, and have petals pointing in many different directions. 'Star Wars' suits most soils, and in time this vigorous plant may grow to form a medium-sized, pyramid-shaped tree. Plant where it has plenty of space to develop unhindered.

☼ ☀ ◊ ◑   Z6–9 H9–5
‡ to 30ft (10m) ↔ to 25ft (8m)

Narcissus 'Passionale'

BULBOUS PERENNIAL

This vigorous, spring-flowering daffodil has milky-white petals and a large pink cup and makes a terrific cut flower. In the late summer or early fall, plant the bulbs in well-drained, fertile soil at one-and-a-half times their depth. They will perform well in a sunny location and can be used in a border planting or a formal bedding design. Deadhead the plants after flowering, and divide large clumps after 3–5 years.

☼ ◊   Z3–9 H9–1

‡ to 16in (40cm) ↔ 6in (15cm)

Paeonia cambessedesii

PERENNIAL

The Majorcan peony is one of the first to bloom in the early spring. It has grayish-green leaves with deep red undersides and wavy margins, while the flowers have five pale magenta-pink petals and deeper pink veins. Plant it in full sun in a well-drained soil. It needs protection from late frosts and is best grown in the shelter of a south-facing wall or under a cloche in the winter.

☼ ◊   Z6–9 H8–5

‡↔ to 22in (55cm)

Prunus 'Accolade'

DECIDUOUS TREE

A beautiful flowering cherry,
'Accolade' has mid-green leaves that
turn orange-red in the fall before they
drop. Its wide-spreading branches
produce clusters of three semidouble,
pale pink flowers in the early spring,
which emerge from deep pink buds. It
needs a sunny location and should be
planted in deep, well-drained, fertile
soil. This tree does not require pruning.

☼ ◊   Z4–9 H9–1
↕↔ to 25ft (8m)

Prunus mume '*Beni-chidori*'

DECIDUOUS TREE

Japanese apricots are spreading trees,
suitable for small gardens. The almond-
scented, double, deep pink flowers of
'Beni-chidori' appear in the late winter
or early spring and become paler as they
age. The tree may also later produce
small orange fruit, which look a little
like apricots but are very bitter. Plant
it in a sunny, sheltered location where
frost is unlikely to damage the blooms
in deep, well-drained, fertile soil. No
pruning is required.

☼ ◊ *f*   Z6–8 H8–6
↕↔ to 28ft (9m)

Prunus 'Okame'
DECIDUOUS TREE

The toothed, oval, dark green leaves of this flowering cherry turn brilliant shades of orange and red in the fall. The cup-shaped, single, deep pink flowers are produced in the early spring. It is best planted in a sunny location in a deep, moist, well-drained, fertile soil and will not need to be pruned.

☼ ◐ ◑   Z5–8 H8–5
↕ to 30ft (10m) ↔ to 25ft (8m)

Prunus x *yedoensis*
DECIDUOUS TREE

The beautiful Yoshino cherry grows to form a medium-sized, round-headed tree with gently arching branches. In the early spring it bears clusters of five or six single, pale pink flowers that gradually fade to white in the sun. It should be planted in deep, fertile, well-drained soil. No pruning is required.

☼ ◐   Z5–8 H8–3
↕ to 50ft (15m) ↔ to 30ft (10m)

Tulipa 'Pink Beauty'
BULBOUS PERENNIAL

Tulips are an invaluable addition to the spring border and are used to create a spectrum of color relatively early in the year. There is plenty of choice with different varieties bursting into flower throughout spring and early summer, providing a range of sizes, colors, and flower shapes. The deep pink petals, with a brush stroke of white, and cup-shaped flowers of 'Pink Beauty' appear early, and it makes a particularly eye-catching bedding plant.

☼ ◊   Z4–7 H7–1

↕ to 24in (60cm) ↔ to 5in (13cm)

Viola x *wittrockiana* Ultima Series
PERENNIAL

These violets, more commonly known as pansies, have been widely hybridized to produce a range of long-flowering plants. The Ultima Series start to flower in the winter and continue through the spring. They are available in a range of bright colors, including pink, and make a superb choice for brightening up the garden during the early spring. Use them as bedding or in tubs and window boxes, and grow them in a sunny spot in fertile, well-drained soil.

☼ ◊   Z8–11 H9–1

↕ to 9in (23cm) ↔ to 12in (30cm)

Camellia japonica '*Coquettii*'

EVERGREEN SHRUB

In the early to midspring the arching stems of this slow-growing shrub are covered with deep red, semidouble or double flowers. It makes an elegant addition to a border and will complement plantings in a woodland garden, but it can also be grown as a specimen in containers or in an open space. Choose a partially shaded spot out of the early morning sun in moist, but well-drained, organic acidic soil. Use an acidic soil mix in containers.

☀ ◐ ◊ ◊   Z7–9 H9–7

‡ to 28ft (9m) ↔ to 25ft (8m)

Chaenomeles x *superba* '*Crimson and Gold*'

DECIDUOUS SHRUB

The deep crimson flowers with golden yellow anthers are produced by this Japanese quince from the spring to early summer and are often followed in the fall by yellow-green fruit. Its wide, spreading style makes it a useful shrub for ground cover, planting against walls or in a border, or it can be grown as an informal, low flowering hedge. Quinces trained against walls or used as hedges should be cut back after flowering.

☀ ◊   Z5–9 H9–5

‡ to 3ft (1m) ↔ to 6ft (2m)

Corydalis solida 'George Baker'

PERENNIAL

This attractive tuberous perennial has deeply dissected, grayish-green leaves. In the spring it produces bright red with a hint of orange, tubular flowers. Plant it in a rock or gravel garden in full sun or partial shade in well-drained, fertile soil. 'George Baker' can be divided in the fall if clumps become too large.

☼ ☀ ◌   Z5–7 H7–3

↕ to 10in (25cm) ↔ to 8in (20cm)

Erysimum 'Blood Red'

PERENNIAL

Although perennial wallflowers are often grown as biennial bedding plants and planted in combination with tall-stemmed tulips. Left alone, they will live for several years but can become woody and leggy with age. This variety has vivid, deep red flowers in the spring and is ideal for growing against a dry wall or to brighten up the front of a sunny border or raised bed. Plant it in the fall in very well-drained, neutral to alkaline soil.

☼ ◌   Z3–7 H7–1

↕↔ to 12in (30cm)

Helleborus orientalis Early Purple Group

PERENNIAL

Often sold under its former name of *H. atrorubens*, this variable hellebore flowers very early in the year. It has deep maroon, saucer-shaped, pendent flowers that emerge from late winter to early spring. The deciduous, palm-shaped leaves are mid-green, flushed with purple. It thrives on rich, moist, well-drained soil, and its preference for partial shade makes it a good choice for a shrub border or a woodland garden.

☀ ◊ ♦   Z4–8 H8–3

‡ to 12in (30cm) ↔ to 18in (45cm)

Paeonia tenuifolia

PERENNIAL

Fernleaf peonies are among the earliest species to flower, producing beautiful deep red, single flowers in the spring, amid dark green, ferny leaves. There are also other types with double white, red, and pink flowers. Plant it in a sunny place in well-drained, sandy soil. This delicate-looking plant may be grown in rock or gravel gardens or an herbaceous border.

☼ ◊   Z3–8 H8–1

‡↔ to 28in (70cm)

Photinia x fraseri 'Red Robin'

EVERGREEN SHRUB

The glossy young leaves of this bush are bright purplish-red and turn dark bronze-green as the season progresses. From midspring it produces clusters of small white flowers. It prefers fertile, well-drained soil; the foliage is easily damaged by cold winds so plant it in a sunny, sheltered location. It can be used as a hedging plant or free-standing shrub. Trim hedges two to three times a year to keep up the display of bright young foliage.

☼ ☀ ◊ ◖   Z7-9 H9-7
‡↔ to 15ft (5m)

Pieris formosa 'Wakehurst'

EVERGREEN SHRUB

The brilliant red young foliage of this beautiful shrub gradually turns various shades of pink and creamy-white and then finally becomes dark green. Small, urn-shaped, white flowers open in midspring and hang in pendent clusters. 'Wakehurst' does best in semi-shade and needs protection from cold winds and frost. Plant it in moist, slightly acidic, organic soil in a shrub or woodland border. Prune lightly after it has flowered to maintain its shape.

☼ ☀ ◊ ◖   Z6-9 H9-6
‡ to 15ft (5m) ↔ to 12ft (4m)

Primula 'Crescendo Bright Red'

EVERGREEN PERENNIAL

Polyanthus are vigorous primulas that should be planted in the fall for a spring bedding display. They produce rosettes of evergreen leaves and often start flowering at the end of the winter. The Crescendo Series is available in a range of bright colors, including vivid red. Polyanthus prefer a sunny location but will tolerate some shade and should be planted in reasonably fertile, moist but well-drained soil.

☼ ◑ ○ ◑   Z5–7 H7–5
‡ to 6in (15cm) ↔ to 12in (30cm)

Pulmonaria rubra 'Redstart'

PERENNIAL

This attractive herbaceous perennial has bright green, hairy leaves and funnel-shaped, coral-red flowers. It begins to flower early in the year with blooms often appearing in the middle of the winter and continuing into the spring. It forms a loose clump and provides excellent ground cover for damp shady locations. Young plants are vigorous and should be divided after four or five years. Cut back after flowering to encourage a flush of bright new foliage.

◑ ◑ ◑   Z5–8 H8–3
‡ to 16in (40cm) ↔ to 36in (90cm)

Tulipa 'Red Riding Hood'
BULBOUS PERENNIAL

The bright red flowers of this striking tulip have black marks at the base of the petals, and its lance-shaped leaves are strongly marked with purple stripes. Plant bulbs in the late fall in a sunny location in well-drained, fertile soil in a border or rock garden, where they can be left for years. Alternatively, plant them in containers and move the bulbs out into the garden after flowering. For a bold bedding display, plant with a deep-yellow tulip, such as 'Yokahama'.

☼ ◊   Z4–7 H7–1
↕ to 8in (20cm) ↔ to 6in (15cm)

Tulipa 'Apeldoorn'
BULBOUS PERENNIAL

Darwin tulips, such as 'Apeldoorn', are easy to grow and their rounded flowers look equally at home in spring bedding displays as they do when used as cut flowers. 'Apeldoorn' has scarlet-red flowers with black centers, surrounded by yellow. Plant bulbs in late fall in a sunny spot in well-drained, fertile soil. It looks superb when partnered with a yellow tulip, such as 'Daydream'.

☼ ◊   Z4–7 H7–1
↕ to 24in (60cm) ↔ to 5in (13cm)

Anemone blanda '**Violet Star**'

PERENNIAL

Spring-flowering anemones make superb border plants, particularly for partially shaded areas under shrubs and trees. Their sunny, daisylike flowers are a welcome sight, and if planted in groups of three or five, they soon spread and naturalize. 'Violet Star' has purple-blue flowers, but consider mixing with other types, such as 'White Splendour' or the magenta 'Radar', to vary the display. Choose a reasonably drained site, and enrich the soil with organic matter.

☀ ☼ ◊ ◗   Z4–8 H8–1
↕↔to 6in (15cm)

Crocus tommasinianus

BULBOUS PERENNIAL

This crocus gives the impression of being rather delicate, but its slender appearance is deceptive. It produces purple, violet, or lilac flowers from the late winter to early spring and grows easily from seed. Choose a sunny spot with well-drained soil, and in the fall plant the corms in groups to create drifts of color at the front of a border, or to naturalize in short grass.

☀ ◊   Z3–8 H8–1
↕ to 4in (10cm) ↔to 1in (2.5cm)

Iris 'George'

BULBOUS PERENNIAL

Dwarf irises are often overlooked when it comes to the early spring garden, but clumps of these bulbs are well worth planting every fall in borders, pots, containers, or window boxes—anywhere where they will be noticed in the garden in the late winter and early spring. 'George' is a rich purple, but try mixing different varieties: colors vary from pale blue to deep, velvety purple, often with yellow crests on the petals. They are ideal underneath larger plants, tolerant of the dry, partially shaded conditions.

☼ ☀ ◊ ◐   Z5–8 H8–4

‡ to 4in (10cm) ↔ to 3ft (1m)

Primula auricula 'Adrian'

EVERGREEN PERENNIAL

A rosette-forming perennial, this alpine auricula has fleshy pale green leaves and in the spring bears beautiful flowers with purple-blue petals, slightly paler edges, and a white eye. Alpine auriculas are extremely hardy plants but will do best in a sunny or partially shaded site in moist, well-drained soil. Grow them in a rock or gravel garden, raised beds, an unheated greenhouse, or in containers with a well-drained potting mix.

☼ ☀ ◊ ◐   Z4–8 H8–1

‡↔ to 4in (10cm)

Rhododendron dauricum

EVERGREEN SHRUB

The leaves of this semi-evergreen shrub are green with a dark brown underside. It starts flowering in the late winter when the funnel-shaped, bright pinkish-purple blooms bring a dramatic burst of color to an otherwise gloomy garden. Plant it in a sunny site in well-drained, organic, acidic soil, and mulch it annually with leaf mold or bark chips. This very hardy rhododendron is suitable for exposed sites and may be used to create an informal screen.

☼ ☀ ◊ ◑   Z4–8 H8–1
↕↔ to 5ft (1.5m)

Rhododendron 'Praecox'

EVERGREEN SHRUB

This is among the first rhododendrons to bloom, flowering from the late winter and continuing into the early spring. It is normally evergreen but sheds some of its leaves during the winter. The flowers are pinkish-purple and appear in clusters of two or three. Although generally hardy, the flowers may be damaged by severe frost. It makes a spectacular flowering hedge but is equally at home in the border. Plant in full sun or partial shade in moist, well-drained, acid soil.

☼ ☀ ◊ ◑   Z6–8 H8–6
↕↔ to 4½ft (1.3m)

Tulipa humilis
Violacea Group
BULBOUS PERENNIAL

This early, spring-flowering tulip has large purple, star-shaped flowers with a bright yellow blotch at the base of the petals and narrow grayish-green leaves. Plant bulbs in the late fall in a sunny location in light, well-drained soil. It is ideal for the rock garden or creates a colorful display in raised beds. Leave it undisturbed so clumps can build up; they like to be dry during the summer.

☼ ◊   Z9–7 H7–1

↕ to 10in (25cm) ↔ to 5in (13cm)

Viola odorata
PERENNIAL

Sweet violets may be small, but their very aromatic bluish-purple or white flowers will perfume the garden from the late winter and throughout the early spring. They self-seed and will quickly become established, particularly when allowed to naturalize in a woodland setting or by deciduous shrubs. Plant in a sunny location or in dappled shade in well-drained, organic soil. They can also be divided and replanted in the spring.

☼ ☀ ◊ *f*   Z6–8 H8–6

↕ to 8in (20cm) ↔ to 12in (30cm)

Ajuga reptans 'Multicolor'
EVERGREEN PERENNIAL

This technicolor version of the blue bugle is an excellent evergreen perennial for ground cover, spreading freely by means of its rooting stems. Dark blue flowers appear on upright stems. While these are a key feature from spring to early summer, the glossy leaves extend the interest much further, particularly early in the year. The foliage color is an unusual mix of purple, green, brown, and white. It is invaluable for border edging under shrubs and robust perennials. It does well in full sun or partial shade.

☼ ☀ ◊ ◖   Z3–9 H9–1
‡ to 5in (12cm) ↔ to 18in (45cm)

Anemone blanda 'Atrocaerulea'
PERENNIAL

The deep-blue, daisylike flowers of this anemone are striking when naturalized in grass or beneath the bare branches of deciduous trees. It is a low, clump-forming plant, which also makes it a suitable plant for the front of a border. Plant the knobby tubers in the fall in full sun or partial shade and organic, well-drained soil.

☼ ☀ ◊   Z4–8 H8–1
‡ to 4in (10cm) ↔ to 6in (15cm)

Anemone nemorosa 'Robinsoniana'

PERENNIAL

This wood anemone bears numerous pale lavender-blue flowers with a light gray underside of the petals. The midgreen leaves die back after flowering. It is a low, creeping plant, useful for underplanting or naturalizing. A native of European woods, it does best in a woodland situation, but it will grow in most locations, given dappled or partial shade and a moist but well-drained, organic soil.

☀ ◊ ◑   Z4–8 H8–1

‡ to 6in (15cm) ↔ to 12in (30cm)

Aubrieta 'Cobalt Violet'

PERENNIAL

A mat-forming perennial with masses of small, hairy leaves. In the spring it produces profuse quantities of small, violet-blue flowers and is ideal for trailing over the edge of a raised bed or stone wall or for growing in a rock garden. Plant it in fertile, well-drained, neutral or alkaline soil, and cut back with pruners after flowering to keep it neat.

☀ ◊   Z5–7 H7–5

‡ to 4in (10cm) ↔ to 8in (20cm)

Chionodoxa luciliae
BULBOUS PERENNIAL

In the spring glory-of-the-snow bears up to three violet-blue, star-shaped flowers, each with a small white eye. It comes from the stony slopes of Turkey and is most at home in a rock garden, raised bed, or naturalized under deciduous trees or at the front of a border. Plant the bulbs in the fall in a sunny spot in well-drained soil. Established clumps benefit from a mulch with well-rotted compost in the fall.

☼ ◊   Z3–9 H9–1

‡ to 4in (10cm) ↔ to 2in (5cm)

Clematis 'Frances Rivis'
CLIMBER

A deciduous, early flowering climber with mid-blue, bell-shaped flowers in the spring to early summer and feathery seedheads in the fall. It is very hardy and tolerates fairly exposed locations. Prune it back after flowering. Provide support in the form of wires or trellis attached to a wall or fence, or train it over an arch or tripod. Grow it in well-drained, fertile, preferably alkaline soil with the roots in shade and its head in the sun.

☼ ☀ ◊   Z4–9 H9–6

‡ to 10ft (3m) ↔ to 5ft (1.5m)

Hepatica nobilis var. *japonica*

PERENNIAL

This is a slow-growing perennial that retains its leathery leaves during most winters. The star-shaped flowers with blue-purple, pink, or white petals that open in the spring sit above three small, dark green leaves. It requires partial shade and moist, organic soil and is well suited to a woodland setting or a shady border.

☀ ◊   Z5-8 H8-4

‡ to 3in (8cm) ↔ to 5in (12cm)

Hyacinthus orientalis 'Blue Jacket'

BULBOUS PERENNIAL

This is one of the best blue flowered hyacinths with wonderfully fragrant, navy blue blooms. The petals have a waxy texture and purple veins. Plant it in the fall in deep, well-drained, fertile soil in sun or partial shade. Hyacinths are perfect for creating colorful spring bedding displays and are also useful container or window box plants. Grow them either outside or forced in bowls of bulb fiber for display in the home.

☀ ☀ ◊ *f*   Z5-9 H9-1

‡ to 10in (25cm) ↔ to 3in (8cm)

Iris histrioides 'Major'
BULBOUS PERENNIAL

The vivid blue flowers of this vigorous dwarf iris open in the early spring. Its lower petals are marked with a bright yellow ridge, which is surrounded by dark blue lines, and the square leaves are very short at the beginning of the year but extend to 12in (30cm) after flowering. Plant it in a sunny location in well-drained, fertile soil. Dwarf irises are an excellent choice for the rock garden, raised beds, or containers.

☼ ◊   Z5–8 H8–4
↕ to 4in (10cm) ↔ to 3in (7cm)

Iris 'Joyce'
BULBOUS PERENNIAL

A perfect plant for a rock garden, this is a reticulata iris that flowers very early in the spring. It bears sky blue flowers with a bold yellow flare down the center of the petals. Plant bulbs in the fall in a sunny location and well-drained, neutral or alkaline soil. 'Joyce' will also grow well in containers or troughs of gritty, soil-based potting mix. Keep the bulbs on the dry side during the summer.

☼ ◊   Z5–8 H8–5
↕ to 5in (12cm) ↔ to 3in (7cm)

Iris 'Katharine Hodgkin'

BULBOUS PERENNIAL

This vigorous dwarf iris flowers from
the late winter. Its upper petals are
covered with fine, deep blue veins,
while the broad lower petals have a
yellow center and are heavily marked
with blue lines and speckles. Plant
the bulbs in the fall, and grow this
iris on a sunny bank or in other well-
drained locations, making sure the
bulbs are kept on the dry side during
the summer. It prefers neutral or
slightly alkaline soil.

☼ ◊   Z5–8 H8–5

‡ to 5in (12cm) ↔ to 3in (7cm)

Iris reticulata 'Cantab'

BULBOUS PERENNIAL

Another reticulata iris (*see* 'Joyce',
opposite), this one has pale blue flowers
with slightly darker lower petals, marked
by a deep yellow crest. The blooms start
to appear in the late winter. These iris
are vigorous, but the bulbs often divide
after it has flowered and then take a
couple of years to grow large enough to
bloom again. Plant the bulbs in the fall in
a sunny location and fertile, well-drained
soil, such as in a rock garden or trough
filled with gritty soil-based potting mix.

☼ ◊   Z5–8 H8–5

‡ to 5in (12cm) ↔ to 3in (7cm)

Muscari armeniacum
BULBOUS PERENNIAL

The grape hyacinth is one of the most widely grown spring-flowering bulbs, used to create spectacular bedding displays and in the border. Each stem carries a dense spike of small, deep blue flowers above narrow, bright green leaves. In the right conditions it spreads quickly and may occasionally be invasive. The bulbs can become overcrowded and will benefit from division in the summer every few years. Plant bulbs in the fall in full sun in fertile, moist but well-drained soil.

☀ ◊ ◊   Z4–8 H8–1

‡ to 8in (20cm) ↔ to 4in (10cm)

Omphalodes cappadocica
EVERGREEN PERENNIAL

The forget-me-not-like flowers of this evergreen are azure blue with white eyes and appear on slender stems in the early spring. It has creeping roots and forms clumps of heart-shaped, slightly hairy leaves and makes ideal ground cover for shady places. Grow it in full or partial shade and slightly moist, well-drained, organic, fertile soil.

☀ ◊ ◊   Z6–8 H8–6

‡ to 8in (20cm) ↔ to 10in (25cm)

Pulmonaria 'Lewis Palmer'
PERENNIAL

This deciduous ground-cover plant has slightly hairy, lance-shaped leaves with greenish-white spots and small funnel-shaped flowers that are pink when they open in the spring and then turn a vibrant blue. Lungwort should be grown in organic, moist soil in partial or full shade. It attracts bees and makes an excellent choice for a wildlife garden, or use it to enhance a shady woodland or shrub border. Cut back or shear after it has flowered to refresh the foliage.

☼ ☀ ◑ Z5–8 H8–5

↕ to 14in (35cm) ↔ to 18in (45cm)

Puschkinia scilloides
BULBOUS PERENNIAL

The pale blue, bell-like flowers of this bulbous perennial are set off by a fine blue line down the center of each petal. Its compact spikes make an attractive addition to the rock garden or a shrub border. Plant it in a sunny or partially shaded site in well-drained, fertile soil.

☼ ☀ ◔ Z3–9 H9–1

↕ to 6in (15cm) ↔ to 2in (5cm)

Rhododendron
Blue Tit Group
EVERGREEN SHRUB

A remarkably compact rhododendron, which in the early spring bears abundant, small, funnel-shaped, grayish-blue flowers. Its leaves are initially yellow-green but darken to a mid-green color as the plant matures. Like many dwarf rhododendrons, 'Blue Tit' will bloom well in a container or in a rock or gravel garden, given full sunshine and moist, well-drained, acid soil or acidic soil mix.

☀ ◐ ◊ ◗   Z5–8 H8–5
↕↔ to 3ft (1m)

Scilla bifolia
BULBOUS PERENNIAL

This is a distinctive early spring flowering bulb that looks wonderful naturalized in grass or under deciduous shrubs and trees. It has narrow strap-shaped, bright green leaves and star-shaped flowers, borne on one side of the stem. This species has blue or violet-blue flowers, but there are also varieties with white ('Alba') and pink ('Rosea') blooms. Plant it in fertile, organic, well-drained soil in full sunshine or partial shade.

☀ ◊   Z3–8 H8–1
↕↔ to 6in (15cm)

Scilla mischtschenkoana

BULBOUS PERENNIAL

The pale blue, bell-shaped flowers of this bulbous perennial have a dark blue stripe down the center of each petal. They are carried above broad, strap-shaped arching leaves on short stems, which grow longer as the flowers open in the early spring. Naturalize it in grass, or plant in a rock or gravel garden or raised bed in a sunny location with well-drained soil. Plant bulbs in the fall.

☼ ◊　　　　　　　Z4–7 H9–6

 ‡ to 4in (10cm) ↔ to 2in (5cm)

Scilla siberica 'Spring Beauty'

BULBOUS PERENNIAL

This bulbous perennial has small spikes of bell-shaped, violet-tinted, deep blue flowers arranged on one side of the stem. Ideal for a rock garden or a mixed herbaceous border beneath deciduous shrubs or trees, it prefers sandy, well-drained, fertile soil in slight shade or full sun. Divide large clumps after flowering during the summer. Plant bulbs in the fall.

☼ ☀ ◊　　　　　　Z5–8 H8–5

 ‡ to 8in (20cm) ↔ to 2in (5cm)

Euphorbia characias subsp. *wulfenii*

EVERGREEN SHRUB

A large rounded bush with grayish-green leaves. The huge, globe-shaped heads pocked with small, yellow-green flowers appear from the early spring. It is ideal for the back of a border, gravel garden, or gaps in paving, but needs a sunny spot and well-drained soil. Buy young plants from a reliable source to avoid inferior, less brightly colored seedlings. Cut out the old flowerheads in the fall, and wear gloves since the sap may cause an allergic skin reaction.

☼ ◊   Z7–10 H10–7

↕↔ to 4ft (1.2m)

Euphorbia myrsinites

EVERGREEN PERENNIAL

This is a sprawling evergreen perennial, suitable for planting in a rock or gravel garden, in gaps in paving, at the edge of a raised bed, or on a stone wall. The fleshy, blue-green leaves are arranged in a spiral around the stems. In the spring the stems are topped with clusters of yellowish-green flowers, which turn a grayish-pink as they fade. Plant it in full sun in well-drained soil. It may self-seed if the deadheads are not removed after flowering.

☼ ◊   Z5–8 H8–5

↕ to 3in (8cm) ↔ to 8in (20cm)

Helleborus argutifolius

EVERGREEN PERENNIAL

The Corsican hellebore bears bright
green, slightly nodding, cup-shaped
flowers from the late winter to early
spring. Its evergreen leaves are divided
into three toothed, grayish-green leaflets.
One of the largest hellebores, it grows
best on moist, well-drained, alkaline or
neutral soil in full sun or partial shade.
Choose it for a mixed border, or allow
to naturalize in a woodland setting
since it self-seeds freely.

☼ ☀ ◑ ◊   Z6–9 H9–6

‡ to 24in (60cm) ↔ to 18in (45cm)

Helleborus foetidus

EVERGREEN PERENNIAL

The stinking hellebore is a vigorous,
clump-forming perennial with dark
evergreen, deeply divided, somewhat
leathery leaves; it is named for the
unpleasant smell that emanates from
them when they are crushed. The bell-
shaped, slightly fragrant, green flowers
are produced in clusters on tall, erect
stems from the late winter to early
spring. Equally at home in full sunshine
or partial shade, it can be planted in
a variety of situations in the garden
and is happy in moist, alkaline soils.

☼ ☀ ◑ ◊ *f*   Z6–9 H9–6

‡↔ to 18in (45cm)

Acacia dealbata
EVERGREEN TREE

The silver wattle is a fast-growing tree that brings a little Australian sunshine into the garden when it is most needed by way of its bright yellow, scented, pom-pom flowers. The gray, evergreen leaves are very finely divided into scores of tiny leaflets. It is slightly tender, so choose a warm and sheltered site. The subspecies *subalpina* is more shrublike but hardier, with paler flowers, and the compact, but very free-flowering variety 'Gaulois Astier' is ideal for a container in sun.

☼ ◊ *f*   Z9–11 H11–1
‡ to 50ft (15m) ↔ to 50ft (15m)

Anemone x *lipsiensis*
PERENNIAL

The pale, sulfur-yellow flowers of this carpet-forming wood anemone appear in the spring. Its dark green leaves are deeply toothed and lie close to the soil surface. Best grown in partially shaded locations beneath deciduous trees or shrubs, this natural hybrid prefers a organic, well-drained soil and will tolerate alkaline or limestone-based soils.

☼ ◊ ◖   Z5–8 H8–5
‡ to 6in (15cm) ↔ to 12in (30cm)

Anemone ranunculoides

PERENNIAL

This spreading perennial received its name because of its similarity to the buttercup. It has deeply divided, mid-green leaves and bright yellow flowers with five or six petals. It enjoys a site in partial shade and is ideal for a mixed border or naturalizing in a woodland or wild garden. Plant it in moist but well-drained, organic soil.

☀ ◊ ◊   Z4–8 H8–1

↔ to 8in (20cm)

Caltha palustris

PERENNIAL

The kingcup, or marsh marigold, is a vigorous, clump-forming perennial with serrated, glossy, green leaves. It is one of the earliest aquatic plants to come into bloom and has large, bright golden yellow flowers. Thriving in full sun in wet soil, it makes an excellent choice for a bog garden but may also be grown in a permanently moist border or shallow water at the edge of a pond, contained in a perforated basket. 'Flore Pleno' is slightly less vigorous and has double yellow flowers.

☀ ◊ ◊   Z3–7 H7–1

‡ to 24in (60cm) ↔ to 18in (45cm)

Corylopsis pauciflora
DECIDUOUS SHRUB

This bushy, deciduous plant produces small, very fragrant, pale yellow, bell-shaped flowers in the spring. The young leaves appear after the flowers and are pink when they open but turn green as they age. Although other corylopsis species tolerate alkaline conditions, *C. pauciflora* requires acid soil. Given plenty of room, it will grow into a pleasing, spreading shape and enhance a woodland garden or a shrub border in dappled shade. The flowers can be damaged by hard frosts.

☀ ◐ ◑ *f*   Z6–9 H9–6
‡ to 5ft (1.5m) ↔ to 8ft (2.5m)

Corylus avellana 'Aurea'
DECIDUOUS SHRUB

In the late winter and early spring this decorative hazel bears dangling yellow catkins. It is a broad, spreading shrub or small tree with bright yellow-green, sharply toothed leaves, and in the late summer the rounded hazelnuts are favorites of squirrels. A relatively small variety, it is suitable for a shrub border and contrasts well with the hazel, *C. avellana* 'Purpurea', which has purple leaves.

☀ ☀ ◐   Z3–9 H9–1
‡↔ to 15ft (5m)

Crocus chrysanthus '**E.A. Bowles**'

BULBOUS PERENNIAL

This dainty crocus has deep lemon-yellow, goblet-shaped flowers with purple feathering on the outer petals. The leaves are dark green with a white stripe. Plant the bulbs in groups in the fall in well-drained soil at the front of a sunny border for an early splash of spring color, or grow in raised beds and containers.

☼ ◊   Z3–8 H8–1

↕ to 3in (7cm) ↔ to 2in (5cm)

Crocus '**Cream Beauty**'

BULBOUS PERENNIAL

A compact, spring-flowering crocus with rich cream-colored flowers that darken at the base to a greenish-gold and have a golden throat. Plant the bulbs as for 'E.A Bowles' (*see above*) in a sunny location in well-drained, gritty soil. It does well in a rock garden and may also be naturalized in grass.

☼ ◊   Z3–8 H8–1

↕ to 3in (7cm) ↔ to 2in (5cm)

Edgeworthia chrysantha
DECIDUOUS SHRUB

In the spring the paper bush never fails to impress passersby, who always pause to admire its unusual bunches of small yellow flowers that appear on the branch tips. Resembling daphne flowers, they are also scented, which makes them attractive to winter insects. The bark is reddish-brown and the leaves pale green. It must be sheltered to thrive with moist but well-drained, organic, clay soil. Plant in full sun. The leaves will drop in hot weather if the soil gets too dry, and late frosts can be damaging.

☼ ◊ ◊ *f*   Z8–10 H10–8
↕↔ to 5ft (1.5m)

Eranthis hyemalis
PERENNIAL

The winter aconite begins flowering in the late winter and continues into the early spring. Its bright yellow blooms perch on a ruff of deeply divided, leaflike bracts. Ideal for naturalizing in grass and woodland borders, it creates a colorful carpet beneath deciduous trees and shrubs. Plant the tubers in the fall in fertile, moist, well-drained soil that does not dry out in the summer. Large clumps can be divided after it has flowered.

☼ ◊ ◊   Z4–9 H9–1
↕↔ to 4in (10cm)

Erythronium 'Pagoda'
BULBOUS PERENNIAL

This dog's-tooth violet bears drooping clusters of up to five sulfur-yellow flowers in the spring. A vigorous plant with mottled, glossy green leaves, it is suitable for planting beneath bushes or in the shade of a woodland garden in moist, organic, well-drained soil. Plant the bulbs in the fall. Large clumps can be divided after the leaves have died; replant immediately to prevent the bulbs from drying out.

☀ ◐ ◊ ◊   Z4–9 H9–1

↕ to 14in (35cm) ↔ to 8in (20cm)

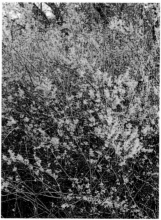

Forsythia x *intermedia* 'Lynwood'
DECIDUOUS SHRUB

Forsythias are free flowering, medium-sized shrubs, the upright branches of which are covered with large, bright yellow flowers during the spring before the leaves unfurl. Plant them in a row to create a spectacular hedge, or grow one as a freestanding bush in a border. Cut hedges and prune back the shoots of shrubs after flowering to promote new growth and flowers the following year. Choose a site in full sun or light shade in fertile, well-drained soil.

☀ ◐ ◊   Z6–9 H9–6

↕↔ to 10ft (3m)

Hyacinthus orientalis 'City of Haarlem'

BULBOUS PERENNIAL

With spikes of primrose-yellow, waxy, bell-shaped flowers, this is one of only a few yellow hyacinths. Its intense scent makes it an appealing houseplant when forced into bloom early in the winter months. Outdoors, it looks wonderful in spring bedding displays and needs full sun and free-draining soil. Forced bulbs grown for indoor display should be fed regularly after flowering and then planted outside. The flowers will be smaller in subsequent years.

☼ ◊ *f*   Z5–9 H9–1

‡ to 10in (25cm) ↔ to 3in (8cm)

Iris danfordiae

BULBOUS PERENNIAL

This is an extremely attractive dwarf iris with bright yellow spring flowers. It is best considered as a disposable plant, because although it flowers well in the first season, the bulb then splits into tiny bulblets that rarely bloom again. Ideal for containers, troughs, or raised beds, the bulbs should be planted in the late summer or early fall in a sunny location and well-drained soil.

☼ ◊   Z5–8 H8–4

‡ to 4in (10cm) ↔ to 2in (5cm)

Narcissus cyclamineus
BULBOUS PERENNIAL

This early-flowering daffodil produces deep yellow, vase-shaped flowers with strongly swept-back petals and bright green leaves. Grow in a sunny location in well-drained, neutral to acidic soil. It makes an excellent choice for containers, a woodland border, or for naturalizing in grass. Plant bulbs as for 'Ambergate' (*see opposite*).

☼ ◊   Z3–9 H9–1
‡ to 8in (20cm) ↔ to 3in (8cm)

Narcissus 'February Gold'
BULBOUS PERENNIAL

A widely grown daffodil, 'February Gold' is extremely vigorous and in the early spring produces nodding, large, golden-yellow flowers with slightly swept-back petals. The flowers are set off by mid-green, strap-shaped leaves. It is suitable for planting in borders or for naturalizing in grass. Plant bulbs as for 'Ambergate' (*see opposite*).

☼ ◊   Z3–9 H9–1
‡ to 12in (30cm) ↔ to 3in (8cm)

Primula palinuri

EVERGREEN PERENNIAL

This is an attractive, rosette-forming primula with fleshy, spoon-shaped leaves. In the early spring it bears often large, cowslip-like clusters of slightly fragrant yellow flowers. Grow it in a sunny site in reasonably fertile, moist, well-drained, preferably alkaline soil, and mulch with grit, a finely ground rock product often sold as a feed additive for poultry. It suffers in cold, wet winters, so it is best to grow it in pots containing a very free-draining, organic-rich soil mix.

☼ ◊ ◑ *f*   Z6–8 H8–1

↕↔to 12in (30cm)

Primula vulgaris

EVERGREEN PERENNIAL

The primrose is often regarded as the true harbinger of spring. Each stem of this rosette-forming perennial carries up to 25 single, pale yellow flowers with an orange spot at the base of each petal. It prefers a location in partial shade and moist, well-drained, organic soil. An excellent plant for growing in containers, it will also be happy in woodland and shrub borders and rock gardens. Propagate it from seed, or divide during the early spring or fall; never collect bulbs from the wild.

☼ ◊ ◑   Z4–8 H8–1

↕ to 8in (20cm) ↔to 14in (35cm)

Ranunculus ficaria 'Brazen Hussy'

PERENNIAL

This celandine boasts glossy, bronze-colored, heart-shaped leaves that lie close to the ground and bright yellow flowers that emerge in the spring. Given wet soil in the winter, it can be invasive, but it is easy to remove unwanted plants, and it dies back completely during the summer. It will thrive in partial shade and moist soil in a shrub border, at the base of a hedge, or in a woodland setting. The variety *R. aurantiacus* bears single orange flowers.

☼ ◖   Z4–8 H8–1

‡ to 2in (5cm) ↔ to 8in (20cm)

Rhododendron lutescens

SEMI-EVERGREEN SHRUB

An attractive, medium-to-large semi-evergreen shrub with bronzy-green leaves, its clusters of primrose-yellow flowers start to open in the late winter and continue into the early spring. Ideal for brightening up a shady woodland location, it should be protected from cold winds and planted in moist, well-drained, organic, acidic soil. Mulch it annually with leaf mold or bark chips.

☼ ☀ ◖ ◖   Z7–9 H9–7

‡↔ to 15ft (5m)

Salix caprea 'Kilmarnock'
DECIDUOUS TREE

Salix caprea is usually a tall, vigorous tree, but the Kilmarnock willow rarely exceeds a height of 6ft (2m), making it ideal for planting in small gardens or large containers. It has a weeping style and bears numerous rounded yellow catkins in the late winter and early spring. Plant it in deep, moist, well-drained soil in a sunny spot. The branches can become congested; in the late winter prune out surplus ones, and remove any shoots that appear on the trunk.

☼ ◐ ◊ ◖   Z6–8 H8–6
↕↔ to 6ft (2m)

Tulipa kaufmanniana
BULBOUS PERENNIAL

The flowers of the water-lily tulip have narrow, pointed, yellow or cream petals that are tinted orange or pink on the outside. Its tall stems bear up to five blooms, carried above lance-shaped grayish-green leaves. A long-lived bulb, it is best grown in a rock garden. Plant the bulbs in the late fall in full sun in fertile, well-drained soil at a depth of at least 4in (10cm).

☼ ◊   Z4–7 H8–1
↕ to 10in (25cm) ↔ to 6in (15cm)

Tulipa urumiensis
BULBOUS PERENNIAL

The cheerful, golden yellow, star-shaped flowers of this low-growing tulip appear in the early spring above a rosette of waxy green leaves; much of its stem remains below ground. Its petals are flushed with green and red on the outside. Grow it in a raised bed or rock garden where clumps can develop undisturbed and the soil is well-drained and fairly dry in the summer. Plant the bulbs in the late fall at a depth of about 4in (10cm).

☼ ◊   Z4–7 H8–1

‡ to 6in (15cm) ↔ to 5in (13cm)

Valeriana phu 'Aurea'
PERENNIAL

The main feature of valerian is its bright butter-yellow foliage, which appears in the early spring. The leaves turn lime-green after a few weeks and then mature to mid-green. After these exciting foliage effects, its small white summer flowers are rather unimpressive. It provides the perfect foil for blue spring flowers in the herbaceous border. Plant it in full sun in any reasonably fertile, well-drained soil, and divide it in the fall.

☼ ◊   Z5–9 H9–5

‡↔ to 15in (38cm)

LATE SPRING

As temperatures rise and light levels increase, the garden seems to burst into life. Blossom buds open, and spring-flowering shrubs with bright new foliage add colour and scent to borders and beds. As the bulbs continue their seasonal show, leaves of perennials pushing through the soil hint at the drama to come.

However, new growth can be damaged by late frosts, so keep fleece handy to protect young plants, and do not be tempted to put out tender bedding or summer displays in containers too early. Slugs and snails are about in the damp conditions and the succulent shoots of many perennials are vulnerable to their attentions. You can entice birds, toads and hedgehogs to help control the pests by providing a pond; with candelabra primulas and other moisture-loving plants in bloom there is plenty for the gardener to enjoy too.

Easy-growing, blossoming ornamental cherries (*Prunus*) and crab apples (*Malus*) are great value; many will reward you with fall interest. The massive blooms of tree peonies make real impact, but the rhododendrons, with hundreds to choose from, and flowers in almost every shade provide the most excitement. If you lack the acid conditions they enjoy, try early-flowering clematis and fragrant lilacs (*Syringa*).

ALPINES AND BULBS

The rock garden is at its best as the season begins, studded with jewel-like flowers of arabis, gold dust (*Aurinia*), spring gentians and small species tulips. Tulips also dominate late spring bulb displays with larger-flowered varieties creating bold swathes of colour in beds, borders and containers. Clumps of quamash (*Camassia*), and tall, stately crown imperials (*Fritillaria imperialis*) make imposing centrepieces in the border, while the delicate snake's head fritillary (*Fritillaria meleagris*) is superb naturalized in grass.

Arabis alpina subsp. *caucasica* 'Variegata'

EVERGREEN PERENNIAL

This mat-forming plant has rosettes of grayish-green, spoon-shaped leaves. The white, fragrant flowers are produced in loose clusters over a long period from the late spring to early fall. It is very hardy and will flower well when grown in poor, well-drained soil in full sun, making it ideal for a rock or scree garden. 'Variegata' has the added bonus of green leaves with pale yellow margins.

☼ ◊ *f*   Z4–8 H8–1
↕↔ to 6in (15cm)

Camassia leichtlinii

BULBOUS PERENNIAL

The white type of quamash flowers from the late spring to early summer. The tall flowering stems make a striking addition to the herbaceous border. The bulbs should be planted at a depth of 4in (10cm) in the fall. Plant quamash in groups in deep, moist but well-drained soil in a sunny or slightly shaded location. In areas prone to long periods of frost, place a thick mulch over the area where the bulbs have been planted.

☼ ☀ ◊ ◑   Z4–11 H11–1
↕ to 5ft (1.5m) ↔ to 12in (30cm)

Cassiope 'Edinburgh'

EVERGREEN SHRUB

This compact plant has small, slightly hairy, dark green leaves and in late spring produces nodding white bell-shaped flowers with swept-back tips, similar to those of the lily-of-the-valley. It is closely related to heathers and needs a moist, fertile, acid soil in a sunny or partially shaded spot. Cassiopes are fairly demanding plants, requiring the right growing conditions to flourish; 'Edinburgh' is the least particular.

☼ ◑ ◊   Z2–6 H6–1

↕↔ to 8in (20cm)

Choisya ternata

EVERGREEN SHRUB

The Mexican orange blossom is a fast-growing shrub with dark green, glossy foliage. The leaves are aromatic when crushed. It produces a profusion of fragrant, star-shaped, white flowers in the late spring—a light pruning after these have faded can often stimulate a second flush of blooms in the fall. Grow in fertile, well-drained soil in full sun. SUNDANCE has bright yellow-green leaves.

☼ ◊ *f*   Z8–10 H10–8

↕↔ to 8ft (2.5m)

Convallaria majalis
BULBOUS PERENNIAL

Lily-of-the-valley is a delightful spring-flowering plant with arching stems of white, sweetly scented, bell-shaped flowers that appear between the dark green leaves. It makes an ideal ground-cover plant for shady, damp situations and spreads very quickly by means of creeping roots. 'Albostriata' has gold-striped leaves, and 'Fortin's Giant' is slightly taller, growing to a height of 12in (30cm).

☀ ☀ ◑ *f*   Z2–7 H7–1
↕ to 6in (15cm) ↔ indefinite

Cornus florida 'White Cloud'
DECIDUOUS TREE

The flowering dogwood forms an attractive spreading tree that looks as if it is adorned with large white flowers in the late spring. In fact, these "blooms" comprise four creamy-white, petal-like bracts surrounding a cluster of tiny green flowers. An additional feature of this beautiful plant is the slightly twisted, green leaves which, in the fall, turn bright orange and red.

☀ ◊   Z5–8 H8–3
↕ to 20ft (6m) ↔ to 25ft (8m)

Davidia involucrata

DECIDUOUS TREE

In the late spring the branches of the pocket handkerchief tree are hung with what look like hundreds of crisp, white linen squares. These are, in fact, showy bracts that surround the tiny flowerheads. Although fully hardy, it needs shelter from strong winds. It will grow in most situations but prefers moist but well-drained, fertile soil and a sunny location. When mature it can become large, making it less suitable for small gardens.

☼ ◊ ◑   Z6–8 H8–6
‡ to 50ft (15m) ↔ to 30ft (10m)

Erythronium oregonum

BULBOUS PERENNIAL

This dog's-tooth violet forms a clump of unusual dark green leaves with paler mottling. In the spring it produces stems bearing two or three pendent flowers with creamy-white reflexed petals and yellow anthers. Suitable for a woodland garden or beneath deciduous shrubs, grow it in fertile, moist but well-drained soil. Divide clumps in the summer after the flowers have faded.

◑ ◊ ◑   Z3–9 H9–1
‡ to 14in (35cm) ↔ to 5in (12cm)

Fraxinus ornus

DECIDUOUS TREE

The manna ash makes a very good specimen tree for a medium to large garden, valued for its fluffy clusters of tiny, fragrant, creamy white flowers that cover the tree in the late spring. It has a rounded crown of divided, dark green leaves that turn dark purple before dropping in the fall. The tree thrives in most fertile, well-drained soils and will tolerate hot, dry sites. Little pruning is required; cut out any badly placed, dead, diseased, or crossing shoots in the winter.

☼ ◊ ◐ *f*   Z6–9 H9–4
↕↔ to 50ft (15m)

Halesia monticola

DECIDUOUS TREE

The fast-growing mountain silverbell grows in an attractive cone shape. In the late spring, often before the leaves emerge, white, bell-shaped blooms appear in clusters along the branches. These are followed in the summer by green, winged fruit, measuring up to 2in (5cm) long. In the fall the leaves take on a strong yellow color before falling. Plant in moist but well-drained, neutral or slightly acidic soil in a sunny or partially shaded, sheltered location.

☼ ☼ ◊ ◐   Z6–9 H9–6
↕ to 40ft (12m) ↔ to 25ft (8m)

Iris confusa
PERENNIAL

This is one of the crested irises with flattened flowers. The leaves, which are green and sword-shaped, are held in fans on bamboolike stems. In the late spring and early summer, it bears abundant, small white flowers, measuring just 2in (5cm) across. *Iris confusa* is not entirely hardy and should be grown in a sunny or slightly shaded, sheltered location. Soil should be moist and fertile. Every year mulch after flowering.

☼ ❂ ◐   Z4–10 H11–9
↕ to 3ft (1m) ↔indefinite

Magnolia wilsonii
DECIDUOUS TREE

This elegant magnolia becomes a large bush or small tree, and in the late spring and early summer produces fragrant, white flowers with a ring of crimson-red in the center. It can be damaged by frost and needs a sheltered spot in full sun or light shade. It also requires a moist, well-drained soil. As with all magnolias, give it plenty of space to develop unhindered.

☼ ❂ ◊ ◐ *f*   Z7–9 H9–7
↕↔to 20ft (8m)

Malus toringo subsp. *sargentii*

DECIDUOUS TREE

This crabapple produces a profusion of white flowers in the spring, giving rise in the fall to bright red fruit. It has dark green, three-lobed leaves. Give it a spot in full sun or light shade and, although tolerant of a wide range of soil types, it prefers moderately fertile, moist, well-drained soil.

☼ ❂ ◐ ◑ ◖   Z4–8 H8–1

↕ to 12ft (4m) ↔ to 15ft (5m)

Narcissus poeticus var. *recurvus*

BULBOUS PERENNIAL

The old pheasant's eye narcissus obtained its common name from the short, red-rimmed, yellow cup in the center of the flower. This particular variety has fragrant, long-lasting flowers with swept-back, pure white petals and greenish-yellow throats. It flowers slightly later in the spring than many other daffodils and can be grown in borders, large containers, or naturalized in grass. Plant it in well-drained soil in full sun or partial shade.

☼ ❂ ◐ *f*   Z3–9 H9–1

↕ to 14in (35cm) ↔ to 4in (10cm)

Osmanthus x *burkwoodii*

EVERGREEN SHRUB

This slow-growing shrub has oval, dark green, slightly glossy, leathery leaves. In the midspring it produces small clusters of fragrant white flowers that, on a still sunny day, will fill the garden with a sweet scent. Plant this shrub in full sun or partial shade in fertile, well-drained soil. It can be used as a hedging plant, which will need clipping once a year in the summer.

☼ ◑ ◊ *f*   Z7–9 H9–7

↕↔ to 10ft (3m)

Osmanthus delavayi

EVERGREEN SHRUB

A large, rounded, evergreen, this plant has arching stems from which hang clusters of tubular flowers in mid- to late spring. The highly, fragrant white blooms are set off by dark green, glossy, toothed foliage. Later in the year, small blue-black berries appear. Grow this bush in well-drained soil in full sun or partial shade, and protect it from drying winds. Prune it after the flowers have faded.

☼ ◑ ◊ *f*   Z7–9 H9–7

↕ to 20ft (6m) ↔ to 12ft (4m)

Paeonia suffruticosa 'Godaishu'

PERENNIAL

This decorative white tree peony is well worth searching for. It has dark green, slightly waxy leaves and large semi-double flowers with pure white, soft petals that surround yellow stamens. For the best results, plant it in well-drained soil in full sun or partial shade.

☼ ☀ ◊   Z5–8 H8–5

↕↔ to 6ft (2m)

Polygonatum x hybridum

PERENNIAL

Solomon's seal is an elegant plant with small, tubular white flowers that hang gracefully from arching green stems. It adds a touch of class to late spring herbaceous borders and woodland gardens and needs a cool, shaded location and fertile, well-drained soil. Solomon's seal may be attacked by sawfly caterpillars, which can quickly reduce the leaves to a skeleton. 'Striatum' has variegated leaves. Divide clumps in the spring.

☀ ◊   Z6–9 H9–6

↕ to 4ft (1.2m) ↔ to 3ft (1m)

Primula denticulata var. alba

PERENNIAL

Drumstick primulas have neat, globe-shaped flowerheads composed of many small blooms. This variety has white flowers, each with a bright yellow eye, although drumstick primulas also come in shades of pale lilac, pink, and deep purple. All thrive in moist, well-drained, neutral to slightly acid soil and fare best if the soil dries out a little in the summer months. They are ideal for use in an herbaceous border or among shrubs and are easy to raise from seed.

☼ ❀ ◊ ◖   Z2–8 H8–1

↕↔to 18in (45cm)

Prunus padus 'Watereri'

DECIDUOUS TREE

The bird cherry has a decorative look with spreading branches that carry pendent stems of cup-shaped, almond-scented, white flowers in the late spring. These are then followed by small black fruits, which are loved by birds. This vigorous tree should be grown in full sun or light shade in a well-drained, moist soil. The bird cherry makes an excellent specimen for the middle of a yard or in a mixed border.

☼ ❀ ◊ ◖ *f*   Z4–8 H8–1

↕to 50ft (15m) ↔to 30ft (10m)

Prunus 'Shirofugen'
DECIDUOUS TREE

One of the best flowering cherries, 'Shirofugen' would make a fine, fast-growing specimen tree for a medium to large garden. Its wide-spreading branches are covered in white blooms in the late spring. Each flower is double, packed with petals that guarantee a massive shower of white as they fall. The flowers fade to a very pale pink as they age, contrasting nicely with the fresh, copper-colored foliage. Plant in full sun.

☼ ◊ ◊   Z6–8 H8–6

↕ to 25ft (8m) ↔ to 30ft (10m)

Pyrus salicifolia 'Pendula'
DECIDUOUS TREE

An ornamental pear, 'Pendula' has attractive weeping branches covered with oval, silvery leaves. These are accompanied in mid- to late spring by clusters of creamy-white flowers. Small, green, inedible fruit may also appear in the late summer. It needs full sun and well-drained soil and can be a decorative specimen for a lawn or a mixed border.

☼ ◊   Z5–9 H9–5

↕ to 25ft (8m) ↔ to 20ft (6m)

Rhododendron 'Fragrantissimum'

EVERGREEN SHRUB

This rhododendron has highly fragrant, white, funnel-shaped, spring flowers that contrast beautifully with the slightly hairy evergreen foliage. It is suitable for mild gardens and warm sheltered sites; where frost is likely, it is better grown in a container and taken under cover for the winter. Grow it in sun or partial shade in a well-drained, acidic to neutral soil, or acidic soil mix. Outdoors, mulch generously with bark or leaf mold.

☼ ☀ ◊ ◗ *f*   Z9–10 H10–9
‡↔ to 6ft (2m)

Rhododendron 'Loderi King George'

EVERGREEN SHRUB

One of the best white rhododendrons, this slow-growing plant can grow to 12ft (4m) in height. The pale pink flower buds open in the late spring to form large trusses of white, fragrant flowers with green markings. It is best planted in a woodland garden and, like most rhododendrons, needs a moist, well-drained, acidic soil. Mulch it every year with bark or leaf mold, especially when young.

☼ ☀ ◊ ◗ *f*   Z7–9 H9–7
‡↔ to 12ft (4m)

Saxifraga 'Southside Seedling'

PERENNIAL

This saxifrage bears densely packed rosettes of pale green, spoon-shaped leaves. It flowers freely and in the late spring produces branched stems of red-centered white blooms. The leaf rosettes die after flowering. 'Southside Seedling' requires a very well-drained, slightly alkaline soil, preferably with gravel added to it, and prefers a sunny location.

☼ ◊   Z4–6 H6–1

‡ to 12in (30cm) ↔ to 8in (20cm)

Smilacina racemosa

PERENNIAL

The false spikenard is a slow-spreading plant with tall stems topped in the late spring with conical clusters of small, slightly scented, white flowers. The large leaves are also an attractive feature. To grow well, false spikenard requires a shady spot and suits a woodland garden setting or a moist shady border. It will perform well in a moist, slightly acidic soil. Divide large clumps in the spring.

☼ ◐ ◊ *f*   Z4–9 H9–1

‡ to 36in (90cm) ↔ to 18in (45cm)

Spiraea 'Arguta'

DECIDUOUS SHRUB

Known as bridal wreath because of its
arching stems that are covered in the
late spring with small, white flowers
that create a light, delicate effect. The
blooms are borne among lance-shaped,
bright green leaves. Bridal wreath is
perfect for a low hedge or in a mixed
shrub border and needs a moist, well-
drained soil in full sun. The flowers are
produced on the previous year's wood,
and the stems should be pruned back
in the early summer after flowering.

☼ ◊ ◐   Z5–8 H8–5

‡ to 6ft (2m) ↔ to 5ft (1.5m)

Syringa vulgaris 'Madame Lemoine'

DECIDUOUS SHRUB

Lilacs are large shrubs with branched,
upright stems, covered with dark green,
heart-shaped leaves. 'Madame Lemoine'
has large, cone-shaped clusters of pure
white, highly scented flowers, which
are produced in abundance during the
spring. Tolerant of pollution and most
soils, except very acid soil, it is ideal
for growing in an urban garden. If lilacs
become leggy, cut them back hard to
3ft (1m) above the ground after they
have flowered.

☼ ◊ ◐ ◗ *f*   Z4–8 H8–1

‡↔ to 22ft (7m)

Trillium grandiflorum

PERENNIAL

The great white trillium produces large flowers with three distinctive, clear white petals and bright yellow stamens, which turn pale pink as they age. The blooms contrast beautifully with the deep green leaves that will eventually form a large clump. Trilliums need moist, well-drained soil and a slightly shaded location. They are best suited to deciduous woodland but can also be used in a rock garden.

☀ ◊ ◊   Z4–7 H7–3
‡ to 15in (38cm) ↔ to 12in (30cm)

Trollius x *cultorum* 'Alabaster'

PERENNIAL

Most globeflowers have bright yellow or orange flowers, but those of 'Alabaster' are much paler. It has bowl-shaped, deep cream-colored flowers held on slim, upright stems. It will grow well in wet soil as long as it dries out slightly in the summer and is suitable for waterside plantings or bog gardens. Large clumps can be divided in the early summer immediately after flowering.

☀ ◐ ◊ ◖   Z5–8 H8–5
‡ to 24in (60cm) ↔ to 18in (45cm)

Tulipa 'White Triumphator'

BULBOUS PERENNIAL

This elegant, lily-flowered tulip
blooms in the late spring and has
pure white flowers. Plant several in
a cluster in a mixed herbaceous border,
or use in bedding plans. Alternatively,
plant a few in a large containers for a
sophisticated patio display. The bulbs
should be planted in the late fall in
full sun and fertile, well-drained soil.
In bedding displays it is often easier
to dig up the bulbs and discard them
after flowering rather than letting
the foliage die naturally.

☼ ◊   Z4–7 H7–1

↕ to 28in (70cm)

Viburnum plicatum 'Mariesii'

DECIDUOUS SHRUB

The broad-spreading branches of
this viburnum are held in several
layers, one above the other. In late
spring it bears clusters of small, fertile
flowers surrounded by sterile, saucer-
shaped flowers with large white petals.
The flowers are followed by small red
fruits, which turn black in the fall.
Plant it in a shrub border or woodland
garden in full sun or partial shade
and moist, well-drained soil.

☼ ☀ ◊ ◐   Z4–8 H8–1

↕ to 10ft (3m) ↔ to 12ft (4m)

Aesculus x *neglecta* 'Erythroblastos'

DECIDUOUS TREE

The emerging spring foliage of the aptly named sunrise horse chestnut is bright pink and later turns pale green. Just after the leaves have unfurled in the late spring, 'Erythroblastos' produces cones of pink or peach flowers. This slow-growing tree also puts on an impressive fall display with bright yellow and orange leaves. Grow it in deep, moist, well-drained soil in full sun or partial shade.

☼ ☀ ◊ ◗   Z5–8 H8–5

‡ to 30ft (10m) ↔ to 25ft (8m)

Anagallis tenella 'Studland'

PERENNIAL

This bog pimpernel forms a low mat of bright green leaves and in late spring is covered with small, lightly scented, deep pink flowers. It requires a moist, free-draining soil to survive and will die if it is allowed to dry out in the summer. Suitable for a rock garden where the soil is moist, this dainty plant can also be used as ground cover. A short-lived plant, it can be propagated by taking cuttings in the late summer.

☼ ◗ *f*   Z5–7 H7–5

‡ to ½in (1cm) ↔ to 6in (15cm)

Aquilegia vulgaris 'Nora Barlow'

PERENNIAL

This unusual aquilegia has double pink and white flowers with pale green-tipped petals, which are slightly swept back when the flower is fully open. It needs a well-drained, moist soil in full sun and makes a stunning addition to a spring herbaceous border. Plant it in bold groups of at least 3–5 plants for the best effect.

☼ ◊ ◊   Z3–8 H8–1

‡ to 30in (75cm) ↔ to 20in (50cm)

Armeria maritima 'Vindictive'

EVERGREEN PERENNIAL

Thrift is a seaside plant and will grow well in a rock garden. It forms a rounded cushion of deep green, grasslike leaves and bears large numbers of bright pink flowers in the spring. Its deep taproot allows it to survive the driest of summers, and care should be taken when weeding to avoid damage to this root, which may kill the plant. Thrift is suitable for either coastal or inland gardens, as long as it is given a sunny site and well-drained soil.

☼ ◊   Z3–9 H9–1

‡ to 4in (10cm) ↔ to 6in (15cm)

Bellis perennis
Pomponette Series
PERENNIAL

A selected form of the common daisy, this perennial is frequently grown as a biennial for spring bedding. The double pink, white, or red flowers have quill-like petals and measure up to 1½in (4cm) across. Grow in a sunny location in a well drained, fertile soil in spring bedding designs, as edging, or in pots or window boxes. Deadhead regularly to extend the flowering period.

☼ ☀ ♦ ◊   Z4–8 H8–1
↕↔ to 8in (20cm)

Clematis 'Elizabeth'
CLIMBER

Like all *Clematis montana*, this vigorous plant is perfect for growing up a large, sturdy trellis, a large, mature tree, or up wires attached to a house or boundary wall. In late spring, just as the lobed leaves unfurl, it produces masses of fragrant pink blooms along its climbing stems. It needs a sheltered situation in full sun and a well-drained soil. It may need pruning after it has flowered to keep it under control.

☼ ☀ ◊ *f*   Z6–9 H9–6
↕ to 22ft (7m)

Clematis 'Markham's Pink'

CLIMBER

Deep pink, semi-double flowers adorn
this beautiful plant in the late spring
and early summer. Not as vigorous
as many early-flowering clematis, it
is ideal for a small urban garden. It
blooms on the previous year's wood
and if necessary should be pruned after
flowering to remove any dead wood
and to keep it within bounds. This
clematis is very hardy and will tolerate
an exposed site in sun or partial shade.
It prefers well-drained soil.

☼ ☼ ◊   Z4–9 H9–3

↕ to 10ft (3m)

Clematis montana var. *rubens*

CLIMBER

This vigorous plant will soon cover
an ugly wall or climb up a large mature
tree. In late spring it produces a huge
number of single, pale pink flowers
with creamy-yellow anthers. Grow
it in free-draining soil in a sunny
or partially shaded site, and prune
it after flowering to keep it in check.

☼ ☼ ◊   Z6–9 H9–6

↕ to 30ft (10m)

Darmera peltata

PERENNIAL

The umbrella plant is a waterside plant that flowers before the large umbrella-shaped leaves emerge. Clusters of tiny, pale pink blooms, held on stout stems, are produced in the late spring. Grow it in permanently wet soil, beside a pool, or in a bog garden in a sunny or partially shaded location. In time it will spread to cover a large area.

☼ ❀ ◊ ♦   Z5–9 H9–5

‡ to 4ft (1.2m) ↔ to 24in (60cm)

Dicentra spectabilis

PERENNIAL

This elegant plant has many common names, including bleeding heart, lady's locket, and lady-in-the-bath. The leaves are pale green and deeply-lobed, and delicate pink and white heart-shaped flowers hang from long arching stems. For the best results plant it in a partially shaded location in moist, well-drained, fertile soil. In hot, dry summers it may die down early.

❀ ◊ ♦   Z3–9 H9–1

‡ to 30in (75cm) ↔ to 20in (50cm)

Epimedium x *rubrum*

PERENNIAL

This carpet-forming plant has attractive, heart-shaped leaves tinted reddish-brown in the spring as they unfurl, which then color yellow in the fall. In the late spring it bears small crimson-pink, star-shaped flowers with long yellow spurs. Epimediums need a partially shaded location and moist but well-drained, fertile soil. Propagate clumps by division in the early spring or fall.

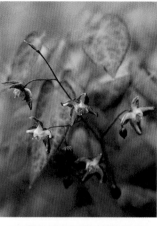

☀ ◊ ◐   Z4–8 H8–1
↕↔ to 12in (30cm)

Erica australis

EVERGREEN SHRUB

The Spanish heath produces small, bell-shaped, purple-pink flowers from midspring to the beginning of summer and has dark green, needlelike foliage. It is not completely hardy, so plant it in a sheltered location. Young plants benefit from some winter protection until they are established. Although tolerant of alkaline conditions, it prefers slightly moist, acidic or neutral soil and full sun.

☼ ◐   Z9–10 H10–9
↕ to 6ft (2m) ↔ to 3ft (1m)

Erythronium dens-canis
BULBOUS PERENNIAL

The dog's-tooth violet has distinctive purple, pink, or white pendent flowers with reflexed petals. The decorative oval-shaped, green leaves have pinkish-brown mottling on the upper surface. Dog's-tooth violets can be planted in woodland or grass and grow best in well-drained, fertile soil in partial shade. To propagate, dig and divide the clumps of bulbs after flowering, and replant them immediately in fertile soil.

☀ ◊   Z3–9 H9–1

‡ to 10in (25cm) ↔ to 4in (10cm)

Geranium cinereum 'Ballerina'
PERENNIAL

This semi-evergreen, mound-forming, hardy geranium, or cranesbill, has deeply divided gray-green leaves. One of the first cranesbills to bloom in the late spring, it bears many cup-shaped, pinkish-purple flowers with distinctive purple veins and dark eyes. It makes a good rock- or gravel-garden plant and flowers over a long period. Plant it in full sun in well-drained soil, and divide plants in the spring.

☀ ◊   Z5–9 H9–5

‡ to 4in (10cm) ↔ to 12in (30cm)

Kolkwitzia amabilis 'Pink Cloud'

DECIDUOUS SHRUB

One of the prettiest of the spring flowering shrubs, *Kolkwitzia* deserves its common name—the beauty bush. It has arching branches, clothed with tapering, dark green leaves. In the late spring it bears clusters of bell-shaped, deep pink flowers with yellow-tinted throats. Plant it in a sunny site in fertile, well-drained soil. Although hardy the new leaves may be damaged by late frosts, so it is best to choose a sheltered site in cold or exposed gardens.

☼ ◊   Z5–9 H9–5

↕ to 10ft (3m) ↔ to 12ft (4m)

Lamium orvala

PERENNIAL

This pretty variety of deadnettle forms clumps of triangular, mid-green leaves. The hooded flowers are bronzy-pink, and borne in tiers around the stem. It needs shade and a moist, well-drained soil to do well and is never invasive, unlike other deadnettles. There is also an attractive white-flowered form called 'Album'.

◐ ◊ ◊   Z4–8 H8–1

↕↔ to 12in (30cm)

Lewisia cotyledon
EVERGREEN PERENNIAL

Lewisias are rosette-forming alpines from the mountains of North America. The funnel-shaped flowers of this species are produced in vivid pink, white, red, apricot, or yellow and bloom from the late spring to early summer. Unlike many lewisias, which need to be grown under glass, *L. cotyledon* can be planted outside in crevices, a drystone wall, or a rock garden. Plant it in full sun and a very well-drained, fertile soil.

☼ ◊   Z3–8 H8–1
‡ to 12in (30cm) ↔ to 6in (15cm)

Magnolia x *soulangeana*
DECIDUOUS TREE

This is probably the most widely grown of all magnolias. Fast growing, it will quickly form a small tree with wide spreading branches. The goblet-shaped flowers are pink to pinkish-purple, but there are also forms with white and reddish-purple blooms. The flowers appear from midspring, before the leaves. Select a planting location in full sun or partial shade where the tree has plenty of space to develop its spreading shape. It also needs a moist, well-drained soil.

☼ ◐ ◊ ◖   Z5–9 H9–5
‡↔ to 20ft (6m)

Malus floribunda
DECIDUOUS TREE

The Japanese crabapple grows into a large shrub or small, spreading tree with graceful, pendent branches. The flower buds are red, opening in the midspring to a very pale pink with small fruits ripening yellow in fall. It does well in any soil conditions, as long as the site is not waterlogged. Grow this crabapple in sun or partial shade, and use it as a specimen tree in a lawn or in a mixed border.

☼ ◑ ◊   Z4–8 H8–1
‡↔to 30ft (10m)

Oxalis adenophylla
PERENNIAL

This mat-forming, tuberous perennial has grayish-green leaves divided into heart-shaped leaflets. In the late spring it produces purplish-pink flowers with conspicuous purple veins. Plant the tubers in a rock or gravel garden or in troughs in well-drained, gritty soil in full sun. It is easily propagated by division in the fall or early spring.

☼ ◊   Z6–8 H8–6
‡to 2in (5cm) ↔to 4in (10cm)

Paulownia tomentosa

DECIDUOUS TREE

The foxglove tree has extremely large, rounded leaves. In late spring the lilac, scented flowers appear. The tree is not entirely hardy, and the flowers may be damaged by frost. In cold areas it can be treated as a foliage plant by cutting it down to ground level in the late winter or early spring, which stimulates growth of even larger leaves the following spring. If this is done annually, apply a balanced fertilizer, and mulch after pruning. Plant it in well-drained soil in a sunny, sheltered site.

☼ ◊ *f*   Z5–8 H8–5

‡ to 40ft (12m) ↔ to 30ft (10m)

Phlox subulata 'Marjorie'

PERENNIAL

A pretty cushion-forming plant with narrow green leaves, the rose-pink flowers of this moss phlox have five notched petals and a dark eye. It is ideal for a spring display in a rock or gravel garden or raised bed and will perform well when planted in well-drained, fertile soil in a sunny location.

☼ ◊   Z3–8 H8–

‡ to 4in (10cm) ↔ to 8in (20cm)

Primula rosea

PERENNIAL

This primula forms a rosette of toothed, bronze-green leaves and produces clusters of beautiful, clear pink flowers in the late spring. It needs moist, neutral to acid, fertile soil and will suit a bog garden or the damp soil beside a pond. It can be grown in full sun, as long as the soil is permanently wet.

☼ ☀ ◐ ◑　　　　　　　Z3–8 H8–1
‡↔to 8in (20cm)

Primula sieboldii

PERENNIAL

This primula has long been cultivated in Japan, and there are many different types from which to choose. The wild plant has pinkish-purple flowers with white eyes, but there are also cultivars with pink or white flowers. The blooms are held above a rosette of bright green leaves. Plant it in a moist, fertile soil, preferably in partial shade, or full sun if the soil remains moist all summer.

☼ ☀ ◐　　　　　　　Z4–8 H8–1
‡ to 12in (30cm) ↔to 18in (45cm)

Prunus 'Kanzan'

DECIDUOUS TREE

This pretty flowering cherry has upright branches when young, which spread more widely as the tree matures, and this growing style must be considered before planting. Double, deep pink flowers are produced just before the reddish-brown leaves appear in mid- to late spring. Grow it in moist, fertile, well-drained soil in full sun.

☼ ◊ ◖   Z6–8 H8–6
‡↔ to 30ft (10m)

Prunus 'Kiku-shidare-zakura'

DECIDUOUS TREE

Often sold as 'Cheal's Weeping', the graceful, weeping branches of this flowering cherry are covered in the spring with clusters of double, bright pink flowers. It is quite tolerant of pollution and is often planted in boulevards along urban roads. Pruning should be avoided to prevent peach leaf curl disease from entering through the wounds. Where pruning has to be carried out, it should be performed in the summer when the sap is rising.

☼ ◊ ◖   Z4–9 H9–1
‡↔ to 12ft (3m)

Rhododendron 'Pink Pearl'
EVERGREEN SHRUB

This is a very popular rhododendron, grown for its large trusses of pale pink, spring flowers. While the plant is generally very vigorous, the branches are rather weak and have a tendency to droop. Plant it among other shrubs or in a woodland garden. It should be grown in a sunny or partially shaded location in deep, moist, well-drained, acid soil. Mulch annually with bark chips or leaf mold.

☼ ❂ ◊ ◖   Z7–9 H9–7

↕↔to 12ft (4m)

Rhododendron yakushimanum
EVERGREEN SHRUB

A compact, hardy rhododendron, this variety forms a domed bush of dark green, glossy leaves. In the late spring it is covered with funnel-shaped, rose-pink flowers, which fade to pale pink and then white. Plant it in full sun or partial shade in moist, well-drained, fertile, acid soil, and mulch annually with bark chips or leaf mold. This shrub is suitable for containers if grown in acidic soil mix.

☼ ❂ ◊ ◖   Z5–9 H9–5

↕↔to 6ft (2m)

Sambucus nigra 'Guincho Purple'

DECIDUOUS SHRUB

This popular elder is an upright shrub with dark green, divided leaves that turn black-purple then red in the fall. In the late spring to early summer fragrant, pink-tinged white flowers emerge on large, flattened clusters, followed by small, black berries. Elders are ideal in new gardens because they establish quickly. Plant in full sun or partial shade. For the best foliage, cut all stems to the ground in the winter, or prune out some of the older stems annually.

☼ ❀ ◊ *f*   Z6–8 H8–6
‡↔ to 20ft (6m)

Syringa meyeri 'Palibin'

DECIDUOUS SHRUB

This slow-growing lilac is the perfect choice for a small garden, where the common species (*Syringa vulgaris*) may grow too large. It forms a compact bush, which is covered from the late spring to early summer with clusters of very fragrant, pale lavender-pink flowers. Plant it in full sun in well-drained soil or in a large container of organic-rich potting soil.

☼ ◊ *f*   Z4–7 H7–1
‡↔ to 5ft (1.5m)

Tulipa 'Don Quichotte'

BULBOUS PERENNIAL

This bright, cherry-pink tulip makes a dramatic statement when planted in large groups and used as a bedding plant. Its vivid color combines well with cream or white tulips, such as 'White Triumphator' (*see p.87*), or forget-me-nots. Plant the bulbs in the late fall in well-drained soil in full sun.

☼ ◊　　　　　　　Z4–7 H7–1

↕ to 18in (45cm)

Tulipa 'Groenland'

BULBOUS PERENNIAL

The viridiflora tulips are named for the bright green stripe in the middle of the outer petals. 'Groenland' has soft pink petals marked with a triangular green brush stroke. It can be used in groups in an herbaceous border or as a bedding plant. Like all tulips, the bulbs need to be planted in the late fall in a sunny location in well-drained soil.

☼ ◊　　　　　　　Z4–7 H7–1

↕ to 18in (45cm)

Acer palmatum '**Corallinum**'

DECIDUOUS TREE

A compact form of *Acer palmatum* that grows slowly to form a bushy shrub or small tree. It is particularly dramatic in the spring when young bright red shoots appear together with vivid shrimp-pink leaves, which gradually turn pale green. In the fall the leaves turn orange, red, and yellow. It is best planted in sun or partial shade in moist, well-drained acidic soil.

☼ ◊ ◖   Z6–8 H8–2

‡ to 4ft (1.2m) ↔ to 3ft (1m)

Anemone x *fulgens*

PERENNIAL

This striking tuberous plant bears vivid scarlet flowers with black centers that resemble poppies. The late spring flowers are held on stout stems above deeply lobed leaves. For the best effect, plant it in groups in sandy, well-drained soil and a sunny location since it can be damaged while dormant in the summer by persistent rain and wet soil conditions.

☼ ◊   Z8–11 H11–8

‡ to 12in (30cm) ↔ to 4in (10cm)

Camellia japonica 'Rubescens Major'

EVERGREEN SHRUB

This is a very old form of the Japanese camellia and produces double crimson-red flowers with darker veins from the midspring. It forms a compact bush with glossy, rounded dark green leaves. There are several other good camellias with red flowers, such as the semi-double 'Paul's Apollo' and 'R.L. Wheeler'. Plant 'Rubescens Major' in a slightly shaded site away from early morning sun in deep, moist, well-drained, acidic soil.

☀ ○ ◐   Z7–9 H9–7

↕↔ to 30ft (10m)

Crataegus laevigata 'Paul's Scarlet'

DECIDUOUS TREE

Similar in shape to the common native hawthorn, this small tree is covered in the late spring with double, deep pink flowers. These are sometimes followed in the late summer by small red fruits. The leaves are shiny and deeply lobed. It will grow well in most soils, as long as they are not waterlogged, in a sunny or lightly shaded location. Mature trees are particularly attractive.

☀ ☀ ○ ◐   Z5–8 H8–3

↕↔ to 25ft (8m)

Dicentra 'Bacchanal'

PERENNIAL

Bleeding hearts are perennial herbs with finely divided leaves. 'Bacchanal' bears its dangling, deep crimson-red flowers on arching stems in the late spring. Plant it in fertile soil in partial shade below shrubs or in a mixed border. Try to combine it with plants that will hide its dying foliage in the summer.

☀ ◐ ◊ ◊   Z3–9 H9–1

↕ to 14in (35cm) ↔ to 18in (45cm)

Geum rivale

PERENNIAL

Water avens grows naturally beside rivers and streams, making them ideal for bog gardens and pond banks. This species produces clumps of hairy, dark green, divided leaves, and in the late spring it bears single, nodding, bell-shaped flowers on arching stems. Plant it in damp soil in full sunshine, and divide clumps in the fall.

☀ ◊ ◊ ◊   Z3–8 H8–1

↕↔ to 24in (60cm)

Paeonia 'Buckeye Belle'

PERENNIAL

'Buckeye Belle' is a spring-flowering peony with semi-double, deep red flowers. It is a vigorous plant and will eventually form a large clump. Peonies need to be grown in well-drained, fertile soil but require relatively little aftercare. They are generally pest free, but may be attacked by the fungal disease, peony blight. *Paeonia* 'Belle Center' is very similar to 'Buckeye Belle', but flowers two weeks later, making them good companions.

☼ ☀ ◊ ◊   Z3–8 H8–1

↨↔ to 34in (85cm)

Primula japonica

PERENNIAL

The Japanese primrose is a robust perennial with a rosette of spoon-shaped, pale green leaves. In the spring it produces a stout stem with up to six tiers of as many as 25 white, pink, red, or purplish-red flowers. It needs organic, damp soil and is ideally suited to the bog garden and areas of damp woodland or waterside plantings.

☼ ☀ ◊ ◊   Z4–8 H8–1

↨↔ to 18in (45cm)

Primula japonica 'Miller's Crimson'

PERENNIAL

Candelabra primulas are ideal for a bog garden or planting by a pool and are grown for their colorful flowers that are arranged in tiers up the stem. The leaves of *Primula japonica* are rounded with finely serrated edges, and in the late spring 'Miller's Crimson' bears striking crimson-red flowers. It prefers a shaded spot in moist soil and looks best when planted in a group. Divide candelabra primulas in the early spring.

✷ ◊ ❖   Z4–8 H8–1

↕↔ to 18in (45cm)

Rhododendron 'Elizabeth'

EVERGREEN SHRUB

'Elizabeth' is a dwarf rhododendron, making it an excellent choice for small gardens. In the late spring it bears trumpet-shaped, bright red flowers that measure up to 3in (7.5cm) across. These large blooms appear in clusters of five or six and create an eye-catching display. Grow this shrub in sun or partial shade in moist, well-drained, acidic soil, and mulch annually with leaf mold or bark chips.

☼ ✷ ◊ ❖   Z7–9 H9–7

↕↔ to 5ft (1.5m)

Rhododendron 'Hotspur'
DECIDUOUS SHRUB

Deciduous azaleas are unsurpassed for vivid spring color, and 'Hotspur' is no exception with its clusters of flame-red flowers. The brightly colored fall foliage adds to this plant's decorative qualities. Plant it in full sun or partial shade in moist, fertile, acidic soil, and mulch annually with leaf mold or bark chips. 'Silver Slipper' is a similar azalea but bears white flowers.

☼ ◐ ◗　　　　　　　Z6–9 H9–6
↕↔ to 6ft (2m)

Rhododendron prunifolium
SEMI-EVERGREEN SHRUB

One of the latest native azaleas to bloom, plumleaf azalea's orange or crimson flower clusters appear in July and August. Though rare and threatened in its native Georgia and Alabama range, it is readily available at nurseries because it grows easily from seed and cuttings. Several cultivars are available such as 'Apricot Glow' with orange flowers and 'Pine Prunifolium' with bright red flowers. Plant in a woodland or naturalized setting. Grow in partial shade in moist, sandy, acidic soil.

◐ ◗　　　　　　　Z6–9 H9–5
↕ to 15ft (5m) ↔ to 10ft (3m)

Ribes sanguineum 'Pulborough Scarlet'

DECIDUOUS SHRUB

The flowering currants create a dazzling display in the late spring when their stems are clothed in masses of tiny flowers, arranged in clusters. This variety has an upright style, dark green, aromatic leaves, and dark red pendent flowers with white centers. It is suitable for an informal hedge that needs only a light trim after flowering. Flowering currants will grow almost anywhere but prefer a sunny site and moderately fertile soil.

☼ ◑ ◊ ◐ *f*   Z6–8 H8–6

↕ to 6ft (2m) ↔ to 8ft (2.5m)

Schisandra rubriflora

CLIMBER

This climber has red shoots and lance-shaped or oval dark green leaves. In late spring it produces striking deep red flowers, measuring up to 1in (2.5cm) across, followed on female plants by red fleshy fruits. Contrary to appearances, it is also fully hardy and grows well in moist, well-drained soil in sun or partial shade.

☼ ◊ ◊ ◐   Z7–9 H9–7

↕ to 20ft (6m)

Trillium sessile

PERENNIAL

Wake robin is a clump-forming plant with three large, irregularly marked leaves. The flowers bloom in late spring and consist of three upright, narrow, maroon-red petals, surrounded by three smaller spreading sepals. It will do well when grown in dappled shade or woodland in moist, fertile, well-drained soil. It benefits from an annual mulch of leaf mold or well-rotted compost. Divide it after the leaves have died.

☀ ◊ ◊   Z4–8 H8–1

↕ to 15in (38cm) ↔ to 18in (45cm)

Tulipa sprengeri

BULBOUS PERENNIAL

The species tulips are very underrated with a simplicity and elegance that is hard to beat. This species is one of the latest to flower in the spring and has single, bright red flowers with sharply pointed petals. It self-seeds and will naturalize if planted in deciduous woodland and prefers a sunny or lightly shaded site and well-drained, acidic soil.

☀ ◊ ◊   Z4–7 H7–1

↕ to 20in (50cm)

Acer palmatum 'Bloodgood'

DECIDUOUS TREE

'Bloodgood' is a strong-growing Japanese maple with beautifully lobed, fingerlike, purple foliage. The leaf color is most vibrant in the spring, intensifying to a rich scarlet in the fall before the leaves drop. Red-winged seeds appear during the summer. It makes a good specimen tree for a medium-sized garden in most soil types, but choose a site that is sheltered from cold or drying winds, which can cause the leaf tips to shrivel. Plant in a sunny or partially shaded area. Very little pruning is required.

☼ ☀ ◊ ◊   Z6–8 H8–2
↕↔ to 15ft (5m)

Allium unifolium

BULBOUS PERENNIAL

This is a decorative ornamental onion from Oregon. Each small bulb produces a single grayish-green leaf, which dies before bright pinkish-purple, six-petalled flowers appear in the late spring. Plant the bulbs in the fall in a sheltered, sunny location in well-drained, fertile soil. It suits a rock or gravel garden and should be grown in bold groups for the best effect.

☼ ◊   Z4–9 H9–1
↕ to 12in (30cm) ↔ to 4in (10cm)

Fritillaria graeca
BULBOUS PERENNIAL

This unusual fritillary is a native of Southern Greece. It has a delicate style, bearing slim flower stems from which hang pendent, brownish-purple, bell-shaped flowers with a bold green stripe down the center of the petals. Despite its place of origin, it is very hardy but needs to be planted in a sunny site and in soil with very good drainage. It will add interest to a rock garden or raised bed, and the bulbs should be planted in groups in the fall.

☼ ◊   Z6–9 H9–6
↕ to 8in (20cm) ↔ to 2in (5cm)

Fritillaria meleagris
BULBOUS PERENNIAL

In the late spring the snake's head fritillary produces pendent, bell-shaped, purple or white flowers with a distinctive checkerboard pattern on the petals. It grows well when naturalized in grass and will often self-seed. Be careful when mowing since the young seedlings look very much like grasses. It should be planted in a moist, well-drained soil, and prefers slightly alkaline conditions. If the bulbs become congested, mark the location, and they can be pulled up in the fall and replanted elsewhere.

☼ ☀ ◊ ◐   Z4–9 H8–2
↕ to 12in (30cm) ↔ to 3in (8cm)

Ipheion uniflorum
BULBOUS PERENNIAL

In the late spring this vigorous clump-forming plant produces violet, blue, or white, star-shaped flowers. The narrow leaves smell like onions when bruised. Plant bulbs in the fall in a sheltered spot where they can naturalize. They prefer a fertile, moist, well-drained soil in a sunny situation. In cold gardens, mulch in the winter since plants may be killed by hard frost.

☼ ◊ ◖   Z5–9 H9–5
↕↔ to 8in (20cm)

Lunaria annua
BIENNIAL

Honesty (or money plant) is a fast-growing biennial that will often flower in its first year. It has tall stems and toothed, heart-shaped, dark green leaves. Small spring flowers with four petals bloom in the late spring and come in shades of either purple or white. It self-seeds and will thrive in a woodland garden or at the bottom of a hedge, preferring a site in partial shade or sun and moist, well-drained soil. Honesty is often grown for its round, silvery seed pods, used in dried flower arrangements.

☼ ☼ ◊ ◖   Z3–9 H9–1
↕ to 30in (75cm) ↔ to 12in (30cm)

Phlox douglasii 'Crackerjack'
PERENNIAL

A reliable plant, this dwarf phlox forms
a mound of narrow dark green leaves
and in the spring is covered with small,
bright purplish-magenta flowers. Grow
this variety in full sun in well-drained,
fertile soil. It is ideally suited to a rock
garden, the cracks of a dry stone wall,
or between the slabs of a stone path.

☼ ◊   Z5–7 H7–5

‡ to 3in (8cm) ↔ to 8in (20cm)

Primula pulverulenta
PERENNIAL

This species is one of the most striking
of the candelabra primulas. In the late
spring it bears tiers of deep reddish-
purple flowers with a bright red
or purple eye. The plants form rosettes
of toothed, mid-green leaves, and their
stems are covered with a grayish-green
downy material called "farina." Plant it
in partial shade in fertile, moist soil. It
will tolerate full sun, as long as the soil
remains damp throughout the summer.
Candelabra primulas look best when
they are planted in a group near water.

☼ ☀ ◊   Z4–8 H8–1

‡ to 3ft (1m) ↔ to 24in (60cm)

Pulsatilla vulgaris

PERENNIAL

This is an extremely beautiful clump-forming pasque flower with attractive divided, feathery foliage. The pendent, bell-shaped flowers have bright purple petals and golden yellow stamens. Ideal for a rock garden, it needs gritty, very well-drained soil and a sunny location and grows best on alkaline soil. Pasque flowers do not like to have their roots bothered and are best left undisturbed after planting. Propagate by seed.

☼ ◊   Z5–7 H7–5
↕↔ to 9in (23cm)

Rhododendron 'Hatsugiri'

EVERGREEN SHRUB

This small, compact evergreen azalea in the late spring produces a profusion of bright reddish-purple flowers in clusters of three blooms. It is suitable for a container on a patio or the front of a border and will tolerate full sun, unlike many of its cousins. Plant it in a free-draining, organic, acidic soil or acidic soil mix. In the open garden, mulch it generously with leaf mold or bark.

☼ ☼ ◊   Z6–9 H9–6
↕↔ to 24in (60cm)

Tulipa 'Blue Parrot'
BULBOUS PERENNIAL

This robust tulip is not truly blue but more violet. It has single flowers with slightly twisted petals and blooms in the late spring. Use it in borders and as a cut flower. *Tulipa* 'Greuze' also has violet-purple flowers, but they are more uniform in shape. The bulbs of both should be planted in the late fall in free-draining soil in full sun.

☼ ◊   Z4–7 H7–1

↕ to 24in (60cm)

Tulipa 'Queen of Night'
BULBOUS PERENNIAL

'Queen of Night' is an elegant hybrid tulip with large, dark maroon-purple flowers. The single cup-shaped blooms are borne on elegant long green stems above lance-shaped, grayish-green leaves. It looks particularly striking when planted with an ivory-colored variety, such as 'Maureen'. Plant bulbs of this reliably perennial tulip in the late fall in a sunny location and free-draining soil.

☼ ◊   Z4–7 H7–1

↕ to 24in (60cm)

Anemone coronaria '**Lord Lieutenant**'

PERENNIAL

This striking plant originates from the Mediterranean region. The cultivar 'Lord Lieutenant' bears velvety, semi-double, deep blue flowers with black eyes, which open in the mid- to late spring and are good for cutting. The divided foliage adds to this plant's charms. Plant the small tubers in the fall, preferably in light, sandy soil in full sun.

☼ ◊ Z8–11 H11–8

‡ to 18in (45cm) ↔ to 6in (15cm)

Brunnera macrophylla

PERENNIAL

This spreading perennial has coarse, long-stalked, heart-shaped leaves and bright blue flowers in the spring. It will eventually become a large clump and is good for providing ground cover in semi-shaded situations. It needs moist, well-drained, organic soil. 'Hadspen Cream' has partially variegated leaves with creamy-white margins, which will brighten a dull corner. Propagate it by seed in the fall or division in the spring.

☼ ◊ ◗ Z3–7 H7–1

‡ to 18in (45cm) ↔ to 24in (60cm)

Ceanothus 'Joyce Coulter'
EVERGREEN SHRUB

Tolerant of drought and clay soils, this
California lilac attracts birds, bees, and
butterflies with its profusion of fragrant
blue blossoms from mid- to late spring.
Left unpruned, the seedheads dry to
a russet color for added fall interest.
This plant works well in a mixed shrub
border or foundation planting. Avoid
overwatering. Grow in full sun in very
well-drained soil.

☼ ◊ *f*   Z7–10 H10–6
‡ to 4ft (1.2m) ↔ to 10ft (3m)

Corydalis flexuosa
PERENNIAL

This plant has waxy, light green, ferny
leaves and produces clusters of long,
tubular, bright blue flowers in the late
spring. Because it tends to go dormant
in late summer, mark the site where
it grows so it won't be accidentally dug
up in the fall. It needs partial shade
and should be grown in fertile, moist,
well-drained soil.

☼ ◊ ◐   Z6–8 H8–6
‡ to 12in (30cm) ↔ to 8in (20cm)

Gentiana acaulis

EVERGREEN PERENNIAL

The trumpet gentian is a beautiful rock plant that bears vivid, trumpet-shaped, deep blue flowers with green spotted throats. The late spring blooms appear above rosettes of evergreen, glossy leaves that form a slightly raised mound. 'Coelestina' has light blue blooms. The trumpet gentian needs to be planted in moist, very well-drained, acid soil in a partly shaded situation.

☀ ◊ ◑   Z5–8 H8–5

‡ to 3in (8cm) ↔ to 12in (30cm)

Hyacinthoides non-scripta

BULBOUS PERENNIAL

In the late spring few sights compare with the beauty of a deciduous wood carpeted with the fragrant flowers of English bluebells. Replicate these shady conditions, and bluebells will self-seed and spread throughout the garden. For the best results, plant the bulbs in the fall in moist, acidic, fertile soil, although they will tolerate slightly alkaline conditions. Cultivars with white and mauve flowers are also available.

☀ ◐ ◑ *f*   Z4–10 H9–1

‡ to 16in (40cm) ↔ to 3in (8cm)

Muscari latifolium
BULBOUS PERENNIAL

This is an unusual grape hyacinth with
a spike of tiny, urn-shaped
flowers. The lower flowers are purplish-
black, while the upper, smaller, infertile
flowers are pale blue. The lance-shaped
leaves are broader than those of most
other muscaris. Plant the small bulbs in
a sunny, sheltered site in a well-drained
soil, and use at the front of a border or
in a rock garden. Established clumps can
be divided, or sow seed in the summer.
This variety is not fully hardy and may
be killed by prolonged, hard frosts.

☼ ◊   Z4–8 H8–1
‡ to 10in (25cm) ↔ to 3in (8cm)

Rosmarinus officinalis 'Sissinghurst Blue'
EVERGREEN SHRUB

Widely grown as a culinary herb and
for its aromatic foliage, rosemary is
a decorative shrub and can be grown
as a low hedge. 'Sissinghurst Blue'
is a dwarf variety that bears small,
pale blue flowers in the late spring. It
does well in a sunny, sheltered location
and well-drained soil. Rosemary will
respond well to pruning, and old
straggly plants can be cut back hard
in the spring. Propagate by semi-ripe
cuttings in the summer.

☼ ◊ *f*   Z8–10 H11–1
‡↔ to 20in (50cm)

Symphytum x *uplandicum* 'Variegatum'

PERENNIAL

Russian comfrey is a vigorous, clump-forming perennial, ideal for ground cover in wild gardens. 'Variegatum' has coarse, hairy green leaves with a broad cream margin. The small, pink, tubular flowers grow on tall stems and eventually turn blue. 'Variegatum' is far less vigorous than the normal green plant and will flourish in moist soil in sun or partial shade. It can be divided in the early spring.

☼ ☀ ◑   Z3–9 H9–1

‡ to 3ft (1m) ↔ to 24in (60cm)

Syringa vulgaris 'Katherine Havemeyer'

DECIDUOUS SHRUB

A double-flowered form of the common lilac that produces clusters of pink buds that develop into lavender-blue, sweetly perfumed flowers. It grows quickly to form a spreading shrub or small tree and will perform well when planted in a moist, well-drained, fertile soil in full sun or partial shade. Young plants do not need pruning, but rejuvenate old lilac bushes by cutting them back hard after they have flowered. Lilacs are also tolerant of pollution.

☼ ☀ ◊ ◑ *f*   Z4–8 H8–1

‡↔ to 22ft (7m)

Veronica peduncularis
PERENNIAL

Masses of small, saucer-shaped, deep blue flowers open over a long period from the spring to early summer on this mat-forming, low-growing veronica. The glossy, purple-tinted green leaves are also an attractive feature. Grow it in a well-drained soil in a sunny location, such as a rock garden or raised bed. Stocks can be increased by dividing it in the fall.

☼ ◊ Z6–8 H8–6

‡ to 4in (10cm) ↔ to 24in (60cm)

Wisteria frutescens
CLIMBER

American wisteria is a vigorous twining vine with long, hanging racemes of fragrant, pale blue summer flowers. Native to the southeastern United States, it thrives in wet woodland settings. Train it on a sturdy trellis or arbor near a patio or pond. Avoid high nitrogen fertilizer. Notable cultivars include fragrant, lavender-blue 'Amethyst Falls', white-flowered 'Nivea', and 'Kate's Dwarf', which has finer foliage and compact purple flower clusters. Plant in full sun or partial shade in moist to wet soil.

☼ ☀ ◊ ● ƒ Z6–9 H9–6

‡ to 30ft (10m)

Adonis vernalis

PERENNIAL

This hardy, clump-forming perennial originates from Europe, where it is often found in rocky, exposed sites. In the spring it produces golden yellow flowers above deeply dissected, bright green leaves. Grow it in a raised bed, rock or gravel garden in full sun and well-drained, preferably alkaline soil.

☼ ◊   Z4–7 H7–1
↕↔to 12in (30cm)

Aurinia saxatilis

EVERGREEN PERENNIAL

Gold dust, formerly known as *Alyssum saxatile*, is an evergreen with grayish-green leaves. In the early spring it produces masses of small, bright yellow flowers. Other gold dusts include 'Citrina', which bears bright lemon-yellow flowers, and 'Compacta', a small variety with golden-yellow blooms. It needs a sunny, well-drained situation and can be grown on a wall to spill over the front of a raised bed or in a rock garden.

☼ ◊   Z4–8 H8–1
↕ to 9in (23cm) ↔to 12in (30cm)

Berberis x *stenophylla*

EVERGREEN SHRUB

This vigorous, spiny plant forms an elegant, spreading bush with arching branches covered with clusters of deep yellow flowers. The blooms appear in the late spring and are followed in the summer by waxy black fruit. Plant it in full sun in a well-drained, fertile soil. It is most useful when grown as a dense intruder-proof hedge, which should be trimmed after flowering has finished.

☼ ◊　　　　　　　Z6–9 H9–6
‡ to 10ft (3m) ↔ to 15ft (5m)

Berberis thunbergii '**Aurea**'

DECIDUOUS SHRUB

A beautiful barberry with bright golden-yellow leaves, it is much shorter than other varieties and is suitable for small gardens. In late spring it bears clusters of pink-tinged, pale yellow flowers, which are followed in the fall by bright red berries. While it needs good light, bright sun can scorch the yellow leaves, but in dense shade the foliage will turn green. It grows well in most soils.

☼ ☀ ◊ ◐　　　　　　Z5–8 H8–5
‡ to 5ft (1.5m) ↔ to 6ft (2m)

Colchicum luteum
BULBOUS PERENNIAL

Colchicums are best known for their bright pink flowers, produced in the fall, but this species is different. It has golden-yellow, goblet-shaped flowers that appear from midspring. It needs very good drainage and should be planted in gritty, fertile soil in full sun. It can be difficult to grow outdoors because the corms need to be kept completely dry when they are dormant. In wet climates, grow it in pots in a cold frame, and take it outside in the spring.

☼ ◊   Z4–9 H9–1

↕ to 4in (10cm) ↔ to 3in (8cm)

Cytisus x praecox 'Allgold'
EVERGREEN SHRUB

This small, free-flowering broom bears a profusion of dark yellow blooms from mid- to late spring. Ideal for growing in a sunny mixed border, it needs a deep, slightly fertile, well-drained soil. After flowering, it can be trimmed back to keep it in shape, although pruning is not essential. 'Warminster' has a similar look to 'Allgold' but produces creamy-yellow flowers.

☼ ◊   Z6–9 H9–6

↕ to 4ft (1.2m) ↔ to 5ft (1.5m)

Dionysia tapetodes
EVERGREEN PERENNIAL

This alpine plant forms a tight cushion of small, grayish-green leaves, and in the late spring and early summer bright yellow, upward facing flowers appear above the foliage. It is hardy but needs dry, very well-drained soil and full sun to succeed. In its natural environment it grows in the crevices of rocks and is best suited to growing in pots of alpine compost under glass to protect it from a damp environment and winter rains.

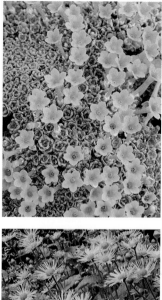

☼ ◊   Z5–7 H7–5

‡ to ½in (1cm) ↔ to 6in (15cm)

Doronicum x *excelsum* 'Harpur Crewe'
PERENNIAL

Bright, golden-yellow, daisylike flowers adorn this leopard's bane in the late spring. The blooms are held on tall erect stems above decorative, heart-shaped, basal leaves. Plant it in a moist, fertile soil in partial shade, and grow it in groups to enliven an early herbaceous border or woodland garden with dazzling color. Leopard's bane can be propagated by division in the fall.

☼ ◐ ◊   Z4–8 H8–1

‡↔ to 24in (60cm)

Epimedium pinnatum subsp. *colchicum*

EVERGREEN PERENNIAL

An attractive clump-former, this plant produces rounded leaves divided into five leaflets, and golden-yellow single flowers, which are relatively large for an epimedium, measuring up to ¼in (18mm) across. It prefers a semi-shaded situation and heavy, moisture-retentive, fertile soil. Although slower to spread than the species, the leaves still make excellent ground cover. The appearance of the plant will be improved if the old foliage is cut back in the late winter.

☀ ◐   Z5–9 H9–4
‡↔ to 12in (30cm)

Erysimum 'Bredon'

EVERGREEN PERENNIAL

The bright, chrome-yellow flowers of this shrubby evergreen perennial appear from the late spring above a mound of gray-green foliage. Ideally planted near the front of a mixed or herbaceous border in poor or not-too-fertile, well-drained soil. Alternatively, try mixing different varieties, such as orange-yellow 'Butterscotch', with tulips to create colorful spring displays in beds or containers. Trim after flowering to keep compact. Erysimums are ideal for hot, sunny, dry sites.

☀ ◇   Z5–8 H8–5
‡↔ to 18in (45cm)

Erysimum 'Moonlight'

EVERGREEN PERENNIAL

A mat-forming, perennial wallflower
with evergreen, grayish-green, lance-
shaped leaves. Throughout the spring
and early summer it produces clusters
of slightly fragrant, pale sulfur-yellow
flowers. It blooms for a short time, but
it is an excellent choice for a dry wall,
gravel or raised bed, or a rock garden.
Plant it in full sunshine in poor, gritty,
very well-drained soil.

☼ ❋ ◊ *f*   Z6–8 H8–6

‡ to 10in (25cm) ↔ to 18in (45cm)

Euphorbia polychroma

PERENNIAL

This plant is guaranteed to brighten up
a dull spring morning. The stems are
clothed in bright green leaves, which
form a rounded clump, and from the
late spring and well into the summer
it bears acid yellow flowers surrounded
by a collar of striking greenish-yellow
bracts. A tolerant plant, it will grow in
most well-drained soils and can be used
at the front of a border or in a woodland
garden. Care should be taken when
pruning the stems because the latex
they secrete can irritate the skin.

☼ ◊ ◐   Z5–9 H9–5

‡↔ to 20in (50cm)

Fritillaria imperialis 'Maxima Lutea'
BULBOUS PERENNIAL

The value of crown imperials in the late spring garden is beyond question. The tall stems carry a tuft of shiny, green leafy bracts at the top, beneath which hang a number of bright yellow, bell-shaped flowers. The bulbs should be planted in late summer in full sun and a deep, well-drained soil where they will not be disturbed. 'Rubra' is more robust with orange-red flowers and purple stems.

☼ ◊   Z5–9 H9–4
‡ to 5ft (1.5m) ↔ to 12in (30cm)

Genista hispanica
DECIDUOUS SHRUB

A mound-forming shrub, Spanish gorse produces a profusion of golden-yellow, pealike, small flowers on green prickly stems in the late spring and early summer. Plant it in a well-drained soil and sunny location, such as the front of a raised bed. Spanish gorse is not totally hardy and may be killed by severe frosts, so in colder gardens, plant it in a sheltered position by a warm wall to prevent it from being damaged.

☼ ◊   Z7–9 H9–7
‡ to 30in (75cm) ↔ to 5ft (1.5m)

Genista tinctoria
DECIDUOUS SHRUB

Dyer's greenweed is a small and
spreading bush that freely bears clusters
of bright yellow pea flowers from the
spring into summer. The narrow, mid-
green foliage is a good foil to the flowers.
Flat seedpods follow the flowers. 'Royal
Gold' and 'Flore Pleno' are both notable
garden varieties that flower profusely.
Trim after flowering, but not into old
wood since this may not grow back.
Good planted in a raised bed or rock
garden or near the front of a border.
Plant in full sun or dappled shade.

☼ ◑ ◊ ◐   Z2–8 H8–1

↔ to 20in (50cm)

Iris 'Golden Harvest'
BULBOUS PERENNIAL

This iris produces pure golden-yellow
flowers that are good for cutting from
the middle of the spring to early
summer. It requires a very well-drained
neutral or slightly alkaline soil and a
sunny site since bulbs may not survive
wet conditions while they are dormant.
Large clumps should be divided as soon
as possible after flowering.

☼ ◊   Z3–9 H9–1

↕ to 32in (80cm) ↔ to 6in (15cm)

Kerria japonica 'Golden Guinea'

DECIDUOUS SHRUB

Kerria is an easy-to-grow and vigorous shrub with graceful, arching green stems. One of the most popular forms is 'Pleniflora', which has double, deep yellow flowers. 'Golden Guinea' is less vigorous with single yellow blooms. It grows best in free-draining soil and full sun but can tolerate light shade. Kerria spreads by suckers, which can be dug up in the fall to propagate it. Cut back the stems after flowering to keep it controlled.

☼ ☀ ◊   Z4–9 H9–1

↕ to 6ft (2m) ↔ to 8ft (2.5m)

Laburnum anagyroides

DECIDUOUS TREE

The laburnum is a widely grown garden plant and in the late spring produces long, pendent clusters of pealike, bright yellow flowers. Laburnums will grow in almost any soil, as long as it is not waterlogged, but they need full sun to flourish. They are easily propagated from seed sown in the fall—but remember that laburnum seeds are very poisonous. *L.* x *watereri* 'Vossii' has larger blooms held in longer clusters.

☼ ◊ ◑   Z6–8 H8–5

↕↔ to 25ft (8m)

Meconopsis cambrica
PERENNIAL

The Welsh poppy has single lemon-yellow or orange flowers and blooms from the late spring to the fall. The flowers are borne on long stems above fernlike, grayish-green foliage. 'Flore-pleno' has double yellow flowers and grows well from seed. Welsh poppies grow best in partial shade and moist, acidic soil, although they will tolerate alkaline conditions. They have a tendency to self-seed and will spread quickly unless the seedheads are cut off before they ripen.

☀ ◊　　　　　　　　　　Z6–8 H8–6

↕ to 18in (45cm) ↔ to 12in (30cm)

Narcissus jonquilla
BULBOUS PERENNIAL

Wild jonquils are valued for their sweet fragrance and small yellow blooms that appear in the spring. Each stem produces five or six bright yellow, single flowers above linear, almost cylindrical leaves. These narcissi look lovely naturalized in grass or beneath deciduous trees and also make wonderful container plants for a patio, where their fragrance can be enjoyed at close range. Plant the bulbs in free-draining soil in sun for the best results.

☀ ◊ *f*　　　　　　　　　Z3–9 H9–1

↕ to 12in (30cm) ↔ to 3in (8cm)

Paeonia delavayi var. *ludlowii*

DECIDUOUS SHRUB

When given the correct conditions, the Tibetan tree peony will eventually become a broad, spreading bush. In the late spring it bears bright yellow flowers and has decorative, lobed, deeply-cut foliage borne on graceful arching stems. Grow this tree peony in full sun or light shade in moist, well-drained soil. It is easily propagated from seed. Cut out one or two of the older stems in the late winter to rejuvenate established plants.

☼ ☀ ◊ ◊   Z3–8 H8–1

‡ to 6ft (2m) ↔ to 9ft (3m)

Paeonia mlokosewitschii

PERENNIAL

There are few more desirable plants than "Molly-the-Witch" with its large primrose-yellow flowers and yellow-green divided foliage. The stems are tinted pink or red. Slow-growing at first, it can eventually form a wide-spreading clump. It grows well in full sun or dappled shade, although a well-drained soil is essential. Propagate it from seed. Although peonies do not like being disturbed, large clumps can be divided in the fall.

☼ ☀ ◊   Z5–8 H8–5

‡↔ to 30in (75cm)

Primula prolifera
EVERGREEN PERENNIAL

This candelabra primula forms rosettes of pale evergreen leaves with serrated edges. The fragrant, golden-yellow flowers appear in the late spring. Like all candelabra primulas, it requires deep, fertile, neutral or slightly acidic soil that does not dry out in the summer. It looks particularly striking when planted in a large group near water. Divide congested clumps in the early spring, or grow plants from seed.

※ ◊ *f*　　　　　　Z4–8 H8–1
↔ to 24in (60cm)

Primula veris
EVERGREEN PERENNIAL

The cowslip is one of the best loved spring flowers and produces clusters of pale yellow, fragrant blooms throughout the season. The erect flower stems are surrounded by a rosette of evergreen, deeply-veined leaves. Cowslips should be planted in a partly shaded site in well-drained, moist soil. They can be grown in full sun as long as the soil remains permanently moist. Grow it from seed in the spring, or divide large clumps in the fall or early spring.

※ ※ ◊ ◊ *f*　　　　　Z3–8 H8–1
↔ to 10in (25cm)

Quercus rubra 'Aurea'

DECIDUOUS TREE

This red oak with yellow leaves makes a striking landscape tree in the spring, when the leaf color is at its most intense. These fade to yellow-green in the summer, becoming yellow-orange in the fall before they drop. Plant in full sun or partial shade. The tree needs little in the way of maintenance, but remove any dead, diseased or crossing branches in the winter. Red oaks are ideal for medium to large gardens, and cope well in urban environments. There is a more compact golden form called 'Magic Fire'.

☼ ☀ ◊ ◖   Z5–9 H9–5

‡ to 25ft (8m) ↔ to 12ft (4m)

Rhododendron luteum

DECIDUOUS SHRUB

In spring, this widely-grown deciduous azalea bears large numbers of strongly fragrant, funnel-shaped, bright yellow flowers. The lance-shaped leaves turn shades of purple, red, and orange in the fall. This azalea prefers full sun but will tolerate a little shade. Plant it with the rootball just above the soil surface in moist, well-drained, acidic soil, and mulch annually with leaf mold or bark chips.

☼ ☀ ◊ ◖ *f*   Z7–9 H9–7

‡↔ to 12ft (4m)

Rhododendron maccabeanum

EVERGREEN TREE

Many people consider this to be the best of all the yellow rhododendrons. In the mid- to late spring it produces large trusses of deep yellow flowers with purple spots on the inside. Very hardy, it eventually grows into a substantial tree, making it only really suitable for large gardens, where it is best planted in partial shade beneath deciduous trees. It enjoys moist, well-drained, acidic soil. Mulch annually with leaf mold or bark chips.

☀ ◊ ◗   Z8–11 H11–10

‡ to 50ft (15m) ↔ to 20ft (6m)

Ribes odoratum

DECIDUOUS SHRUB

The buffalo currant is an upright bush with attractive three-lobed, bright green leaves. From the mid- to late spring clusters of small fragrant, tubular, golden-yellow flowers with bright red anthers appear, followed in the summer by black berries. In the fall its foliage turns various shades of red and purple. Plant it in full sun or light shade in well-drained soil. It is easy to propagate by taking hardwood cuttings during the winter.

☀ ☀ ◊ *f*   Z5–8 H8–5

‡↔ to 6ft (2m)

Trillium luteum

PERENNIAL

This clump-forming plant has silver-green mottled leaves with pointed tips. Its yellow, fragrant flowers appear in the late spring and are composed of three narrow green sepals and three upright, pale yellow petals. It is a good choice for a woodland garden and should be grown in a shaded location in moist, well-drained, acidic soil. In the fall, mulch it with well-rotted leaf mold.

☼ ☀ ◑ ◐ *f*   Z5–7 H7–4

‡ to 16in (40cm) ↔ to 12in (30cm)

Trollius europaeus

PERENNIAL

The European globeflower is a reliable plant for moist soils. Resembling a large buttercup, the spherical, lemon-yellow flowers appear in the late spring and early summer. It also has attractive, glossy, divided foliage. This globeflower can be planted in full sun or partial shade and is suitable for bog gardens because it does particularly well in fertile soil that never dries out. 'Canary Bird' is one of the best cultivars. European globeflowers can be grown from seed or divided in the fall.

☼ ☀ ◑   Z5–8 H8–5

‡ to 24in (60cm) ↔ to 18in (45cm)

Tulipa 'Golden Apeldoorn'

BULBOUS PERENNIAL

A widely grown single-flowered tulip
with bright golden-yellow flowers. The
base of the inner petals is marked with
a large black patch that disguises the
black stamens. Plant it in well-drained,
fertile soil in a sunny location. Most
tulips look best when grown with a
contrasting color; this yellow variety
would look good with the cherry-red
'Apeldoorn' or scarlet 'Oxford' in a
bedding design.

☼ ◊   Z4–7 H7–1

‡ to 24in (60cm)

Tulipa 'West Point'

BULBOUS PERENNIAL

This is a striking lily-flowered tulip,
the late spring primrose-yellow flowers
of which have pointed petals that curve
slightly outward at the tips. It should
be planted in a sunny situation in well-
drained, fertile soil and looks stunning
when combined with a bright red tulip,
such as the lily-flowered 'Mariette'. It is
particularly well suited for containers.

☼ ◊   Z4–7 H7–1

‡ to 20in (50cm)

Uvularia grandiflora

PERENNIAL

An unusual spreading plant, the large merrybells has erect stems that droop at the tip and in the late spring have narrow, bell-shaped, yellow flowers. It should be planted in deep, moist, well-drained soil. Merrybells is a hardy plant and will perform well when grown in a shady border or in the partial shade of a woodland garden. It is vulnerable to slug and snail damage and will need to be protected from these pests during the growing season.

☀ ◊ ◊   Z3–7 H7–1
‡ to 24in (60cm) ↔ to 12in (30cm)

Vancouveria chrysantha

PERENNIAL

Golden inside-out flower is a semi-evergreen perennial native to California and Oregon. From the late spring to early summer loose panicles of dainty yellow flowers appear above the thick, dark green, diamond-shaped leaves. Best planted as a ground cover in a woodland or naturalized setting. Grow in partial shade in moist soil.

☀ ◊   Z6–8 H8–6
‡ to 12in (30cm) ↔ to 24in (60cm)

Viola biflora

PERENNIAL

A dwarf violet with attractive kidney- or
heart-shaped leaves, this plant spreads
slowly by creeping roots. In the spring
and early summer it produces solitary
or pairs of small, deep lemon-yellow
flowers, the lower petals of which have
purple-brown streaks that radiate out
from the center. It performs well when
planted in well-drained, moist soil in a
partially shaded situation and is suitable
for a woodland garden.

☼ ◐ ◊ ◖   Z4–8 H8–1

‡ to 3in (8cm) ↔ to 8in (20cm)

Viola 'Jackanapes'

EVERGREEN PERENNIAL

This violet has toothed, bright green
leaves and spreading stems that bear
bicolored flowers in the late spring and
throughout the summer. The small
blooms are deep maroon-purple at the
top and bright yellow at the base with
purple streaks radiating from the
center. 'Jackanapes' should be grown in
moist, well-drained soil in full sun or
partial shade. It is short-lived and needs
to be propagated regularly by taking
stem-tip cuttings in the late summer.

☼ ☼ ◊ ◖   Z4–8 H8–1
‡ to 5in (12cm) ↔ to 8in (20cm)

Berberis linearifolia 'Orange King'

EVERGREEN SHRUB

This attractive barberry has glossy, dark green leaves and strong, upright, spiny stems. The cup-shaped, bright orange flowers, borne in small clusters, appear in the late spring and are then followed in the late summer by waxy black fruit. It will grow well in full sun and deep, moist, well-drained soil. To propagate it, take softwood cuttings in the late summer.

☼ ◊ ◖   Z6–9 H9–6
↕↔ to 8ft (2.5m)

Primula x bulleesiana

EVERGREEN PERENNIAL

This beautiful candelabra primula is a hybrid between *P. bulleyana* and *P. beesiana*. Plants may have orange, yellow, pink, red, and purple flowers borne in tiers around stout stems. Plant it in a slightly shaded situation in moist, neutral or slightly acidic soil. The plant overwinters as a rosette of mid-green leaves and can be divided or grown from seed in the spring.

☽ ◖   Z5–8 H8–5
↕↔ to 24in (60cm)

Primula bulleyana
PERENNIAL

Clusters of crimson flowers that quickly
fade to bright orange bloom on this
striking candelabra primula in the late
spring. The toothed, rounded, lance-
shaped, mid-green leaves form a tight
rosette at the base of the plant. It suits
waterside plantings and bog gardens
since it enjoys partial shade and deep,
moist, fertile, neutral or slightly acid soil
that does not dry out in summer. It can
be propagated by division in the spring.

 Z5–8 H8–5
↕↔ to 24in (60cm)

Rhododendron 'Frome'
DECIDUOUS SHRUB

A medium-sized deciduous azalea, this
type has orangy-yellow, frilly, funnel-
shaped flowers with red marks on their
throats. It forms a large, dome-shaped
bush and is suitable for the middle
or back of a mixed border or beneath
deciduous trees. It needs a moist, well-
drained, fertile, acidic soil in partial
shade. Mulch it annually with leaf
mold or bark chips.

Z5–8 H8–5
↕↔ to 5ft (1.5m)

EARLY SUMMER

Not a day goes by without more flowers opening somewhere in the garden. Hanging baskets and containers, brimming with pelargoniums, verbenas and other tender bedding, can be put out now all danger of frost has passed. The herbaceous border reaches a peak of perfection: peonies and delphiniums surround their supports, holding their flowers up against the weather for pure enjoyment, while bearded irises, daylilies, starry alliums and hardy geraniums bloom in profusion and dazzling shades.

In the light shade of trees, making cool leafy ground cover, grow hostas, heucheras and bugle (*Ajuga*). Monkshood (*Aconitum*) and the feathery clumps of goatsbeard (*Aruncus*) will thrive in moist conditions, but for permanently wet soil and pond margins the beauty of the Japanese iris is without peer.

Mediterranean shrubs such as genistas, thymes and phlomis revel in the hot dry conditions.

More dramatic bursts of colour are provided by sun-loving annuals, especially those sown in the fall, like eschscholzia. Half-hardy salvias can be used for bedding or to fill gaps, perhaps replacing oriental poppies after their flowers have gone. All will flower into the fall if they are deadheaded; the key to extending the display of many annuals and, of course, roses.

SUMMER ROMANCE

Most evocative of summer are the roses, gracing many garden situations with fragrance and colour throughout the season. Modern shrub roses are easier going than hybrid teas, often having the characteristics of old roses but flowering for longer. Ground cover roses are healthy and very versatile; for example, **SURREY** trails over sunny banks or walls, but is also at home in a large pot or hanging basket, while 'Madame Knorr' makes a spectacular thorny hedge.

Achillea ptarmica 'The Pearl'

PERENNIAL

Sneezewort is a slender perennial with narrow, serrated, dark green leaves. From the early to late summer 'The Pearl' bears abundant small, pom-pom shaped flowers with tiny, white petals. It thrives when planted in a sunny location in well-drained, fertile soil. Propagate it by division in the fall. The flowerheads dry well.

☼ ◊   Z3–8 H8–1
‡↔ to 30in (75cm)

Actinidia kolomikta

CLIMBER

This deciduous, woody-stemmed climber with its green, white, and purple-red variegated leaves is ideal for covering a pergola or a wall. Fragrant white flowers are borne in clusters in the early summer and are sometimes followed by yellow-green fruits. Plant in fertile, well-drained soil, and provide shelter from strong winds. It will grow in partial shade, but full sun will give the best leaf color. Propagate by semi-ripe cuttings in the late summer. Prune lightly in the early spring to keep it contained.

☼ ◑ ◊ *f*   Z5–8 H11–1
‡ to 12ft (4m)

Aesculus parviflora

DECIDUOUS SHRUB

A close relative of the horse chestnut, the bottlebrush buckeye has similar leaves, which are divided into several long, slightly waxy, bronze-green leaflets. From the early summer it produces tall spikes of white flowers. In the fall the leaves turn bright yellow. It is a very tolerant plant and can be grown in full sun or partial shade, preferring fertile, slightly moist but well-drained soil. The bush spreads by suckers, which can be separated and replanted or removed to control the spread.

☼ ☀ ◊ ◐　　　　　　Z5–9 H9–4

‡ to 10ft (3m) ↔ to 15ft (5m)

Aruncus dioicus

PERENNIAL

Goatsbeard forms large clumps of fernlike, mid-green foliage. From early to midsummer tiny, star-shaped, white flowers appear on fluffy plumes up to 20in (50cm) long. An easygoing plant, it is tolerant of sun or shade and moist or dry, reasonably fertile soil. It does well in a sunny border or damp ground by water or a woodland border. Divide plants in the early spring or fall.

☼ ☀ ◊ ◐　　　　　　Z3–7 H7–1

‡ to 6ft (2m) ↔ to 4ft (1.2m)

Cardiocrinum giganteum
BULBOUS PERENNIAL

The giant lily is an impressive plant, with up to 20 fragrant, trumpet-shaped blooms on top of a tall, stout stem that does not require staking. It forms a rosette of dark green, glossy leaves at the base. For the best results, give it a shady, sheltered location in moist, organic soil. Although the lily dies after flowering, the bulb forms plenty of small bulblets that can be dug up and replanted immediately. They will be ready to flower in three to five years. Protect new growth in the winter with a dry mulch.

☼ ◊ *f*   Z7–9 H9–7
‡ to 10ft (3m) ↔ to 3½ft (1.1m)

Cistus ladanifer
EVERGREEN SHRUB

This is a substantial, though often short-lived, upright bush. The branches are covered with aromatic leaves, and from the early summer, it bears large quantities of white, saucer-shaped flowers with yellow centers. Each papery petal carries a crimson spot at its base. A native of the Mediterranean, this shrub thrives in full sun and well-drained soil and suits a gravel garden or a site close to a sunny wall. It also grows well in coastal gardens. Established plants will not tolerate being moved.

☼ ◊ *f*   Z7–10 H10–7
‡ to 6ft (2m) ↔ to 5ft (1.5m)

Clematis florida var. sieboldiana

CLIMBER

This clematis is widely grown for its striking early summer flowers with their creamy-white petals and rich purple stamens. Severe winters may damage early top growth, so plant it in a sheltered spot in organic, well-drained soil or in a container of soil-based potting mix. In the early spring, prune stems back to a strong pair of buds, approximately 8in (20cm) above the ground. Train it along supporting wires, a trellis, or over a tripod.

☀ ☽ ◊   Z6–9 H9–6

to 8ft (2.5m)

Clematis 'Silver Moon'

CLIMBER

Large, silvery-white flowers with a hint of mauve make this among the most attractive of the early summer-flowering clematis. Rarely growing taller than 6ft (2m), it is ideal for a small garden. It needs a sheltered spot in sun or partial shade with its roots in the shade and well-drained, organic, fertile soil. Provide it with a support, or allow it to wind through bushes. In early spring, remove dead stems and prune back the other shoots to a couple of strong buds.

☀ ☽ ◊   Z4–11 H9–1

to 6ft (2m)

Cornus canadensis

PERENNIAL

Spreading by means of underground stems, the creeping dogwood will provide a low-growing carpet of lush greenery beneath shrubs or trees. The bright green, oval leaves, which grow in opposite pairs, are a perfect foil for the creamy-white, petal-like bracts that surround the tiny green-red flowers. It does best on moist but well-drained, slightly acidic soil in partial shade. Divide established plants in the early spring or fall.

☀ ◊   Z2–7 H7–

‡ to 6in (15cm) ↔ to 12in (30cm)

Cornus 'Norman Hadden'

DECIDUOUS TREE

'Norman Hadden' bears masses of large creamy-white, petal-like bracts in the early summer that, after a few weeks, turn a deep shade of pink. The blooms are followed in the fall by strawberrylik fruits. Yet another of its attractions is that, with age, its bark will start to peel, creating a handsome effect. For best results, plant in a sunny or partially shaded location, protected from strong winds in well-drained, neutral to acidic fertile soil.

☀ ☀ ◊   Z5–8 H8–

‡↔ to 25ft (8m)

Crambe cordifolia
PERENNIAL

This extremely vigorous perennial has large, dark green, crinkled leaves. In wonderful contrast small, highly fragrant, star-shaped flowers are borne in a white froth on stiffly branching, slender stems. To accommodate its sprawling style, provide it with plenty of space. Although it will tolerate poor soil, it prefers a sunny location in well-drained, fertile soil. Plant it in a gravel garden or herbaceous border.

☼ ☀ ◊ *f*   Z6–9 H9–6

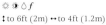 ‡ to 6ft (2m) ↔ to 4ft (1.2m)

Delphinium 'Butterball'
PERENNIAL

In the summer this vigorous perennial bears tall spikes of white, semi-double flowers with deep yellow eyes. For the greatest impact, plant in groups of up to ten in well-drained, fertile soil in full sun. The stems will need supporting with canes from a young age to prevent them from snapping in strong winds. Feed the plants in the spring and remove the faded flowerheads, and you may be rewarded with a second burst of flowers.

☼ ◊   Z3–7 H8–3

‡ to 5ft (1.5m) ↔ to 36in (90cm)

Deutzia gracilis
DECIDUOUS SHRUB

An upright, spreading shrub, it bears clusters of fragrant, pure white flowers in the early summer. Plant it in a sunny site in fertile, well-drained soil, and provide protection from late-spring frosts that can damage the flowers. Prune back the old shoots after flowering has finished. Take softwood cuttings in the summer and hardwood cuttings in the fall.

☼ ◊ *f* Z5–8 H8–5
↕↔to 3ft (1m)

Dianthus 'Haytor White'
PERENNIAL

This white, modern pink is widely grown for cutting and will fill a room with its delicious clove scent. The double flowers have deeply serrated petals. Pinks do best in a sunny position at the front of a border or by paving and should be planted in reasonably fertile, well-drained soil. In the spring, pinch off the growing tips to promote bushy growth. Deadheading will help prolong flowering. Take cuttings from non-flowering stems in the early spring.

☼ ◊ *f* Z7–10 H10–7
↕ to 18in (45cm) ↔ to 16in (40cm)

Digitalis purpurea
f. *albiflora*

BIENNIAL

This foxglove will grow easily in most gardens, provided you give it moist but well-drained soil and a little shade. In the first year it produces a large rosette of oval-shaped, deep green leaves, followed, in the early summer of the next year, by a tall spire of pure white flowers. Sow seed in the spring, and plant out the young seedlings in the fall. Foxgloves look best when planted in groups in front of a dark background by shrubs or in a dappled woodland.

☀ ○ ◐   Z4–8 H9–1

↕ to 5ft (1.5m) ↔ to 18in (45cm)

Dryas octopetala

EVERGREEN SHRUB

The dainty flowers of the mountain avens belie its tough nature—this plant can cope with the harsh conditions on top of windswept, stony slopes and cliffs. What it lacks in height it more than makes up for in spread; its glossy, dark green leaves will quickly fill crevices between rocks, gaps in drystone walls, or form large mats in a gravel garden. Grow it in well-drained, gritty soil in sun or partial shade.

☀ ☀ ○   Z3–6 H6–1

↕ to 2½in (6cm) ↔ indefinite

Erica carnea '*Springwood White*'

EVERGREEN PERENNIAL

Early-flowering heathers can bring a beautiful carpet of color to the garden in the spring and early summer, sometimes flowering even in the late winter. This trailing variety produces a profusion of white flowers for up to two months above bright, evergreen foliage. It tolerates acid soils in a sunny location and can be grown in a container or trough. The flowers are good for cutting. Trim as soon as the flowers begin to fade to ensure that next year's flower buds are not damaged.

☼ ◊ ◑   Z6–8 H8–6
↕ to 10in (25cm) ↔ to 22in (55cm)

Galega officinalis '*Alba*'

PERENNIAL

An ideal plant for the back of a sunny border, this goat's rue bears small, pealike, white flowers in the early summer. For the best results, plant it in sun or partial shade in moist, well-drained soil. If the soil is rich, the stems will be floppy and the plant will need supporting, either with stakes inserted in the late spring, or by allowing it to grow through other open, sturdy shrubs. Propagate by dividing established plants between the late fall and spring.

☼ ◐ ◊ ◑   Z5–10 H10–5
↕ to 5ft (1.5m) ↔ to 36in (90cm)

Gillenia trifoliata

PERENNIAL

This is an upright, herbaceous perennial with red-tinted, branched stems and small, single, white to pinkish-white flowers that are good for cutting. Plant it in a well-drained, fertile soil. Native to North American woodlands, it needs the light or dappled shade of a woodland garden or shady border beneath deciduous trees. The tall, wiry stems will need supporting early in the year if the site is exposed. Divide large clumps in the spring or fall.

☀ ◊ ◊　　　　　　　　　Z5–9 H9–5

‡ to 4ft (1.2m) ↔ to 24in (60cm)

Gladiolus callianthus

BULBOUS PERENNIAL

This half-hardy gladiolus may be sold under its former name of *Acidanthera*. The fragrant white flowers, borne on tall, arching stems, have deep red or purple throats and are good for cutting. Plant the corms in a sunny border in well-drained, fertile soil. They will rot quickly in wet conditions, and it is advisable to mix organic matter with heavier soil when planting. They will not survive a cold winter, so dig up the corms in the early fall, dry them, and store in a frost-free place until planting in the spring.

☀ ◊ *f*　　　　　　　　　Z8–10 H11–1

‡ to 3ft (1m) ↔ to 2in (5cm)

x *Halimiocistus sahucii*
EVERGREEN SHRUB

A spreading shrub with narrow, dark green, downy leaves, this species bears a profusion of saucer-shaped, white flowers from early summer to fall. It makes a welcome addition to a gravel or rock garden or a raised bed, where it will enjoy basking in the full heat of the sun. It does well in poor soils, and very well-drained conditions are a must. If in doubt, improve drainage by adding grit to the soil.

☀ ◊   Z7–9 H9–7

↕ to 18in (45cm) ↔ to 36in (90cm)

Hebe 'Pewter Dome'
EVERGREEN SHRUB

A rounded, spreading shrub, it has grayish-green leaves and spikes of small white flowers for several weeks from the early summer. Grow in reasonably fertile, well-drained soil in sun or partial shade. Provide some shade from strong sun, which can burn the leaves. It is suitable for a rock garden or a mixed border and is good for seaside gardens. In mild areas it can be used as a low hedge. It needs no pruning, but hedges can be clipped lightly after flowering.

☀ ☀ ◊   Z9–11 H11–9

↕ to 16in (40cm) ↔ to 24in (60cm)

Helianthemum 'Wisley White'

EVERGREEN SHRUB

Rock roses are attractive dwarf shrubs that bear an abundance of small, saucer-shaped flowers all summer. The papery flowers of 'Wisley White' are pure white with yellow stamens, offset by grayish-green leaves. Rock roses thrive in well-drained soil on sun-baked banks, cracks in paving, and in gravel gardens. Trim after flowering to keep the shape of the bush neat. Propagate by semi-ripe cuttings in the early summer.

☼ ◐   Z6–8 H8–6

↕ to 9in (23cm) ↔ to 12in (30cm)

Hesperis matronalis var. albiflora

PERENNIAL

The tall flower spikes of sweet rocket are a favorite of butterflies. Make the most of the heavenly scent—which, incidentally, grows stronger after dusk—by planting it along a path or patio. It is short-lived and best grown as a biennial. Plants are easy to raise from seed sown in the same area outdoors every year. Grow in full sun, in fertile, moist, well-drained soil. It is also tolerant of poor soil.

☼ ◐ ◐ *f*   Z4–9 H9–1

↕ to 30in (75cm) ↔ to 24in (60cm)

Hydrangea petiolaris

CLIMBER

The climbing hydrangea is a woody-stemmed, deciduous, self-clinging climber. It is a useful flowering plant for shady walls, where it bears large and attractive, lacecaplike heads of creamy white flowers in the summer. The mid-green leaves are oval and coarsely toothed. Plants can sometimes be slow to establish, but once the space is filled, trim back overlong shoots after flowering. Grow in any reliably moist, fertile soil in sun or partial shade, and in areas with very cold winters, choose a sheltered site.

☼ ◑ ◐   Z4–9 H9–1
‡ to 50ft (15m)

Iberis amara

ANNUAL

In the summer this fast-growing annual produces masses of white to purplish-white scented flowers that are borne in dense, flat clusters. Grow in a sunny site and well-drained soil. It is perfect for edging a path or planting in a gravel garden or raised bed. Sow seed in the same area each spring or fall.

☼ ◊ *f*   Z11 H11–1
‡ to 12in (30cm) ↔ to 6in (15cm)

Iris 'Bold Print'

PERENNIAL

Bearded iris come in a huge range of colors and subtle color combinations. 'Bold Print' has striking white flowers that are edged and lightly veined with deep purple. Grow it in full sun in a well-drained, neutral to slightly acid soil. Divide congested clumps in the late summer. When planting, make sure that the tops of the rhizomes are exposed to the sun.

☼ ◊　　　　　　　Z3–9 H9–1

↕ to 22in (55cm) ↔ indefinite

Lamium maculatum 'White Nancy'

PERENNIAL

Ideal as ground cover in shady areas and beneath trees and shrubs, this attractive deadnettle retains its green-edged, silver leaves throughout most winters. In the early summer it produces dainty spikes of hooded, white flowers. Plant it in moist but well-drained soil in full or partial shade. Divide large clumps in the fall or early spring.

☼ ☀ ◊ ◊ 　　　　　Z4–8 H8–1

↕ to 6in (15cm) ↔ to 3ft (1m)

Lavandula angustifolia 'Nana Alba'

EVERGREEN SHRUB

This is a compact, white-flowering variety of the classic English lavender—known for its spikes of fragrant flowers in the early summer. English lavenders establish easily in most well-drained soils in full sun, and 'Nana Alba' makes a fine low hedge or border edge. Prune lavenders back hard each year to sideshoots in the late winter, or they will grow leggy and bare in the middle. After flowering, trim off dead flowerheads, but save hard pruning until later.

☼ ◊ *f*   Z5–8 H8–5

↕↔ to 12in (30cm)

Lavatera x *clementii* 'Barnsley'

SEMI-EVERGREEN SHRUB

The tree mallow is a vigorous, free-flowering, semi-evergreen shrub with lobed green leaves. From the early summer until the first frosts, 'Barnsley' steadily produces clusters of funnel-shaped, white flowers with distinctive red eyes. Choose a spot for it in full sun in well-drained, ideally light, fertile soil. Provide shelter from strong winds since the branches are brittle. Propagate by taking softwood cuttings in the summer. It is suitable for gardens in coastal areas.

☼ ◊   Z6–9 H9–5

↕↔ to 6ft (2m)

Leucanthemum x *superbum* 'Wirral Supreme'

PERENNIAL

A stalwart of the herbaceous border, this vigorous plant produces masses of double, daisylike flowers on stiff, erect stems held above dark green, lance-shaped leaves. The blooms make good cut flowers. In exposed sites the tall stems may need support. Happiest in fairly fertile, well-drained but moist soil in full sun or partial shade, it will eventually spread to form a large clump. Divide established plants in the early spring or late summer.

☼ ◑ ◊ ◖   Z5–8 H8–1

‡ to 36in (90cm) ↔ to 30in (75cm)

Leucojum aestivum 'Gravetye Giant'

BULBOUS PERENNIAL

If left undisturbed in a lightly shaded spot in damp, fertile soil, the summer snowflake will quickly spread to form a large clump of glossy, dark green leaves. From spring to early summer, 'Gravetye Giant' produces up to eight slightly pendent, white flowers tipped with green that have a faint chocolate scent. Plant the bulbs in the fall.

☼ ◖ *f*   Z3–9 H9–1

‡ to 36in (90cm) ↔ to 3in (8cm)

Lilium 'Mont Blanc'

BULBOUS PERENNIAL

From early to midsummer, this sturdy Asiatic lily produces bunches of ivory-white flowers with brown-spotted throats. Its compact stems make it ideal for growing in containers or in a raised bed. Plant bulbs in full sun in fertile, well-drained soil from late fall to early spring. The flowers are good for cutting, but care must be taken because the pollen stains clothing and damages polished surfaces.

☼ ◊   Z5–8 H8–5

↕ to 28in (70cm)

Matthiola 'Hansens Park'

PERENNIAL

Their sweet fragrance makes stocks a popular bedding plant and cut flower. Most have narrow, grayish-green leaves and erect stems. Sow seed in the spring in containers of light potting soil, and overwinter young plants in a cold frame before planting outside the following spring in moist but well-drained, slightly fertile soil. There are a few white-flowering forms available. *M. fructiculosa* 'Alba' is a compact form that is ideal for containers.

☼ ◊ ◖ *f*   Z6–10 H10–6

↕ to 18in (45cm) ↔ to 12in (30cm)

Paeonia lactiflora 'Baroness Schröder'

PERENNIAL

This superb Chinese peony produces a bold clump of dark green leaves and very large, almost globe-shaped flowers. The petals are blushed pink when they first open but turn snow-white as they mature. Plant in fertile, moist but well-drained soil in full sun or partial shade. The blooms are heavy, so provide support for them before they open. The fragrant flowers are excellent for cutting.

☼ ☀ ◊ ◖ *f*   Z3–8 H8–1
‡↔ to 36in (90cm)

Papaver orientale 'Black and White'

PERENNIAL

This white-flowered, oriental poppy has crimson-black markings at the base of the petals. The flowers are borne in the early summer above the mid-green foliage with white-bristled, upright stems; they are followed by distinctive seed pods, which should be cut back at the base to encourage further flowering. Like other oriental poppies, it is a mainstay of the English-style garden border, and its color would suit a border made up of cooler shades. Plant in full sun.

☼ ◊ ◖   Z3–9 H9–1
‡↔ to 36in (90cm)

Philadelphus 'Belle Etoile'

DECIDUOUS SHRUB

Mock orange is a free-flowering shrub with sprays of large, white fragrant flowers. When weighted down with blossoms, the branches arch over, giving the shrub a graceful spreading outline. Plant it in full sun or partial shade in fertile, well-drained soil. Each year, when it has finished flowering, prune some of the older branches down to the ground to encourage new, young shoots.

☼ ☽ ◊ *f*   Z5–8 H8–5
↕ to 4ft (1.2m) ↔ to 8ft (2.5m)

Potentilla fruticosa 'Groneland'

DECIDUOUS SHRUB

Shrubby cinquefoils produce an abundance of charming small flowers over a long period from the late spring to mid-fall. This variety has white flowers, but there are varieties available with red, yellow, or pink flowers. The dark green leaves are composed of several leaflets, and they fall in the winter. This is a dependable, undemanding shrub that would make a useful addition to a mixed or shrub border, or as a low flowering hedge. It prefers to be planted in full sun.

☼ ◊ ◐   Z3–7 H7–1
↕ to 3ft (1m) ↔ to 5ft (1.5m)

Prunus lusitanica subsp. *azorica*
EVERGREEN TREE

This vigorous Portugal laurel forms an evergreen shrub or small tree and bears large glossy leaves. It produces free-flowering spikes of small, white, scented blooms in the late spring and early summer. In the fall it bears red cherrylike fruits that turn black when ripe. This plant grows well even on poor, alkaline soil and will flourish when planted in a sheltered location in full sun. It makes a good specimen plant.

☼ ◊ ◑ *f*   Z7–9 H9–4
 to 70ft (20m)

Pyracantha 'Watereri'
EVERGREEN SHRUB

This upright shrub combines glossy, dark green leaves with an abundance of small, white, early summer flowers. These are followed in the fall and winter by shiny red berries. A good choice for a hedge, its sharp thorns will deter intruders; or train it against a wall. Plant it in a sheltered location in well-drained, fertile soil in full sun or shade. Shorten side shoots to two or three leaves after flowering, and trim hedges in the spring and summer.

☼ ◐ ● ◊   Z7–9 H9–7
↔ to 8ft (2.5m)

Romneya coulteri
DECIDUOUS SHRUB

The California tree poppy is a vigorous bush with large, poppylike, fragrant flowers and gray-green leaves. It can be difficult to establish but in the right conditions will spread extensively. Plant it in a sunny situation in deep, well-drained soil, and provide protection during cold winters—in frost-prone areas, grow plants in the shelter of a sunny wall or fence. It usually dies down each year but should regrow in the spring. Mature plants resent being moved and are best left to grow unhindered.

☼ ◊ *f*   Z8-10 H9-2
↕↔to 6ft (2m)

Rosa 'Blanche Double de Coubert'
DECIDUOUS SHRUB

This shrub rose flowers from early summer to early fall, producing semi-double, fragrant, white blooms. Occasionally it will go on to develop bright red hips in the fall. Suitable for a mixed border, it can also be used as a hedge. It tolerates a wide range of conditions but prefers full sun and an open site on fairly fertile, moist but well-drained soil. In the early spring, remove a few of the oldest stems, and lightly trim back flowering shoots.

☼ ◊ ◗ *f*   Z3-9 H9-1
↕ to 5ft (1.5m) ↔to 4ft (1.2m)

Rosa 'Madame Hardy'

DECIDUOUS SHRUB

Ideal for a mixed border, this attractive shrub rose has vibrant green, leathery foliage and a rounded shape. It flowers only once, producing rosette-shaped blooms that have a green button eye and a spicy fragrance. A sunny site and fertile, moist but well-drained soil is ideal, although it will tolerate a wide range of growing conditions. Prune it in the early spring, removing only the old stems, or lightly trimming it into shape.

☼ ◊ ◐ *f*   Z4–9 H9–1

↕ to 5ft (1.5m) ↔ to 4ft (1.2m)

Styrax hemsleyanus

DECIDUOUS TREE

The snowbell tree is a small and graceful, deciduous tree grown for both its white flowers and its fall foliage color. In the early to midsummer the delicate bell-shaped flowers hang in clusters from the branches. In the fall the leaves turn red and yellow. Snowbells are good trees for small to medium gardens and grow best in a well-drained, neutral to acid soil in full sun or partial shade with shelter from cold winds. *S. japonicus*, the Japanese snowbell, is similar.

☼ ◐ ◊   Z7–9 H9–7

↕ to 15ft (5m) ↔ to 12ft (4m)

Tanacetum parthenium 'Aureum'

PERENNIAL

In the summer, feverfew produces clusters of daisylike, white flowers with dark yellow centers, borne on upright stems above aromatic, golden-yellow leaves. Grow in a sunny border, herb, or rock garden in well-drained soil. Deadhead regularly since it will self-seed liberally.

☼ ◊ *f*   Z4–9 H9–1
↕↔ to 18in (45cm)

Veratrum album

PERENNIAL

A statuesque plant with large, pleated, green leaves in the early summer, it sends up a tall spike of small, star-shaped, white flowers lightly tinged with green. Tolerant of shade and happy in organic, moist but well-drained soil, it is ideal for a woodland garden or shady border. Provided the soil never dries out, it will also adapt to full sun. Protect it from cold, drying winds, and divide congested clumps in the fall or early spring. All parts of this plant are toxic.

☼ ◑ ◊ ◊   H11–10
↕ to 6ft (2m) ↔ to 24in (60cm)

Zantedeschia aethiopica 'Crowborough'

BULBOUS PERENNIAL

The calla lily has shapely flowers held on stiff stems above luxuriant, dark green leaves. 'Crowborough' is hardy and can be planted in shallow water at the edge of a pond or in a border in deep, moist, fertile soil in sun or dappled shade. In the latter situation, protect the root area in the winter with a thick layer of mulch. Where not hardy, overwinter calla lilies in a frost-free location.

☼ ◑ ◊ ◊   Z8–10 H10–4
‡ to 36in (90cm) ↔ to 18in (45cm)

Zenobia pulverulenta

DECIDUOUS SHRUB

From early to midsummer, this attractive shrub produces aniseed-scented, bell-shaped, white flowers that are similar to those of lily-of-the-valley. Its leaves are glossy green above and waxy beneath, turning attractive shades of yellow tinged with red or purple in fall. Give it a sheltered spot, and it may retain some leaves in the winter. It prefers a organic, acidic, moist soil, preferably in partial shade. It will grow in a sunny location, provided the soil never dries out.

☼ ◑ ◊ *f*   Z5–9 H9–5
‡ to 6ft (2m) ↔ to 5ft (1.5m)

Acer negundo 'Flamingo'
DECIDUOUS TREE

This round-headed maple is known for its pink-tinted, white-margined oval leaflets, which appear in the spring and early summer. For larger, more exotic-looking leaves with intensified color, prune the tree to a shrub size every year or two in winter. Kept in this way, the tree will suit a small garden or mixed border. The bare stems in the winter are also attractive. Remove any branches with all-green leaves. Best planted in full sun in an acid to neutral soil.

☼ ◊ ◐   Z5–8 H8–3
↕ to 50ft (15m) ↔ to 30ft (10m)

Allium schoenoprasum
BULBOUS PERENNIAL

Chives are widely grown as a kitchen herb, but the plant is pretty enough to use in an herbaceous border or to edge a bed. In the summer small, dark pink or occasionally lavender-white flowers appear on the top of narrow stems among the grayish-green leaves. Cut back after flowering to encourage fresh leaves to sprout. Chives prefer full sun and well-drained soil. Large clumps may be divided in the spring.

☼ ◊   Z5–11 H11–1
↕ to 10in (25cm) ↔ to 4in (10cm)

Argyranthemum 'Vancouver'

PERENNIAL

With its fernlike foliage and unusual, rose-pink blooms, 'Vancouver' is a particularly striking argyranthemum. It has a long flowering period from early summer until early fall, making it excellent for borders, bedding, and container displays. Pinching off the growing tips will help maintain a neat, bushy shape. It is not fully hardy and is best planted in a sheltered spot in well-drained soil and full sun. Potted up, it can be easily grown in a greenhouse in winter.

☼ ◊   Z7–11 H11–1

↕ to 36in (90cm) ↔ to 32in (80cm)

Astilbe 'Straussenfeder'

PERENNIAL

The dark green leaves—bronze tinted when young—of this astilbe will provide attractive ground cover for a permanently moist border by water or in a bog garden. Sprays of coral-pink flowers are produced in the summer. Astilbes prefer wet, fertile soil in full sun. Plant in groups of four or five for maximum impact. A fast grower, clumps will need to be divided every few years in the early spring to thrive. The faded flowerheads remain attractive through the fall.

☼ ◐ ◑ ◆ ◆   Z3–8 H8–2

↕↔ to 3ft (1m)

Astilbe 'Venus'

PERENNIAL

The limited spread of this astilbe makes
it ideal for a small garden. In the early
summer tall sprays of bright pink flowers
are borne above vibrant green foliage.
It grows best in moist, fertile soil in full
sun and is excellent for a bog garden or
damp soil beside a pond. In drier soils,
grow in partial shade. Divide clumps
every few years in the early spring to
keep plants strong and to encourage
more flowers. The bleached flowerheads
dry well and continue to look attractive
on the plants through the fall.

☼ ☀ ◐ ◖   Z3-8 H8-2
‡↔ to 3ft (1m)

Astrantia major

PERENNIAL

Masterwort is a clump-forming plant
with toothed, mid-green leaves. The
tiny, early summer flowers are pink
or green and surrounded by a pinkish-
white, papery collar. Astrantias prefer
moist, fertile soil in full sun or light
shade. They are good for a slightly
shaded herbaceous border, a woodland
garden, or damp ground beside a pond
or stream. Deadhead to prevent self-
seeding. Large clumps may be divided
in the spring.

☼ ☀ ◐ ◖   Z4-7 H7-1
‡ to 24in (60cm) ↔ to 18in (45cm)

Campanula lactiflora 'Loddon Anna'

PERENNIAL

The milky bellflower is a tall herbaceous plant that bears large clusters of bell-shaped, lilac-pink flowers throughout the summer. They may need staking since they are inclined to fall over in strong winds. It enjoys full sun or dappled shade in a fertile, neutral to alkaline, moist, well-drained soil. It self-seeds and can be divided in the spring or fall. 'Prichard's Variety' is not as tall and has violet-blue flowers.

☼ ◑ ◊ ◊   Z5–7 H7–5

↕ to 4ft (1.2m) ↔ to 24in (60cm)

Campanula punctata

PERENNIAL

This low-growing bellflower thrives in moist but well-drained, fertile, fairly light soil, particularly if it gets plenty of sun. In the early summer, dusky- to shell-pink flowers hang from erect stems. Their inner surfaces are freckled red and covered in a fuzz of soft hairs. The dark green, semi-evergreen leaves are heart-shaped at the base. To encourage a second flush of blooms and prevent self-seeding, cut back after flowering.

☼ ◑ ◊ ◊   Z4–8 H8–1

↕ to 12in (30cm) ↔ to 16in (40cm)

Centaurea hypoleuca '*John Coutts*'

PERENNIAL

This upright plant has grayish-green, wavy-edged leaves. The long-lasting, fragrant flowers are borne singly on long stems throughout the early summer. The outer florets are star-shaped with bright pink thistlelike centers. Plant in a border or rock garden in full sunshine and well-drained soil. Divide big clumps in the spring or fall.

☼ ◊ *f*   Z3–9 H9–1

‡ to 24in (60cm) ↔ to 18in (45cm)

Centranthus ruber

PERENNIAL

Red valerian will grow in some of the most exposed places: on cliffs, walls, and at the edge of roads. It is also grown successfully as a border perennial, where it is valued for its long flowering season. It has fleshy, bright-green leaves and, throughout the summer, branching stems covered with small, star-shaped, pink, red, or white flowers. Plant in poor, well-drained soil in full sun and deadhead regularly. Suitable for coastal gardens.

☼ ◊   Z5–8 H8–5

‡ to 36in (90cm) ↔ to 24in (60cm)

Cistus x *argenteus* 'Peggy Sammons'

EVERGREEN SHRUB

Each bloom on a rock rose lasts for only one day, but they are produced constantly from early to late summer. 'Peggy Sammons' has large, purplish-pink flowers and grayish-green leaves. It thrives on well-drained soil, or even poor soil, in full sun and will survive most winters in a sheltered location. Grow in containers around paved areas, on sunny banks, in a border, or in coastal gardens.

☼ ◊   Z8–10 H10–8

↔ to 3ft (1m)

Clematis 'Comtesse de Bouchaud'

CLIMBER

A vigorous, deciduous clematis with pale green leaves. In the summer many pinkish-mauve flowers are produced with dark lines radiating out from their yellow centers. Grow in well-drained, fertile soil in sun or partial shade with the roots in shade. Cut back in early spring to a pair of strong buds 8in (20cm) above soil level since this will encourage flowers. Clematis are often grown through roses and other shrubs or trees, or used to clothe a trellis, walls, or arches.

☼ ☽ ◊   Z4–11 H9–1

↔ to 10ft (3m)

Clematis 'Nelly Moser'

CLIMBER

In the early summer this deciduous clematis bears large, pinkish-purple flowers with a reddish stripe down the center of each petal. The foliage is a pretty, pale green. It is best grown in well-drained fertile soil in a slightly shaded location since the blooms fade in strong sun. Let it scramble through a tree or shrub, or over a trellis or an arch. To encourage plenty of flowers, remove any dead stems in the early spring and prune remaining shoots back to a pair of strong buds.

☀ ◐ ◊   Z4–11 H9–1
↕ to 10ft (3m)

Cordyline 'Southern Splendour'

PERENNIAL

This cultivar of New Zealand cabbage palm features an upright, arching look with pink, gray-green, and bronze-striped, sword-shaped, evergreen leaves. It is a great choice for containers—inside or out. Also suitable as a specimen plant in a mixed or shrub border or in a courtyard garden. Apply a balanced fertilizer when planting. Grow in full sun to partial shade in well-drained soil.

☀ ◐ ◊   Z9–11 H11–8
↕ to 10ft (3m) ↔ to 24in (60cm)

Cornus kousa 'Miss Satomi'

DECIDUOUS TREE

This dramatic dogwood has many attractive features, including decorative bark, deep purplish-red leaves in the fall, and a handsome shape. Perhaps most striking, though, is the early summer display of masses of dark pink bracts against the dark green foliage. The bracts surround a cluster of tiny flowers. Plant in a sunny or partially shaded location in neutral or acidic, well-drained, organic soil.

☼ ◑ ◊   Z5–8 H8–5

↕ to 22ft (7m) ↔ to 15ft (5m)

Daboecia cantabrica 'Bicolor'

EVERGREEN SHRUB

The leaves of the Cantabrian heath are larger than other heathers. The urn-shaped flowers are borne over a long period from early summer to mid-fall, and 'Bicolor' produces blooms in purple-pink, white, or striped on the same flower spike. Plant it in full sun or light shade in neutral or acid, well-drained soil. It is suitable for a rock or heather garden and forms a colorful carpet when used as ground cover.

☼ ◑ ◊   Z6–8 H8–6

↕ to 18in (45cm) ↔ to 24in (60cm)

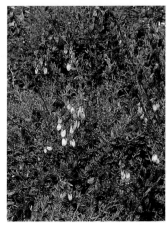

Deutzia x *elegantissima* 'Rosealind'

DECIDUOUS SHRUB

Deutzias are stunning when grown in the border or as a specimen plant; choose a location in full sun and fertile, well-drained soil. Thousands of star-shaped, pale pink flowers are borne in the early summer. Maintain this shrub's neat shape by pruning out old and flowered shoots when the blooms have faded.

☼ ◊   Z6–8 H8–6

‡ to 4ft (1.2m) ↔ to 5ft (1.5m)

Dianthus alpinus 'Joan's Blood'

PERENNIAL

Alpine pinks are compact, tuft-forming evergreens with narrow, shiny, dark green leaves. In summer, 'Joan's Blood' is almost completely covered by large, deep pink flowers with toothed petals. This decorative plant is ideal for planting at the front of borders, in raised beds, rock gardens, and between paving slabs. Choose a sunny spot in organic, well-drained soil.

☼ ◊   Z4–8 H8–1

‡ to 3in (8cm) ↔ to 4in (10cm)

Dianthus 'Doris'

PERENNIAL

With its pale pink, wavy-edged petals and raspberry-colored center, this is one of the prettiest pinks. Often two or three flushes of clove-scented blooms will be borne from the early summer to the fall above a mound of gray-green leaves. The flowers are decorative in a border and very long lasting when cut. Pinks thrive in well-drained soil and full sun.

☼ ◊ *f*　　　　　　Z5–9 H8-1

‡ to 18in (45cm) ↔ to 16in (40cm)

Dianthus 'Houndspool Ruby'

PERENNIAL

This bold pink has double, rose-pink flowers with a splash of red at their center and delicately fringed petals. Modern pinks bloom throughout the summer, are good in a border, and excellent for cutting. They also form dense mounds of narrow, gray-green, evergreen leaves. Choose a location in full sun with well-drained soil.

☼ ◊　　　　　　Z4–10 H10-1

‡ to 18in (45cm) ↔ to 12in (30cm)

Dictamnus albus var. *purpureus*

PERENNIAL

The burning bush produces aromatic oils that can, very occasionally, ignite on a hot summer's day. Long spikes of large pink flowers with dark purple veins are produced in the early summer. The foliage is lemon-scented, but be careful since contact with its leaves may irritate the skin. Plant in well-drained soil in sun or partial shade, and avoid transplanting because it does not like to be disturbed.

☼ ☀ ◊ *f*   Z3–8 H8–3

↕ to 36in (90cm) ↔ to 24in (60cm)

Dierama pulcherrimum

BULBOUS PERENNIAL

Angel's fishing rod is so named because the bright pink, bell-shaped flowers hang from graceful, arching stems in the summer. The narrow leaves are grayish-green and grasslike. It is especially pretty grown beside a pond, where the water will reflect its slender form, or in a border. Choose a sunny situation in reliably moist but well-drained soil, planting the bulbs 2–3in (5–7cm) deep, in the spring.

☼ ◊ ◖   Z8–10 H10–8

↕ to 5ft (1.5m) ↔ to 24in (60cm)

Digitalis x *mertonensis*
PERENNIAL

This foxglove has large, strawberry-
colored, funnel-shaped flowers borne
on sturdy spikes in the early summer.
It forms clumps of handsome, glossy
green leaves. Foxgloves prefer moist,
well-drained soil in partial shade but
will tolerate a wide range of conditions.
They do equally well in a border or
naturalized beneath deciduous trees.
Allow plants to self-seed or sow seed
in late spring.

☼ ☀ ◊ ◐   Z3–8 H8–1

↕ to 36in (90cm) ↔ to 12in (30cm)

Eremurus robustus
PERENNIAL

From a clump of strappy, bluish-green
leaves, this impressive plant produces
a tower of pale pink flowers on top of
a tall, leafless stem. Foxtail lilies look
best when several are grouped together
in a border. Grow in a sunny location in
sandy, very well-drained soil since the
roots will die if they get too wet in
the winter. The flower spikes may need
support, especially in exposed areas. In
late winter and spring, if frost threatens,
mulch with straw or cover with garden
fabric to protect emerging shoots.

☼ ◊   Z5–8 H8–5

↕ to 10ft (3m) ↔ to 4ft (1.2m)

Escallonia 'Apple Blossom'
EVERGREEN SHRUB

A bushy shrub with rounded, glossy green leaves, this escallonia bears small, clear pink flowers with white centers in the early summer. Grow it in a border, against a wall, or as a hedge or windbreak. If the wind is not too cold, it will also thrive in coastal areas. To help maintain a neat shape, trim lightly in mid- to late spring.

☼ ◊　　　　　　　　　　　　　Z8–9 H9–8
↕↔to 8ft (2.5m)

Filipendula rubra 'Venusta'
PERENNIAL

Queen of the prairies is a spreading perennial with architectural, deeply-cut, mid-green foliage. In the summer it produces branched stems bearing clusters of tiny, fragrant, deep rose-pink flowers. It is a bog plant and needs to be planted in partial shade, although it tolerates full sun in permanently moist soil. Grow close to a pond margin or in damp ground beneath deciduous trees; it will only thrive in an herbaceous border if the soil never dries out.

☼ ◑ ◊ ◕ *f*　　　　　　　　　Z3–9 H9–1
↕ to 8ft (2.5m) ↔to 4ft (1.2m)

Fragaria PINK PANDA ('Frel')

PERENNIAL

This vigorous ground-cover plant is related to the strawberry but rarely fruits. Deep pink flowers are produced for a long period during summer. The leaves are bright green, deeply veined, and almost evergreen. It does well in full sun or partial shade and prefers moist but well-drained, fertile soil. Ideal for the front of an herbaceous border, if it threatens to spread out of bounds, control it by removing unwanted runners (the horizontal stems).

☀ ◐ ◊ ◑　　　　　　　　Z5–9 H9–5

‡ to 6in (15cm) ↔ indefinite

Geranium endressii

PERENNIAL

A clump-forming hardy geranium, or cranesbill, with trumpet-shaped, pale pink flowers with notched petals. The evergreen leaves are hairy and wrinkly. Cranesbills tolerate a wide range of soil types and growing conditions, coping well in full sun or partial shade—a rock garden, the front of a mixed border, or a wild garden are ideal. Cut back after flowering to encourage fresh growth and more flowers. *G. endressii* combines well with a blue-flowering geranium such as *G. ibericum*.

☀ ◐ ◊ ◑　　　　　　　　Z5–8 H9–1

‡ to 18in (45cm) ↔ to 24in (60cm)

Geranium x riversleaianum 'Russell Prichard'

PERENNIAL

This hardy geranium, or cranesbill, has trailing, creeping stems, making it a good ground-cover plant. In the summer it has deeply divided, slightly hairy, grayish-green leaves and deep magenta flowers. It prefers to be planted in full sun in well-drained, slightly fertile soil but will tolerate a wide range of conditions. Cut back after flowering to encourage fresh growth and more flowers.

☼ ◊   Z6–8 H8–6

↕ to 12in (30cm) ↔ to 3ft (1m)

Gladiolus 'Rose Supreme'

BULBOUS PERENNIAL

This is one of the largest gladioli available; the tall spikes can hold as many as 24 flowers above a fan of sword-shaped leaves. Each rose-pink bloom has a cream throat and dark pink edges. Plant it in full sun in fertile, well-drained soil, and support with a stake. Gladioli are superb for adding height to a border and make excellent cut flowers. Lift corms in fall, store dry over the winter, and replant in the spring in soil enriched with organic matter.

☼ ◊   Z8–10 H11–1

↕ to 5ft (1.7m) ↔ to 10in (25cm)

Helianthemum 'Rhodanthe Carneum'

EVERGREEN SHRUB

A wide-spreading rock rose with silver-gray leaves. In the summer it produces numerous flat, pale pink flowers marked with yellow in the center. Grow it at the front of a border, in a raised bed, alongside paving, or in a rock garden. Choose a location in fertile, well-drained soil and full sun. Prune after flowering to keep the bush compact and prevent it from becoming leggy.

☼ ◊   Z6–8 H8–6

↕↔to 12in (30cm)

Iberis umbellata Fairy Series

ANNUAL

The abundant and colorful flowers of this candytuft are invaluable in the spring and summer. They flower freely in an interesting mix of pink shades, from almost white to lilac-purple or reddish-pink. They are hardy annuals so will grow from seed each year, but they are also readily available as bedding plants. Useful for containers, large gaps in patio paving, and the fronts of borders, they do best in full sun, in poor to moderately fertile soil that is moist but well drained.

☼ ◊ ◑   H11–1

↕↔to 8in (20cm)

Impatiens walleriana 'Tempo Lavender'

PERENNIAL

With its vivid, lavender-pink, long-lasting flowers and light green leaves, 'Tempo Lavender' is a particularly pretty summer bedding plant. Available in a wide range of colors, impatiens are tender perennials that are usually grown as annuals. For the best flowers, choose a spot in partial shade in moist but well-drained soil. They also make good container plants.

☀ ◊ ◑   Z10–11 H11–1
↕↔to 10in (25cm)

Incarvillea delavayi

PERENNIAL

An exotic-looking plant with large flowers held on strong stems above a rosette of lush, mid-green leaves. The flowerhead consists of up to 10 trumpet-shaped, rose-pink or purple blooms. Grow it in fertile, moist, well-drained soil in a bright, sunny location but, preferably, one that avoids direct midday sun. A good choice for a rock garden or mixed or herbaceous border.

☼ ◊ ◑   Z6–10 H9–3
↕ to 24in (60cm) ↔ to 12in (30cm)

Indigofera amblyantha
DECIDUOUS SHRUB

A medium-sized, spreading shrub grown
for its long display of pealike flowers and
elegant foliage. The small, purplish-pink
flowers begin to appear in dense clusters
in the early summer and continue into
the fall. Its arching stems carry gray-
green leaves made up of many leaflets.
It prefers a sunny site and suits most
well-drained soil types. Train it against
a warm wall in cold climates. Prune
established plants in the early spring,
cutting back to just above ground level. *I.
heterantha* is similar, also recommended.

☼ ◊　　　　　　　Z6–9 H9–6
↕↔ to 6ft (2m)

Iris
'Carnaby'
PERENNIAL

Bearded irises are mostly grown for
their flamboyant flowers that come in
a huge range of colors; however their
sword-shaped leaves are attractive, too.
This variety has large flowers with peach-
pink upper petals and pink-purple lower
petals that are furred with an orange
"beard." Divide congested clumps of iris
after flowering, replanting only plump
sections of rhizome in a sunny spot in
well-drained, fertile soil, ensuring their
tops are exposed to the sun.

☼ ◊　　　　　　　Z3–9 H9–1
↕ to 3ft (1m) ↔ indefinite

Kalmia latifolia
EVERGREEN SHRUB

The calico bush is an excellent choice for slightly acid soil, where your reward will be large heads of pink or white flowers. It is a rounded bush with oval, dark green leaves. Kalmias prefer organic, moist but well-drained, acidic soil in partial shade, although they will tolerate full sun where the ground remains damp in the summer. Deadhead regularly and lightly trim after flowering to maintain its shape. Mulch annually with leaf mold or bark chips.

☼ ◐ ◊ ◊   Z5–9 H9–5
↨ to 10ft (3m)

Lupinus 'The Chatelaine'
PERENNIAL

The stately, pink-and-white flowered spires of this lupine are excellent for lending height and color to a border from early to midsummer. They are also good for cutting. The palmlike, mid-green leaves are beautiful in their own right, and after drops of rain collect on their surface. Lupines are generally short-lived but last longest in sunshine in slightly acid to neutral soils with good drainage. Protect the young growth from slugs and snails. Varieties are available in a range of colors.

☼ ◊   Z5–8 H8–5
↕ to 4ft (1.2m) ↔ to 18in (45cm)

Lychnis flos-jovis

PERENNIAL

The upright stems of the flower of Jove are covered with white hairs, giving them a silvery appearance, while the spoon-shaped, soft basal leaves are also silver-gray. From early to late summer clusters of pink, scarlet, or white flowers with deeply divided petals appear. This species is a good choice for the front of a sunny border or a rock garden. Plant it in well-drained, slightly fertile soil, and sow seed in the spring.

☼ ◊   Z4–8 H8–1

↔ to 18in (45cm)

Matthiola incana Cinderella Series

PERENNIAL

Stocks are extremely fragrant flowers that, despite being perennial, are usually grown as a biennial or annual. The Cinderella Series has double white, deep pink, purple, or lavender flowers, produced from the early summer. Plant in a sunny location in fertile, well-drained, neutral or slightly alkaline soil. Stocks are excellent as annual bedding and as cut flowers.

☼ ◊ *f*   Z5-8 H8-5

↔ to 10in (25cm)

Nectaroscordum siculum subsp. *bulgaricum*
BULBOUS PERENNIAL

An elegant perennial with pendulous, pink-flushed, bell-shaped flowers that are borne on tall stems. These emerge from a clump of garlic-smelling, linear leaves. It can be grown in full sun or partial shade and prefers a slightly fertile, well-drained soil. This bulb is ideal for a wild garden, where it may freely self-seed. In an herbaceous border, to help control its spread simply deadhead regularly.

☀ ☀ ◊   Z6–10 H10–1

‡ to 4ft (1.2m) ↔ to 18in (45cm)

Neillia thibetica
DECIDUOUS SHRUB

This shrub grows well in a border or beneath deciduous trees, spreading by suckers to form a dense thicket. The arching branches have glossy green leaves and long clusters of bright pink, bell-shaped flowers. Grow in full sun or partial shade in fertile, well-drained soil. To encourage strong new growth the following year, prune after flowering by cutting branches back to a strong pair of buds, and removing a quarter of the stems right to the base of the plant.

☀ ◊   Z6–9 H9–6

‡↔ to 6ft (2m)

Onoportdum acanthium
BIENNIAL

The Scotch thistle is an architectural
plant that is good for a large border or
a wild or gravel garden. In its first year,
an impressive rosette of spiny, grayish
green leaves is formed. During the
second year, a strong, prickly stem,
which is covered with white hairs, is
produced. The stem is crowned with
thistlelike flowerheads, composed of
many small deep pink or occasionally
white flowers. Grow in full sun in
fertile, well-drained, neutral or alkaline
soil. It will readily self-seed.

☼ ◊   Z6–8 H11–7
‡ to 6ft (1.8m) ↔ to 3ft (1m)

Osteospermum jucundum
PERENNIAL

Free-flowering and extremely decorative,
this is an excellent perennial for any
border. It has pretty mauvish-pink or
magenta, daisylike blooms that are
produced throughout summer above
a clump of grayish-green leaves. Grow
in well-drained, fertile soil in full sun.
Regular deadheading will help extend
the flowering period.

☼ ◊   Z9–11 H6–1
‡↔ to 12in (30cm)

Paeonia lactiflora 'Monsieur Jules Elie'

PERENNIAL

A large, herbaceous peony with bold clumps of glossy, dark green leaves. In the early summer it produces deep pink, double flowers that are good for cutting. Grow in a border in sun or partial shade in deep, fertile, well-drained soil. For the best blooms, mulch generously with organic matter in the fall. The blooms, which reach over 8in (20cm) across, may need some support—encircling stakes are ideal. Clumps are best left undisturbed.

☼ ❂ ◊ ◗   Z3–8 H8–1

↕↔ to 3ft (1m)

Papaver orientale 'Cedric Morris'

PERENNIAL

The Oriental poppy is a vigorous plant that will provide a spectacular splash of color in any border. It forms a large clump of lobed, gray-haired leaves, and in the summer tall stems bear very large, soft-pink flowers with a black mark at the base of each petal. After the decorative seed pods appear, the plant dies down—make sure it is hidden by other plants during this unattractive phase. Plant in full sun in fertile, well-drained soil; sow seed in the spring.

☼ ◊   Z3–9 H9–1

↕↔ to 36in (90cm)

Papaver somniferum '**Paeony Flowered**'

ANNUAL

Although grown mainly for its beautiful flowers, the opium poppy also has handsome blue-green leaves and decorative pepper-pot seed pods. In the summer the 'Peony Flowered' type bears huge, rounded, frilly blooms in shades of pink or purple. Sow in the same area in the spring in a sunny location. It does best in very well-drained soil in an annual border or in gaps in an herbaceous or mixed border.

☼ ◊　　　　　　　　Z3–8 H8–1
‡ to 4ft (1.2m) ↔ to 12in (30cm)

Persicaria bistorta '**Superba**'

PERENNIAL

Bistort is a vigorous plant that is often used in a border or wild garden or as ground cover. Numerous flower spikes are held well above clumps of broad, mid-green leaves in early summer. They are made up of many tiny, densely packed, soft-pink flowers. Although it will tolerate dry soil, it prefers moist ground in full sun or partial shade. Divide large clumps in the spring or fall.

☼ ◐ ◊ ◐　　　　　　Z4–8 H8–1
‡ to 30in (75cm) ↔ to 24in (60cm)

Petunia SURFINIA PINK VEIN ('Suntosol')

PERENNIAL

The Surfinia Series is well known for its large summer flowers and vigorous growth. Their trailing style makes them ideal for containers and hanging baskets. They can also be used as bedding, but the flowers may be damaged by heavy rain. In a border, provide a sunny location and well-drained soil. Deadhead regularly and feed container-grown plants with a tomato fertilizer every 10–14 days to prolong flowering. Petunias are usually grown as annuals.

☼ ◊   Z11 H11–1

‡ to 16in (40cm) ↔ to 36in (90cm)

Primula vialii

PERENNIAL

Grow this unusual-looking primula beside a pond or in any moist site in sun or, preferably, partial shade. In the summer, from a rosette of hairy leaves, it produces a stout stem topped with a tight spike of small pink flowers that emerge from crimson buds. *P. vialii* performs best in organic, neutral or acid soil. Although perennial it can be rather short-lived; sow, or allow to self-seed, in the spring to renew your stock.

☼ ◑ ◊   Z5–8 H8–5

‡ to 24in (60cm) ↔ to 12in (30cm)

Robinia 'Idaho'
DECIDUOUS TREE

The Idaho locust is a beautiful, fast-growing, deciduous tree grown for its wisterialike clusters of pale pinkish-purple flowers. These appear in the early summer while the foliage is still a lovely fresh green, and their fragrance is very attractive to pollinating insects. The fernlike foliage only casts light shade, which allows for planting beneath this tough, drought-tolerant tree. The loosely columnar canopy retains its elegance even after flowering. Choose a sunny site sheltered from strong winds.

☼ ◊ ◐ *f*   Z6–10 H10–6
↕ to 50ft (15m) ↔ to 25ft (8m)

Rosa 'Blessings'
DECIDUOUS SHRUB

If deadheaded regularly, this hybrid tea rose will produce many urn-shaped, pink, scented blooms through the fall. Prune the main stems to 10in (25cm) above the ground in the early spring, then apply a balanced fertilizer and mulch generously with well-rotted manure to encourage the production of lots of flowers. Roses should be planted in a sunny location in fertile, organic, well-drained soil, preferably slightly acid or neutral.

☼ ◊ ◐ *f*   Z5–9 H9–5
↕ to 3ft (1m) ↔ to 30in (75cm)

Rosa 'Frühlingsmorgen'

DECIDUOUS SHRUB

A healthy, upright shrub rose with dark, grayish-green leaves. The single, blossom-pink, hay-scented flowers are produced in the early summer. It can be grown up a pillar, in mixed borders, or as hedging and will even tolerate light shade. It needs less rich conditions than hybrid teas and other bush roses. To maintain a neat shape, lightly trim the bush after flowering.

☼ ◊ ◑ *f*   Z4–9 H9–4

↕ to 6ft (2m) ↔ to 5ft (1.5m)

Rosa GERTRUDE JEKYLL ('Ausbord')

DECIDUOUS SHRUB

Named after the famous Edwardian garden designer, this is a slender, large-flowered shrub rose. It is grown for its deep pink flowers, which are extremely fragrant and start to appear in the early summer. With regular deadheading, flowering may continue into the early fall. This disease-resistant rose needs rich growing conditions, so mulch deeply in the early spring with well-rotted manure after lightly pruning it to shape—although this is not essential.

☼ ◊ ◑ *f*   Z5–9 H9–1

↕ to 6ft (2m) ↔ to 4ft (1.2m)

Rosa 'Madame Knorr'

DECIDUOUS SHRUB

An old variety of Portland rose with large, lilac-pink, very fragrant flowers throughout the summer months. It is an easygoing rose with mid-green foliage and thorny stems. It does well on most well-drained soils and even in poor conditions. When used as hedging, trim it back in the late winter or early spring.

☼ ◑ ◊ *f*   Z5–9 H9–5

‡ to 4ft (1.2m) ↔ to 3ft (1m)

Rosa SURREY ('Korlanum')

DECIDUOUS SHRUB

Ground-cover roses are chosen for their low, spreading style and abundant, healthy foliage. They can be used in many situations: in a border, trailing down a bank or over a wall, and in a container or large hanging basket. Surrey is disease resistant, grows quickly, and is very free flowering with double soft-pink blooms. Grow in moist but well-drained, fertile soil in full sun. Trim in the late winter or early spring to keep it within bounds.

☼ ◊ ◑   Z5–9 H9–5

‡ to 32in (80cm) ↔ to 4ft (1.2m)

Salvia viridis Claryssa Series

ANNUAL

Clary is an aromatic plant with upright, branching stems. Seed is available in single shades or in rainbow mixtures. The bracts of 'Claryssa Pink' are a particularly bright, rose-pink hue and appear from early summer. Sow seeds in the same area in midspring in well-drained soil. It can be used as a long-lasting cut or dried flower.

☼ ☀ ◊ ◖ *f*   H9–1

‡ to 16in (40cm) ↔ to 9in (23cm)

Sidalcea 'Elsie Heugh'

PERENNIAL

This false mallow forms clumps of rounded, basal leaves. In the early summer upright stems hold purple-pink, fringed flowers that have the texture of satin. They are excellent for cutting. Grow in a sunny border in well-drained, neutral to slightly acid, fertile soil.

☼ ☀ ◊ ◖   Z5–7 H8–2

‡ to 36in (90cm) ↔ to 18in (45cm)

Spiraea japonica var. *albiflora*

DECIDUOUS SHRUB

This compact, deciduous shrub would suit a mixed or shrub border but could also be grown as a low, informal, flowering hedge. The bronze-tinted new leaves emerge in the spring. As they fade to mid-green in the early summer, dense clusters of tiny pale pink flowers gradually emerge with the full display in midsummer. Grow in a sunny location in well-drained soil, and prune established plants back to a framework before the leaves emerge in the spring.

☼ ◊ ◑   Z5–8 H8–5

↔ to 3ft (1m)

Tanacetum coccineum 'Eileen May Robinson'

PERENNIAL

The painted daisy is a bushy plant with silver-haired, balsam-scented leaves that can be used as a cut flower and to make potpourri. In the early summer it produces an abundance of soft-pink flowers. Cut back after the flowers fade to encourage a second flush. It will tolerate any light, well-drained soil in full sunshine.

☼ ◊ *f*   Z5–9 H9–5

↕ to 30in (75cm) ↔ to 18in (45cm)

Thymus serpyllum 'Annie Hall'

EVERGREEN SHRUB

This thyme forms a mat of creeping branches covered in the summer with numerous tiny, pale pink flowers. Its small, dark green leaves are highly aromatic when crushed, making it ideal for planting in paving crevices where its pungent oils are released each time it is stepped on. Alternatively, plant it in an herb or rock garden or in containers, choosing a sunny location and very well-drained soil.

☼ ◊ *f* Z4–9 H9–1

↕ to 10in (25cm) ↔ to 18in (45cm)

Verbascum 'Helen Johnson'

PERENNIAL

This mullein produces tall spikes of pinkish-brown, saucer-shaped flowers in the early to midsummer. They emerge from an evergreen rosette of downy, grayish-green leaves. Plant in a border or rock garden in a sunny location in well-drained soil. 'Helen Johnson' can be short-lived, so propagate new plants by division in the fall.

☼ ◊ Z6–9 H9–5

↕ to 36in (90cm) ↔ to 12in (30cm)

Verbena 'Sissinghurst'

PERENNIAL

This sprawling verbena is ideal for
containers and especially hanging
baskets. It has dark green leaves and
during the summer and into fall, large,
round clusters of bright, magenta-pink
flowers. Usually grown as an annual
in cooler regions, it can be potted
and taken into a greenhouse for the
winter. It is easily grown from semi-
ripe cuttings of non-flowering shoots
taken in the late summer.

☼ ◊ ◑   Z7–11 H11–1

‡ to 8in (20cm) ↔ to 3ft (1m)

Veronica spicata 'Rotfuchs'

PERENNIAL

Also known as 'Red Fox', this clump-
forming perennial is a valuable plant for
the herbaceous border because it bears
striking spires of rich rose-pink flowers
for many weeks in the summer. In full
bloom it has a spiky appearance, so it
would be useful mixed in with plants
of other shapes and textures to create
interest. The lance-shaped, deciduous
leaves are deep green. Choose a moist
but well-drained site in full sun, and cut
back after flowering.

☼ ◊ ◑   Z3–8 H8–1

‡↔ to 22in (50cm)

Aesculus x *carnea* 'Briotii'
DECIDUOUS TREE

This red-flowered horse chestnut is a spreading, rounded tree admired in the early summer for its large, upright cones of dark rose-red flowers, which are followed by spiny fruits. The dark green, palmlike leaves are divided into 5–7 leaflets. It is a large tree, only good for big gardens, but its resistance to horse chestnut leaf miner makes it a good alternative to the increasingly affected common horse chestnut. The yellow horse chestnut, *A.* x *neglecta* 'Autumn Fire' is smaller. Plant in sun or partial shade.

☼ ☀ ◐ ◑   Z7–8 H8–6
‡ to 70ft (20m) ↔ to 50ft (15m)

Astilbe 'Fanal'
PERENNIAL

This dramatic herbaceous plant bears plumes of tiny red flowers in the early summer. Its divided, toothed, deep green foliage contrasts well with the blooms and is a feature in its own right. Astilbes flourish in organic, fertile soil in a permanently damp border at the edge of a woodland garden, in a bog garden, or by water. They prefer a location in partial shade, although they will grow in full sun as long as the soil never dries out.

☼ ☀ ◐ ◑   Z3–8 H8–2
‡ to 24in (60cm) ↔ to 36in (90cm)

Astrantia 'Hadspen Blood'

PERENNIAL

Growing to two feet tall, this masterwort selection forms a clump of deeply lobed green leaves, and bears sprays of tiny, dark red flowers surrounded by petal-like bracts for many months from early to midsummer. Plant astrantias beside a stream, in a damp border or a deciduous woodland garden in moist, fertile soil in full sun or partial shade. Large clumps can be divided in spring.

☼ ☀ ◐   Z4–7 H7–1

↕ to 36in (90cm) ↔ to 18in (45cm)

Cirsium rivulare 'Atropurpureum'

PERENNIAL

The thistlelike flowers and informal look of this plant make it ideal for growing in a naturalized garden, a damp meadow, or in association with ornamental grasses. It forms clumps of narrow, lance-shaped leaves, covered beneath with soft hairs and in early summer produces tall stems of reddish-purple blooms. It needs to be planted in a sunny location in moist, well-drained soil. To propagate, divide it in the fall or early spring.

☼ ◐ ◐   Z4–8 H8–1

↕ to 4ft (1.2m) ↔ to 24in (60cm)

Clematis 'Jackmanii Rubra'

CLIMBER

Mid-season clematis come in many shapes and colors with a flowering season that is concentrated during the early part of the summer. They look very attractive trailing through shrubs like roses or along a trellis, especially if they bloom just before or after their hosts or neighbors. 'Jackmanii Rubra' has crimson, velvety blooms aboout 4in (10cm) across. Plant in full sun. Mulch around the roots in the late winter, and train young growth carefully. Trim lightly in the late winter.

☼ ◊ ◐ Z4–11 H9–1
↕ to 10ft (3m)

Clematis 'Niobe'

CLIMBER

Possibly the best of all the red clematis, 'Niobe' has single, velvety, deep ruby-red flowers with yellow stamens, and blooms for a long period in the summer. It will brighten up a trellis, or train it over an arch or up a post. Plant 'Niobe' in a fertile, well-drained soil in sun or partial shade with the roots in shade. It does particularly well in alkaline soil. In the early spring remove any dead or damaged growth, and cut the rest of the stems back to a strong pair of buds.

☼ ◐ ◊ Z4–11 H9–1
↕ to 10ft (3m)

Dianthus barbatus 'Dunnet's Dark Crimson'

BIENNIAL

Sweet Williams are valued for their early summer flowers and wonderful perfume, and 'Dunnet's Dark Crimson' is a particularly decorative variety. Its dark, bronzy-green leaves contrast well with the dense clusters of deep red flowers. Sweet Williams will grow well in a sunny herbaceous border in fertile, well-drained, neutral to alkaline soil. Good for cutting.

☼ ◊   Z3–9 H9–1

↕ to 24in (60cm) ↔ to 12in (30cm)

Embothrium coccineum Lanceolatum Group

EVERGREEN SHRUB

The Chilean firebush is an eye-catching shrub in the early summer, when it bears clusters of showy, tubular, flaming scarlet flowers that stand out brilliantly against the shiny, dark green, narrow leaves. If allowed to grow, it can become a large shrub for a medium to large garden— either as a free-standing specimen or as part of a shrub border. Choose a sheltered site with moist but well-drained, acid to neutral soil in full sun or partial shade. Needs minimal pruning.

☼ ◐ ◊ ◊   Z8–11 H11–8

↕ to 30ft (10m) ↔ to 15ft (5m)

Geum 'Red Wings'

PERENNIAL

'Red Wings' is considered to be one of the best geums available. It is an herbaceous perennial, forming clumps of hairy, fresh green, divided leaves. In the early and midsummer bowl-shaped, semi-double, bright scarlet flowers rise up on long, branching stems; these last well when cut. Geums are best suited to mixed or herbaceous borders in full sun in most fertile, moist but well-drained soils. Varieties with yellow and orange flowers are also available. Cut back after flowering.

☼ ◊ ◑   Z5–9 H9–5

‡ to 24in (60cm) ↔ to 16in (40cm)

Helianthemum 'Fire Dragon'

EVERGREEN SHRUB

This rock rose flowers for many months from the early summer and quickly spreads to form a dense mound of linear, gray-green leaves, which set off the bright orange-red, cup-shaped blooms. It will inject color into a sunny bank, rock garden, or a raised bed. It will flourish in full sun and a well-drained, alkaline soil and should be trimmed after flowering to maintain its shape.

☼ ◊   Z6–8 H8–6

‡ to 12in (30cm) ↔ to 18in (45cm)

Heuchera 'Cherries Jubilee'

EVERGREEN PERENNIAL

Heucheras are invaluable little plants with neat mounds of foliage and long-lasting flowers. While there are many varieties to choose from with brilliant leaf colors and pretty flowers, 'Cherries Jubilee' is notable for its dark, chocolate-green foliage. Spires of coral-red flowers appear in the early summer. Heucheras are ideal for containers and shady borders. They tolerate most soils, but perform best in slightly acid conditions in a site with partial shade.

☀ ◐ ◊   Z4–9 H9–1

↕ to 8in (20cm) ↔ to 16in (40cm)

Leptospermum scoparium 'Kiwi'

EVERGREEN SHRUB

This New Zealand tea tree has aromatic, lance-shaped, purple-tinged leaves and produces masses of dark, crimson-red flowers from the late spring to early summer. It is not hardy and may need to spend the winter in a container in a cool greenhouse. In mild areas grow it outside in well-drained soil next to a sunny, south-facing wall, ideally on a sheltered patio or terrace where the flowers can be fully appreciated. Suitable for coastal gardens.

☀ ◊ *f*   H11–3

↕↔ to 10ft (3m)

Lilium chalcedonicum
BULBOUS PERENNIAL

The scarlet turkscap lily is a tall plant with deep green leaves arranged in a spiral up the stem. It flowers from early to midsummer and has bright scarlet petals that are strongly swept back, while the long stamens with bright red anthers drop down from the center of the flower. This unusual lily makes a valuable addition to a sunny or partially shaded herbaceous border and will grow in almost any well-drained soil.

☼ ◊   Z7–9 H8–1

↕ to 5ft (1.5m)

Lupinus 'Inverewe Red'
PERENNIAL

Bold spikes of deep red flowers appear on this lupine in the early summer above clumps of palmate leaves. Plant in groups in an herbaceous border or as an excellent addition to a English-style garden. Encourage a second flush of flowers by deadheading. Lupines need a spot in full sun or partial shade and should be planted in well-drained, fertile soil. They usually benefit from staking, and the succulent new growth is a favorite of slugs and snails.

☼ ◐ ◊   Z5–8 H8–5

↕ to 4ft (1.2m) ↔ to 18in (45cm)

Lychnis x *arkwrightii* 'Vesuvius'

PERENNIAL

This dramatic but often short-lived perennial has lance-shaped, dark maroon leaves that form a perfect foil for its cross-shaped, brilliant scarlet flowers. These are borne freely from the early to midsummer. Good for a sunny, mixed or herbaceous border, especially those with a hot-colored theme. The plants are fairly low-maintenance and drought tolerant, and they will grow in coastal conditions.

☼ ◐ ◊ ◊   Z5–8 H8–5
↕ to 18in (45cm) ↔ to 12in (30cm)

Meconopsis napaulensis

PERENNIAL

The satin poppy is a very large plant that can take several years to grow to flowering size. When mature, it will produce clusters of large red, purple, or pink, bowl-shaped flowers from early to midsummer, after which the plant will die. It is suitable for a woodland garden or the back of a mixed border. Plant it in semi-shade in neutral or acid, moist soil. Sow new seed annually in the fall or spring to provide a continual supply of mature plants that will be ready to bloom in the summer.

◐ ◊ ◊   Z8–9 H9–8
↕ to 8ft (2.5m) ↔ to 36in (90cm)

Paeonia delavayi
DECIDUOUS SHRUB

The flowers of this tree peony bloom in the early summer and have dark red petals and yellow stamens. The handsome, deeply dissected, blue-green foliage provides color and texture long after the flowers have faded. It is perfect for the back of an herbaceous or mixed border and prefers a sunny or partially shaded location in moist, well-drained soil. It does best when left alone, apart from occasionally removing one or two of the oldest stems in the fall.

☼ ❂ ◊ ◗ *f*   Z3–8 H8–1
↕↔ to 6ft (2m)

Papaver commutatum 'Ladybird'
ANNUAL

A distinctive annual poppy with numerous glossy, bright red flowers. Grow it in groups in a rock garden or a border with a fiery color theme in full sun and well-drained soil. It does not need staking. It will self-seed naturally, or seed can be collected and sown in the spring where it is to flower. Alternatively, remove the deadheads to prevent the seed from setting and to prolong the flowering season.

☼ ◊   H8–1
↕ to 18in (45cm) ↔ to 6in (15cm)

Papaver orientale 'Beauty of Livermere'

PERENNIAL

Large scarlet blooms with black centers are borne on the long, sturdy stems of this poppy from early to midsummer. Its vibrant colors contrast well with gravel, or plant it in a sunny border, where it can help to disguise the dying foliage of spring bulbs. It dies back early after flowering and should be grown close to late flowering perennials that will fill the gap later in the year. Plant it in well-drained soil.

☼ ◊   Z3–9 H9–1

↕ to 4ft (1.2m) ↔ to 3ft (1m)

Papaver rhoeas

ANNUAL

Field poppies are well known summer-flowering annuals, ideal for creating a splash of color in any sunny part of the garden. They are easily grown from seed if sown in the spring onto a prepared seedbed with poor to moderately fertile soil. Various flower colors are available from white to pink and mauve or mixed shades. Once established, the plants may self-seed in successive years. Alternatively, collect the ripe seedheads, and save the seed for the next season.

☼ ◊   H11–1

↕ to 24in (60cm) ↔ to 6in (15cm)

Pelargonium 'Caligula'

PERENNIAL

This miniature zonal geranium has dark green leaves and double, bright scarlet flowers, which are produced from the early summer up to the first frost if they are deadheaded regularly. Its compact size and long flowering season combine to make it an excellent plant for containers, although it can also be used as bedding in the garden if planted in full sun in free-draining soil. It is tender and must be kept in a frost-free place in the winter.

☼ ◌ ◁   H11–1

‡ to 5in (12cm) ↔ to 4in (10cm)

Potentilla fruticosa 'Red Ace'

EVERGREEN SHRUB

This shrublike cinquefoil bears orange-red, saucer-shaped, single flowers, which contrast well with the small, divided leaves. It blooms from late spring to mid fall and makes a wonderful low informal hedge or gravel-garden plant. Grow it in a sunny location in well-drained, poor to moderately fertile soil, and trim after flowering, removing weak shoots and cutting dead wood back to the base.

☼ ◁   Z3–7 H7–1

‡ to 3ft (1m) ↔ to 5ft (1.5cm)

Potentilla 'Gibson's Scarlet'

PERENNIAL

A profusion of single, bright scarlet flowers appear on this cinquefoil from early to late summer. The blooms are produced on long stems above clumps of soft green, palmate foliage. It is an excellent plant for the front of a sunny border, or use it in a raised bed or gravel garden. It needs a sunny location in poor or moderately fertile, well-drained soil.

☼ ◊   Z5–8 H8–5

↕ to 18in (45cm) ↔ to 24in (60cm)

Rheum palmatum 'Atrosanguineum'

PERENNIAL

Chinese rhubarb is a large, spreading plant with huge, deeply-cut, rough-textured, green leaves that are crimson-purple when young. In the early summer the spectacular foliage is accompanied by tall stems of feathery, pinkish-red flowers that provide a focal point in a damp border or beneath deciduous trees. This plant is happy in full sun or partial shade in moist soil. Mulch plants annually in the spring with well-rotted compost.

☼ ◑ ◊   Z5–9 H9–1

↔ to 6ft (2m)

Rhododendron 'Spek's Brilliant'

DECIDUOUS SHRUB

Mollis-type deciduous azaleas like 'Spek's Brilliant' are tough plants and are popular not only for their late flowers, which can be used to extend the rhododendron season, but also for their fall leaf color. This variety bears full trusses of funnel-shaped, bright scarlet-orange flowers with deeper-colored flares inside. It tolerates full sun but must have organic, neutral to acid soil. Similar varieties include 'Fireball' and 'Dracula'.

☼ ☀ ◑ ◊   Z5–8 H8–5
↕↔ to 8ft (2.5m)

Rosa gallica var. *officinalis*

DECIDUOUS SHRUB

The crimson damask rose produces lightly scented, pinkish-red flowers from the early summer. These are followed in the fall by orange-red hips. Plant this compact rose with other old-fashioned roses or in a shrub or mixed border alongside hardy geraniums. Alternatively, use it as a low hedge that can be cut back lightly in the early spring. Plant it in full sun in fertile, moist, well-drained soil.

☼ ◊ ◑ *f*   Z3–9 H9–1
↕ to 32in (80cm) ↔ to 3ft (1m)

Rosa KNOCK OUT ('RadRazz')
DECIDUOUS SHRUB

This easy-to-grow, deciduous shrub rose can form an informal hedge or work well in a mixed perennial or shrub border. The fragrant, cherry-red flowers appear from the late spring to the first frost and attract butterflies. In the fall orange-red hips develop as the dark green foliage turns burgundy. Drought tolerant once established, this rose features excellent disease resistance. Grow in full sun to partial shade in average soil.

  Z4–9 H9–1

↔ to 4ft (1.2m)

Rosa L.D. BRAITHWAITE ('Auscrim')
DECIDUOUS SHRUB

This modern shrub rose is covered from the early summer to fall with crimson flowers. The blooms are slightly scented when they first open but develop a stronger fragrance as they age. This rose has a compact style and is ideally suited to small gardens, where it can be planted as a specimen or in a border. It will do best when grown in full sun in fertile, moist, well-drained soil. Lightly prune to shape in the late winter or early spring.

☼ ◊ ◑ *f* Z5–9 H9–5

 to 36in (90cm) ↔ to 4ft (1.2m)

Rosa 'Roseraie de l'Haÿ'

DECIDUOUS SHRUB

A rugosa shrub rose with heavily scented, purple-red flowers from the early summer through to the fall. The blooms are complemented by its light green, healthy foliage. It makes a thorny-stemmed hedge or it can be used as a specimen plant or grown in a mixed border. It prefers full sun and a deep, fertile, moist but well-drained soil. Clip hedges to shape in the early spring, otherwise little pruning is required.

☼ ◊ ◑ *f*   Z4–9 H9–1

‡ to 7ft (2.2m) ↔ to 6ft (2m)

Salvia splendens 'Van-Houttei'

PERENNIAL

Throughout the summer this variety of scarlet sage bears long spires of vibrant red, tubular flowers above the dark green, toothed foliage. Its long-lasting, brilliant flowers are a valuable addition to any summer bedding or container display, but they will not survive the winter unless protected in a frost-free place. Plant in a sunny location. The flowers are also good for cutting. 'Scarlet King' is similar, and varieties with pink, white, or bicolored flowers are available.

☼ ◊   Z11 H12–5

‡ to 3ft (1m) ↔ to 30in (75cm)

Sempervivum tectorum
PERENNIAL

Often overlooked as a garden plant, the common houseleek forms rosettes of pointed, bristle-tipped, blue-green leaves, which often turn a rich purple-red in the summer. The star-shaped, reddish-purple flowers appear in the early summer, after which the leafy rosettes die but are quickly replaced by new growth. Plant houseleeks in a sunny location in a rock garden or a trough or on a drystone wall. Good drainage is also important, and they should be grown in a porous soil.

☼ ◊   Z4–8 H8–1

↕ to 6in (15cm) ↔ to 8in (20cm)

Tropaeolum speciosum
CLIMBER

The flame nasturtium has beautiful rounded leaves that resemble flower petals. Throughout the summer and into the fall it bears long-spurred, vermilion flowers, which are followed by round, blue fruit. It looks best grown against a trellis or through an evergreen bush, which has the benefit of providing some winter protection since it is not totally hardy. Otherwise use a thick winter mulch. Plant it in moist but well-drained, fertile, neutral to acid soil in full sun or dappled shade.

☼ ◑ ◊ ◑   Z8–11 H11–8

↕ to 10ft (3m)

Acanthus spinosus

PERENNIAL

The distinctive, purple-hooded, white tubular flowers of bear's breeches are held on tall spikes. Its deeply divided leaves are a glossy dark green. Grow it in fertile, well-drained soil, close to a warm wall or in an herbaceous border in full sun. In partial shade it will produce lusher foliage. Divide clumps in the spring or fall. When given plenty of space, this clump-forming perennial makes a striking architectural plant. The flowers dry well when left on the plant or cut.

☼ ☀ ◊   Z5–9 H9–5

‡ to 4ft (1.2m) ↔ to 24in (60cm)

Allium 'Globemaster'

BULBOUS PERENNIAL

The large flowerheads of this ornamental onion are made up of numerous small, intense-purple flowers grouped together in a huge globe that can reach 8in (20cm) across. The gray basal leaves are slightly hairy and arch over at the tips. For maximum impact plant the bulbs in the fall in groups of at least five in a sunny border in well-drained, fertile soil. Although good for cutting fresh, the globes look most dramatic when left to dry on the plant.

☼ ◊   Z6–10 H8–1

‡ to 32in (80cm) ↔ to 8in (20cm)

Allium 'Purple Sensation'
BULBOUS PERENNIAL

This is a terrific ornamental flowering onion with long, strap-shaped, grayish-green leaves. In the late spring and early summer it produces large flowerheads that are good for cutting, comprised of 50 or more tiny, star-shaped, deep violet florets. The decorative seedheads last well into the late summer, although any self-sown plants that result may be inferior to the original. Plant the bulbs in the fall in a sunny location in fertile, well-drained soil.

☼ ◊   Z4–9 H9–1

‡ to 32in (80cm) ↔ to 3in (7cm)

Brassica oleracea 'Azur Star'
BIENNIAL

The purple kohlrabi makes a fabulous early summer foliage plant, useful for temporarily filling gaps in border displays. The plants mix well with blues and purples, like wild onions and lupines, due to their richly purple-tinted leaves and stems. It is best known as a vegetable with an oddly swollen, yet pleasantly flavored stem. When this reaches the size of a tennis ball, the plants can be uprooted, and the round stems peeled and cooked. Plant in full sun.

☼ ◐   Z7–11 H6–1

‡↔ to 24in (60cm)

Buddleja alternifolia
DECIDUOUS SHRUB

Clusters of the sweetly scented, pale lilac flowers wreath the arching branches of this bush in the early summer. So many are produced that they nearly hide the silvery-green, lance-shaped leaves. It flowers on the previous year's wood and should be pruned back to a strong bud after flowering. Prune out around a quarter of the old branches each year to stimulate new growth. It can also be trained as a standard tree, as shown here. Grow in fertile, well-drained, preferably alkaline soil in full sun.

☼ ◊ *f*   Z6–9 H10–1
‡↔ to 12ft (4m)

Campanula carpatica 'Jewel'
PERENNIAL

Forming low, dome-shaped mounds of heart-shaped leaves, this pretty plant bears masses of bright blue-purple, upward-facing bellflowers in the summer. The greatest concentration of flowers appear in the early summer, but the display often continues or repeats into the late summer. This bellflower grows well on dry stone walls and crevices, in rock gardens, containers, or as ground cover. It tolerates alkaline soils and does well in sun or partial shade.

☼ ☀ ◊ ◑   Z4–7 H7–1
‡↔ to 6in (15cm)

Campanula glomerata 'Superba'

PERENNIAL

The clustered bellflower is a fast-growing, clump-forming perennial carrying pretty, dense heads of large, bell-shaped, purple-violet flowers from the early summer. The lance-shaped to oval, mid-green leaves are arranged in rosettes at the base of the plant and along the stems. This super plant suits herbaceous borders or informal, English-style gardens; it prefers full sun or partial shade and neutral to alkaline soil. Cut back after flowering to encourage a second flush of flowers.

☼ ☽ ◊ ◑   Z3–8 H8–1

‡ to 30in (75cm) ↔ to 3ft (1m)

Clematis 'The President'

CLIMBER

This free-flowering clematis deserves a prominent spot on a pergola or decorative trellis where it can show off its amazing silver-backed, deep purple-blue blooms. These can measure up to 6in (15cm) across. It should be planted in fertile, well-drained soil in full sun or partial shade. Clematis grow best when their roots are in the shade. Remove any dead shoots in early spring, and prune the others back to a strong pair of buds.

☼ ☽ ◊   Z4–11 H9–1

to 10ft (3m)

Corylus maxima '**Purpurea**'

DECIDUOUS SHRUB

This filbert forms a large, upright shrub or small tree with dangling purple catkins in the winter. In the spring the dark purple leaves appear. Later in the summer and early fall there are edible, purple-husked nuts. It makes an attractive specimen tree. Grow in full sun for good foliage color and abundant nuts. It does best in fertile, well-drained soil and grows well in alkaline soil.

☼ ◊　　　　　　　　　　　Z4–9 H9–1

↕ to 20ft (6m) ↔ to 15ft (5m)

Cotinus '**Royal Purple**'

DECIDUOUS SHRUB

This purple-leaved smoke bush is grown for its rounded leaves. The fresh foliage looks good right from the outset, but this is heightened in the late summer when cloudlike plumes of tiny, pink-purple flowers appear. In the fall its appearance changes again when the leaves turn a brilliant scarlet. 'Royal Purple' is good in a shrub border, at the back of a mixed border, or as a specimen tree; where space permits, plant in groups. Plant in full sun or partial shade. Prune to size in the spring before the leaves emerge.

☼ ◐ ◊ ◑　　　　　　　　Z5–9 H9–3

↕↔ to 15ft (5m)

Delphinium 'Bruce'

PERENNIAL

A mixed summer border would be incomplete without delphiniums. 'Bruce' produces deep violet-purple flowers on tall spires in the early summer. A fall flowering can often be encouraged if the faded flowering stems are cut back. Easily damaged by winds and rain, the plants should be securely staked when young and the tall stems tied in as they grow. Plant in a well-drained, fertile soil in full sun. Protect emerging foliage from slugs and snails.

☼ ◊   Z3–7 H8–3

‡ to 7ft (2.2m) ↔ to 36in (90cm)

Echium vulgare

PERENNIAL

Viper's bugloss is a bushy, short-lived perennial with bristly, hairy leaves, stems, and flowers. It is grown for its early summer flowers, which are borne in short, curved spikes amid and above the narrow leaves. The broadly bell-shaped flowers are purple in bud and open into purple-blue and sometimes pink or white. They are attractive to bees. Vipers bugloss can be grown as temporary bedding or in containers and prefers partial shade.

◑ ◊   Z3–8 H8–1

‡ to 12in (30cm) ↔ to 8in (20cm)

Erodium manescavii

PERENNIAL

The delicate magenta-purple, saucer-shaped blooms of this clump-forming plant are very similar to those of the hardy geranium. Throughout the summer, they are borne on long stalks in profuse clusters of up to 20. The top two petals of each flower are darkly freckled. The leaves are attractive, too, being deeply divided, lance-shaped and slightly hairy. Plant it in gritty, very well-drained soil in full sun. A rock garden would suit it well, or plant it at the front of the herbaceous border. It self-seeds freely.

☼ ◊   Z6–8 H8–6

↕ to 18in (45cm) ↔ to 24in (60cm)

Erysimum '**Bowles's Mauve**'

EVERGREEN PERENNIAL

A long-flowering wallflower, 'Bowles's Mauve' produces tall spikes of mauve blooms throughout the year; but the early summer is when they are most profuse. The flowers are set off by narrow, gray-green leaves. Plant it in well-drained, poor to moderately fertile, preferably alkaline soil in full sun. A lovely border plant, in cold areas give it the shelter of a warm wall. Trim after flowering and take cuttings to transplant since it tends to be short lived.

☼ ◊   Z6–10 H10–3

↕ to 30in (75cm) ↔ to 24in (60cm)

Geranium psilostemon

PERENNIAL

One of the largest hardy geraniums, this fast-growing plant has deep magenta-purple flowers with an almost black eye. The toothed, mid-green leaves are infused with crimson in the spring and fall. A useful ground-cover plant to fill in around bushes in a border, it grows well in most well-drained soils in sun or partial shade. Trim it back after flowering to encourage new growth. In the right conditions it will self seed freely; alternatively, divide large clumps in the spring.

☼ ◑ ◊   Z5–8 H8–5

‡↔to 4ft (1.2m)

Geranium sylvaticum 'Mayflower'

PERENNIAL

With its white-centered, rich violet-blue, upward-facing flowers, 'Mayflower' is one of the most attractive geraniums available. Its deeply lobed, mid-green leaves form a shapely mound. It is a good naturalizer in open ground or under trees and shrubs. Plant it in moist, but well-drained soil; although it tolerates shade it would prefer full sun. Trim the plant back after flowering to encourage new growth.

☼ ◑ ◊ ◊   Z8 H9–8

‡ to 3ft (1m) ↔to 24in (60cm)

Gladiolus communis subsp. *byzantinus*

BULBOUS PERENNIAL

The tall flower spikes of this gladiolus carry up to 20 magenta flowers that add zest to an early summer border and are good for cutting. The rich-green, strappy leaves reach 28in (70cm) long. Unless you want huge swathes of these plants, be careful when working in the soil around them since small corms will break off and spread. Plant in full sun in fertile, well-drained soil. Corms do not need to be dug up in the winter, but in cold gardens cover the soil with a mulch

☼ ◌　　　　　　　　　　Z7–10 H11–1

‡ to 28in (70cm) ↔ to 6in (15cm)

Heliotropium arborescens 'Marine'

EVERGREEN SHRUB

The heliotrope is a tender, short-lived bush often grown as an annual bedding plant. With its clusters of fragrant, violet-blue flowers, it looks good in pots and windowboxes or as front-of-the-border edging. Plant it in full sun in moist, but well-drained, fertile soil. Take softwood cuttings in the summer and overwinter them in a cool greenhouse. You can also grow heliotropes as sunroom plants. Use a soil-based potting mix and provide shading from strong sunlight.

☼ ◌ ◊ *f*　　　　　　　　　　H11–9

‡↔ to 18in (45cm)

Heuchera
'Palace Purple'
EVERGREEN PERENNIAL

Heucheras are evergreen, or nearly evergreen, clump-forming plants, which are grown primarily for their attractive foliage. 'Palace Purple' has glossy, deeply lobed, purplish-red leaves and airy spikes of tiny greenish-cream flowers. It is a lovely ground-cover plant in an herbaceous or shrub border. Plant in full sun or partial shade in moist, but well-drained, neutral fertile soil.

☼ ☀ ◐ ◑ ◔   Z3–8 H8–1

↔ to 18in (45cm)

Iris ensata
'Hue and Cry'
PERENNIAL

The Japanese iris is a beautiful aquatic marginal plant. The purple 'Hue and Cry' has flat flowers with six large, white-veined, lower petals, each with a yellow stripe down the center. Short periods of flooding are tolerated, but rather than total immersion, this plant prefers permanently moist or wet, acid soil and is suitable for a bog garden. There are many other attractive varieties to choose from.

☼ ☀ ◐ ◑   Z3–9 H9–1

‡ to 36in (90cm)

Iris x *robusta* 'Gerald Darby'

PERENNIAL

Another stunning water iris, 'Gerald Darby' has narrow, sword-shaped leaves that are covered at the base with purple spots. Its stems, which are dark violet, produce four bluish-purple flowers, each marked with a patch of yellow. Plant it in a moist border or at the edge of a pond. Given the right conditions, this vigorous clump-former can reach the spectacular height of 6ft (1.8m); however, it usually measures just under half that.

☀ ☼ ◊ ◆   Z3–9 H9–1

‡ to 30in (75cm)

Iris versicolor

PERENNIAL

The richly colored petals of the blue flag iris have beautiful markings, with heavy purple veining and a large white patch at their base. Together with the vibrant green, sword-shaped leaves, this is an attractive plant for a bog garden, the shallow margins of a natural pond, or a moisture-retentive border. Plant the rhizomes in permanently moist or wet soil, but not underwater.

☀ ☼ ◊ ◆   Z3–9 H9–1

‡ to 32in (80cm)

Lavandula angustifolia 'Hidcote'

EVERGREEN SHRUB

This English lavender has narrow, silver-gray, aromatic leaves, and in mid- to late summer it produces spikes of highly fragrant, small purple flowers loved by bees. 'Hidcote' makes a good low hedge or is suitable for planting in a gravel garden. It needs a site in full sun and a slightly fertile, well-drained soil. Lavenders are easily propagated by taking semi-ripe cuttings in the summer. Trim hedges in the spring and lightly after flowering to remove the dead heads.

☼ ◊ *f* Z5–8 H8–5

‡ to 24in (60cm) ↔ to 30in (75cm)

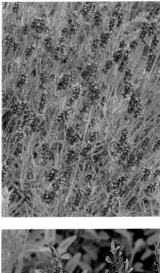

Lavandula stoechas

EVERGREEN SHRUB

French lavender forms an attractive rounded shrub with branching stems covered with narrow, grayish-green, slightly fragrant leaves. It is smaller and flowers slightly earlier than English lavender, but the blooms are not as fragrant. The small purple flowers, each topped by a tuft of pinkish-mauve, petal-like bracts, are produced throughout the summer. It is not completely hardy and should be grown in a warm, sheltered location in slightly fertile, well-drained soil or in containers.

☼ ◊ *f* Z8–9 H9–8

‡↔ to 24in (60cm)

Polemonium 'Lambrook Mauve'

PERENNIAL

Jacob's ladder is a free-flowering plant that produces clusters of lilac-blue flowers on upright, branched stems. A compact, mound-forming perennial, it is ideally suited to the front of a mixed or herbaceous border. It also makes a lovely feature plant in formal planting or among low-growing grasses. Give it a spot in full sun or partial shade in a moist, but well-drained, fertile soil. Deadhead regularly and divide large clumps during the spring.

☼ ☽ ◊ ◖   Z4–8 H8–1

↕↔ to 18in (45cm)

Roscoea humeana

PERENNIAL

This unusual tuberous plant has orchidlike flowers with a prominent, hooded upper petal. The lush, deep-green, rounded leaves set the blooms off perfectly. A sheltered woodland garden would be the ideal home for this plant, since it grows best in damp shade in a cool climate. It is not fully hardy, so where frosts are likely in the winter, cover the root area with a deep mulch, such as leaf mold.

☀ ◖   Z7–9 H9–7

↕ to 10in (25cm) ↔ to 8in (20cm)

Stachys macrantha 'Superba'

PERENNIAL

Erect spikes of pinkish-purple, hooded flowers are held above rosettes of wrinkled, dark green, heart-shaped leaves. An easy-going plant for the front of an herbaceous border, it flowers over a long period from the early summer until the early fall. Plant it in well-drained, fertile soil. It does best in full sun but will tolerate a certain amount of shade.

☀ ☀ ◊   Z7–9 H9–7

‡ to 18in (45cm) ↔ to 24in (60cm)

Thalictrum aquilegiifolium 'Thundercloud'

PERENNIAL

Meadow rues are clump-forming plants with fernlike foliage composed of small, rounded leaflets. 'Thundercloud' has erect, waxy stems, and clusters of tiny flowers are borne in the summer. The outer part of the flower quickly falls away to leave the colorful, dark purple stamens that give the blooms a frothy appearance. It may take some time to become established and prefers partial shade and deep, moist soil.

☀ ◐   Z5–9 H9–5

‡ to 3ft (1m) ↔ to 12in (30cm)

Aconitum napellus

PERENNIAL

Monkshood is an upright plant, much like a delphinium, with spires of very attractive, hooded, violet-blue flowers that begin to appear in the early to midsummer. Behind this beauty lies a dark secret: all parts of this plant are highly poisonous. This makes them ideal for the back of a border where they won't be disturbed. Plant in groups of five or more for the best display, in organic, moist but well-drained soil in a sunny or partially shaded site. They will not need staking. When handling the plants, wear gloves.

☀ ◐ ◊ ◊   Z3–8 H8–3

↕ to 5ft (1.5m) ↔ to 12in (30cm)

Ageratum houstonianum 'Adriatic'

ANNUAL

The floss flower forms a mound of downy, oval, green leaves, above which frothy-looking heads of tiny mid-blue flowers are borne in the summer and up to the first frosts. It is widely grown as a bedding plant and complements low-growing annuals with bright yellow flowers, such as calceolarias. It is also suitable for containers and hanging baskets. Plant it in full sun in a moist, well-drained soil. In containers, keep it well watered when in flower.

☀ ◊ ◊   Z10–11 H11–1

↕ to 8in (20cm) ↔ to 12in (30cm)

Ajuga reptans 'Variegata'

EVERGREEN PERENNIAL

Bugle is a useful, easygoing ground-cover plant which forms a carpet of evergreen leaves, borne on spreading stems. 'Variegata' has gray-green leaves with a cream edge and cream markings. From the late spring to early summer, bugle produces upright stems of small, dark blue tubular flowers. Plant it in any moist soil in partial shade. It will also tolerate full sun if the soil does not dry out during the summer.

☼ ☽ ◊   Z3–9 H9–1

‡ to 6in (15cm) ↔ to 36in (90cm)

Allium caeruleum

BULBOUS PERENNIAL

A beautiful ornamental onion, this species produces one- to two-inch wide spherical heads of bright blue, star-shaped flowers in late spring or early summer. The blooms are produced after the narrow leaves have died down on triangular, stiff green stems. Plant groups of bulbs in the fall in a herbaceous border, rock garden, or a large container, in full sun and well-drained, fertile soil..

☼ ◊   Z4–10 H10–1

‡ to 32in (80cm) ↔ to 6in (15cm)

Anchusa azurea '**Loddon Royalist**'

PERENNIAL

This beautiful, early summer-flowering plant forms a clump of lance-shaped leaves and robust branched stems of deep blue flowers. The blooms are attractive to bees, making it a good candidate for a wild garden or an herbaceous border. Plant it in groups in full sun and moist, well-drained soil. Young plants should be cut back after flowering to promote the growth of basal leaves. Deadhead mature plants to encourage a second flush of flowers.

☼ ◊ ◖   Z3–8 H8–1
‡ to 4ft (1.2m) ↔ to 24in (60cm)

Aquilegia alpina

PERENNIAL

The alpine columbine is an upright plant and is suitable for planting in an herbaceous border, rock garden, or raised bed. It blooms in the late spring and early summer and produces long stems that bear slightly nodding, deep blue flowers. The stems thrust up above finely-divided, bluish-green, ferny foliage. Grow it in a sunny or partially shaded location in fertile, moist, well-drained, gritty soil.

☼ ☽ ◊ ◖   Z4–7 H7–1
‡ to 18in (45cm) ↔ to 12in (30cm)

Baptisia australis

PERENNIAL

False indigo is a spreading plant with mid-green leaves divided into three egg-shaped leaflets. In the summer it produces tall spikes of dark-blue pealike flowers, which are often marked with white or cream. The flowers are followed in the fall by large seed pods, suitable for drying. Plant it in an open, sunny site in deep, very free-draining, neutral to acid soil. It is suitable for an herbaceous border, but once planted is best left undisturbed. Stake tall plants unless the planting site is sheltered.

☼ ◊   Z3–9 H9–1

‡ to 30in (75cm) ↔ to 24in (60cm)

Borago officinalis

ANNUAL

This important herb annual produces intensely blue, star-shaped, early summer flowers, borne in drooping clusters. When in full bloom, bumblebees are often seen around the bristly oval foliage in search of nectar. Borage is well suited to informal, cottage-garden style plantings. Its flowers, once considered edible, are no longer fit for consumption. It needs to be sown from seed each year, but established clumps may self-seed. It does best in full sun or partial shade. A white-flowered form, 'Alba' is available.

☼ ◐ ◊ ◊   H11–1

‡ to 36in (90cm) ↔ to 12in (30cm)

Brachyscome iberidifolia
ANNUAL

The Swan River daisy is a bushy, sprawling plant with deeply divided, grayish green, ferny foliage. In the summer it produces blue, violet, or white, slightly scented, daisylike flowers. An excellent plant for edging summer containers, including hanging baskets, it will also bring color to the front of an herbaceous border. The seed should be sown under glass in the spring, then young plants moved outdoors after the last frost in a sunny location and well-drained, fertile soil.

☼ ◊ ◗ *f*　　　　　　　　　　H11–1
‡↔ to 18in (45cm)

Campanula barbata
PERENNIAL

The bearded bellflower is so named because of the unusual hairs that edge the pendent, lavender-blue flowers that appear in the early summer. A short-lived perennial, it forms rosettes of hairy, lance-shaped, mid-green leaves beneath the erect flower stems. It is a suitable plant for a rock or gravel garden and should be planted in full sun or partial shade in moist, but well-drained soil.

☼ ◐ ◊ ◗　　　　　　　　Z5–8 H8–5
‡ to 8in (20cm) ↔ to 5in (12cm)

Campanula persicifolia 'Telham Beauty'

PERENNIAL

One of the most vigorous bellflowers, this form bears rosettes of evergreen lance-shaped, bright green leaves. In the early summer pale-blue, bell-shaped flowers appear for many weeks on tall stems. Flowering can be prolonged by regular deadheading. It is best planted in groups in an herbaceous or mixed border or in a woodland or wild-flower garden. Grow it in full sun or partial shade in fertile, well-drained, neutral or slightly alkaline soil.

☼ ☽ ◊   Z3–8 H8–1

↕ to 3ft (1m) ↔ to 12in (30cm)

Ceanothus 'Gloire de Versailles'

DECIDUOUS SHRUB

Hardier than many other California lilacs, 'Gloire de Versailles' has oval dark green leaves and clusters of tiny, deep sky-blue flowers, held in open spikes at the end of the stems. It flowers in the early summer and again in the fall. A good shrub for a mixed border or a Mediterranean-style garden, it prefers a location in full sun and a well-drained soil. Overgrown specimens can be cut back hard in spring.

☼ ◊   Z7–11 H11–7

↕↔ to 5ft (1.5m)

Centaurea montana

PERENNIAL

This perennial cornflower is a vigorous plant that is easy to grow on most soils. It looks very pretty in the early summer with its vivid, purple-blue flowers from the late spring to midsummer. They have a spidery, thistlelike appearance and are attractive to butterflies and bees. This is a creeping plant that forms soft, woolly mats or clumps of broad and pointed, mid-green leaves. In exposed sites, stakes may be needed to support the stems. Plant in full sun or dappled shade.

☀ ◑ ◊ ◗   Z3–9 H9–1

‡ to 20in (50cm) ↔ to 24in (60cm)

Clematis 'H.F. Young'

CLIMBER

This reliable purple-blue, mid-season clematis freely produces very big, pale yellow-centered flowers in the early summer. A second, less profuse, flowering may occur in the late summer. Its compact size makes it a good choice for containers in a sunny location as long as the roots are in shade. Alternatively train it up a support or grow it through bushes, such as roses. Mulch in the late winter, and tie in young growth carefully, ideally to fill gaps in the display. Trim lightly in the late winter or early spring.

☀ ◊ ◗   Z4–11 H9–1

‡ to 6ft (2m)

Consolida ajacis

ANNUAL

The annual delphiniums, otherwise
known as larkspurs, are fast-growing
herbaceous plants with deeply divided,
feathery leaves. They look similar to
perennial delphiniums but tend to have
shorter flowering stems. In the summer
they produce spikes of violet-blue, pink,
or white flowers with long spurs and are
good for cutting. Ideal for filling gaps left
by spring bulbs in a border, they grow
best in full sun in light, well-drained soil.
Sow the seeds where they are to grow in
the spring, or fall in mild winter regions.

☼ ◌   H9–1
‡ to 4ft (1.2m) ↔ to 12in (30cm)

Cynoglossum nervosum

PERENNIAL

Hairy hound's-tongue is an herbaceous
perennial closely related to borage,
admired for its bright blue, forget-me-
not flowers that are carried in small
clusters on upright stems. They are
good for supplying color to early
summer beds and borders, and they
are good for cutting. The plant gets
its name from its narrow, mid-green,
hairy leaves. Plant in full sun.

☼ ◌   Z5–8 H8–5
↔ to 24in (60cm)

Delphinium grandiflorum 'Blue Butterfly'

PERENNIAL

A short-lived plant, this delphinium is often grown as an annual. It has deeply divided leaves, and in the summer it bears spikes of bright blue flowers. Grow it in a bedding plan, or at the front of an herbaceous border. It also makes a good cut flower. Plant this delphinium in well-drained, fertile soil in full sun. It is less demanding than the large-flowered varieties, such as 'Blue Nile'.

☼ ◊   Z3–8 H8–1

‡↔ to 12in (30cm)

Echium vulgare 'Blue Bedder'

BIENNIAL

The dwarf form of viper's bugloss has an upright habit, and produces bristly, lance-shaped, dark-green leaves. In the early summer it bears an abundance of blue flowers, which turn pink as they age. Plant it in a wild-flower garden or use it as bedding. Viper's bugloss likes a sunny situation and reasonably fertile, well-drained soil.

☼ ◊   Z3–8 H8–1

‡ to 16in (40cm) ↔ to 12in (30cm)

Erigeron 'Dunkelste Aller'

PERENNIAL

Daisylike flowers always look so cheerful and the blooms of the fleabane are no exception. This one has a sunny yellow center, fringed with violet blue, semidouble petals. A clump-forming plant with lance-shaped, grayish-green leaves, it would do well in a mixed herbaceous border or rock garden. It will also thrive in a coastal garden but will need staking on exposed sites. As a cut flower, it also has great lasting qualities. Plant in fertile soil that does not dry out in the summer.

☼ ◊   Z5–8 H8–5

‡ to 32in (80cm) ↔ to 24in (60cm)

Festuca glauca 'Blaufuchs'

PERENNIAL

This bright blue fescue is a densely tufted, evergreen, perennial grass. It is excellent in a border or rock garden as a foil to other cool-colored plants or for providing a contrast in shape and form. Spikes of not particularly striking, violet-flushed flowers are borne in the early summer above the foliage. The narrow, bright blue leaves are its chief attraction. Grow in any dry, well-drained soil in full sun. For the best foliage color, divide and replant clumps every three years.

☼ ◊   Z4–8 H8–1

‡ to 12in (30cm) ↔ to 10in (25cm)

Geranium clarkei 'Kashmir Blue'

PERENNIAL

This tough geranium can be a useful, herbaceous ground cover for a sunny site, flowering profusely in the early summer. The flowers are a lovely dark blue, but varieties in white, purple, and pink are also available. It thrives in most garden soils. Grown in a border, either as edging or mixed in with other low plants, it will need occasional cutting back after flowering to keep it within bounds. To establish it as ground cover, plant in groups of five or more.

☼ ◐ ◊ ◑   Z5–8 H8–4

‡ to 18in (45cm) ↔ indefinite

Geranium 'Johnson's Blue'

PERENNIAL

This is one of the most widely-grown geraniums, favored for its deeply lobed, mid-green leaves and long flowering season in the summer. It bears deep lavender-blue, saucer-shaped flowers with pink centers. Plant it at the front of an herbaceous border or use it as underplanting in a rose bed. It will grow in most soils, but does best in well-drained, fertile soil in a sunny or partially shaded situation. Divide large clumps in the fall.

☼ ◐ ◊ ◑   Z4–8 H8–

‡ to 12in (30cm) ↔ to 24in (60cm)

Geranium pratense 'Mrs Kendall Clark'

PERENNIAL

The meadow cranesbill is a clump-forming plant with deeply lobed, mid-green leaves. The single flowers appear from early to midsummer and are bluish-gray flushed with pale pink, or sometimes violet-blue with delicate white veining. The meadow cranesbill is a beautiful plant for the front of a border, or use it as ground cover. It grows well in most soils, but prefers a well-drained, fertile soil in full sun or partial shade.

☼ ☀ ◊ ◑　　　　　　　Z4–8 H8–1

‡ to 36in (90cm) ↔ to 24in (60cm)

Hosta 'Halcyon'

PERENNIAL

The thick, heart-shaped, blue-green leaves of this hosta may be slightly less susceptible to slug damage than some other varieties. In the summer it bears spikes of grayish-lavender, funnel-shaped flowers. The color of the foliage may fade in bright sun, so it is advisable to plant it in partial shade beneath shrubs or trees in moist, well-drained soil. In the spring mulch hostas with organic matter, such as composted bark to conserve moisture in the summer.

☀ ◊ ◑　　　　　　　Z3–9 H9–2

‡ to 16in (40cm) ↔ to 28in (70cm)

Hosta 'Krossa Regal'

PERENNIAL

'Krossa Regal' lives up to its royal name with its stately style. It is tall and vigorous, bearing lovely blue-green, heavily veined leaves that emerge rapidly from underground buds in the spring. Plant it in a sunny or partially shaded site. As with all hostas, protect it from slugs and snails, although this variety shows greater resistance than most. Long stems that bear beautiful, short-lived, pale violet flowers emerge from the center of each clump in the summer. Remove the flowers once they fade.

☼ ☀ ◐   Z3–9 H9–2

↕ to 18in (45cm) ↔ to 24in (60cm)

Iris ensata 'Flying Tiger'

PERENNIAL

Japanese irises are beautiful plants with striking, large flat blooms. The flowers of 'Flying Tiger' measure up to 12in (30cm) across and have rounded petals marked with bold violet-blue veins and a splash of yellow radiating from the center. Although it is an aquatic plant, it will grow in a bog garden or moist border, as long as the roots do not dry out in the summer. When grown in a border, it prefers a rich, moist, acid soil.

☼ ☀ ◐ ◐   Z3–9 H9–1

↕ to 36in (90cm) ↔ indefinite

Iris 'Jane Phillips'

PERENNIAL

An elegant, tall bearded iris, this variety
has bluish-green, sword-shaped leaves,
and mid-blue, fragrant flowers. To
ensure a good show of flowers year after
year, plant it in front of a sunny wall or
in a hot border where its rhizomes can
enjoy the summer sun. It also grows
well in neutral or slightly alkaline,
fertile, well-drained soil. Divide large
clumps after flowering and replant
plump sections so that the top of the
rhizomes are exposed to the sun.

☼ ◊ *f*   Z3–9 H9–1
‡ to 36in (90cm) ↔ to 24in (60cm)

Iris laevigata

PERENNIAL

The deep purple-blue flowers of this
beardless water iris appear in the early
summer and make an excellent addition
to a sunny or partially shaded bog
garden or the margins of a pond in acidic
soil. The blooms are set off by broad,
mid-green, straplike leaves. This is
a vigorous iris, and large clumps can
be divided in the spring. 'Variegata' is
an attractive cultivar with white- and
green-striped leaves.

☼ ◔ ◊ ◈   Z3–9 H9–1
‡ to 36in (90cm) ↔ indefinite

Iris pallida 'Variegata'

PERENNIAL

The dramatic, variegated sword-shaped leaves of this iris provide structure, color, and form in a sunny herbaceous border from spring to fall. The beautiful bearded, mid-blue flowers, which appear in the early summer, are a bonus and magnify this plant's charms. For the best results, plant it in groups in well-drained, neutral or alkaline soil.

☼ ◊   Z1–9 H9–1

‡to 4ft (1.2m) ↔indefinite

Linum perenne

PERENNIAL

The perennial flax is a clump-forming plant with narrow, bluish-green, lance-shaped leaves and slender flower stems. Although each pale blue flower lasts for just one day and fades before evening, the blooms are produced in succession from early to midsummer. Grow it in groups in full sun and a well-drained, fertile soil, and use it in a flower garden or herbaceous border. It can be raised from seed sown in pots in a cold frame in the fall or early spring.

☼ ◊   Z7–9 H9–7

‡to 12in (30cm) ↔to 6in (15cm)

Lithodora diffusa 'Heavenly Blue'

EVERGREEN SHRUB

This prostrate plant produces trailing branches covered with small, elliptic, deep green leaves. In the summer it bears large numbers of rich azure-blue flowers. It can be planted in a raised bed or a rock or gravel garden, and to grow well it needs an acidic, fertile soil and a sunny situation.

☼ ◊　　　　　　　　Z8–11 H11–10
‡ to 12in (30cm) ↔ to 18in (45cm)

Lobelia erinus 'Sapphire'

PERENNIAL

This dainty plant is usually treated as an annual and raised from seed each year. It is grown for its trailing stems of small, mid-green leaves and abundant bright blue flowers with striking white eyes. It flowers through the summer and is an excellent plant for containers, hanging baskets, and edging borders. It should be planted in full sun or partial shade in moist, well-drained soil. When grown in containers, feed it every two weeks with a liquid fertilizer.

☼ ☼ ◊ ◑　　　　　　Z2–8 H8–1
‡ to 8in (20cm) ↔ to 6in (15cm)

Lupinus albifrons
EVERGREEN SHRUB

A decorative tree lupine, this variety has a rounded look and attractive foliage covered with silvery hairs. Throughout the summer it produces spikes of pealike, blue or reddish-purple flowers. Although reasonably hardy, to survive the winter it needs to be planted in a sunny location in very well-drained soil, such as by a wall, in a sheltered raised bed, or rock garden. Apply inorganic mulch, such as gravel.

☼ ◊   Z9–10 H10–9
↕↔ to 30in (75cm)

Malva sylvestris 'Primley Blue'
PERENNIAL

This spreading, almost ground-hugging perennial produces very lovely, upright spires of funnel-shaped, pale blue-violet flowers with darker veins. The blooms appear from the late spring to mid-fall and can be used as cut flowers throughout the seasons. It is useful in a mixed or herbaceous border, tolerating most garden soils. Plant in a sunny site.

☼ ◊ ◖   Z4–8 H8–1
↕ to 8in (20cm) ↔ to 24in (60cm)

Nepeta 'Six Hills Giant'

PERENNIAL

This imposing catmint forms large clumps of strongly aromatic, grayish-green foliage and spires of vivid blue flowers that cover the plant through the summer. It is a good, drought-tolerant plant for the middle of a sunny border or near paths where its lemony scent can be enjoyed. Cats, bees, and butterflies find the plant irresistible. Cut back in the fall when the foliage is looking tired.

☼ ◐ ◊ *f*   Z3–8 H8–1

↕ to 3ft (1m) ↔ to 4ft (1.2m)

Nigella damascena 'Miss Jekyll'

ANNUAL

A widely-grown, self-seeding annual, love-in-a-mist has highly decorative, finely divided green leaves and early summer blooms. 'Miss Jekyll' bears sky-blue flowers surrounded by a "ruff" of threadlike leaves, which are followed by attractive seedheads. In the spring or fall, sow the seed where it is to grow in bold groups at the front of a mixed border or with other annuals in a wild-flower meadow. It needs to be grown in full sun and a well-drained soil.

☼ ◊   H11–1

↕ to 18in (45cm) ↔ to 8in (20cm)

Polemonium caeruleum

PERENNIAL

Jacob's ladder has decorative, divided foliage, and in the early summer bears erect stems of clear blue, bell-shaped flowers. It is very adaptable and can be grown in an informal planting among low-growing grasses or at the front of an herbaceous border, where it can help to disguise the dying foliage of early spring bulbs. Plant it in full sunshine or partial shade in fertile, moist, well-drained soil. Deadhead regularly and divide large clumps in the spring.

☼ ☀ ◊ ◗　　　　　　　　Z4–9 H9–1
‡↔ to 24in (60cm)

Salvia x *sylvestris* '**Mainacht**'

PERENNIAL

This enigmatic, deep-colored herbaceous perennial forms neat clumps of pleasantly aromatic, softly hairy, mid-green foliage; it provides strong contrast for silver-leaved plants in a border. It is highly valued for its tall and dense, upright spikes of vibrant, indigo-blue flowers that appear in the early and midsummer. It grows well in most garden soils in a sunny location and copes well with drought. Cut back after the first flush of flowers to encourage further blooms.

☼ ◊ *f*　　　　　　　　　Z5–9 H9–4
‡ to 28in (70cm) ↔ to 18in (45cm)

Solanum crispum 'Glasnevin'

CLIMBER

The Chilean potato vine is a fast-growing, woody-stemmed, evergreen, climbing shrub. It is grown for its lightly fragrant, deep purple-blue flowers, which are borne in clusters at the tips of the stems during early and midsummer and are followed by small, yellow-white fruits. The leaves are oval and dark green. Prune after flowering or in the spring, tying in any new shoots. In areas with cold winters, grow it against a sheltered, warm, and sunny wall.

☼ ◑ ◊ ◑ *f*　　　　　Z9–11 H11–1

‡ to 20ft (6m)

Veronica prostrata

PERENNIAL

The prostrate speedwell forms a low-growing mat of small, toothed leaves, and in the late summer short, upright stems are clothed with tiny pale or deep blue blooms. It is ideally suited to a rock garden or raised bed, but will also add interest planted among the rocks in a gravel garden or a dry-stone wall. Plant it in full sun in slightly fertile, well-drained soil. To propagate it, divide it in the fall or spring.

☼ ◊　　　　　Z5–8 H8–5

‡ to 12in (30cm) ↔ indefinite

Carex pendula
PERENNIAL

The weeping sedge forms substantial clumps of relatively wide, straplike, mid-green leaves that are blue-green underneath. In early summer arching, triangular stems bear pendent, catkinlike flower spikes, which look attractive when hanging over water at the edge of a pool or in a damp border or woodland setting. Grow this sedge in permanently moist or wet soil in partial shade or sun. It can self-sow profusely.

☼ ☀ ◐ ♦　　　　　　　Z5–9 H9–5
‡ to 3ft (1m) ↔ to 12in (30cm)

Dryopteris affinis
PERENNIAL FERN

The golden male fern is a useful foliage plant for shady or partially shady sites where its upright plumes of feathery fronds are a welcome sight when they begin to unfurl from coppery brown fiddleheads in the spring. The young fronds are a delightful fresh green in the early summer, maturing to a darker green. They continue through the winter and should be cut back in the early spring to allow for new growth. There are several varieties available, such as 'Cristata' and the shorter 'Crispa Gracilis'.

☼ ☀ ◐　　　　　　　Z6–8 H8–6
‡↔ to 36in (90cm)

Hosta 'Frances Williams'

PERENNIAL

A widely-grown hosta, this variety is
favored for its large, thick, blue-green,
heart-shaped leaves with yellow-green
margins. It has very pale lavender-gray
flowers, borne in clusters on tall stems
in the early summer. It is best to grow
it in moist soil in a partially shaded
situation because the leaves have a
tendency to scorch in bright sun. Plant
it to provide interest beneath deciduous
trees or in a mixed or herbaceous border.
Take measures to prevent slug damage.

☼ ◐   Z3–9 H9–2
↕ to 24in (60cm) ↔ to 3ft (1m)

Hosta plantaginea
var. *japonica*

PERENNIAL

The large oval, light green leaves of
this hosta have a glossy texture and
distinctive raised veins. It grows well
in sun or partial shade in moist but
well-drained soil, and it can be used
in an herbaceous or mixed border or in
the light shade underneath deciduous
trees. Most hostas are grown for their
foliage, but this one also has attractive,
trumpet-shaped, fragrant white flowers,
borne on long stems in the midsummer.
Slugs may cause leaf damage.

☼ ◐ ◊ ♦ *f*   Z3–9 H9–2
↕ to 24in (60cm) ↔ to 3ft (1m)

Hosta undulata var. *albomarginata*

PERENNIAL

The clumps of relatively small, bright green leaves of this hosta are enlivened with creamy-white margins that define their elliptical shape. Lavender, funnel-shaped flowers are borne on long stems from early to midsummer. This hosta will lighten up a partially shaded site in an herbaceous or mixed border or use it in deciduous woodland. It prefers a moist, well-drained soil. Grow it in soil-based potting mix in a pot to reduce the chance of slug damage.

☀ ◐ ◊   Z3–9 H9–2

‡ to 22in (55cm) ↔ to 24in (60cm)

Liriodendron tulipifera

DECIDUOUS TREE

The tulip tree has a conical shape and bears unusual lobed, square leaves, which appear as though they have been chopped off at the tips. The tulip-shaped flowers are yellowish-green with a hint of orange at the base of the petals but are only produced on mature trees. In the fall the foliage turns wonderful shades of golden-yellow. Grow the tulip tree in a large garden where it can reach its full size unhindered, in full sun or partial shade and fertile, moist, well-drained soil.

☀ ◐ ◊ ◊   Z4–9 H9–2

‡ to 100ft (30m) ↔ to 50ft (15m)

Matteuccia struthiopteris

PERENNIAL

In the spring the shuttlecock fern produces a cluster of brilliant green fronds arranged in a tight funnel. In the late summer dark brown, fertile fronds appear at the center of the shuttlecock. Plant in partial shade in moist, neutral to acidic, organic soil, particularly in woodland or near water. It spreads by underground stems to form large colonies. It can be increased by lifting and separating young plants from the parent plant in the spring.

☀ ◐ 　　　　　　　　　　Z2–8 H8–1

‡ to 3ft (1m) ↔ to 18in (45cm)

Osmunda regalis

PERENNIAL

The elegant royal fern forms a substantial clump of upright, finely divided, bright green fronds that turn shades of apricot-yellow before they die down. In the summer distinctive rusty brown, tassel-like fronds rise from the center of the clump. Grow in partial shade in moist, organic, preferably acidic soil. It can be planted in full sun in permanently damp soils. The royal fern makes a beautiful specimen in damp woodland or beside a stream or pond.

☀ ◐ ◗ 　　　　　　　　　Z2–10 H9–1

‡ to 6ft (2m) ↔ to 3ft (1m)

Acer shirasawanum 'Aureum'

DECIDUOUS TREE

Japanese maples are a group of deciduous trees, but they all have beautiful foliage that turns to fiery shades in the fall. 'Aureum' also has wonderful spring color because the foliage emerges almost neon yellow and then fades to a golden green. The handsomely rounded but prominently toothed leaves may shrivel at the tips in dry conditions, so keep the soil moist in hot weather. It prefers a partially shaded site. The varieties 'Autumn Moon' and 'Palmatifolium' are also notable.

☀ ◐ ◊   Z5–7 H7–5
↕↔ to 20ft (6m)

Achillea 'Coronation Gold'

PERENNIAL

The bright-yellow flowerheads of yarrow are made up of numerous tiny flowers gathered together in broad, flat clusters. The gray-green, deeply cut leaves provide a perfect foil for them. This vigorous plant tolerates a wide range of growing conditions but does best in a sunny situation in well-drained, fertile soil. It is a lovely plant for a wildflower garden. When cut and dried, the flowerheads retain their color well. Propagate by division in the fall.

☀ ◊ ◖   Z3–9 H9–1
↕ to 3ft (1m) ↔ to 24in (60cm)

Alchemilla mollis

PERENNIAL

After rain or heavy dew, the downy leaves of lady's mantle glisten with water droplets captured in the hairs on their surface. From the early summer to early fall, large, airy sprays of tiny yellow-green flowers are produced, which are good for cutting. Fairly drought resistant, it is tolerant of most soil conditions, and although it prefers full sun, it will also grow in partial shade. Plant it along the edge of a path or in a wildflower border, where it will self-seed freely.

☼ ◐ ○ ◖   Z4–7 H7–1

↕↔to 20in (50cm)

Allium flavum

BULBOUS PERENNIAL

A large clump of these alliums would look wonderful at the front of a border. A satisfyingly fast-growing bulb, it produces stems topped with up to 60 delicately scented, bright yellow flowers. These dangle on slender stalks but turn upward when the seed is developing. The bluish-green leaves are waxy and cylindrical. Plant bulbs in fall in a sunny location in well-drained soil.

☼ ○ *f*   Z4–10 H9–1

↕ to 14in (35cm) ↔ to 3in (8cm)

Allium moly

BULBOUS PERENNIAL

The golden garlic produces clusters
of up to 30 golden-yellow, star-shaped
flowers on slender stems. Its waxy,
lance-shaped leaves are usually
produced in pairs. Plant in a sunny
situation in fertile, well-drained soil. It
often self-seeds freely and can become
invasive, which, if grown in a wild
garden or naturalized in woodland, is
more of an asset than a problem. Plant
bulbs and, if necessary, divide large
clumps in the fall.

☼ ◊   Z3–9 H9–5

‡ to 14in (35cm) ↔ to 5in (12cm)

Anthemis tinctoria 'E.C. Buxton'

PERENNIAL

Filigree foliage and a long-flowering
season make the golden marguerite
a great-value border plant. A clump-
forming evergreen, it produces masses
of lemon-yellow, daisylike flowers with
deep yellow centers. The leaves are
mid-green above and a soft downy-
gray on the reverse. Cut back hard after
flowering to reinvigorate the plant and
encourage it to produce a neat clump
of leaves for next spring. Plant it in a
sunny location in well-drained soil.

☼ ◊   Z3–8 H8–3

‡↔ to 3ft (1m)

Argyranthemum 'Jamaica Primrose'

PERENNIAL

In frost-free areas this plant will just keep on flowering; elsewhere it is usually grown as summer bedding or in containers. Beautiful, soft-yellow, daisylike flowers and deeply divided, fern-like, mid-green leaves are a winning combination. Grow in moderately fertile, well-drained soil in full sun. Pot the whole plant and move under glass for the winter, or take stem cuttings in the early fall and grow them under cover for next year. Easy to train as a standard.

☼ ◊　　　　　　Z7–11 H11–1

↔ to 3ft (1m)

Bidens ferulifolia

PERENNIAL

The trailing stems of this plant can be best appreciated when tumbling over the edges of a windowbox or used to plump up the planting in a hanging basket. It has large, daisylike, golden-yellow flowers and bright green, filigree foliage and stems. A short-lived perennial, it is usually grown as an annual and is best propagated by taking cuttings at the end of the year. It needs moist, but well-drained, fertile soil. Plants grown in a sunroom or heated greenhouse may flower until the winter.

☼ ◊　　　　　　Z8–11 H11–8

‡ to 12in (30cm) ↔ indefinite

Brachyglottis 'Sunshine'

EVERGREEN SHRUB

A free-flowering look and attractive silvery-gray, slightly woolly foliage make this mound-forming plant a useful addition to any shrub border. From early to midsummer it produces a profusion of bright yellow, daisylike flowers. Plant it in a sunny situation in well-drained, fertile soil. It does well in coastal areas but needs to be protected from strong cold winds inland. Prune in the early spring to keep the bush neat and well shaped.

☼ ◊   Z9–10 H10–9

↕ to 5ft (1.5m) ↔ to 6ft (2m)

Buddleja globosa

DECIDUOUS SHRUB

The orange ball tree forms a large shrub or small tree with spherical clusters of dark orange or yellow, fragrant flowers. It has lance-shaped leaves, which may be semi-evergreen in sheltered areas. It can be used in a shrub border or makes a good specimen plant, although it tends to get leggy with age. It prefers a sunny site in well-drained, preferably alkaline soil. Pruning is unnecessary.

☼ ◊ *f*   Z7–9 H9–7

↕↔ to 15ft (5m)

Buphthalmum salicifolium
PERENNIAL

Yellow ox-eye has dark green, narrow leaves and deep yellow, daisylike flowers held on long, willowy stems. In the late spring insert supports so they are in place before the flowers open. When cut, the flowers are long lasting. It is best grown in full sun in well-drained, poor soil. If given richer soil it may become invasive, in which case, divide plants regularly to keep them in check. In certain situations, however, its spreading habit would be useful, such as on a bank or in a wild garden.

☼ ◊   Z5–8 H8–5

‡ to 24in (60cm) ↔ to 36in (90cm)

Calceolaria 'John Innes'
PERENNIAL

Curiously pouch-shaped and often beautifully marked, the flowers of the slipper flower are a delight. 'John Innes' has intense yellow flowers with red-brown spots. It is a vigorous, clump-forming plant that needs a well-drained, moderately fertile, acid soil in sun or partial shade; it is best grown as a container plant. It is not fully hardy, so pot it and place under glass in the winter, or take softwood cuttings in the summer and keep the plants in a cold frame during the winter as an insurance policy.

⁜ ☼ ◊   Z8–9 H6–1

‡ to 8in (20cm) ↔ to 12in (30cm)

Callistemon pallidus

EVERGREEN SHRUB

Aptly named, the yellow bottle brush bristles with stiff-stemmed, greenish-yellow flowers. Its graceful arching branches are covered with grayish-green leaves that are tinged with pink when they are young. Plant in full sun in well-drained, neutral to acid soil. Not entirely hardy, it needs a sheltered spot against a south- or west-facing wall. Alternatively, plant it in a container of soil-based potting mix and overwinter in a cool greenhouse.

☼ ◊   Z10–11 H11–1C
↕↔ to 12ft (4m)

Carex elata 'Aurea'

PERENNIAL

A vibrantly colored, ornamental sedgelike plant, Bowles' golden sedge is an evergreen that is grown for its gently arching, green-margined, bright yellow leaves. In the early summer, it may send up long, brown, male flower spikes. It requires a site in full sun in a fertile, moist, but well-drained soil. To keep the tufts neat, cut out dead leaves in the summer. Plant in a container, or in groups near water or a in mixed border.

☼ ☀ ◊ ◗   Z5–9 H9–3
↕ to 16in (40cm) ↔ to 6in (15cm)

Cephalaria gigantea

PERENNIAL

The giant scabious is a clump-forming perennial with large green leaves divided into many small lance-shaped leaflets. In the summer it produces tall, branched, erect stems that hold large primrose-yellow flowers, the outer petals of which surround a pincushion of smaller blooms. Plant this scabious in full sun and fertile, moist, well-drained soil. It makes an excellent plant for the back of an herbaceous border, but unlike other scabious it needs plenty of space to grow to its full potential.

☼ ◊ ◖   Z3–7 H7–1

‡ to 8ft (2.5m) ↔ to 24in (60cm)

Coreopsis grandiflora '**Badengold**'

PERENNIAL

Bees love the daisylike flowers of tickseeds, as do flower arrangers who value them for their long life after cutting. 'Badengold' is a short-lived perennial that is most often grown as an annual. Sow seed in the same area from the early spring to early summer. Its orange-centered, yellow blooms are held aloft on tall stems above bright green, lance-shaped leaves. It needs a sunny spot in well-drained, fertile soil. Deadheading helps prolong flowering.

☼ ◊   Z4–9 H11–1

‡ to 30in (75cm) ↔ to 24in (60cm)

Coreopsis verticillata '**Grandiflora**'

PERENNIAL

A good choice for a sunny herbaceous border, this cheerful tickseed bears masses of single, yellow flowers. Deadheading helps prolong the flowering period. Plants raised from seed sown in the early to midspring in a prepared seedbed will go on to flower the same year, while the feathery, mid-green leaves quickly knit together to form a good-sized clump. Plant in fertile, well-drained soil in full sun or light shade. A good cut flower and bee plant.

☼ ◊   Z4–9 H9–1

‡ to 24in (60cm) ↔ to 12in (30cm)

Delphinium '**Sungleam**'

PERENNIAL

In the early summer, this stunning delphinium sends up tall, tapering spires of creamy-yellow flowers with strong yellow eyes. A second flush of flowers can be encouraged by cutting down the flower spikes as soon as they fade. Plant it in groups in a sunny location in well-drained, organic, fertile soil. To prevent wind damage, especially on exposed sites, insert strong canes when planting and tie in the flower stems as they grow.

☼ ◊   Z3–7 H8–3

‡ to 6ft (2m) ↔ to 36in (90cm)

Dicentra scandens
CLIMBER

Very pretty yellow, charmlike flowers hang freely from the rambling stems of this herbaceous climber from the early summer. The flowers sometimes have white, purple, or pink tips. Each winter it dies back to ground level, at which point the old growth should be removed. New growth soon appears again in spring, climbing quite high in a good year. Best in humus-rich, neutral to slightly alkaline soil in a partly shaded spot. Provide a means of support, such as a small trellis or netting..

☀ ◐   Z4–8 H8–1
↕↔ to 3ft (1m)

Digitalis grandiflora
PERENNIAL

Overwintering as a rosette of deep green leaves, the yellow foxglove is an upright, short-lived perennial that produces its spikes of pale lemon, tubular flowers in the early summer. It prefers a semi-shaded situation and damp, well-drained soil, where it will happily self-seed. Deadheading after flowering will control its spread. Grow the slightly smaller *D. lutea* if you have an alkaline soil. Both varieties would suit a wild garden or a less formal mixed border.

☀ ◊ ◐   Z3–8 H8–1
↕ to 3ft (1m) ↔ to 18in (45cm)

Eremurus stenophyllus
PERENNIAL

The foxtail lily produces canary-yellow flowers, fading to copper, on spikes that soar above other early summer border plants. Although fairly hardy, they start to grow early in the year, and the young buds are prone to frost damage. Cover the crowns in the winter and spring with fabric or straw to protect the emerging shoots. The bent, strappy leaves will die down when the flower spike starts to emerge. Plant in very well-drained, sandy soil in full sun. An excellent cut flower.

☼ ◊   Z7–9 H8–1

‡ to 3ft (1m) ↔ to 24in (60cm)

Eriophyllum lanatum
PERENNIAL

The woolly sunflower has silvery-green, slightly furry, deeply divided leaves that knit together to form a dense mat. The deep yellow, daisylike flowers are produced right through summer. Plant in full sun in well-drained, light soil. Fairly drought tolerant, it is a good plant for rock gardens and crevices in walls and paving. To keep it compact, trim back after it has finished flowering. Divide plants in the spring.

☼ ◊   Z5–8 H8–5

‡↔ to 12in (30cm)

Eschscholzia californica
ANNUAL

Perfect for a sun-drenched spot in a Mediterranean-style or gravel garden, the California poppy has decorative finely-divided, feathery, blue-green foliage and bright yellow-orange cup-shaped flowers. The blooms open in full sun and close as the light dims at the end of the day, and appear from early to midsummer. Sow them in the same area in the spring, or the fall where winters are mild in poor, free-draining soil, and deadhead them regularly to stimulate new flowers to develop.

☼ ◊   H9–1

‡ to 12in (30cm) ↔ to 6in (15cm)

Euphorbia palustris
PERENNIAL

Needing soil that is permanently moist, this spurge would make an unusual waterside plant for an informal pond. The strong stems are covered with narrow, lime-green leaves topped, from late spring to early summer, by clusters of greenish-yellow flowers. In the fall the leaves turn various shades of yellow and orange. Choose a site in full sun. Avoid skin contact with the milky sap.

☼ ◖   Z7–9 H7–6

‡↔ to 36in (90cm)

Fremontodendron '*California Glory*'

EVERGREEN SHRUB

While not completely hardy, this shrub
will survive most winters if it is trained
against a sheltered, south-facing wall.
The large golden-yellow flowers bloom
from the late spring to mid-fall and are
set off by dark green, five-lobed foliage,
making this plant a valuable addition
to any garden. It grows happily in
alkaline, free-draining soil and can
be pruned lightly in the early spring.
Contact with the foliage may cause
an allergic reaction.

☼ ◊   Z8–10 H10–8

‡ to 20ft (6m) ↔ to 12ft (4m)

Genista lydia

DECIDUOUS SHRUB

Ideally suited to the well-drained
conditions of a rock garden or raised
bed, this dome-shaped, low-growing
shrub will trail over sunny walls and
rocks. In the early summer its prickle-
tipped, gray-green, arching branches
are covered in bright yellow, pealike
flowers. It prefers hot sites in poor, light
soils that have not been enriched. Take
semi-ripe cuttings in the summer or sow
seed in the fall. Pruning is unnecessary,
and straggly plants are best replaced.

☼ ◊   Z6–9 H9–3

‡ to 24in (60cm) ↔ to 24in (60cm)

Geum 'Lady Stratheden'

PERENNIAL

Geums are especially suitable for the front of an herbaceous border. They form clumps of arching, kidney-shaped leaves that have a covering of fine hairs. The cup-shaped, semidouble, golden-yellow flowers are carried on branching stems. Plant in full sun in moist but well-drained soil. Divide large clumps in fall. Unlike many geums, 'Lady Stratheden' will grow true from seed.

☀ ◊ ◑   Z5–9 H9–5

‡ to 24in (60cm) ↔ to 18in (45cm)

Halimium 'Susan'

EVERGREEN SHRUB

A small, spreading, evergreen shrub valued for its single or semi-double summer flowers, which are bright yellow with deep purple markings. They are a good contrast with the grayish foliage. 'Susan' grows well in sun in any light, well-drained soil, and would suit a rock garden in a warm, coastal area. Provide shelter at the foot of a warm wall where winters are cold, and trim lightly in the spring, if necessary. The flowers are best during long, hot summers. *H. ocymoides* is similar but more upright.

☀ ◊   Z9–11 H11–9

‡ to 18in (45cm) ↔ to 24in (60cm)

Helichrysum italicum subsp. *serotinum*

PERENNIAL

The curry plant is grown for its aromatic, evergreen, sage-green foliage and clusters of yellow flowers. Despite its common name, the leaves of this plant are not used in curry powder; however, they are edible and their savory tang can be used to liven up cream cheese, egg, or chicken dishes. It can suffer during wet winters and should be planted in a raised bed or open, sunny situation in very well-drained soil.

☼ ◊ *f*   Z7–10 H10–7

‡ to 16in (40cm) ↔ to 30in (75cm)

Hemerocallis lilioasphodelus

PERENNIAL

There are thousands of cultivated daylilies to choose from, but this species is up there with the best of them. It is vigorous and easy to grow with funnel-shaped, fragrant flowers that only last for a day or two but are soon replaced. They open in the afternoon and last through the night, so plant a clump close to the patio or other area in the garden that you use in the evening. Plant in full sun in moist but well-drained soil. Divide large clumps in the spring.

☼ ◊ ◑ *f*   Z3–10 H11–2

‡↔ to 3ft (1m)

Hemerocallis
'Stella de Oro'

PERENNIAL

Daylilies are perfect herbaceous border
plants. Their narrow, arching leaves
quickly form an attractive clump; and
while their colorful flowers may only
last a day or so, they appear in rapid
succession over several weeks. Happiest
in full sun in moist but well-drained
soil, daylilies will tolerate the damp
margins of a pond. 'Stella de Oro'
is a compact form that is very free-
flowering and powerfully fragrant.
Propagate by division in the spring.

❁ ◊ ♦ *f*   Z3–10 H11–2
‡to 12in (30cm) ↔to 18in (45cm)

Humulus lupulus
'Aureus'

CLIMBER

An herbaceous climber that will quickly
cover a pergola or fence. Male and
female flowers grow on separate plants
with the female producing the hops.
The yellow color of 'Aureus'—which is
far less vigorous than commercially
grown hops—is transitory because
the leaves turn green later in the year.
Grow in moist but well-drained soil.
Full sun will enhance leaf color.
Remove remains of old growth in the
early spring. Dry hops for decoration.

❁ ◊ ♦   Z4–8 H8–1
‡to 20ft (6m)

Iris '*Brown Lasso*'

PERENNIAL

Bearded irises come in a wide range of colors. 'Brown Lasso' is a lovely combination of yellow upper petals and lilac lower petals edged with butterscotch. Each stem carries 6–12 of these three-toned flowers. Plant in fertile, well-drained, neutral to acid soil in full sun. Divide clumps when they become congested, usually after 3–5 years. The upright, sword-shaped leaves remain after the flowers have faded to add form to the herbaceous border.

☼ ◊   Z3–9 H9–

↕ to 22in (55cm) ↔ indefinite

Iris innominata

PERENNIAL

This attractive Pacific Coast iris is native to the western United States. It has pale yellow to cream flowers with bold brown veining. Other colors include purple and pale lavender. It is a very small plant, rarely exceeding a height of 10in (25cm), with narrow, dark green, evergreen leaves that flush to purple at their base. Plant it in full sun or partial shade, in neutral or slightly acid soil; it is best suited to a raised bed or a woodland garden.

☼ ☀ ◊   Z7–9 H9–

↕ to 10in (25cm) ↔ to 12in (30)

Jasminum humile 'Revolutum'

EVERGREEN SHRUB

This variety of jasmine is treasured for its fragrant, rich yellow flowers from the late spring to early summer. It is fairly versatile and can be trained against a wall or support; it will tolerate shade, although it flowers more freely in sun. After flowering, shorten flowered shoots to a strong bud; when mature, remove one in five of the oldest, flowered stems. It is also good in a border or as ground cover. The flowers are good for cutting.

☼ ❋ ◊ ◐ *f*   Z7–9 H9–7

‡ to 8ft (2.5m) ↔ to 10ft (3m)

Kniphofia 'Buttercup'

PERENNIAL

A robust red hot poker, 'Buttercup' will hold its own in a busy herbaceous border. It forms a large clump of narrow, strappy leaves and, in the early summer, produces several tall spikes of clear yellow flowers that open from green buds. They are very attractive to bees. For best results, plant in full sun or light shade in fertile, moist but well-drained soil. Old foliage offers protection over the winter; remove it in the spring and divide large clumps.

❋ ❋ ◊ ◐   Z6–9 H9–6

↔ to 30in (75cm)

Ligularia przewalskii

PERENNIAL

Tall, narrow spikes of yellow flowers on purple-green stems rise in stately fashion above a robust clump of deeply divided leaves. A lover of deep, moist soil, this plant would look wonderful beside a large pond. Another situation recommended is tucked toward the back of a permanently moist, mixed or herbaceous border where, sheltered among other plants, it is less vulnerable to strong, gusting winds. Although it is happy in full sun, light shade during the middle of the day would be ideal.

☼ ☀ ◐ ◑   Z4–8 H8–1

↕ to 6ft (2m) ↔ to 3ft (1m)

Limnanthes douglasii

ANNUAL

The two-tone petals of this fast-growing, hardy annual inspired its common name of poached-egg plant. It has deeply divided, slightly succulent, glossy green leaves, and stays in flower over a long period right through the summer. Sow seed in the same area during the spring or late summer in moist but well-drained, fertile soil. Use it to edge a path or dot it among rows of vegetables where it will attract hoverflies, which help control aphids.

☼ ◑   H9–

↕ to 6in (15cm) ↔ to 4in (10cm)

Lupinus arboreus

EVERGREEN SHRUB

Tree lupines are strong shrubs, often evergreen in mild winters, with sprawling branches of grayish-green leaves. They make wonderful specimen plants in a hot, dry border. The species has fragrant, sulfur-yellow flowers, but there are also lavender or white types. The tree lupine is not fully hardy and may be damaged by hard frost, so plant it in a sunny location in sandy, well-drained soil, preferably by the coast where it grows very well. Propagate by seed in the spring.

◊ *f*   Z9–10 H10–9

↕ to 6ft (2m)

Luzula sylvatica 'Aurea'

PERENNIAL

This golden type of greater woodrush is a clump-forming, evergreen rush with narrow, grasslike leaves. They are a bright golden yellow in the winter, fading to yellow-green in the summer. It is happy in deep or partial shade in organic, moist but well-drained, poor to moderately fertile soil. It tolerates dry soils. Use as ground cover or in a woodland garden. It can be increased by division in the fall and spring.

☀ ◊ ◊   Z4–9 H9–4

↕ to 32in (80cm) ↔ to 18in (45cm)

Mimulus guttatus
PERENNIAL

The monkey flower is at home in the deep, moist soil beside a stream or pond where it forms a spreading mat of toothed, mid-green leaves. Through the summer until fall it produces tall, narrow spikes of deep yellow flowers, which are often freckled with reddish brown spots. Their shape resembles the intricate flowers of the snapdragon (*Antirrhinum*). Plant in full sun or in dappled shade. Monkey flowers tend to be short lived, so propagate plants by dividing them in the spring.

☀ ☼ ◊ ◖   Z6–9 H9–
↕ to 12in (30cm) ↔ to 24in (60cm)

Oenothera fruticosa 'Fyrverkeri'
PERENNIAL

The scented, deep yellow flowers of the evening primrose open at dusk and are pollinated by night-flying insects. While they may last only a day or so, the flowers are produced in abundance all summer long. The plant has striking red stems and, when young, the lance-shaped leaves are flushed red, too. It is a good plant for a raised bed, gravel garden, or the front of an herbaceous border. Grow it in full sun or partial shade in well-drained, sandy soil.

☀ ☼ ◊ *f*   Z4–8 H8–
↕↔ to 15in (38cm)

Phlomis fruticosa

EVERGREEN SHRUB

Jerusalem sage forms a mound of
aromatic, felted, gray-green leaves.
From early to midsummer, short stems
of golden-yellow, hooded flowers are
produced in bunches. A cluster planting
would suit a sunny border or a gravel
garden with well-drained, light soil.
Although generally hardy, there is a
risk it may be killed by particularly
cold, damp winters—in cold areas, give
it the shelter of a warm wall. Propagate
by taking cuttings in the summer.

◊ *f*   Z8–9 H9–8

↕ to 3ft (1m) ↔ to 5ft (1.5m)

Primula florindae

PERENNIAL

The giant Himalayan cowslip is one of
the largest primulas with a handsome
basal rosette of mid-green, toothed
leaves. The freshly fragrant, sulfur-
yellow, bell-shaped flowers are borne
on tall stems up to 4ft (1.2m) high. It
should be planted in full sun or partial
shade in moist, organic, neutral or
slightly acid soil. Plant in swathes along
a stream bank or in large groups in a
bog or woodland garden or around the
margins of a natural pond.

☀ ◐ ◊ *f*   Z3–8 H8–1

↕ to 4ft (1.2m) ↔ to 3ft (1m)

Ranunculus constantinopolitanus 'Plenus'

PERENNIAL

This cultivated buttercup has neat, double, yellow-green pom-pom flowers in the early summer. It has deeply divided leaves, which are often dotted with grayish-white spots. It is a well-behaved plant that would suit a rock garden or mixed border. Plant it in full sun in moist but well-drained soil. Propagate by dividing the woody roots after flowering has finished.

☀ ◊ ◐   Z7–9 H9–
‡ to 20in (50cm) ↔ to 12in (30cm)

Rhodiola rosea

PERENNIAL

The waxy-covered, triangular-shaped leaves of roseroot clump together to form a neat mound of stiffly erect stems. In early summer it produces large heads of pink buds that open to greenish-yellow, star-shaped flowers. Give it a sunny spot in well-drained, moderately fertile soil in a rock garden, dry walls, or at the front of a raised bed or herbaceous border.

☀ ◊   Z4–8 H8–
‡↔ to 12in (30cm)

Rosa GRAHAM THOMAS
('Ausmas')
DECIDUOUS SHRUB

This excellent modern shrub rose forms
a nicely rounded bush. It never gets out
of control and is one of the best yellow
roses available. All through the summer
until fall, it has deep golden-yellow,
cup-shaped, fragrant flowers. If space
allows, plant in a group of 4–5 in full
sun in well-drained, organic, fertile soil.
Shrub roses are suitable for growing
in mixed borders and need less rich
growing conditions than bush roses
such as Mountbatten.

☼ ◊ *f*　　　　　　　　Z5–9 H9–1

↕ to 4ft (1.2m) ↔ to 5ft (1.5m)

Rosa MOUNTBATTEN
('Harmantelle')
DECIDUOUS SHRUB

A very vigorous, repeat-flowering
floribunda rose with double, fragrant,
deep yellow flowers. It is a nice bush
with plenty of glossy green foliage. Plant
it in a sunny location in well-drained
soil, enriched with plenty of organic
matter. Remove dead flowers to
encourage the production of new buds.
Prune main stems to about 12in (30cm)
above the ground in the early spring,
then apply a balanced fertilizer and a
thick mulch of well-rotted manure.

☼ ◊ *f*　　　　　　　　Z5–9 H9–5

↕ to 4ft (1.2m) ↔ to 30in (75cm)

Rosa xanthina 'Canary Bird'

DECIDUOUS SHRUB

This is a very decorative, but rather large, shrub rose suitable for a wild garden since it needs a lot of space to develop well. It produces long, arching branches covered in the early summer with single, saucer-shaped, lightly fragrant, deep-yellow flowers. A smattering of flowers may appear until fall. In exposed areas it is vulnerable to severe frost, and the young buds may be damaged by cold winds. Grow in moist but well-drained, fertile soil in full sun.

☼ ◊ *f* Z5–9 H9–5
↕↔ to 7ft (2.1m)

Sedum acre 'Aureum'

PERENNIAL

A mat-forming plant with upright or sprawling stems that are covered with small fleshy, green leaves with yellow variegated tips. The bright yellow, star-shaped flowers bloom throughout the summer. Given the right conditions— full sun and a very well-drained soil—it may become invasive, but it is easily controlled. It makes a colorful plant for a trough filled with gritty compost, a raised bed, or a rock garden. Take cuttings in the spring or late summer.

☼ ◊ Z3–8 H8–1
↕ to 2in (5cm) ↔ to 9in (23cm)

Thermopsis rhombifolia var. *montana*

PERENNIAL

An upright plant with divided leaves and tall spikes of bright yellow, pealike flowers that are attractive to bees. Although tolerant of a wide range of conditions, it prefers a sunny spot in fertile, light, sandy soil. Often used to provide vertical accents in an herbaceous border, it is perhaps best suited to an informal wildlife garden where its invasive tendencies are more easily accommodated. Propagate by division in the spring or sow seed in the fall.

☀ ☼ ◊ ◖   Z3–8 H8–1

‡ to 36in (90cm) ↔ to 24in (60cm)

Verbascum 'Gainsborough'

PERENNIAL

This mullein is one of the Cotswold hybrids and overwinters as a large rosette of downy, grayish-green leaves. In the early summer it springs into action and produces a stately spire of saucer-shaped, pale-yellow flowers. Further flowers often appear on side branches. A long-flowering plant for an herbaceous border, it is, unfortunately, rather short-lived. Plant in a sunny location in well-drained, fertile soil.

☼ ◊   Z5–9 H9–3

to 4ft (1.2m) ↔ to 24in (60cm)

Calendula officinalis

ANNUAL

Pot marigold is a vigorous, erect plant with hairy, aromatic, spoon-shaped leaves. The bright orange-yellow, daisylike flowers are produced from the summer to fall. Excellent as bedding, it can also be used in pots or as a cut flower. Plant it in sun or partial shade in well-drained, fertile soil. Sow seed in fertile soil where the plants are to grow. For strong orange shades choose 'Fiesta Gitana' (a dwarf cultivar), 'Orange King' (double blooms), or 'Indian Prince' (reddish flowers). Deadhead to keep the show going.

☼ ◊ *f* H6–1

‡ to 30in (75cm) ↔ to 18in (45cm)

Eccremocarpus scaber

CLIMBER

The Chilean glory flower is a vigorous evergreen with tubular, bright orange-red flowers, which appear early in the summer and continue through the fall. A short-lived, tender perennial, it will only survive the winter outside if planted in a sunny, sheltered location, such as against a south-facing wall that is protected from hard frosts. Alternatively, grow it as an annual. Use it to cover a trellis or pergola, or train it on wires up a house wall. Plant it in full sun in well-drained, fertile soil.

☼ ◊ Z11 H11–1

‡ to 10ft (3m)

Eremurus x *isabellinus* 'Cleopatra'

PERENNIAL

This is a dramatic foxtail lily with tall, stately spikes of deep orange flowers held above mid-green, lance-shaped leaves. It needs to be grown in very well-drained, fertile, sandy soil in full sun. The fleshy roots will quickly rot if the soil becomes too wet, so it is advisable to plant it in a raised bed, where any excess water will quickly drain away. Mulch them over in winter with straw or pine needles to protect the emerging shoots.

☼ ◊   Z5–8 H8–5

‡ to 5ft (1.5m) ↔ to 20in (50cm)

Geum coccineum 'Cooky'

PERENNIAL

Geums are sturdy, clump-forming perennials for the herbaceous border or English-style garden. They bear pretty, five-petalled flowers in warm colors, from yellow to red. 'Cooky' has bright orange flowers from the early to midsummer above bunches of hairy, fresh green foliage. The flowers last well when cut. Most garden soils are suitable. Plant in a sunny spot.

☼ ◊ ◐   Z5–8 H8–5

‡ to 20in (50cm) ↔ to 12in (30cm)

Gladiolus 'Solveiga'

BULBOUS PERENNIAL

If you are looking for a show-stopping gladiolus, 'Solveiga' is one to consider. It can be hard to come by, but the effort is worthwhile. It bears tall spires of large, ruffled yellow flowers with orange centers and rosy marking on the lower petals—a very pleasing combination. They flower from the early to midsummer. 'Solveiga' is a good variety for displaying as a cut flower. Choose a sunny site with good drainage, and allow them to sprout on a sunny windowsill before planting them outside in the spring.

☼ ◊   Z8–10 H12–4

↕ to 3ft (1m) ↔ to 3in (8cm)

Iris 'Blue Eyed Brunette'

PERENNIAL

The name of this bearded iris accurately brings to mind the color of its distinctive flowers. The petals are tinted orange-brown with the lower set highlighted with a bright lilac spot, surmounted by a golden-yellow "beard." Use it in a mixed or herbaceous border and combine it with bronze grasses, such as *Carex flagellifera*, to create an unusual color theme. Plant in a sunny site in well-drained, fertile, neutral to acid soil (*see* 'Bold Print' *p.159*).

☼ ◊   Z3–9 H9–1

↕ to 3ft (1m) ↔ indefinite

Kniphofia 'Bees' Sunset'

PERENNIAL

A beautiful red hot poker, 'Bees' Sunset'
produces tall spikes of pale orange,
tubular flowers over a long period from
the early summer. Grow it in groups in
a fiery color-themed border or gravel
garden. It complements pale yellow
and bright red flowers, such as dahlias.
Plant it in moist, well-drained soil in full
sun or partial shade. Leave the remains
of the old foliage over the winter for
protection, and remove it in the spring,
when large clumps can also be divided.

☼ ☀ ◊ ◖   Z6–9 H9–6

↕ to 36in (90cm) ↔ to 24in (60cm)

Lonicera x *tellmanniana*

CLIMBER

This twining, deciduous, woody-
stemmed honeysuckle bears clusters
of coppery orange, tubular flowers that
open from the late spring to midsummer.
They are a pleasing shade against the
deep green, oval leaves with blue-white
undersides. Train the climbing growth
onto a fence or wall or up into a large
shrub, and after flowering, trim shoots
back by one-third. This honeysuckle
will grow in any moist but well-drained,
organic soil, and provides the best
flowering displays in light shade.

☼ ☀ ◊ ◖   Z7–9 H9–7

↕ to 15ft (5m)

Papaver nudicaule Gartenzwerg Group

PERENNIAL

Iceland poppies are short-lived perennials and do best in neutral to acid soils in full sun. In appearance they are much like the common field poppy, but with flowers in very bright and cheerful shades of orange, pink, red, peach, yellow, and white. Mixtures like Gartenzwerg Group are very popular and can either be bought as plug plants or as seed, which can be sown in the fall or spring in beds or containers. Unlike field poppies, their flowers last well when cut.

☼ ◊ ◓   Z2–7 H9–2
‡ to 24in (60cm) ↔ to 12in (30cm)

Rosa FLOWER CARPET AMBER ('Noa97400a')

DECIDUOUS SHRUB

This compact, low-growing shrub rose features pale orange, lightly fragrant flowers from the early summer into fall. Relatively disease resistant and tolerant of heat and humidity, this low maintenance rose is well suited to containers and planting in small groupings as a ground cover. Grow in full sun in well-drained soil with organic matter added. Apply slow release fertilizer, or top dress with compost in the early spring.

☼ ◓ *f*   Z5–9 H9–5
‡ to 24in (60cm) ↔ to 36in (90cm)

Tagetes 'Tangerine Gem'

ANNUAL

An upright Signet marigold with ferny, dark green leaves. It is very free flowering, producing vast numbers of single, orange flowers throughout the summer. These marigolds make excellent edging and bedding plants, or use them in hanging baskets and containers. Plant them in full sun in fertile, well-drained soil, and deadhead regularly. They are easily raised from seed sown in the early spring in pots on a windowsill or under glass.

☼ ◇   H11–1
‡ to 8in (20cm) ↔ to 12in (30cm)

Tropaeolum majus

CLIMBER

Nasturtiums are colorful summer annuals with rounded, pale green leaves, held on climbing or scrambling stems. They come in a range of colors, including orange, yellow, and red. Their edible leaves, flower buds, and flowers are often used to garnish salads. Plant in pots and hanging baskets, or use them in borders trained up a tripod. Grow in a sunny or lightly shaded situation and moist, well-drained soil. Check plants regularly for caterpillars and black fly, and remove them before the plants become infested.

☀ ☼ ◇ ◐   H11–1
‡ to 12in (30cm)

LATE SUMMER

Many of the plants that bless the hottest and driest time of year are annuals. Sweet peas, sunflowers, marigolds, and nasturtiums are just a few that can make a cheerful show in a border. Other plants, used as annuals, can join them, like salvias and *Ricinus communis* 'Carmencita'. Unlike most annuals, which are sun-lovers, tobacco plants (*Nicotiana*) also thrive in shade where their pastels and lime-greens glow alluringly. As with sweet peas, not all are scented, so check the variety if fragrance is required.

Fuchsias bloom continuously; the large frilly flowers of many are favourites for pots and hanging baskets, along with pelargoniums. As temperatures soar, water containers on a daily basis. It is also vital to water new plants in dry periods. Give priority to trees, shrubs and climbers planted less than a year ago and water generously so moisture penetrates deep below the soil surface.

Borders and gravel gardens are aglow with coneflowers (*Echinacea* and *Rudbeckia*) and red-hot pokers (*Kniphofia*), but for sheer elegance a white colour theme is hard to beat. Combine *Anemone* x *hybrida* 'Honorine Jobert', *Epilobium angustifolium* var. *album*, and tall white dahlias, hollyhocks and lilies for a display that takes on a luminous quality at dusk. To extend the show into the fall, keep deadheading and fill any gaps with fast growers like penstemon.

HOT TROPICAL STYLE

Mirror the heat of summer days with vibrant combinations of red and orange flowers. *Phygelius* x *rectus* 'African Queen' and dahlias like 'Hillcrest Royal' and 'Wootton Impact' will set the garden alight. Punctuate them with red-hot pokers, and choose *Ensete ventricosum*, cannas, agaves and yuccas to increase the tropical flavour with their flamboyant foliage.

Abelia x *grandiflora*
EVERGREEN SHRUB

This large rounded plant has arching branches and glossy, dark green leaves. It flowers from mid- to late summer and produces fragrant, funnel-shaped, pink-flushed white flowers. Plant in a sunny site in a sheltered location or against a west-facing wall, where it will be protected from cold, damaging winds. Grow it in fertile, well-drained soil, and to rejuvenate established plants, cut out some of the older stems after flowering.

☼ ◊ *f*　　　　　　　　　Z6–9 H9–6
‡ to 10ft (3m) ↔ to 12ft (4m)

Achillea ageratum 'W.B. Childs'
PERENNIAL

This variety of yarrow becomes a clump of feathery foliage as it emerges from the ground in the spring. From midsummer these clumps are topped by flat heads of long-lasting, small, white daisy flowers with darker centers. Apart from needing to be cleaned up each winter, like most herbaceous perennials, it is relatively trouble-free and is a good choice for any partially shaded border.

☀ ◊　　　　　　　　　　Z5–7 H7–5
‡↔ to 24in (60cm)

Agapanthus 'Snowy Owl'

PERENNIAL

This white-flowered agapanthus is good for late borders or large containers. With its large, round heads of tubular flowers, it makes an excellent late-summer perennial, and established clumps can be very impressive when in flower, although they can take up a lot of room. The lush green, strap-shaped foliage dies back in the winter. Plant in full sun. In pots, grow in soil-based compost, and water and fertilize weekly in the summer. Divide large clumps in the spring, and protect the roots with a mulch in cold winters.

☼ ◊ ◖   Z8–10 H10–8
↕ to 4ft (1.2m) ↔ to 24in (60cm)

Anemone x *hybrida* 'Honorine Jobert'

PERENNIAL

The Japanese anemone is a popular late-flowering plant, perfect for growing in a summer or fall herbaceous border. It is also good for cutting. This is one of the prettiest varieties, bearing single, pure white flowers with bright green centers surrounded by golden-yellow stamens. Plant it in sun or light shade in moist, fertile, well-drained soil. It spreads quickly to form large clumps and can be invasive. Divide the plants in the early spring.

◖ ☼ ◊ ◖   Z4–8 H8–1
↕ to 5ft (1.5m) ↔ to 24in (60cm)

Campanula alliariifolia
PERENNIAL

Ivory bells is an elegant, herbaceous plant that forms clumps of grayish-green, hairy, heart-shaped leaves. The white, bell-shaped, pendent flowers are held on branched, wiry stems. It prefers a slightly shaded situation and is ideal for planting beneath a light canopy of deciduous trees or shrubs in a mixed border. It blooms from summer to early fall and can be cut to the ground after flowering to prevent self-seeding. Grow it in moist, well-drained, fertile, neutral or alkaline soil.

☀ ◊ ◖   Z3–7 H7–1
↕ to 24in (60cm) ↔ to 20in (50cm)

Clerodendrum trichotomum var. *fargesii*
DECIDUOUS SHRUB

In the late summer this upright large shrub or small tree produces clusters of very fragrant, white flowers with persistent green sepals. The flowers are followed later in the year by bright blue berries. The young leaves are also a feature, opening bronze before turning green. In cold areas plant it against a west- or south-facing wall in moist, well-drained, fertile soil. Pruning is rarely required, except to remove crossing branches.

☀ ◊ ◖ *f*   Z7–9 H9–
↕↔ to 20ft (6m)

Dahlia 'Angora'

PERENNIAL

This dahlia has double white flowers, and creates a stunning display when planted in front of a dark background, or in a white border. The blooms also make excellent cut flowers. Dahlias need a sunny location in fertile, moist, well-drained soil. Plant it in the spring, and insert a supporting cane when planting. Dig up the tubers after the first frost, allow them to dry, and then store them in boxes of dry sand or compost in a frost-free, cool place.

☼ ◊ ◖   Z8–11 H12–1

‡ to 36in (90cm) ↔ to 24in (60cm)

Echinacea purpurea 'White Swan'

PERENNIAL

Coneflowers originate from the western prairies and have daisylike flowers with raised conelike centers. The flowers of 'White Swan' are borne on tall, erect stems above lance-shaped leaves and are composed of white petals with an orange-brown cone. Plant it in a sunny site in an herbaceous border in deep, well-drained soil. It will also tolerate little shade. Cut the stems back after flowering to encourage a second flush of blooms.

☼ ◊   Z3–9 H9–1

to 24in (60cm) ↔ to 18in (45cm)

Epilobium angustifolium f. *album*

PERENNIAL

The common rosebay willow herb is an invasive thug of a plant and is not suitable for growing in the garden. However, this beautiful white form is less aggressive and perfect for a wild area of the garden or the herbaceous border. Narrow, lance-shaped leaves provide a foil for the tall spikes of white summer flowers. It tolerates most soil conditions and will grow in full sun or partial shade. It self-seeds, so deadhead it after flowering.

☼ ❁ ◊ ◗ ◖   Z3–7 H7–1

‡ to 5ft (1.5m) ↔ to 20in (50cm)

Erica tetralix 'Alba Mollis'

EVERGREEN SHRUB

The cross-leaf heath is a spreading bush with small, silvery-gray leaves, which are arranged in the shape of a cross. In the late summer, it is covered with small, bell-shaped, white flowers. It grows naturally on wet moorland and needs damper soil conditions than other species of heather. It also requires an acid soil and should be grown in full sun for the best results. Cut back the plant in the spring to keep it neat.

☼ ◗   Z5–7 H7–

‡ to 8in (20cm) ↔ to 12in (30cm)

Eucomis bicolor

BULBOUS PERENNIAL

An exotic-looking bulb, the pineapple lily has large, strap-like, light green leaves and purple-spotted flower stems. In late summer it bears dense spikes of purple-edged white flowers topped by a rosette of small leaves that inspired its common name. Plant bulbs about 6in (15cm) deep in full sun in fertile, well-drained soil. The bulbs may survive the winter in mild areas, but in cold climates, lift them and store in a frost-free place, then replant them in the spring. Alternatively, grow them in pots.

☼ ◊   Z8–10 H10–8

‡ to 20in (50cm) ↔ to 24in (60cm)

Fallopia baldschuanica

CLIMBER

The mile-a-minute plant, or Russian vine, is a rampant climber which grows rapidly up to a height of 40ft (12m). It has woody, twining stems covered with heart-shaped, pale green leaves. In the late summer it bears masses of small, pink-flushed, creamy-white flowers. Although unsuitable for a small garden, it is useful for covering an ugly wall or a dead tree. Grow it in full sun or partial shade in poor or slightly fertile, well-drained soil. Don't be afraid to cut it back hard in the spring.

☼ ◑ ◊   Z5–9 H9–5

‡ to 40ft (12m)

Fuchsia '*Annabel*'

EVERGREEN SHRUB

'Annabel' is a free-flowering, trailing fuchsia that produces delicate white flowers and is well suited for hanging baskets and tall containers. It can also be trained as a standard, if provided with a permanent supporting stake. Feed it regularly throughout its growing season. This fuchsia is not hardy, so move it indoors for the winter into a frost-free greenhouse. To propagate it, take softwood cuttings in the spring.

☼ ☀ ◊ ◑   Z9–11 H11–9
↕↔to 24in (60cm)

Galtonia candicans

BULBOUS PERENNIAL

Valued for its late summer blooms, this bulbous plant has long, grayish-green, straplike leaves and white, pendent, slightly fragrant, tubular flowers, which are produced on tall spikes. It is very hardy, but in areas that experience very cold winters, the bulbs should be dug up in the fall and stored in a frost-free place or covered with a deep mulch. Plant the bulbs in spring in full sun and fertile, moist soil that never dries out.

☼ ◑ *f*   Z7–10 H10–7
↕ to 4ft (1.2m) ↔to 9in (23cm)

Gaura lindheimeri

PERENNIAL

This graceful, clump-forming perennial with tall and slender stems will more than earn its keep in any sunny garden. Not only is it easy to grow, it flowers over a very long period in the summer up until the first frost of fall. These flowers are carried in loose spires and open from pinkish-white buds each morning to display white flowers. It is a graceful plant for a mixed flower border, tolerating both heat and drought, and some part-day shade. Divide clumps in the spring, if necessary.

☼ ☀ ◊ ◊　　　　　　　Z6–9 H9–6

‡ to 5ft (1.5m) ↔ to 36in (90cm)

Hydrangea macrophylla '**Veitchii**'

DECIDUOUS SHRUB

Lacecap hydrangeas have flat-topped flowerheads composed of a cluster of small fertile blooms surrounded by larger sterile flowers. 'Veitchii' has white sterile flowers that become pink as they age and forms a mound of dark green foliage. The flowerheads can be cut and dried or left over the winter and removed in the spring, when a few of the oldest stems can also be pruned to the ground. Plant in sun or partial shade in moist, well-drained, fertile soil.

☼ ☀ ◊ ◊　　　　　　　Z6–9 H9–6

‡ to 6ft (2m) ↔ to 8ft (2.5m)

Hydrangea quercifolia 'Snowflake'

DECIDUOUS SHRUB

This double-flowered variety of the oak-leaved hydrangea is a mound-forming, deciduous shrub bearing arching clusters of white flowers that fade to pink from midsummer to fall. The distinctive oaklike, mid-green leaves turn bronze-purple in the fall. It is useful in a range of sunny or partially shaded garden sites, including large containers, but the leaves may become yellow if grown in shallow, alkaline soil. Keep any pruning to a minimum, in the spring, if necessary.

☼ ◐ ◊   Z5–9 H9–5

↕ to 6ft (2m) ↔ to 8ft (2.5m)

Jasminum officinale 'Argenteovariegatum'

CLIMBER

This jasmine is semi-evergreen with cream-edged, green leaves. The highly fragrant, pure white flowers appear in clusters from early summer to early fall. Grow it in full sun or partial shade in fertile, well-drained soil. Once the flowering is over, thin old or congested stems. During the summer, take semi-ripe cuttings. It is not fully hardy so plant it in a sheltered location or by a warm wall. It can also be grown in containers of soil-based potting mix.

☼ ◐ ◊ *f*   Z9–10 H10–9

↕ to 40ft (12m)

Lathyrus latifolius 'Albus'

CLIMBER

The everlasting pea is an herbaceous perennial, which can be used to climb up a support or as ground cover. 'Albus' produces white to creamy-white flowers that appear from the summer to early fall. It grows well in full sun or light shade in well-drained, fertile soil that has been enriched with well-rotted manure. Cut back any dead stems in the spring, but otherwise leave it undisturbed.

☼ ☀ ◊   Z5–9 H9–5

‡ to 6ft (2m)

Lilium regale

BULBOUS PERENNIAL

One of the best lilies for perfume, the regal lily is a vigorous plant with erect or arching stems clothed with shiny, grayish-green leaves. In midsummer it produces up to 25, intensely fragrant, trumpet-shaped white flowers. The petals have purple streaks on the back and golden-yellow throats. Regal lilies grow well in containers, although they need the support of tall canes. Plant them in well-drained, fertile soil in full sun with the lower part of the plant shaded by other planting.

☼ ◊ *f*   Z4–7 H8–5

‡↔ to 6ft (2m)

Lonicera periclymenum 'Graham Thomas'

CLIMBER

A vigorous climber with white flowers that turn yellow with age and are followed by glossy, red berries. Grow it through trees and over pergolas or trellis, or it can be used as gound cover and over banks. The flowers are highly fragrant and attract night-flying moths and insects. Bear this in mind if you are considering planting it near the house. Plant in sun or partial shade in any reasonable soil. Cut established plants back by up to a third after flowering.

☼ ☀ ◊ ◗ *f*   Z5–9 H9–5
‡ to 23ft (7m)

Magnolia grandiflora

EVERGREEN TREE

Given a warm, sheltered location, the bull bay eventually becomes a large tree with glossy, leathery, dark green leaves. In late summer it bears large, creamy-white flowers, up to 10in (25cm) across. Flowers may also appear sporadically at other times of the year. It is not fully hardy, and in cold areas it should be grown against a west- or south-facing wall in moist, well-drained soil. Grow it in full sun or partial shade.

☼ ☀ ◊ ◗ *f*   Z7–9 H9–1
‡ to 60ft (18m) ↔ to 50ft (15m)

Myrtus communis

EVERGREEN SHRUB

Myrtle has an upright style and bears rounded, glossy, dark green, aromatic leaves. The attractive, fragrant white flowers have frothy centers created by long white stamens. It blooms from the middle of the summer to the beginning of the fall. A Mediterranean plant, myrtle is not completely hardy and is more likely to survive cold winters if planted against a sunny wall. Grow it in slightly fertile, moist, well-drained soil.

☼ ◊ ◕ *f*   Z8–9 H9–8

‡↔ to 10ft (3m)

Nicotiana sylvestris

PERENNIAL

A vigorous, short-lived perennial, the tobacco plant is frequently grown as an annual in cool climates. The flowers of this species are borne on long stems above a rosette of elliptic, dark green, sticky leaves. The long, white, highly fragrant flowers resemble shooting stars and are produced from midsummer. It is easily damaged by frost but may survive a mild winter if protected by a thick layer of mulch. Plant it in a sunny or partially shaded site in moist, well-drained soil.

☼ ◑ ◊ ◕ *f*   Z10–11 H11–1

‡ to 5ft (1.5m) ↔ to 30in (75cm)

Rhododendron 'Polar Bear'

EVERGREEN SHRUB

'Polar Bear' is unusual for a rhododendron —instead of flowering in the spring, like most, it bears its huge trusses of fragrant, waxy, white flowers in the late summer. It makes a sturdy, treelike shrub with large, oval leaves. In a medium to large garden it is ideal for adding color to a shaded area, and it will also grow in a large container. Acid soil is essential. Little pruning is required.

☀ ◐ *f*   Z7–9 H9–7
↕ to 15ft (5m) ↔ to 12ft (4m)

Rodgersia aesculifolia

PERENNIAL

A sizable, clump-forming plant with creeping roots and large, dark, bronzy-green leaves that are similar in shape to a horsechestnut leaf. In the summer it produces tall plumes of fragrant, white or pinkish-white flowers. Plant in moist, fertile soil in full sun. A perfect pondside plant, it will also grow well in a bog garden. If given partial shade, it will tolerate slightly drier soil. Propagate by dividing established plants in the fall.

☀ ☀ ◐ *f*   Z5–8 H8–1
↕↔ to 3ft (1m)

Schizophragma hydrangeoides

CLIMBER

Japanese hydrangea vine is cloaked in oval to heart-shaped, dark green leaves. In mid- to late summer, creamy white flowers bloom in terminal clusters. It attaches to surfaces by aerial roots and is ideal for planting at the base of a large tree or a wall. Grow in moderately fertile, well drained soil in part or dappled shade; it may tolerate full sun in cool regions.

☼ ☀ ◊ ◐ Z6–9 H9–6
‡ to 40ft (12m)

Yucca filamentosa

EVERGREEN SHRUB

The Spanish dagger is an architectural plant and bears stiff, lance-shaped, spiky leaves with razor-sharp points. Cut off these points if growing yuccas in gardens used by children. In the late summer it produces a tall spike of bell-shaped, creamy-white flowers. Plant it in well-drained soil in a sunny position, such as in a gravel garden, where it has space to grow to its full size. Protect young plants during cold, wet winters with a straw mulch or fabric.

☀ ◊ Z4–11 H11–5
‡ to 6ft (2m) ↔ to 5ft (1.5m)

Achillea 'Cerise Queen'

PERENNIAL

This pretty, pink-flowered yarrow is ideal for a sunny, herbaceous border. Its flat, dishlike flowerheads appear through midsummer and are very attractive to many flying insects, such as butterflies. They are also good cut for an indoor arrangement. The flowerheads may flop over, so place a support over the plant in the spring. Divide large clumps in the spring or fall, and remove old flowerheads to promote reflowering. This is a tough plant that can tolerate drought and hot weather.

☼ ◊ ◊   Z3–9 H9–1

↕↔to 24in (60cm)

Agrostemma githago 'Milas'

ANNUAL

Corn cockle used to be a cornfield annual weed, but the widespread use of herbicides has made it a rare plant in the wild. It has lance-shaped, grayish-green leaves, and in the summer 'Milas' has vibrant plum-pink flowers with white centers. Plant corn cockles in full sun in poor, well-drained soil. They can be grown in an English-style garden, in containers, or planted in a summer flower meadow. The species self-seeds freely.

☼ ◊   H9–

↕ to 36in (90cm) ↔to 12in (30cm)

Alcea rosea

PERENNIAL

Hollyhocks are tall, vigorous plants, with rounded, slightly hairy leaves. In the summer they produce a long spike of funnel-shaped pink, white, purple, or creamy-yellow flowers. 'Chater's Double' is a beautiful double type. Hollyhocks need a sunny location and well-drained, fertile soil. They look good grown by a wall. Rust can be a problem, so look out for resistant types; they are often grown as biennials to reduce the effects of this disease. They may need staking in open sites.

☼ ◊   Z3–9 H10–3

‡ to 6ft (2m) ↔ to 24in (60cm)

Androsace lanuginosa

PERENNIAL

The fine, silky hairs that clothe the evergreen leaves of this low-growing perennial give the plant a soft-textured appearance. The primroselike, pink flowers appear in mid- to late summer or early fall. Rosettes of tiny, deep gray-green leaves are arranged along the length of the trailing stems. It needs a sunny location and very well-drained soil. Add plenty of gravel to heavy clay soils to improve drainage. Good for a rock garden, trough, or along the top of a drystone wall.

☼ ◊   Z5–7 H7–3

‡ to 1½in (4cm) ↔ to 7in (18cm)

Anemone hupehensis 'Hadspen Abundance'

PERENNIAL

This late-flowering anemone produces deep pink flowers over a long period that are good for cutting. The edges of the petals fade to white as the flower ages. The long-stalked leaves have three leaflets. This anemone enjoys a sunny or partially shaded site. Plant it in moist soil in an herbaceous border. In cold areas mulch it well in the fall.

☼ ◐ ◌ ◊　　　　　　　　　Z5–7 H7–5
‡ to 4ft (1.2m) ↔ to 18in (45cm)

Anemone x *hybrida* 'Elegans'

PERENNIAL

The Japanese anemone is a vigorous late-flowering plant with upright, branched stems. From late summer to mid fall, 'Elegans' produces masses of beautiful single, light pink flowers, which become darker as they age. It looks great in an herbaceous border, and is good for cutting. It does best in a moist, fertile soil in full sunshine or partial shade. 'Margarete' has double, pale pink flowers.

☼ ◐ ◌ ◊　　　　　　　　　Z4–8 H8–5
‡ to 5ft (1.5m) ↔ indefinite

Begonia
'Roy Hartley'
PERENNIAL

The glossy leaves provide the perfect foil for this tuberous begonia's large, salmon-pink flowers, which are borne from midsummer. Its upright growth makes it an excellent bedding plant. Tubers can be planted in the garden when all risk of frost has passed; it flowers better in a partially shaded site and moist, well-drained soil. For an indoor display, plant 'Roy Hartley' in a large container of soil-based potting mix in bright light, away from direct sun.

☀ ◯ ◐   H10–1

‡ to 24in (60cm) ↔ to 18in (45cm)

Callistephus chinensis
Ostrich Plume Series
ANNUAL

China aster flowers resemble chrysanthemums with double blooms. The Ostrich Plume Series are tall plants with flowers in shades of pink, purple, and red. They bloom from late summer until the middle of fall, and can be deadheaded to prolong flowering. Plant them in a sunny, sheltered site in moist, well-drained soil. China asters make good bedding plants and cut flowers.

☀ ◯ ◐   H9–1

to 24in (60cm) ↔ to 12in (30cm)

Calluna vulgaris 'County Wicklow'

EVERGREEN SHRUB

There are over 500 different cultivars of ling, or heather. All are evergreen shrubs and can be used in heather gardens or as ground cover. 'County Wicklow' is compact with slightly prostrate stems and mid-green foliage. It bears spikes of small, double shell-pink flowers and blooms from late summer to late fall. Plant it in full sun in well-drained, acidic soil. Cut it back in the spring to keep it neat and bushy.

☼ ◊   Z5–7 H7–5

‡ to 12in (30cm) ↔ to 14in (35cm)

Chelone obliqua

PERENNIAL

The turtlehead plant bears stiff stems sparsely covered with lance-shaped, mid-green leaves. From late summer to mid fall it produces clusters of pink flowers with turtle mouthlike openings, which explain its common name. It will perform well, planted in a sunny border or partial shade in deep, fertile, moist soil. To propagate it, divide clumps in the spring.

☼ ◑ ◊   Z3–9 H9–3

‡ to 3ft (1m) ↔ to 20in (50cm)

Chrysanthemum 'Clara Curtis'

PERENNIAL

Unlike many chrysanthemums, this variety has simple, single daisylike flowers with pale pink petals and greeny-yellow centers. Their perfume comes as something of a surprise, because many chrysanthemums are unscented. Plant it in well-drained soil that has previously been enriched with well-rotted manure. It is hardy, but in cold, wet areas it should be dug up and overwintered in a frost-free place.

☀ ◊ *f*　　　　　　Z5–9 H9–1

↕ to 30in (75cm) ↔ to 18in (45cm)

Cleome hassleriana 'Rose Queen'

ANNUAL

Spider flowers are tall, handsome plants with handlike leaves. They flower in the midsummer, producing large clusters of spidery, pink, white, or purple blooms that are good for cutting. They are ideal for the back of an herbaceous border since they do not need staking and for filling spaces created when spring flowering perennials are over. Sow seeds in the spring in a heated propagator, and plant out after all risk of frost has passed, in full sun and fertile, well-drained soil.

☀ ◊　　　　　　Z11 H11–1

↕ to 5ft (1.5m) ↔ to 18in (45cm)

Cosmos bipinnatus **Sensation Series**

ANNUAL

This elegant hardy annual is perfect for an annual or mixed border where it is valued for its feathery, mid-green leaves and large, showy blooms. The long-stemmed, daisylike flowers come in a range of pinks and whites and are good for cutting. Prolong flowering with regular deadheading. It prefers a sunny location in moist but well-drained soil. For early flowering, sow seed in the fall.

☼ ◊ ◊   H11–1
‡ to 36in (90cm) ↔ to 24in (60cm)

Crinum x powellii

BULBOUS PERENNIAL

From late summer to fall tall stems of large, slightly fragrant, funnel-shaped, pale pink flowers appear on this vigorous, clump-forming perennial. The straplike leaves can measure up to 5ft (1.5m) in length. Crinums are not completely hardy, and in cold areas protect them with a thick mulch during the winter. They should be planted with the neck of the bulb just above the ground, preferably in the shelter of a sunny wall in fertile, moist, well-drained soil.

☼ ◊ ◊ *f*   Z7–10 H11–8
‡ to 3ft (1m) ↔ to 24in (60cm)

Dahlia 'Fascination'

PERENNIAL

Dahlias provide a late burst of color after early-flowering perennials are past their best. 'Fascination' is a dwarf form with bronze-tinged leaves and purple-pink flowers. It can be used as a bedding plant at the front of a border and makes a good cut flower. Grow it in full sun in fertile, well-drained soil. Dig up the tubers after the first frost, pack them in boxes of dry sand or compost, and overwinter them in a frost-free place. Plant out in the late spring.

☼ ◊　　　　　　　　　　Z9–11 H11–1

‡ to 18in (45cm) ↔ to 12in (30cm)

Dianthus gratianopolitanus

PERENNIAL

The Cheddar pink is a compact, low-growing evergreen that forms a carpet of waxy, narrow, gray-green leaves. In late summer solitary, very fragrant, pink or red flowers with toothed petals are borne on short stems. It will flourish in a rock garden, raised bed, or trough and should be planted in well-drained, gritty soil in full sun.

☼ ◊ *f*　　　　　　　　Z4–8 H8–1

‡ to 6in (15cm) ↔ to 12in (30cm)

Diascia barberae '**Blackthorn Apricot**'

PERENNIAL

This mat-forming plant produces masses of apricot-pink flowers in the summer and fall and is ideal for the front of an herbaceous border, a rock garden, or a container. Diascias grow well in full sun in moist, well-drained, fertile soil and need protection in cold, wet winters. Other excellent forms include 'Salmon Supreme', with larger, pale apricot flowers, and 'Ruby Field', which produces deep salmon-pink flowers.

☼ ◊ ◖   Z8–9 H9–8
‡to 10in (25cm) ↔to 20in (50cm)

Echinacea purpurea

PERENNIAL

The coneflower has tall, erect stems that bear slightly hairy, lance-shaped leaves. In the late summer and early fall it produces large, purplish-pink, daisylike flowerheads with cone-shaped centers comprised of tiny golden-brown flowers. It is ideal for the middle or back of a border, and to grow well, it needs full sun and a deep, well-drained soil. Good for cutting.

☼ ◊   Z3–9 H9–1
‡to 5ft (1.5m) ↔to 18in (45cm)

Erica ciliaris 'Corfe Castle'

EVERGREEN SHRUB

The Dorset heath 'Corfe Castle' bears rose-pink flowers from midsummer to the middle of fall. In the winter the mid-green foliage has a bronze tone, and its spreading stems make good ground cover. *Erica ciliaris* and its cultivars should be planted in an open, sunny situation in acidic, well-drained soil. Although hardy, it may suffer during very cold winters. Cut back the plants in the spring to keep them neat, and remove dead flowers.

☀ ◊　　　　　　　　Z8–9 H9–8

↕ to 9in (22cm) ↔ to 14in (35cm)

Erica vagans 'Birch Glow'

EVERGREEN SHRUB

This summer-flowering heather is a low, spreading, evergreen shrub that looks good on its own in a container or trough filled with bark-based, acidic soil mix. Its deep pink flowers continue well into the fall. In the open garden, grow in acid soil, although it will tolerate alkaline soil. Plant in a sunny site. It can be grown as ground cover and is tolerant of coastal conditions. Trim in the early spring.

☀ ◊ ◊　　　　　　　Z5–7 H7–5

↕ to 12in (30cm) ↔ to 20in (50cm)

Erigeron karvinskianus
PERENNIAL

This carpeting plant produces spreading stems and grayish-green, lance-shaped leaves. The pretty, daisylike flowers, which appear in the summer, are solitary or produced in groups of up to five white or pink blooms, which darken to reddish-purple as they age. It should be planted in full sun, in moist but well-drained soil. The blooms will liven up a rock garden or the front of a border, and it is ideal for planting in cracks and crevices in walls and paving. Once established it spreads freely.

☼ ◊   Z5–7 H7–5

‡ to 6in (15cm) ↔ indefinite

Eupatorium maculatum Atropurpureum Group
PERENNIAL

Joe Pye weed is tall with very strong, reddish-purple stems and pointed, lance-shaped, purple-tinged green leaves. The large heads of pinkish-purple flowers appear from midsummer to early fall. It is a useful plant for the back of a large, late summer border and blends well with grasses such as *Miscanthus*. It enjoys damp, slightly alkaline soil in full sun or partial shade.

☼ ◐ ◊   Z3–9 H9–1

‡ to 7ft (2.2m) ↔ to 3ft (1m)

Filipendula purpurea
PERENNIAL

This close relative of meadowsweet
is a pretty perennial for moist or wet
ground. It forms upright clumps of
elegant, dark green foliage that is topped
by feathery clusters of red-purple
flowers on purple-tinged stems in the
summer. It looks good planted in groups
to form drifts and would be suitable for
a waterside planting or a bog garden.
It can also be naturalized in a damp
woodland. The plant will tolerate full
sun as long as the soil is reliably moist.

☼ ☀ ◐ ●   Z4–9 H9–1
↕ to 4ft (1.2m) ↔ to 24in (60cm)

Fuchsia 'Leonora'
DECIDUOUS SHRUB

A free-flowering, upright fuchsia that
has bell-shaped, soft pink flowers with
reflexed outer sepals. It is a good choice
for a patio container; use soil-based
potting mix and position it in full sun
or light shade. In the summer water
well, and feed regularly with a balanced
fertilizer, or use a slow-release fertilizer
when planting. Keep it frost-free over
the winter, moving it outside after frosts
are over. New plants are easy to raise
from softwood cuttings in the spring.

☼ ☀ ◐ ◐   Z9–11 H11–9
↕ to 5ft (1.5m) ↔ to 3ft (1m)

Gaura lindheimeri 'Siskiyou Pink'

PERENNIAL

This robust plant has branched stems and forms a clump of narrow lance- or spoon-shaped leaves. The flowers of 'Siskiyou Pink' are white, but heavily flushed with deep pink. They first appear in the late spring but reach their peak in the late summer and continue into the early fall. This long-flowering plant is perfect for the front of a sunny border and needs a fertile, moist, well-drained soil. It will tolerate partial shade and dry soil during the summer.

☼ ☼ ◊ ◊   Z6–9 H9–6

‡ to 4ft (1.2m) ↔ to 3ft (1m)

Hebe 'Great Orme'

EVERGREEN SHRUB

There are over 75 species of hebe, all suitable for coastal gardens. This one forms a rounded bush with purple shoots and glossy leaves. From midsummer to mid-fall it produces spikes of pink flowers, which fade to white as they age. It is a medium-sized shrub, and will add year-round interest to a mixed border. Plant it in a sunny or partially shaded location, sheltered from cold winds and frost in well-drained soil. No pruning is necessary.

☼ ☼ ◊ ◊   Z9–11 H11–9

‡↔ to 4ft (1.2m)

Hemerocallis 'Jolyene Nichole'

PERENNIAL

The daylily is so called because its flowers open for just one day. 'Joylene Nichole' is unusual because it unfurls its flowers late in the afternoon and they stay open throughout the night. It has large, pink flowers with a yellowish-green throat, lined with deep pink veins. The flowers are borne above a large clump of almost evergreen, bluish-green leaves. Plant in moist but well-drained soil, in a sunny border near the house or patio to enjoy its blooms fully.

☼ ◊ ◐   Z3–10 H11-2
‡ to 20in (50cm) ↔ to 3ft (1m)

Hydrangea paniculata PINK DIAMOND ('Interhydia')

DECIDUOUS SHRUB

In the late summer and early fall this spreading hydrangea bears large, cone-shaped flowerheads that open creamy-white but then turn deep pink as they age. It should be planted in a moist, well-drained, fertile soil in sun or partial shade. It will also benefit from some protection against cold, drying winds. No pruning is necessary, but flowering is improved by cutting back stems in the early spring to a permanent framework of branches.

☼ ☀ ◊ ◐   Z4–8 H8–1
‡ to 22ft (7m) ↔ to 8ft (2.5m)

Hydrangea serrata 'Rosalba'

DECIDUOUS SHRUB

This upright yet compact, deciduous shrub is valued for its flat flowerheads, which appear from the summer to fall. These are made up of tiny pink flowers in the center, surrounded by larger white flowers that become red-marked as they age. The leaves are oval, mid-green, and pointed. 'Rosalba' is ideal as a specimen plant or in a shrub border and can be planted in full sun or partial shade. The flowers may turn blue in acid soils. Very little pruning is necessary.

☼ ❀ ◐   Z6–9 H9–6

↕↔ to 4ft (1.2m)

Indigofera dielsiana

DECIDUOUS SHRUB

The dark green leaves of this medium-sized bush are composed of many small opposite leaflets and contrast well with the pealike, pale reddish-pink flowers that are produced from summer to early fall. *Indigofera* is not completely hardy and should be grown in full sun in a sheltered shrub border or against a warm, south- or west-facing wall. It will do well when planted in fertile, moist, well-drained soil. The stems produce an orangy-yellow latex when they are cut, which may irritate the skin.

☼ ◇   Z6–9 H9–6

↕↔ to 5ft (1.5m)

Lathyrus latifolius

CLIMBER

The everlasting pea is an herbaceous climber with branched stems and pairs of blue-green leaflets. The leaves terminate in tendrils, which allows it to scramble or climb over banks or through shrubs. In late summer and early fall it bears clusters of pealike, magenta-purple flowers. Plant it in fertile, well-drained soil in full sun or partial shade, and prune it to the ground in the spring to encourage new stems, otherwise leave it undisturbed. Sow seed in the fall.

☀ ☀ ◊   Z5–9 H9–5
to 6ft (2m)

Lavatera maritima

EVERGREEN PERENNIAL

This shrublike perennial has rounded, grayish-green leaves with shallow lobes. In the summer it bears solitary, saucer-shaped, pink flowers with deep magenta veins radiating out from the center. It prefers a spot in full sun in fertile, well-drained soil, sheltered or staked against the wind. To encourage healthy growth the following year, cut back to a strong bud close to the base after it flowers. Mallows tend to be short lived. Well suited to seaside gardens.

☀ ◊   Z6–8 H8–6
to 5ft (1.5m) ↔to 3ft (1m)

Lilium
Pink Perfection Group

BULBOUS PERENNIAL

These Asiatic lilies have large, slightly nodding, trumpet-shaped flowers held on tall, robust stems. The blooms are fragrant and have deep pinkish-purple petals with swept-back tips. Plant Asiatic lilies in well-drained, fertile soil that has been enriched with leaf mold or well-rotted garden compost. They need a sunny location to thrive with the base of the plant in shade. If using them as cut flowers, snip off the orange anthers since the pollen stains.

☼ ◊ *f*   Z3–8 H8–1

‡ to 6ft (2m)

Lonicera periclymenum
'Serotina'

CLIMBER

The late Dutch honeysuckle has woody, twining stems and grayish-green leaves In mid- to late summer it produces clusters of pink buds opening to display highly perfumed, creamy-white and purplish-pink flowers. It is very hardy and can be grown over fences and pergolas or through trees and shrubs, or as ground cover over a bank. Plant it in full sun or partial shade in fertile, mois but well-drained soil. Prune back after flowering to keep within bounds.

☼ ◑ ◊ ◓ *f*   Z5–9 H9–

‡ to 22ft (7m)

Lychnis coronaria
BIENNIAL

The rose campion has lance-shaped, soft, downy, silver-gray leaves and stems, which in mid- to late summer contrast beautifully with the bright magenta, rounded, flat-topped flowers. It self-seeds with abandon and is a welcome addition to any garden bed or border. Plant rose campion in full sun in slightly fertile, well-drained soil. Sow the seed in the spring to flower the following year.

☀ ◊   Z3–8 H8–1

‡ to 24in (60cm) ↔ to 18in (45cm)

Monarda 'Croftway Pink'
PERENNIAL

This pink-flowered variety of bergamot is a clump-forming, herbaceous perennial primarily grown for its round heads of tubular pink flowers that appear in the late summer. These are carried above the small, deliciously aromatic, light green leaves, which betray the plant's use as an herb. Bergamot would suit a mixed or herbaceous border in sun or partial shade, or even a kitchen garden. Another common name for the plant is bee balm because the flowers are attractive to bees.

☀ ◑ ◊ f   Z4–9 H9–2

‡ to 3ft (1m) ↔ to 18in (45cm)

Morina longifolia

PERENNIAL

A spiny-toothed, evergreen perennial with dark-green, aromatic leaves that overwinter as a thistlelike rosette. In the early summer it produces a spike of small, dangling, tubular flowers—these open white, turn pink after they have been fertilized, then eventually change to red before falling. Plant in a sunny location in poor, very well-drained soil. The roots will rot if the soil is wet during the winter months so mulch with grit or gravel.

☼ ◊ *f*   Z6–9 H9–6
‡ to 30in (75cm) ↔ to 12in (30cm)

Nicotiana 'Domino Salmon-pink'

ANNUAL

This tobacco plant is grown as an annual in cooler climates. It has large, sticky basal leaves and narrow, lance-shaped stem leaves. In mid- to late summer, 'Domino Salmon-pink' is clothed with star-shaped, salmon-pink flowers that open up in the early evening and emit a delicate scent. Grow tobacco plants in full sun or partial shade in fertile, moist well-drained soil near a window or path where the fragrance can be enjoyed.

☼ ◐ ◊ ◗ *f*   Z10–11 H11–1
‡ to 18in (45cm) ↔ to 16in (40cm)

Nymphaea 'René Gérard'

PERENNIAL

Waterlilies are aquatic perennials grown for their showy flowers and rounded, floating leaves. The shade cast by the leaves is useful in reducing the growth of pond algae and providing shelter for fish and other pond creatures. The star-shaped flowers of 'René Gérard' are rosy pink. Plant in aquatic planting baskets in still water in a sunny site, and divide plants in the spring if necessary. The plants retreat underwater in the winter.

☼ ◗　　　　　Z3–11 H11–1
↔ to 5ft (1.5m)

Origanum 'Kent Beauty'

DECIDUOUS SHRUB

A semi-evergreen herb with creeping roots and a prostrate style with aromatic, rounded, bright green leaves. From midsummer it produces masses of small, tubular, pale-pink or mauve flowers surrounded by deep pink bracts. 'Kent Beauty' is perfect for an herb or gravel garden, patio pot, or the front of an herbaceous border. Plant it in full sun in slightly fertile, well-drained soil.

☼ ◊ *f*　　　　　Z5–8 H8–5
↕ to 8in (20cm) ↔ to 12in (30cm)

Pelargonium '**Bird Dancer**'

PERENNIAL

This frost-tender plant bears decorative rounded green leaves with wavy edges and a darker zone in the center. The flowers are pale salmon-pink and borne on long stems in ball-headed clusters from the summer to fall. Its compact, neat shape makes it ideal for a patio container or a sunny window box. Plant it in fertile, well-drained potting compost or outside in a bed with free-draining garden soil. Move under cover for the winter and keep fairly dry.

☼ ◐ ◊   H11–1

‡ to 8in (20cm) ↔ to 6in (15cm)

Pelargonium '**Clorinda**'

PERENNIAL

This vigorous, scented-leaved geranium has crinkled, evergreen foliage that smells of cedar. Rounded clusters of deep rose-pink flowers appear from the summer to fall. Grow it in containers in well-drained potting compost in a location in sun or light shade. A tender plant, this geranium must be overwintered in a frost-free greenhouse or indoors. Alternatively, take softwood cuttings of non-flowering shoots from the spring to fall.

☼ ◐ ◊ *f*   H11–1

‡ to 20in (50cm) ↔ to 10in (25cm)

Penstemon 'Apple Blossom'
PERENNIAL

This penstemon bears spikes of elegant, tubular, light pink flowers with white throats from midsummer right through to fall if the blooms are deadheaded regularly. It prefers a moist but free-draining soil in full sun or light shade and is perfect for a border with a pastel color theme. Although it may survive the winter in a sheltered site, it is not fully frost hardy. As a precaution take softwood cuttings from the middle of the summer.

☀ ◐ ◊   Z7–10 H10–7

↔ to 24in (60cm)

Persicaria affinis 'Donald Lowndes'
EVERGREEN PERENNIAL

This vigorous plant is popular for its dense spikes of long-lasting, pale pink flowers that appear in midsummer on long, slender stems. These will enliven a border in the late summer, and as the flowers age to dark pink, a range of lovely pink shades continues until the fall, when the mats of lance-shaped, deep green leaves turn rich brown. Plant in a sunny or partially shaded spot in groups or use as groundcover. Dig out invasive or spreading roots in the spring or fall.

☀ ◐ ◊   Z3–8 H8–1

↕ to 6in (15cm) ↔ to 6in (15cm)

Phlox paniculata '**Windsor**'

PERENNIAL

The dense, conical heads of carmine-rose flowers with distinctive, deep red eyes are borne on this phlox in the late summer above oval, mid-green leaves. Grow it in full sun or partial shade in well-drained, moist soil, and stake where necessary. Plant groups of this tall phlox in an herbaceous border or behind shorter plants in a gravel garden. Deadhead regularly in summer, and thin out weak shoots in the spring for improved flowering.

☼ ☀ ◑   Z4–8 H8–1

‡ to 4ft (1.2m) ↔ to 3ft (1m)

Physostegia virginiana '**Variegata**'

PERENNIAL

The obedient plant is unusual because its flower stalks are hinged, so that when the blooms are moved, they stay in position. In the summer, tall spikes bear small, mauve-pink, tubular flowers, which will brighten up a border and are also good for cutting. The leaves are lance-shaped and mid-green, edged with white. Plant in sun or partial shade in moist soil.

☼ ☀ ◑   Z2–8 H8–1

‡ to 4ft (1.2m) ↔ to 24in (60cm)

Physostegia virginiana 'Vivid'

PERENNIAL

Commonly known as the obedient plant because the flowers will remain in position after they are moved on their stalks. Tall spikes of small, tubular, vivid purple-pink flowers appear from midsummer to fall and are ideal for cutting. The mid-green leaves are lance-shaped and toothed and form dense clumps. Grow in full sun in well-drained, moisture-retentive soil. Overcrowded clumps can be divided in the spring.

☼ ◊ ◖   Z2–8 H8–1

↕↔ to 24in (60cm)

Rodgersia pinnata 'Superba'

PERENNIAL

This clump-forming plant has upright clusters of star-shaped, bright pink flowers. These grow in mid- to late summer above the equally attractive, heavily veined and palmate, large, dark green foliage. Each leaf can measure up to 36in (90cm) across and has a purplish-bronze tint when young. It is good in sun or partial shade near water, such as in a bog garden, or for naturalizing at a woodland margin, as long as the soil is moist. Shelter from cold, drying winds.

☼ ☼ ◖   Z3–7 H7–1

↕ to 4ft (1.2m) ↔ to 30in (75cm)

Sanguisorba obtusa
PERENNIAL

Burnet is a clump-forming plant with bold, grayish-green leaves. In the summer, thin wiry stems, tipped with spikes of tiny pink flowers like bottle-brushes, are produced. Grow them in a border or next to a pond in moist but well-drained soil in full sun or partial shade. Both the flowers and leaves are good for cutting.

☼ ◑ ◊ ◐   Z4–8 H8–3
‡ to 4ft (1.2m) ↔ to 24in (60cm)

Saponaria officinalis 'Rosea Plena'
PERENNIAL

Before commercial detergents became available, soapwort was used as a soap substitute for washing delicate fabrics. Today it is still often used in natural shampoos. A robust plant with rough, rounded leaves, this type has double, pale pink flowers. It can spread rapidly and may need to be kept in check in a border to prevent it from smothering other plants. It does best in well-drained neutral to alkaline soils in a sunny location.

☼ ◊   Z3–9 H9–1
‡ to 24in (60cm) ↔ to 20in (50cm)

Spiraea japonica 'Anthony Waterer'

DECIDUOUS SHRUB

This medium-sized, twiggy shrub has small, lance-shaped leaves that emerge red and gradually turn dark green as they age. The foliage is occasionally tinged with cream or pink, too. The flat heads of purple buds open to frothy, dark pink flowers from mid- to late summer. Grow this spirea in a shrub or mixed border in full sun and any moderately fertile soil that does not completely dry out. Cut back lightly after flowering.

☼ ◊ ◐　　　　　　Z4–9 H9–1

↕↔to 5ft (1.5m)

Tamarix ramosissima 'Pink Cascade'

DECIDUOUS SHRUB

This tamarisk is an attractive small tree with graceful, arching branches and feathery foliage. In the summer it is covered with tiny pink flowers. It makes an excellent windbreak or hedge in coastal areas; in inland areas it will need a more sheltered location. To prevent plants from becoming straggly, cut back shrubs and hedges in the early spring. It grows best in sandy, well-drained soil in full sun.

☼ ◊　　　　　　　Z3–8 H8–1

↕ to 12ft (4m) ↔to 11ft (3.5m)

Achillea 'Summerwine'

SEMI-EVERGREEN PERENNIAL

This yarrow has beautiful wine-red, flat flowerheads, which look striking in a border, and in mid- to late summer are alive with insects, who seem to use them as landing platforms. They are also good for cutting, which encourages further blooms. The feathery foliage is grayish-green. Place a support over the emerging clump in the spring to prevent the flowers from flopping, and divide large clumps in the spring or fall. This plant can tolerate periods of drought and hot weather. It prefers a sunny location.

☼ ◊ ◗   Z4–9 H9–2

↕↔to 32in (80cm)

Aster novae-angliae 'Andenken an Alma Pötschke'

PERENNIAL

New England asters are clump-forming perennials with erect, woody stems covered with mid-green, narrow, lance-shaped leaves. This variety has dense sprays of salmon-red, daisylike flowers and is an excellent plant for a late summer border. It is also good for cutting. Plant in full sun or light shade and fertile, moist, well-drained soil. They also benefit from support with twigs or canes and string. Divide clumps regularly in the spring.

☼ ☀ ◊ ◗   Z4–8 H8–1

↕ to 4ft (1.2m) ↔to 24in (60cm)

Begonia Nonstop Series

PERENNIAL

These compact tuberous begonias have heart-shaped, mid-green leaves and double flowers, measuring up to 3in (8cm) across. They are available in a wide range of bright colors, including red, pink, yellow, and orange. Use them as bedding plants or in pots, and grow them in full sun in fertile, moist, well-drained soil. They are not hardy, and the tubers must be dug up before the first frost. Store them in dry sand in a cool room indoors.

☼ ◊ ◑   H11–1

↔ to 12in (30cm)

Campsis radicans

CLIMBER

The common trumpet creeper has dark green leaves divided into many leaflets and in late summer produces clusters of orange-red, trumpet-shaped flowers. It is not fully hardy and is best planted in full sun against a warm wall, to which it will cling with aerial roots. Plant it in fertile, moist, well-drained soil. In warm areas it will grow vigorously to cover a large area within a few seasons, and it suits a tropical-style garden. Keep it clear of roofs and gutters, and hard prune it in the winter to keep it in check.

☼ ◊ ◑   Z5–9 H9–3

↕ to 30ft (10m)

Canna 'Assaut'

PERENNIAL

Cannas are grown for their large, broad leaves and exotic-looking flowers. 'Assaut' has impressive purple-brown foliage and spikes of scarlet blooms. Cannas grow quickly and make a dramatic addition to a late summer border, tropical-style garden, or they can be grown in pots. Plant them in the late spring in full sun and moist, well-drained soil. They are not hardy, and the rhizomes should be overwintered in just-moist compost in a frost-free place.

☼ ◊ ◖   Z8–11 H11–1

‡ to 4ft (1.2m) ↔ to 24in (60cm)

Chrysanthemum 'Cherry Chintz'

PERENNIAL

'Cherry Chintz' produces huge, double blooms composed of many red petals in the late summer. Plant it in a sheltered site in fertile, moist, well-drained soil with well-rotted manure incorporated into it before planting. It is mostly grown for cutting and needs staking. Often grown in pots of soil-based potting mix under glass, it is also suitable for a sheltered, sunny patio or deck. Remove all but the terminal bud for the largest flowers to flourish.

☼ ◊ ◖   Z4–9 H9–1

‡ to 4½ft (1.3m) ↔ to 30in (75cm)

Cosmos atrosanguineus

PERENNIAL

This Mexican plant has green, deeply-lobed leaves and from midsummer to early fall produces masses of dark red, chocolate-scented, single flowers on reddish-brown stems. While it is not completely hardy, it should survive most winters if covered with a thick layer of mulch. In very cold locations, dig up the tubers in the fall and store them during the winter in trays of slightly damp sand or compost. Plant it in full sun in moist, well-drained soil.

☼ ◊ ◗ *f*   Z7–11 H11–1
‡ to 24in (60cm) ↔ to 18in (45cm)

Crocosmia 'Lucifer'

PERENNIAL

This widely-grown plant has dramatic mid-green leaves and from mid- to late summer produces arching stems bearing clusters of bright-red flowers. For maximum effect, plant it in groups in a gravel garden or herbaceous border. It prefers full sun or partial shade and a moist, well-drained soil. When clumps become congested after a few years, divide them in the fall and replant the corms elsewhere. In cold gardens apply a protective mulch in the winter.

☼ ☀ ◊ ◗   Z6–9 H9–6
‡ to 3ft (1m) ↔ to 10in (25cm)

Dahlia 'Hillcrest Royal'
PERENNIAL

The red-purple, cactus-type flowers of this striking dahlia are held on strong stems and make a dramatic statement in the middle of an herbaceous border. It needs a sunny site and fertile, moist, well-drained soil. Deadhead it regularly to promote the development of more flowers, and in the summer feed it with a general-purpose fertilizer. Dig up the tubers, and store them over the winter in a frost-free place. Plant in mid- to late spring, and insert a stake at the same time.

☼ ◊ ◑   Z9–11 H11–1
↕ to 3½ft (1.1m) ↔ to 24in (60cm)

Dahlia 'Whale's Rhonda'
PERENNIAL

A dark purple-red, pom-pom dahlia, the petals of 'Whales Rhonda' have silver undersides, giving them a two-tone appearance. It is often grown for cut flower arrangements or for shows and should be planted in full sun in a moist, well-drained soil. It can also be planted in a large container. Lift and store the tubers as described for the 'Hillcrest Royal' (*see above*).

☼ ◊   Z9–11 H11–1
↕ to 3ft (1m) ↔ to 24in (60cm)

Escallonia rubra 'Woodside'

EVERGREEN SHRUB

This dwarf escallonia is a small-leaf shrub with abundant clusters of miniature red flowers in the summer amid the attractive, glossy foliage. It thrives in relatively mild, coastal sites, but it would also suit an inland garden as a low, formal or informal, evergreen hedge, or as a sunny mixed border. Trim annually in the spring for a formal shape. Overly vigorous shoots should be cut out as they appear; this is the plant reverting to the large species form, which can reach 15ft (5m) tall.

☀ ◊ ◑ Z8–9 H9–8

↕ to 30in (75cm) ↔ to 5ft (1.5m)

Fuchsia 'Golden Marinka'

DECIDUOUS SHRUB

From midsummer to early fall, this trailing fuchsia produces bright red flowers set off by variegated green and yellow foliage. Grow it in full sun or partial shade. It can be used as ground cover, or planted in hanging baskets in soil-less potting compost or containers of soil-based potting mix. In the garden grow it in moist, well-drained soil. Feed fuchsias in containers every two weeks with a balanced liquid fertilizer, or mix in slow-release fertilizer when planting.

☀ ◑ ◊ ◑ Z9–11 H11–9

↕ to 12in (30cm) ↔ to 18in (45cm)

Fuchsia magellanica 'Thompsonii'

DECIDUOUS SHRUB

A hardy fuchsia with small red flowers that appear in midsummer, this plant can be grown as a hedge or a shrublike specimen in a border. In cold areas mulch it over the winter since the top growth may be damaged by frost. Cut out dead stems in the spring, and pinch off the soft tips of the stems to encourage bushy growth. It is suitable for training as a standard, or grow it in a large pot. Plant it in a sheltered location in moist, free-draining soil in sun or partial shade.

☼ ❂ ◊ ◗   Z6–9 H9–6
‡ to 10ft (3m) ↔ to 6ft (2m)

Gaillardia x *grandiflora* 'Dazzler'

PERENNIAL

As the name suggests, the flowers of this plant will certainly catch the eye in a bed or border. Their petals are deep orange-red, tipped with yellow, while the centers resemble a maroon pincushion. The blooms appear from the early summer and continue up until the early fall. Grow 'Dazzler' in a sunny location in fertile, well-drained soil, and remove the dead flowers to prolong blooming. Good for cutting.

☼ ◊   Z3–8 H8–1
‡ to 24in (60cm) ↔ to 20in (50cm)

Helenium
'Moerheim Beauty'

PERENNIAL

This undemanding, yet very rewarding, summer perennial is a firm garden favorite for its beautiful, rich coppery-red, daisylike flowers that appear toward the end of summer when many other flowers are fading. Combined with ornamental grasses and coneflowers, it can bring a late summer garden to life. It prefers a sunny location. Deadhead regularly, and divide large clumps in the spring or fall to maintain vigor.

☀ ◊ ◊   Z4–8 H8–1

↕ to 3ft (1m) ↔ to 24in (60cm)

Hemerocallis
'Stafford'

PERENNIAL

A beautiful daylily, this variety produces deep red flowers with golden-yellow centers, borne above a clump of straplike, mid-green leaves. It flowers from early to midsummer and will help to perk up a gravel garden or the front of a border. Alternatively, it can be grown in a large container if well watered in the summer. Plant it in full sun in moist, well-drained soil.

☀ ◊ ◊   Z3–10 H11–2

to 28in (70cm) ↔ to 3ft (1m)

Knautia macedonica

PERENNIAL

This clump-forming, often short-lived plant forms a rosette of hairy, lobed, basal leaves and in the summer produces branched stems that bear deeply divided leaves and small, pincushion-shaped heads of tiny, dark red flowers. Attractive to bees, it is perfect for a wild garden, herbaceous border, or English-style garden. It will flourish in full sun in a well-drained, preferably alkaline soil.

☼ ◊   Z5–9 H9–5

‡ to 30in (75cm) ↔ to 24in (60cm)

Lathyrus odoratus 'Red Ensign'

CLIMBER

This sweet pea bears sweetly scented, scarlet-red flowers from the summer to late fall. It can be grown up a cane pyramid in a border for instant height, or train it against a trellis. Cut the flowers regularly for the home and to stimulate more to develop. Grow sweet peas in full sun in moist, well-drained soil with well-rotted manure incorporated into it. Sow the seeds in pots in the fall to overwinter in a cold frame for planting outdoors in the spring, or sow in the same area in the spring.

☼ ◊ *f*   Z9–10 H8–

‡ to 6ft (2m)

Lilium speciosum var. *rubrum*

BULBOUS PERENNIAL

This tall lily has erect, purple-flushed stems and lance-shaped, dark green leaves. In late summer it produces up to a dozen fragrant, slightly pendent, turk's-cap flowers with swept-back petals. The deep carmine-red blooms are marked with darker red spots and have very long stamens. This lily grows well in moist, well-drained, slightly acid soil in partial shade and will thrive in a woodland garden.

❀ ○ ◊ *f*   Z5–7 H10–8

↕ to 5½ft (1.7m)

Lobelia 'Cherry Ripe'

PERENNIAL

'Cherry Ripe' has narrow, deep green leaves and in the summer has spikes of bright cherry-red flowers. It will bring a splash of color to a damp, herbaceous border, woodland, or the margins of a pool. For a spectacular effect, plant a group of five or more in moist soil and full sun. Lobelias are very vulnerable to damage by slugs and snails in the spring—sharp sand around the new shoots may deter these pests.

❀ ◊   Z3–8 H8–1

↕ to 3ft (1m) ↔ to 9in (23cm)

Lychnis chalcedonica

PERENNIAL

The Maltese cross forms a clump of evergreen basal leaves, above which domed heads of small, scarlet flowers appear in the summer borne on tall, hairy flower stems. The stems of this hardy plant are weak and will need to be staked if it is grown in an exposed site. It is ideal for an herbaceous border or a gravel or wild garden and should be planted in moist, well-drained soil in full sun or dappled shade.

☼ ✷ ◊ ◉   Z3–8 H8–1

‡ to 4ft (1.2m) ↔ to 18in (45cm)

Monarda 'Cambridge Scarlet'

PERENNIAL

Bergamot, or bee balm, is a clump-forming herb with aromatic, toothed leaves. 'Cambridge Scarlet' has vivid red, hooded, spidery-looking flowers and, like all bergamot, it is attractive to bees. Perfect for a border or prairie-style garden, it spreads quickly in a moist but well-drained soil that does not dry out in the summer or become waterlogged in the winter and a sunny situation. It can be divided in the spring.

☼ ◊ ◉ *f*   Z3–9 H9–1

‡ to 3ft (1m) ↔ to 18in (45cm)

Penstemon 'Chester Scarlet'

PERENNIAL

In the late summer and up to the first frost, this beautiful penstemon produces tall spikes of bell-shaped, scarlet flowers. It should be planted in full sun or partial shade in fertile, well-drained soil and is suitable for a warm herbaceous border. Deadhead it regularly to prolong the flowering period. Since this plant is not reliably hardy, protect it during the winter with a thick layer of mulch. It is easy to propagate from softwood cuttings taken in the early summer.

☼ ☀ ◊   Z7–10 H10–7

↕ to 36in (90cm) ↔ to 30in (75cm)

Persicaria amplexicaulis 'Firetail'

PERENNIAL

This Himalayan bistort is a vigorous, clump-forming plant with decorative, large, dark green, lance-shaped leaves. From midsummer to fall 'Firetail' produces tall spikes of small, bright red flowers. It likes moist soil conditions and offers a long season of interest in a damp border or an area partially shaded by deciduous trees. Its foliage also makes good ground cover.

☼ ☀ ◊   Z3–8 H8–1

↔ to 4ft (1.2m)

Phygelius x rectus 'African Queen'

EVERGREEN SHRUB

In the late summer this upright plant bears tall spires of pendent, pale red flowers above lance-shaped, dark green leaves. It should be planted in fertile, free-draining soil in a border among hardy shrubs or against a sunny wall. In cold locations it is best to treat this frost tender shrub as an herbaceous perennial. To protect it in the winter, cover with a thick mulch in the fall, and cut the stems down to the ground in the spring.

☼ ◊ ◑   Z8–9 H9–8

↕ to 3ft (1m) ↔ to 4ft (1.2m)

Ricinus communis 'Carmencita'

ANNUAL

The castor oil plant is usually grown for its large, architectural, palm-shaped leaves. This variety has dark bronzy-red foliage, and in the late summer it may produce tall spikes of small, bright red flowers. It should be planted in full sun in fertile, well-drained soil and is useful in bedding designs and tropical-style gardens. It can also be grown in a large container. All parts of this plant are highly toxic.

☼ ◊   Z11 H11–1

↕ to 5ft (1.5m) ↔ to 3ft (1m)

Salvia coccinea 'Lady in Red'
PERENNIAL

This tender South American perennial is usually treated as an annual in colder countries. It has erect stems and oval or heart-shaped dark green leaves, and in the summer and fall it produces spikes of bright red flowers. Plant it in a sunny location in light, well-drained soil. This bushy salvia works well at the front of an herbaceous border, or use it as a bedding or container plant. The seeds should be sown in the spring for flowers the same year.

☼ ◊ H11–1

↕ to 24in (60cm) ↔ to 12in (30cm)

Salvia x jamensis 'Hot Lips'
EVERGREEN SHRUB

This eye-catching salvia has extremely pretty red and white flowers that appear throughout the summer. Unlike many salvias, it is reasonably hardy to frost, but in areas with cold winters it is sensible to restrict it to a very sheltered location. Plant in full sunshine in the early summer, to allow the roots to establish well before the winter. The aromatic leaves smell of mint when crushed.

☼ ◊ *f* Z7–10 H10–1

↕↔ to 30in (75cm)

Solenostemon scutellarioides

PERENNIAL

Better known as coleus, the flame nettle is a tender plant grown primarily for its foliage. The most decorative varieties have toothed, hairy variegated leaves in a range of bright colors, including red, yellow, burgundy, and green. They bear spikes of small blue or white flowers, which should be removed before they open to retain the foliage effect. Plant them in light shade in pots of soil-based potting mix or as part of a bedding plan in moist, well-drained soil.

☀ ◊ ◗   Z11 H11–1

↕ to 18in (45cm) ↔ to 12in (30cm)

Tagetes 'Cinnabar'

ANNUAL

One of many varieties of fast-growing French marigold, this has feathery, deeply-divided, dark green leaves. From midsummer to early fall it bears rusty-red, single flowers with bright yellow eyes. Usually grown as a half-hardy annual bedding plant or for containers, it should be planted in a sunny location in fertile, well-drained soil. Easy to raise from seed, it can be sown under glass in the early spring, or sow in the same area in the late spring.

☀ ◊   H11–1

↕↔ to 12in (30cm)

Zauschneria californica 'Dublin'

PERENNIAL

The California fuchsia forms a clump of slightly hairy, grayish-green, lance-shaped leaves and in the late summer bears large numbers of bright red, tubular flowers on slightly arching stems. Plant it in a gravel or rock garden at the front of a mixed border or in the gaps of a drystone wall in full sun and reasonably fertile, well-drained soil. It is very hardy but needs a protected site out of cold winds.

☼ ◊   Z8–11 H11–8

‡ to 12in (30cm) ↔ to 18in (45cm)

Zinnia elegans 'Ruffles'

ANNUAL

A striking, upright, bushy plant with egg- or lance-shaped, mid-green leaves, 'Ruffles' lives up to its name, bearing frilly, pom-pom, fully double flowers in a wide range of colors, including red. Plant it in sun in any well-drained soil. Use it as bedding, or plant it in groups in an herbaceous border. Zinnias are also good for cutting, for use in the home.

☼ ◊   H11–1

‡ to 24in (60cm) ↔ to 12in (30cm)

Allium sphaerocephalon
BULBOUS PERENNIAL

The round-headed leek sends up golf-ball-sized flowerheads in midsummer. They are a rich, bright purple and are a magnet to bees. These bulbs are of tremendous value and worth mixing into any sunny, perennial border since they take up no space at all, yet rise above most other plants to add an extra dimension to flower displays. They come up year after year requiring little or no effort. They are also ideal for wildlife gardens.

☼ ◊ ◑   Z4–11 H11–1
‡ to 36in (90cm) ↔ to 2in (5cm)

Angelica gigas
PERENNIAL

The double pleasures of purple flowers and burgundy flower stems make this short-lived perennial well worth growing in a large border. Closely related to culinary angelica, be sure to give its lush, mid-green leaves plenty of room to spread. It is ideally suited for an informal woodland garden, and as a lover of moist but well-drained, fertile soil, it is at home around the margins of a large pond. It will tolerate sun and partial shade. Grow from seed because mature plants dislike being moved.

◑ ● ◑   Z4–9 H8–2
‡ to 6ft (2m) ↔ to 4ft (1.2m)

Aster x *frikartii* '**Mönch**'

PERENNIAL

Considered by many people to be one of the best of the perennial asters, this type has bright lavender-blue, daisylike flowers held on tall sturdy stems that rarely need staking. It flowers over a very long period from midsummer until the first frost. An excellent addition to an herbaceous border, this aster needs a sunny site and well-drained, fertile soil. It can be propagated by division in the spring.

☼ ◊　　　　　　　　Z5–8 H8–1

‡to 28in (70cm) ↔to 16in (40cm)

Buddleja crispa

DECIDUOUS SHRUB

The arching stems of this attractive, late-flowering shrub are covered with toothed, white-felted leaves. From midsummer to early fall it produces large, fragrant, clustered spikes of lilac flowers. It is very attractive to beneficial insects and butterflies. Grow in a mixed border or in a shrub border. It is not completely hardy and is sometimes damaged by hard frosts, so plant in a sheltered location in cold or exposed gardens. Plant it in full sunshine in fertile, well-drained soil.

☼ ◊ *f*　　　　　　Z8–9 H9–8

‡↔to 10ft (3m)

Buddleja davidii 'Dartmoor'

DECIDUOUS SHRUB

This butterfly bush has long, arching branches and gray-green leaves. From mid- to late summer, it produces large conical clusters of small, magenta-purple, fragrant flowers. Its flowers attract butterflies, and it is ideal for a wildlife garden. Alternatively, plant it close to a path or the house where the butterflies can be seen. It prefers full sun and a well-drained soil. Prune it hard in the spring to the ground or to a low permanent framework.

☼ ◊ *f*   Z6–9 H9–1

‡ to 10ft (3m) ↔ to 15ft (5m)

Campanula latiloba 'Hidcote Amethyst'

PERENNIAL

The pale mauve of this rosette-forming bellflower is a good mixer in the busy color palette of the herbaceous border. Tall flower stems carry the large, bell-shaped flowers well above the bed of broad, lance-shaped leaves. Plant in any fertile, neutral to alkaline soil that is moist but well drained. Light shade is preferable, although a spot in full sun is fine, but the flower color may fade. Divide large clumps in fall.

☼ ☀ ◊ ◊   Z5–7 H7–5

‡ to 36in (90cm) ↔ to 18in (45cm)

Cercis canadensis 'Forest Pansy'

DECIDUOUS TREE

The eastern redbud, or Judas tree, is remarkable for its pale pink flowers that adorn the bare tree in the spring before the heart-shaped leaves emerge. This variety is chosen for its reddish-purple, velvety foliage that turns purple and gold in the fall. Standing alone, the tree will develop a rounded shape, but it can be trained against a wall or as a foliage plant in a sunny or lightly shaded, mixed border, making it suitable for a small to medium garden. Prune after flowering, if necessary.

☼ ◑ ◊　　　　　　　　Z4–9 H9–2
↕↔to 15ft (5m)

Clematis 'Etoile Violette'

CLIMBER

'Etoile Violette' is one of the Viticella Group of clematis, which are known for their late summer displays. This old variety is truly tried and tested, freely bearing good-sized, very attractive, violet-purple flowers for many weeks. The growth can be very vigorous. Since it should be cut back to ground level each year in the late winter to a pair of strong buds, it can be allowed to grow into and over large shrubs and trees where it will never pose a risk of taking over. It does well in sun or partial shade.

☼ ◑ ◊ ◐　　　　　　　Z4–11 H9–1
↕ to 15ft (5m) ↔to 5ft (1.5m)

Clematis 'Jackmanii'
CLIMBER

From midsummer to the middle of fall, this widely grown clematis bears an abundance of large, single, velvety, purple-violet flowers. Team it with roses on a pergola or arch, or train it up trellis for late summer color. It will flourish in full sun or partial shade in fertile, moist, well-drained soi l with the roots in shade. Flowering on the current year's stems, it should be pruned back to about 8in (20cm) from the ground in the early spring.

☼ ☀ ◊ ◊　　　　　　　Z4–11 H9–1

↕ to 10ft (3m)

Clematis 'Purpurea Plena Elegans'
CLIMBER

This variety of clematis has leathery, lobed leaves. In the late summer it produces double, reddish-mauve flowers with unusual ruffled petals. Plant it in full sun or partial shade in fertile, moist, well-drained soil, and train it over a pergola or arch, or grow it through a large shrub. It flowers on the current year's stems and should be cut back to just above the ground in the early spring.

☼ ☀ ◊ ◊　　　　　　　Z4–11 H9–1

↕ to 12ft (4m)

Cynara cardunculus
EVERGREEN PERENNIAL

Closely related to the globe artichoke,
the cardoon is a fast-growing, large
architectural plant with grayish-green,
deeply divided, arching evergreen
leaves. The purple, thistlelike flowers
are borne on tall, robust stems from the
summer until fall. For real impact, if
space allows, plant it in groups of 3–4
in a sheltered, sunny spot by a wall
or fence in fertile, well-drained soil.
A useful plant, it attracts bees, the
flowers dry well, and, when blanched,
the leaf stalks and midribs are edible.

☼ ◊   Z7–10 H9–1

‡ to 6ft (2m) ↔ to 3ft (1m)

Fuchsia **'Auntie Jinks'**
DECIDUOUS SHRUB

From midsummer to mid-fall this
trailing plant produces flowers with
deep pink tubes, pink-edged white
sepals, and purple petals. For hanging
baskets use a soilless potting mix, but
plants in containers are better grown in
soil-based potting mix. Feed every two
weeks with a balanced fertilizer. It does
well in full sun or partial shade, but it is
not hardy and should spend the winter
in a light, frost-free place. Easy to raise
from softwood cuttings in the spring.

☼ ◐ ◊ ◑   Z9–11 H11–9

‡ to 8in (20cm) ↔ to 16in (40cm)

Fuchsia '**La Campanella**'

DECIDUOUS SHRUB

The trailing branches of this fuchsia bear mid-green leaves and masses of blooms from midsummer up to the first frost. The semidouble flowers are pale pink and deep purple. In the summer plant it outside in full sun or partial shade in hanging baskets filled with soilless potting mix. It can also be grown in a container filled with a soil-based potting mix. Feed every two weeks with a balanced fertilizer. It should be overwintered in a cool greenhouse.

☼ ☀ ◊ ◑　　　　　　　　Z9–11 H11–9

‡ to 12in (30cm) ↔ to 18in (45cm)

Hemerocallis '**Prairie Blue Eyes**'

PERENNIAL

The majority of daylilies have yellow or orange blooms, but this one has deep lavender-blue flowers, produced from early to midsummer. Semi-evergreen, it forms a clump of narrow mid-green leaves, which add structure and form to a sheltered border throughout the year. It can also be used in a large container or in gravel beds and prefers a sunny site and fertile, moist, well-drained soil.

☼ ◊ ◑　　　　　　　　Z3–10 H11–2

‡ to 28in (70cm) ↔ to 30in (75cm)

Hydrangea villosa
DECIDUOUS SHRUB

This delightful spreading plant is much loved by garden designers for its lance-shaped, velvety, mid-green leaves and large, flat flowerheads. In the summer masses of tiny, bluish-purple fertile flowers are borne, surrounded by larger, lilac-pink sterile blooms. It can be grown as a specimen plant or in a mixed border. This hydrangea will thrive when grown in sun or partial shade and moist, well-drained soil. Little pruning is needed apart from deadheading in the spring.

☼ ❀ ◐ ◑   Z7–9 H9–7

↔ to 10ft (3m)

Liatris spicata
PERENNIAL

Gayfeather is an attractive plant native to North American prairies. It forms a tuft of narrow leaves, measuring up to 16in (40cm) in length, and in late summer and early fall it produces tall spikes of feathery, pinkish-purple flowers that are attractive to bees. The flower buds at the top of the spike open before those further down. Plant it in full sun and very well-drained, reasonably fertile soil. It is not suitable for heavy clay soils since the roots will rot if they get too wet.

☼ ◐   Z4–9 H9–1

‡ to 24in (60cm) ↔ to 12in (30cm)

Limonium platyphyllum

PERENNIAL

Sea lavender forms a rosette of large, elliptic- or spoon-shaped, dark green leaves, and in the late summer it produces dense, wiry, branched stems covered with clusters of tiny, tubular, lavender-blue flowers. It grows well in coastal areas, but the frothy sprays of flowers are a valuable addition to any mixed or herbaceous border. Plant four or five plants together for maximum impact, and grow them in full sun and sandy, well-drained soil. The cultivar 'Violetta' has deep violet flowers.

☼ ◌   Z7–9 H9–7

‡ to 24in (60cm) ↔ to 18in (45cm)

Lobelia erinus 'Cascade Blue'

PERENNIAL

This small, trailing lobelia flowers from the summer to the middle of fall. It is grown as an annual. It produces hundreds of tiny, two-lipped, dark blue flowers, although similar plants with white, pink, red, purple, and violet flowers are available. All lobelias make excellent plants for hanging baskets and trailing over the edges of containers or window boxes. Plant them in full sun or in partial shade, which they last longer in, and do not let them dry out.

☼ ◐ ◑   Z2–8 H8–

‡↔ to 6in (15cm)

Lobelia x *gerardii* 'Vedrariensis'

PERENNIAL

This tall, stately plant forms a rosette of elliptic- or lance-shaped deep green leaves. The flower spikes appear in the late summer and bear small, violet-purple, tubular flowers. Cluster four or five plants together in a group to maximize their impact, and plant them in moist, fertile soil that does not dry out, in full sun or partial shade. This lobelia is perfect for a late-summer border or for the margins of a water garden.

☼ ◑   Z8–9 H9–8
‡ to 3ft (1m) ↔ to 12in (30cm)

Monarda 'Prärienacht'

PERENNIAL

A member of the mint family, this vigorous, clump-forming beebalm selection has square stems and lance-shaped leaves. Its lilac-purple flowers bloom from midsummer into early fall, attracting butterflies, hummingbirds, and other pollinators. It is drought tolerant once established and is a good choice for a mixed border. Powdery mildew can develop in humid regions. Grow in moderately fertile, well-drained soil in full sun.

☼ ◊   Z4–9 H9–1
to 4ft (1.2m) ↔ to 24in (60cm)

Passiflora 'Amethyst'

CLIMBER

This fast-growing passion flower bears distinctive purple-blue flowers in the late summer followed by large, oval, orange fruits. It is not hardy, and in cold areas, it is best to grow this climber in a warm greenhouse or a sunroom where it will form a leafy canopy when trained on wires or support. Plant it in a container filled with soil-based potting mix, and water well in the summer. Prune back the vigorous growth in the spring to keep it within bounds.

☼ ◊ ◑　　　　　　　　　　H11–10
‡ to 12ft (4m)

Passiflora caerulea

CLIMBER

The blue passion flower has woody stems and dark green divided foliage. The exotic-looking flowers have white petals, which are sometimes tinged with pink, and a ring of purple-blue banded strands that radiate out from the center. In hot summers the blooms may be followed by round, yellow fruit. Plant it in a sunny, sheltered site in moist, well-drained soil. It is not fully hardy and may be killed by hard frosts, but young shoots often appear from the base if the root area is mulched for the winter

☼ ◊ ◑　　　　　　　　Z6–9 H9–◖
‡ to 30ft (10m)

Penstemon 'Stapleford Gem'

PERENNIAL

The bell-shaped flowers of this lilac-purple penstemon are suffused with shades of mauve, pink, and purple, giving it a multi-colored effect. It blooms from midsummer to early fall, and needs full sun and a well-drained soil. Penstemons are wonderful plants for an herbaceous border, and this one works well as part of a pastel color palette. 'Stapleford Gem' is one of the hardiest penstemons but will need a sheltered spot and winter mulch in cold areas.

☼ ◒ ◊   Z6–9 H9–6

‡ to 24in (60cm) ↔ to 18in (45cm)

Stachys officinalis

PERENNIAL

Wood betony is an attractive perennial that produces ground-covering rosettes of deeply veined leaves with scalloped edges. From early summer to early fall it is adorned with spikes of tubular, reddish-purple flowers. Its long flowering season makes it an ideal candidate for the front of an herbaceous border, or use it in a wild garden. Easy to grow, this betony prefers a sunny or lightly shaded location in well-drained, slightly fertile soil. Divide in the fall or spring.

☼ ◒ ◊   Z5–8 H8–4

‡ to 24in (60cm) ↔ to 18in (45cm)

Thalictrum delavayi 'Hewitt's Double'

PERENNIAL

This upright, clump-forming perennial produces sprays of long-lasting, pompomlike, rich mauve flowers from midsummer to early fall. Its finely divided, mid-green leaves are carried on slender, purple-tinted stems. 'Hewitt's Double' makes an excellent foil in a sunny or partially shaded, herbaceous border to plants with bolder leaves and flowers. Divide large clumps, and replant every few years to maintain vigor.

☼ ❀ ◊ ◑   Z4–7 Z7–1

‡ to 5ft (1.5m) ↔ to 24in (60cm)

Tradescantia 'Purple Dome'

PERENNIAL

This clump-forming, hardy plant belongs to the Andersoniana group of tradescantias and has branching stems and narrow, strappy leaves. In the summer to early fall it produces clusters of small, deep purple flowers with three triangular petals and fluffy purple stamens. Plant it *en masse* in a mixed or herbaceous border, in full sun or partial shade and a moist, fertile soil. Divide large clumps in the fall or spring.

☼ ❀ ◑   Z5–9 H9–

‡ to 24in (60cm) ↔ to 18in (45cm)

Tulbaghia violacea
BULBOUS PERENNIAL

This South African plant forms clumps of narrow, grayish-green leaves, and from midsummer to early fall it produces stout stems that bear clusters of fragrant, star-shaped, lilac-blue flowers. In mild areas it can be grown outside in a sunny location in slightly fertile, well-drained soil. In cold climates where temperatures dip well below freezing for long periods, pot it in a container filled with soil-based potting mix, and overwinter it in a cool greenhouse or sunroom.

☼ ◊ *f*   Z7–10 H10–7
‡ to 24in (60cm) ↔ to 12in (30cm)

Verbena bonariensis
PERENNIAL

The tall, airy, branched stems of this verbena hold aloft small, domed clusters of tiny, lilac-purple, scented flowers, which appear from midsummer to early fall. Individual plants come into their own when planted in a group and can be positioned at the front as well as the back of the border or in a gravel garden. They need full sun and fertile, well-drained soil and a sheltered position. In cold gardens, mulch with garden compost for winter protection.

☼ ◊ *f*   Z7–11 H11–7
‡ to 5ft (1.5m) ↔ to 24in (60cm)

Aconitum 'Bressingham Spire'

PERENNIAL

Monkshood is a tall, striking plant that thrives in woodland gardens and in herbaceous borders. It has glossy, dark green, deeply-lobed leaves, and in the late summer and early fall produces large spikes of deep violet-blue flowers. It can be grown in full sun, but will perform better in partial shade and moist soil. To maintain its vigor, dig it up and divide it after 3–4 years. All parts of this plant are very toxic.

☼ ◑ ◐   Z3–7 H8–3

↕ to 3ft (1m) ↔ to 20in (50cm)

Agapanthus 'Blue Giant'

PERENNIAL

The African blue lily is impossible to overlook in the late summer garden. It forms a clump of arching, deep green, strap-shaped leaves and large spherical flowerheads held on tall, stiff stems. 'Blue Giant' is exceptionally large with huge balls of deep blue, bell-shaped flowers. It should be grown in a sunny, sheltered location in fertile, moist, well-drained soil. It is borderline hardy, so in cold areas, protect it with a thick layer of mulch in the winter.

☼ ○ ◐   Z8–11 H11–1

↕ to 4ft (1.2m) ↔ to 24in (60cm)

Aster amellus 'King George'
PERENNIAL

This species prefers drier conditions than the popular New England and New York asters and thrives in alkaline soil. It has small, mid-green leaves and from the late summer to late fall produces loose clusters of light violet-blue, daisylike flowers. Plant it in groups in a sunny, herbaceous or mixed border in reasonably fertile, well drained soil. Divide clumps every three to four years in the spring to rejuvenate them and to keep the plants growing vigorously.

☼ ◊   Z5–8 H8–1

↨ to 20in (50cm)

Campanula cochleariifolia
PERENNIAL

Known as fairies' thimbles, this dwarf campanula forms rosettes of toothed, bright green leaves and in the summer produces masses of slightly pendent, pale blue or white flowers. It will add color and interest to a rock garden or the gaps in paving or a drystone wall, flourishing in the well-drained soil both these sites afford. It can be grown in full sun or partial shade, and although it may become rather invasive, it is easy to control by pulling up surplus growth.

☼ ◐ ◊   Z5–7 H7–1

↨ to 3in (8cm) ↔ indefinite

Caryopteris x *clandonensis* 'Heavenly Blue'

DECIDUOUS SHRUB

This free-flowering plant with aromatic, grayish-green foliage forms clusters of deep blue flowers in the late summer. It provides color and form in a mixed border or gravel garden and needs full sun and a sheltered site in well-drained soil. In cold gardens, plant it by a sunny wall to give some extra protection during the winter. Prune it back hard in the spring, being careful not to cut into old wood, or it may not regrow.

☼ ◊ *f*   Z6–9 H9–1
↕↔to 3ft (1m)

Catananche caerulea 'Major'

PERENNIAL

Cupid's dart is a short-lived perennial that is often grown as biennial. It looks similar to a cornflower with oblong, lilac-blue petals with serrated tips and a dark blue center. Plant it in a sunny location in well-drained soil at the front or in the middle of a flower or herbaceous border. It does not grow very well in heavy soils and may die at the end of the year.

☼ ◊   Z3–8 H8–1
↕ to 24in (60cm) ↔to 12in (30cm)

Ceratostigma plumbaginoides

PERENNIAL

This rhizomatous, spreading plumbago features upright, wiry red stems and bright green leaves that develop a reddish hue in the fall. From the late summer to the first frost clusters of blue flowers appear above the foliage. It makes a good ground cover, edger, or rock garden plant. It may spread aggressively in ideal conditions. Grow in moderately fertile, well-drained soil in full sun to partial shade.

☼ ☀ ◊   Z5–9 H9–4

‡ to 18in (45cm) ↔ to 12in (30cm)

Clematis 'Perle d'Azur'

CLIMBER

This late-flowering clematis has sky blue, open bell-shaped flowers approximately 4in (10cm) in diameter. They are carried in profusion on vigorous growth, which benefits from the support of a large bush, such as a shrub rose. This growth should be cut back to ground level each year in the late winter to a pair of healthy-looking buds. Specimens often take a year or two to get well established in a sunny or partially shaded site. During this time, give the young stems some support, and protect them from slugs and snails.

☼ ☀ ◊ ◑   Z4–11 H9–1

‡ to 10ft (3m) ↔ to 3ft (1m)

Echinops ritro 'Veitch's Blue'
PERENNIAL

Grown partly for its architectural, spiny, grayish-green leaves, in the summer this vigorous plant also produces spherical dark blue flowerheads on woolly gray stems. The lollipop-shaped flowerheads contrast well with flat-headed blooms, such as those of achillea, in a gravel garden or an herbaceous border. The flowers are frequently used, fresh or dried, in floral arrangements. Plant it in groups of four or five in poor, well-drained soil in full sunshine.

☼ ◐ ◊   Z3–9 H11–1
‡ to 4ft (1.2m) ↔ to 30in (75cm)

Eryngium x *oliverianum*
PERENNIAL

This striking sea holly forms a clump of heart-shaped, mid-green, spiny leaves with distinctive silver veining. In the summer and early fall branched stems produce lavender-blue, thistlelike flowers, surrounded by spiny, linear, leaflike bracts. The whole plant is steel-blue in color. Plant it in a sunny location in well-drained soil, and use it in an herbaceous border or gravel garden. The flower stems make excellent cut flowers, too, or they can be left to stand in the winter.

☼ ◊   Z5–8 H8–5
‡ to 36in (90cm) ↔ to 18in (45cm)

Felicia amelloides 'Santa Anita'

EVERGREEN SHRUB

This tender blue daisy is often grown as an annual in cooler climates. It is bushy and compact with oval, deep green leaves. From the middle of the summer to fall, it bears bright blue, daisylike flowers with yellow centers. It can be grown in containers or is mostly used as an annual, although it may survive in mild, sheltered areas in the garden. Plant it in full sun in any well-drained soil. Pinch off the shoot tips in the spring to promote side shoots.

☼ ◊   H11–9

‡↔ to 24in (60cm)

Geranium ROZANNE ('Gerwat')

PERENNIAL

The summer-long display of this geranium makes it one of the best for a sunny, mixed border. From clumps of prettily divided foliage emerge the most perfect saucer-shaped, vibrant violet-blue flowers. Because it keeps on flowering from the early summer right until the first frost in the fall, this has to be one of the best value for money plants on the market. The foliage dies back in the winter, and it suits most well-drained soils.

☼ ◊ ◊   Z4–8 H8–3

‡↔ to 20in (50cm)

Hibiscus syriacus **'Oiseau Bleu'**

DECIDUOUS SHRUB

This hardy hibiscus is an exotic-looking addition to a shrub or mixed border. It has upright branches and toothed, lobed, mid-green leaves that appear late in the spring. In the late summer it produces large, deep blue, trumpet-shaped flowers. Plant it in full sun and moist, well-drained, fertile soil. It will survive most winters, but in very cold areas plant it against a warm wall, and cover the root area with a thick mulch during the winter.

☼ ◊ ◊   Z5–9 H9–1

↕ to 10ft (3m) ↔ to 6ft (2m)

Hydrangea macrophylla **'Blue Wave'**

DECIDUOUS SHRUB

This lacecap hydrangea is a rounded shrub with large green leaves and flat flowerheads that appear from mid- to late summer. The blooms are made up of small, dark blue, fertile flowers surrounded by large pale blue sterile flowers. In acid soil the flowers turn a rich shade of lavender-blue, but in alkaline soil they are mauve-pink. Plant it in full sun or partial shade in moist, well-drained, fertile soil, rich in organic matter. Suitable for coastal gardens.

☼ ☼ ◊ ◊   Z6–9 H9–6

↕ to 6ft (2m) ↔ to 8ft (2.5m)

Hydrangea serrata 'Bluebird'

DECIDUOUS SHRUB

This compact hydrangea has bright green leaves. From the late summer to early fall it bears large flat flowerheads of tiny, deep blue fertile flowers, surrounded by larger, pale-blue, infertile flowers, which may become pink in alkaline soil. Ideal for a shrub or mixed border in a small garden, it grows well in full sun or partial shade and moist but well-drained, fertile soil, preferably neutral or slightly acid for the best flower color.

☼ ☀ ◊ ◖   Z6–9 H9–6

↕↔ to 4ft (1.2m)

Hyssopus officinalis

SEMI-EVERGREEN SHRUB

Hyssop is a pretty garden plant that can also be used for medicinal and culinary purposes. It has small, aromatic leaves, and the flowers vary in color from blue to violet, pink, and white. It blooms from early or midsummer to early fall and will add color and form to an herb bed or the front of a border. It can also be grown in a large container or a gravel garden. Plant it in a sunny situation in well-drained soil.

☼ ◊ *f*   Z6–9 H9–6

↕ to 24in (60cm) ↔ to 3ft (1m)

Ipomoea tricolor 'Heavenly Blue'

CLIMBER

Morning glory, grown as an annual, has fast-growing, twining stems and heart-shaped, light green leaves. In the late summer it produces large, sky-blue, funnel-shaped flowers with white throats. Plant this eye-catching climber outside in the late spring or early summer in full sun and well-drained soil. Provide support in the form of a tripod. Use ipomeas to clothe an arch or a trellis, or grow in a large container.

☼ ◊   H11–1
‡ to 10ft (3m)

Lathyrus nervosus

CLIMBER

Lord Anson's blue pea, a perennial, is often grown as an annual. In the late summer it bears fragrant, indigo-blue flowers. Each leaf is split into a pair of grayish-green leaflets. It will quickly climb a support when grown in full sun and a well-drained, fertile soil. This pea is not fully hardy and will be killed by winter wet and hard frosts unless protected with a cloche and a deep, dry mulch. Grow it from seed in the early spring, and plant it outside in the late spring or early in the summer.

☼ ◊ *f*   Z3–10 H10–1
‡ to 15ft (5m)

Lathyrus odoratus 'Noel Sutton'

ANNUAL

'Noel Sutton' is a vigorous sweet pea that can be grown up supporting canes or a trellis. If shoot tips are pinched off while the plant is young, it will become a much smaller bush suitable for a container. In the summer the stems are covered with sweetly perfumed, mauve-blue flowers, which should be picked regularly for the home to promote new blooms. Plant it in sun or light shade in moist, well-drained soil rich in organic matter.

☼ ☀ ◊ ◑ *f*　　　　　Z9–10 H8–1

↕ to 8ft (2.5m)

Lobelia siphilitica

PERENNIAL

The blue cardinal flower has a rosette of egg-shaped, light green leaves. In the summer it produces tall stems that bear tubular, bright blue blooms with double lips. It needs permanently moist, fertile soil and is happy in full sun or partial shade. It adds grace and elegance to a damp border or an area beneath deciduous trees, or plant it beside a pool. To propagate this lobelia, divide it in the spring.

☀ ☀ ◑　　　　　　　Z4–8 H8–1

↕ to 3ft (1m) ↔ to 9in (23cm)

Nemesia strumosa '**Blue Gem**'

ANNUAL

This vigorous, compact, bushy annual has spoon- or lance-shaped, toothed and slightly hairy leaves. In the late summer it bears vast numbers of small, bright blue flowers and makes a colorful bedding or container plant. It needs a site in full sun and moist, well-drained soil. It must be watered regularly during the summer if it is to produce a good display of flowers. Nemesias come in other colors including red, yellow, and pink.

☼ ◊ ◊   H7–1

‡ to 12in (30cm) ↔ to 6in (15cm)

Nepeta sibirica

PERENNIAL

This relative of catmint is a vigorous plant with branched, upright stems and dark green, lance-shaped, toothed, aromatic foliage. In the late summer lavender-blue flowers appear on tall spikes and make a bold statement in a gravel garden or an herbaceous bed. As its name suggests, this plant comes from Siberia and is very hardy. It should be planted and divided in the spring in a sunny location in well-drained soil.

☼ ◊ *f*   Z3–8 H8–1

‡ to 36in (90cm) ↔ to 18in (45cm)

Perovskia 'Blue Spire'
DECIDUOUS SHRUB

This is an attractive, late flowering bush with tall stems and silver, deeply dissected, aromatic foliage. In the late summer it produces branched spikes of small, lavender-blue flowers. It prefers a sunny location and should be planted in very well-drained soil in a gravel bed or an herbaceous border, or use it in a low hedge to edge a path. To keep it bushy, cut back stems in the spring. It will tolerate alkaline soil and coastal conditions.

☼ ◊ *f*   Z6–8 H9–6

↕ to 4ft (1.2m) ↔ to 3ft (1m)

Platycodon grandiflorus
PERENNIAL

The balloon flower is often mistaken for a campanula, to which it is related. The leaves appear late in the spring but eventually grow to form a clump of toothed, blue-green foliage. In the late summer bell-shaped, purplish-blue flowers open from balloon-shaped buds. Ideal for a rock garden or the front of a border, it does not like to be disturbed and should not be divided. Plant it in full sun or partial shade in moist, well-drained soil.

☼ ☼ ◊ ◐   Z4–9 H9–1

↕ to 24in (60cm) ↔ to 18in (45cm)

Salvia patens 'Cambridge Blue'

PERENNIAL

From summer to fall this form of sage produces delicate pale blue flowers. Beneath the flower stems it forms a clump of oval, mid-green leaves. Plant it in a sunny, sheltered border or by a wall in well-drained soil. Not fully hardy, this salvia is unlikely to survive a hard frost and is better treated as an annual in cold areas. Sow seed under glass in the spring, or overwinter mature plants in a frost-free greenhouse.

☼ ◊   Z8–9 H9–8
‡ to 24in (60cm) ↔ to 18in (45cm)

Salvia uliginosa

PERENNIAL

The bog sage prefers damp conditions. It forms a clump of lance-shaped mid-green leaves, above which tall flower spikes bear clusters of pale blue flowers. A good source of color for the back of a damp late summer border, it should be planted in full sun and moist soil. The bog sage is not totally hardy, but it can survive winters in mild areas if protected with a thick layer of mulch or grown in a pot and moved under glass.

☼ ◊   Z8–11 H11–7
‡ to 6ft (2m) ↔ to 36in (90cm)

Scabiosa caucasica 'Clive Greaves'

PERENNIAL

A beautiful scabiosa, 'Clive Greaves' has gray-green basal leaves, and violet-blue flowers with cream-colored centers, which attract bees and butterflies. It is perfect for a wildflower garden or an herbaceous border and needs a sunny location and well-drained, reasonably fertile, neutral to alkaline soil to thrive. Young plants flower most freely, so divide and replant them every spring to ensure a good display each summer. Deadhead the plants regularly, too.

☼ ◊   Z4–9 H9–1

↔ to 24in (60cm)

Scaevola aemula 'Saphira'

EVERGREEN PERENNIAL

The fairy fan flower is a vigorous, trailing plant ideal for the edge of a container or basket. It bears a profusion of pretty blue flowers, and purple and mauve varieties are also available. In frost-free areas scaevolas grow as short-lived evergreen perennials, but in cold climates they are treated as bedding annuals, fed every two weeks to maintain a prolific flowering display. Grow in moist but well-drained, fertile soil in a sunny location.

☼ ◊ ◖   Z11 H11–1

↔ to 20in (50cm)

Stokesia laevis
EVERGREEN PERENNIAL

Stokes' aster is an evergreen, clump-forming plant with long, lance-shaped leaves with a distinctive pale green midrib. From midsummer to early fall, it bears solitary cornflowerlike blooms on stout stems. The outer petals are purplish-blue, pink, or white—the pale varieties exhibit a darker center, while the dark forms have pale centers. 'Blue Star' has deep blue petals and a pale blue eye. Plant Stokes' asters in a sunny border in well-drained soil.

☼ ◊   Z5–9 H9–5
↕↔to 18in (45cm)

Symphyandra wanneri
PERENNIAL

As the pretty, hanging clusters of deep violet-blue flowers suggest, the ring bellflower is a close relative of the true bellflowers (*Campanula*). These flowers are carried in profusion over a long period in the summer amid the toothed, mid-green leaves. The plants may not flower in their first year and will usually die once the display is over and the seed has set. Collect the seed for sowing again in the same area, or allow to self-seed. This plant is good for a sunny or lightly shaded rock garden.

☼ ◑ ◊   Z7–9 H9–7
↕↔to 12in (30cm)

Tradescantia '*J.C. Weguelin*'

PERENNIAL

This clump-forming, hardy plant has narrow, lance-shaped, mid-green leaves held on branching stems. The blooms appear in the late summer and are composed of pale blue petals that surround fluffy stamens. It can be used at the front of a mixed or herbaceous border and should be planted in full sun or partial shade in moist, well-drained, fertile soil. It can be divided in the spring or fall.

☀ ☀ ◑   Z5–9 H9–5

↕ to 24in (60cm) ↔ to 18in (45cm)

Veronica longifolia

PERENNIAL

The long-leaf veronica is a tall perennial that has upright spikes of bright blue flowers in the late summer. It is ideal for a sunny or lightly shaded, mixed or herbaceous border, planted in groups of three or five. The pointed, mid-green leaves are carried in twos or threes along the stems. Cut the plant back in the late winter to prepare for the new growth in the spring.

☀ ☀ ◐ ◑   Z4–8 H8–1

↕ to 4ft (1.2m) ↔ to 12in (30cm)

Agave americana '**Variegata**'

PERENNIAL

This plant, ideal for a patio or tropical-style garden, forms a basal rosette of fleshy, lance-shaped, cream-edged leaves with spiny margins and pointed tips. The leaves grow upright, then arch over and finally lie flat on the ground. Plant in a large container of soil-based potting mix. Place it outside in summer, and move it indoors in winter. It may survive outside in mild, very well-drained, sheltered conditions provided it is protected when young.

☼ ◊   Z9–11 H11–5

↕↔ to 5ft (1.5m)

Deschampsia cespitosa '**Goldtau**'

PERENNIAL GRASS

Tussock grass is a robust, evergreen plant with rigid, rough-edged green leaves. In late summer 'Goldtau' bears arching stems of yellow-green that turn golden-brown as they age. This type is much more compact than other tussock grasses and is perfect for an herbaceous or wildflower garden. It is happy in full sun or partial shade and a moist or well-drained soil. Leave the dried flowerheads to decorate a winter garden, but remove them in spring.

☼ ☼ ◊ ◊   Z5–9 H9–1

↕ to 28in (70cm) ↔ to 20in (50cm)

Ensete ventricosum

PERENNIAL

The Ethiopian banana is a tender plant and bears huge, paddle-shaped leaves. Grow it in a large pot of soil-based potting mix. It will add an exotic look when moved outside and placed in a late summer border or tropical-style garden in full sun or light shade. It also needs to be fed and watered regularly when growing. At the end of the summer it must be moved indoors and to a heated greenhouse or sunroom with a minimum temperature of 45°F (7°C).

☼ ◐ ◊ ◊   Z10–11 H11–1

↕ to 20ft (6m) ↔ to 10ft (3m)

Melianthus major

EVERGREEN SHRUB

The honey bush is usually treated as an herbaceous perennial. Grown for its foliage, it has beautiful, bluish-green, featherlike leaves, which are divided into several sharply-toothed leaflets. The brown flowers are rather uninspiring. Plant it in a sunny location, sheltered from cold winds in moist, well-drained, fertile soil. Frost destroys the upper growth, but if it is protected during the winter with a thick mulch, it should resprout again in the spring.

☼ ◊ ◊   Z8–11 H11–8

↕↔ to 10ft (3m)

Moluccella laevis

ANNUAL

Bells of Ireland has deeply-veined, rounded, pale green leaves, and in the summer and fall it produces stems of tiny white flowers, surrounded by large, pale green cups. Its architectural flower spikes make a dramatic statement in an herbaceous border and are very useful in flower arrangements, fresh or dried. Plant it in full sunshine, in fertile, moist, well-drained soil. It is easy to grow from a spring sowing of the seed.

☼ ◊ ◐ *f*   Z9–11 H9–1

↕ to 24in (60cm) ↔ to 8in (20cm)

Nicotiana langsdorffii

ANNUAL

This tobacco plant forms a rosette of large egg-shaped leaves at the base and in the summer produces apple-green flowers that dangle like slender bells from the tall, branched, sticky stems. It adds interest to the middle of an herbaceous border and is ideal for disguising the space left by spring bulbs. Plant it in a sunny or lightly shaded location in fertile, moist, well-drained soil, and stake if necessary.

☼ ◑ ◊ ◐   Z10–11 H11–1

↕ to 5ft (1.5m) ↔ to 12in (30cm)

Pennisetum macrourum

PERENNIAL GRASS

Well-drained soil is vital for this pretty grass with its foxtail-like, fluffy plumes of seedheads that appear in the late summer and last well into the fall. They fade from green to pale brown as they age with a strawlike quality that gives a long season of interest. Cut back plants in the late winter to allow for the new growth. Grow in a sunny, mixed border in a sheltered location. The flowerheads are also good for cutting.

❀ ◊   Z7–11 H12–4

‡ to 6ft (1.8m) ↔ to 4ft (1.2m)

Zinnia elegans 'Envy'

ANNUAL

Most zinnias stand out because of their brightly colored flowers, but 'Envy' is more subtle with semidouble, yellow-green blooms. It makes a good bedding or container plant and will perform well when grown in a sunny or lightly shaded location and fertile, moist, well-drained soil. The seed should be sown indoors in the early spring, or in the same area outside in the late spring. It is useful in flower arrangements because of its unusual color.

❀ ☀ ◊   H11–1

‡ to 24in (60cm) ↔ to 12in (30cm)

Achillea filipendulina 'Cloth of Gold'

PERENNIAL

Although this plant grows nearly double the height of 'Coronation Gold', it is actually less vigorous. It has attractive, feathery, light green leaves and bears large, golden-yellow flowerheads, up to 5in (12cm) across from early summer right through until early fall. It is ideal for growing in an herbaceous border and will thrive in any well-drained soil. By the late spring the tall stems will need supporting with canes. Good for cutting fresh or for drying.

☼ ◊ ◑   Z3–9 H9–
↕↔ to 5ft (1.5m)

Catalpa bignonioides 'Aurea'

DECIDUOUS TREE

The golden type of the Indian bean tree has spreading branches and large, heart shaped leaves. The young foliage is bronze in the spring but turns golden-yellow by the time the flowers appear in midsummer. The candle-shaped spikes of fragrant, white flowers with yellow and purple marks are followed by dangling pods that last through the winter and give this tree its name. Plant it in full sun away from strong winds in deep, fertile, moist, well-drained soil.

☼ ◊ ◑ *f*   Z5–9 H9–
↕↔ to 30ft (10m)

Celosia argentea 'Century Yellow'

ANNUAL

From the summer to the first frost this vigorous cockscomb cultivar produces large, golden-yellow, feathery plumes that attract bees and butterflies. The flowers make excellent cut or dried flowers. It will self-sow readily. It works well as a container plant or in a mixed annual bed. Grow in full sun in moist, well-drained soil.

※ ◊ ◊   H9–2

↕ to 36in (90cm) ↔ to 24in (60cm)

Chrysanthemum 'Mary Stoker'

PERENNIAL

In the late summer and early fall this hardy chrysanthemum bears single, apricot-yellow, daisylike flowers with green centers that turn yellow as they mature. The flowers are set off by the bed, deep green leaves that have a light silvery sheen. Plant it in a sunny, sheltered herbaceous or mixed border in well-drained soil. It will benefit from a protective, thick mulch in the winter.

※ ◊   Z5–9 H11–1

↕ to 4ft (1.2m) ↔ to 30in (75cm)

Crocosmia 'Solfatare'
BULBOUS PERENNIAL

The bronze-green leaves and clusters of apricot-yellow flowers that appear on slender, arching stems make this a very desirable plant for a border or gravel garden. It will grow well in full sun or partial shade and prefers moist, well-drained soil. The individual plants are small and are best planted in groups of three or five. It is not fully hardy and needs a sheltered site and thick mulch to survive a harsh winter.

☼ ◐ ◊ ◖   Z6–9 H9–(

‡ to 28in (70cm) ↔ to 3in (8cm)

Cytisus battandieri
DECIDUOUS SHRUB

In the summer the pineapple broom produces tight clusters of fruit-scented, bright yellow, lupinelike flowers. Its silvery-green leaves are carried on arching, spreading branches, giving the bush an open shape. Although not fully hardy, it should overwinter successfully if it is planted in a sunny, sheltered spot by a wall in well-drained, sandy, moderately fertile soil. Other than to remove shoots that spoil the symmetry of the bush—do this in the early spring—it does not really need pruning

☼ ◊ *f*   Z7–9 H9–

‡↔ to 15ft (5m)

Dahlia 'Yellow Hammer'

PERENNIAL

This tender perennial is usually grown as an annual bedding plant and has bronze-green leaves and clear yellow flowers. For a dazzling bedding display, plant it with other dwarf dahlias, or use it in an herbaceous border or in containers. Providing it is deadheaded regularly, 'Yellow Hammer' will flower continuously up to the first frosts. Plant it in full sun in fertile, well-drained soil or soil-based potting mix.

☼ ◊   Z9–11 H11–1

‡ to 24in (60cm) ↔ to 18in (45cm)

Euphorbia sikkimensis

PERENNIAL

This spreading perennial is recommended for its heads of yellow flowers that appear from midsummer, but the spring growth, which is bright pink, is just as attractive. These upright shoots are covered in narrow leaves that become paler with red veins and margins as they age. The flowers are followed by blue-green pods, which are also attractive. Ideal for a shady border. When handling this plant, wear gloves since the milky sap can irritate the skin.

☼ ◊   Z6–9 H9–6

‡ to 4ft (1.2m) ↔ to 18in (45cm)

Genista aetnensis

DECIDUOUS TREE

The Mount Etna broom forms a large shrub or medium-sized tree with green, arching, almost leafless branches. In the summer it explodes into color, producing masses of fragrant, yellow, pealike flowers. It makes a spectacular specimen tree for a sunny situation, with a canopy that is light enough to allow underplanting. Pruning is unnecessary, except to remove damaged stems. Plant in well-drained, light, poor to moderately fertile soil.

☼ ◊ *f*   Z9–10 H10–9
↕↔ to 25ft (8m)

Helenium 'Butterpat'

PERENNIAL

Unlike many heleniums, which tend to have muddy-colored flowers, those of 'Butterpat' are a clear, bright yellow. Very free flowering, it is a good clump-forming plant for an herbaceous border. The blooms, which are usually crowded with bees, are held on tall stems and make excellent cut flowers. Remove the deadheads to encourage more blooms. Grow it in sun in moist, well-drained, fertile soil, and divide it in the early spring every 2–3 years to maintain its vigor.

☼ ◊ ◖   Z4–8 H8–1
↕ to 36in (90cm) ↔ to 24in (60cm)

Helianthus annuus
ANNUAL

A fast-growing, unfussy flower that is a
favorite with children. The growth spurt
of some of the giant sunflowers is
spectacular—in one season they can
reach 10ft (3m). The large daisylike
flowers have long yellow petals and a
dark purply-brown center. If left to dry,
the seedhead will provide valuable food
for birds in the winter. Sunflowers need
a sunny location in well-drained, fertile
soil. Grow them from seed each year.
Tall-growing plants will need staking
and a sheltered site.

❀ ◊　　　　　　　　　　H11–1
‡ to 10ft (3m) ↔ to 18in (45cm)

Helianthus 'Lemon Queen'
PERENNIAL

In the late summer 'Lemon Queen'
bears large quantities of acid yellow,
daisylike flowers with darker centers.
This is a vigorous, herbaceous
perennial with erect stems and slightly
hairy, lance-shaped, dark green leaves.
Plant it in a sunny location in fertile,
moist but well-drained, neutral or
alkaline soil. A good plant for cutting,
it also combines well with other plants
in an herbaceous border. To maintain
its vigor, divide plants in the early
spring every 2–4 years.

❀ ◊ ◊　　　　　　　Z5–9 H9–5
‡ to 5ft (1.5m) ↔ to 24in (60cm)

Helichrysum 'Schwefellicht'

PERENNIAL

Clusters of small, fluffy, sulfur-yellow flowers that turn orange-yellow as summer progresses make this an interesting plant for a well-drained rock, gravel, or scree garden. Its spreading stems, which are covered with white hairs and narrow, silvery white leaves, form an attractive, weed-suppressing mound. Plant it in a sunny situation in reasonably fertile, well-drained, neutral to acid soil.

☼ ◊   Z10–11 H11–1
↕ to 24in (60cm) ↔ to 12in (30cm)

Heliopsis helianthoides 'Sommersonne'

PERENNIAL

A terrific plant for the herbaceous border, the ox eye is a clump-forming perennial with erect, branched stems and egg- or lance-shaped, mid-green leaves. In the late summer it produces semi-double flowerheads that look similar to small sunflowers with deep-golden petals and a brownish center. Grow it in full sun in fertile, moist but well-drained soil. Established clumps need dividing in the early spring every 2–3 years to maintain vigor.

☼ ◊ ◗   Z4–9 H9–1
↕ to 36in (90cm) ↔ to 24in (60cm)

Hemerocallis 'Corky'
PERENNIAL

One of the more compact daylilies, 'Corky' is suitable for planting in a small garden or in containers. Clusters of reddish-brown buds appear on long, erect stems among the evergreen, mid-green leaves. These buds open one or two at a time to reveal bright yellow flowers. Although each flower lasts only for one day, they are quickly replaced. Plant it in full sun in fertile, moist but well-drained soil. Propagate daylilies by dividing large clumps in the spring.

☼ ◐ ○ ◑   Z3–10 H11–2

↕ to 28in (70cm) ↔ to 16in (40cm)

Hypericum calycinum
EVERGREEN SHRUB

Through the summer to mid-fall the St. John's wort produces yellow, cup-shaped flowers with showy stamens. It is a low-growing shrub that quickly spreads by means of trailing stems. It is hardy, and not surprisingly, it makes excellent ground cover for a bank or area where little else will grow. It can become invasive; to keep it neat and bushy, cut it back to the ground in the spring. Plant in full sun or partial shade in any well-drained soil. It is easily propagated by division in the spring.

☼ ◐ ○ ◑   Z5–9 H9–4

↕ to 24in (60cm) ↔ indefinite

Hypericum 'Hidcote'

EVERGREEN SHRUB

The arching, spreading branches of 'Hidcote' are covered with handsome, lance-shaped, dark green leaves. Through the summer to early fall clusters of bright golden-yellow flowers, up to 2½in (6cm) across, are produced in profusion. Plant in a reasonably fertile, moist but well-drained soil in full sun. This is a good choice for a shrub or mixed border.

☼ ◊ ◭   Z6–9 H9–6

↕ to 4ft (1.2m) ↔ to 5ft (1.5m)

Inula hookeri

PERENNIAL

A wonderful plant for a shady border, this perennial from the Himalayas will soon form large clumps where conditions suit. It has slender, erect, softly hairy stems and lance-shaped, mid-green leaves. From the late summer to fall it produces clusters of pale yellow flowers with a darker, brownish-yellow center. Plant it in partial shade in fertile, moist but well-drained, soil. To propagate, divide established clumps in the spring or fall.

☼ ◊ ◭   Z4–8 H8–1

↕ to 30in (75cm) ↔ to 18in (45cm)

Kniphofia 'Royal Standard'

PERENNIAL

Although 'Royal Standard' has been around for a long time, it is still one of the best red hot pokers for the herbaceous border. Green, strappy leaves form a large clump from which rise tall, robust, flower spikes. These are studded with scarlet-red buds that open to bright yellow, tubular flowers. Kniphofias are a favorite of bees. Plant them in fertile, moist but well-drained soil in sun.

☼ ◊ ◑   Z6–9 H9–6

↕ to 4ft (1.2m) ↔ to 24in (60cm)

Kniphofia 'Wrexham Buttercup'

PERENNIAL

A yellow red hot poker, 'Wrexham Buttercup' bears tapering spikes of tubular flowers, lightly tipped with orange. It is similar to, but rather larger than, 'Buttercup' (*see p.273*). Grow in full sun or light shade in fertile, moist but well-drained soil. Red hot pokers are classic herbaceous border plants and a favorite of bees. Leave remains of old foliage in place over the winter for protection and remove in the spring, when large clumps can also be divided.

☼ ☀ ◊ ◑   Z6–9 H9–6

↕ to 4ft (1.2m) ↔ to 24in (60cm)

Koelreuteria paniculata
DECIDUOUS TREE

The golden-rain tree deserves a rest over the winter because for the other three seasons it puts on an amazing show. In the late summer this wonderful specimen tree produces spikes of small yellow flowers followed in the fall by pink or red seed capsules. Early spring foliage is a bright pinkish-red, turning through mid-green to a rich, buttery yellow in the late summer and early fall. Plant it in full sun in fertile, well-drained soil. No pruning is needed.

☼ ◊   Z6–9 H9–1
‡↔ to 30ft (10m)

Ligularia 'Gregynog Gold'
PERENNIAL

In the late summer, from a base of large, heart-shaped leaves, 'Gregynog Gold' throws up pyramids of daisylike golden flowers on very tall, stiff stems. Each flower is delicately flecked with chocolate brown filaments. Choose a site where the soil is moderately fertile and permanently damp—around the margins of a natural pond would be ideal—in full sun or partial shade.

☼ ☀ ◊ ●   Z6–9 H9–6
‡ to 6ft (1.8m) ↔ to 3ft (1m)

Lilium
Golden Splendor Group

PERENNIAL BULB

In midsummer stout stems bear long, plump buds that open to large, trumpet-shaped, rich yellow flowers. Like many lilies, the scent is exquisite, and they are ideal for cutting, but be careful not to get the bright orange pollen on your clothes. Lilies are wonderful plants to scatter about in sunny borders, ideally close to paths where they can be really appreciated. Remove lily beetle excrement from the mid-green leaves on sight. Plant bulbs in the fall or spring.

☼ ◊ *f*   Z5–8 H8–1

↕ to 6ft (2m) ↔ to 12in (30cm)

Linaria dalmatica

PERENNIAL

The bright yellow, spurred flowers of this toadflax bear more than a passing resemblance to those of the snapdragon (*Antirrhinum*). The slightly erect, lance-shaped, waxy, green leaves grow up to 7in (18cm) long. Plant it in full sun in a light, preferably sandy, fertile, well-drained soil. Its upright stature will ensure it stands out in the middle of a busy herbaceous border; it would also do well in a gravel garden.

☼ ◊   Z5–8 H8–5

↕ to 3ft (1m) ↔ to 24in (60cm)

Lysimachia nummularia '**Aurea**'

PERENNIAL

The golden form of creeping Jenny is a vigorous evergreen that readily roots when its stems touch the soil. It can become rampant and may need to be controlled by weeding. The leaves are a bright yellow, lime green in the shade, and during the summer it has small, yellow, upright, cup-shaped flowers. Choose a spot in full sun or partial shade in a moist, well-drained soil that won't dry out during the summer. Propagate by division in the spring or fall.

☼ ☼ ◊   Z4–8 H8–1

‡ to 2in (5cm) ↔ indefinite

Lysimachia punctata

PERENNIAL

This is an extremely vigorous perennial that quickly spreads by means of underground rhizomes. The upright stems have tiers of lance-shaped leaves and numerous bright yellow, cup-shaped flowers. It makes an attractive plant for a damp border, but be careful because it can become invasive. It grows best in partial shade but will tolerate full sun. Plant it in fertile, moist but well-drained soil.

☼ ☼ ◊ ◊   Z4–8 H8–1

‡ to 30in (75cm) ↔ to 24in (60cm)

Nymphaea 'Marliacea Chromatella'

PERENNIAL

'Marliacea Chromatella' is a beautiful
waterlily with canary yellow flowers
that appear among the rounded, floating
leaves in the summer. The shade cast by
its leaves is useful in reducing the growth
of pond algae and providing shelter for
fish and other pond creatures. It is an
aquatic perennial and should be grown in
a sunny spot in aquatic planting baskets
where the water is reliably tranquil. The
plants retreat underwater in the winter.
Divide plants in the spring if necessary.

☼ ◗　　　　　　　Z3–11 H11–1

↔ to 5ft (1.5m)

Oenothera biennis

BIENNIAL

The clear yellow, cup-shaped flowers of
the evening primrose are a true delight.
As their name would suggest, they seem
to glow with the warmth of the day in
the failing light on late summer
evenings. The plants are biennial, which
means that they form a large rosette of
foliage in their first year, then sending
up a tall flowering stem in the second.
After this, the plant dies, but from the
seeds new plants will usually come up
again on their own in successive years.
They prefer a sunny location.

☼ ◌　　　　　　　Z4–8 H8–1

↔ to 5ft (1.5m)　↔ to 24in (60cm)

Robinia pseudoacacia 'Frisia'

DECIDUOUS TREE

Dramatic leaf color is what makes this fast-growing, spreading tree so special. In the spring the leaves are bright yellow, in the early summer they take on a dash of lime, then, in the late summer they turn a rich orange-yellow. The tree has fragrant, white flowers in the spring and thorny branches. A wonderful specimen tree with a canopy light enough for underplanting. Give it a spot in full sun in fertile, moist but well-drained soil. No pruning is required.

☼ ◊ ◑ *f*   Z4–9 H9–3

‡ to 50ft (15m) ↔ to 25ft (8m)

Rudbeckia fulgida 'Goldsturm'

PERENNIAL

The dark-centered flowers of the black-eyed Susan are produced in abundance from the late summer to mid-fall. The deep green leaves are lance-shaped. It will grow in any reasonably fertile, well-drained soil as long as it does not dry out in the summer; it also suits clay soil. A good mixer in an herbaceous or woodland border, it is also perfect for natural plantings with ornamental grasses.

☼ ❁ ◊ ◑   Z4–9 H9–1

‡ to 30in (75cm) ↔ to 12in (30cm)

Rudbeckia laciniata '**Herbstsonne**'
PERENNIAL

The cheerful coneflower is one of the
mainstays of the late-summer garden.
'Herbstsonne' has yellow, daisylike
flowers with conical greenish-brown
centers that are carried aloft on tall,
upright stems. The rich, glossy green
leaves are deeply veined. It does best in
fertile, moist but well-drained soil,
including clay. This clump-forming
plant is perfect for the back of an
herbaceous border where it will act as a
foil for smaller plants. Good for cutting.

☼ ❋ ◊ ◐   Z3–9 H9–1

‡ to 7ft (2.3m) ↔ to 30in (75cm)

Silphium perfoliatum
PERENNIAL

From the summer through to early fall
the upright, branching stems of the cup
plant are crowned with sunny-yellow,
daisylike flowers. Its deeply toothed
leaves are attractive too, if a little
bristly to touch. This clump-forming
herbaceous perennial prefers a rather
heavy, neutral or alkaline soil, including
clay, that is moist but well-drained. It
would be at home in a partially shaded
wild or woodland garden.

☼ ❋ ◐ ◊   Z5–9 H9–5

‡ to 8ft (2.5m) ↔ to 3ft (1m)

Solidago 'Goldenmosa'

PERENNIAL

With its upright, yellow-stalked, golden
flowerheads and wrinkled, mid-green
leaves, this is a select form of goldenrod.
Compact and bushy, it is much less
invasive than the species. Plant it in
a late-summer border in full sunshine
in well-drained, slightly fertile, sandy
soil. It is an ideal plant for a wild garden
and is also good for cutting.

☀ ◊   Z5–9 H9–5

↕ to 3ft (1m) ↔ to 24in (60cm)

Solidago rugosa 'Fireworks'

PERENNIAL

From late summer to mid-fall this
goldenrod cultivar's long, arching
stems bear dense panicles of tiny yellow
blooms in such a way that they resemble
fireworks. The flowers attract bees and
butterflies. It works well in a mixed
perennial border or in a wild garden,
meadow, or naturalized area. Plant in
full sun in average soil.

☀ ◐   Z4–9 H9–1

↕↔ to 36in (90cm)

Tropaeolum peregrinum
CLIMBER

The Canary creeper is a vigorous annual
climber with deeply lobed, gray-green
leaves. In the summer it produces
clusters of bright yellow flowers. These
have three small lower petals and two
larger, deeply fringed, upper petals,
which give it a birdlike appearance.
Plant it in a sunny location in moist
but well-drained, slightly fertile soil.
Canary creeper is ideal for growing
against a trellis, over a fence or pergola,
or through a deciduous tree. Sow seed
in the same area in the early spring.

☼ ◊ ◖   Z9–10 H10–9

↕ to 12ft (4m)

Verbascum nigrum
PERENNIAL

The elegant dark mullein bears 20in
(50cm) tall flower spikes dotted with
yellow, saucer-shaped blooms that have
purple filament hairs. The heart-shaped
leaves are fuzzy and gray underneath
and form a rosette at the base, gradually
becoming smaller as they grow up the
stem. Grow in poor, well-drained,
alkaline soils; in richer soils the plant
grows larger and needs staking. Ideal
for planting in gravel or naturalizing in
a wild garden, this mullein also mixes
well in a sunny herbaceous border.

☼ ◊   Z3–8 H8–1

↕ to 36in (90cm) ↔ to 24in (60cm)

Antirrhinum majus 'Trumpet Serenade'

PERENNIAL

In a range of vibrant colors, including this rich gold, the freesialike blooms of 'Trumpet Serenade' are very different from the usual "squeeze-open, snap-shut" flowers of most snapdragons. As short-lived, tender perennials they are usually grown as annual bedding plants, filling gaps at the front of an herbaceous border or used as a cut flower. Plant in full sun in fertile, preferably sandy soil. Avoid wet soil since it encourages rust, although this is a resistant variety.

☼ ◊   Z9–11 H11–1
↕↔to 12in (30cm)

Arctotis fastuosa

PERENNIAL

The deeply lobed leaves of the African daisy are silvery white and covered with hairs. In the late summer it bears orange, daisylike flowers with a black or dark maroon center. It is a tender perennial, and it is usually treated as a half-hardy annual used in bedding designs, gravel gardens, and containers. Outside it needs a moist but very well-drained soil in an open, sunny site. It can be kept from year to year in a pot of gritty, well-drained compost and overwintered under glass.

☼ ◊   Z11 H9–1
↕ to 24in (60cm) ↔to 12in (30cm)

Begonia 'City of Ballarat'

PERENNIAL

Bright orange flowers, up to 7in (18cm)
across, adorn this tuberous begonia.
Grow it in containers of soil-based
potting mix as a houseplant, and move
it outside in summer. It can be used as
bedding if the tubers are lifted in the
fall before the first frost and stored in
trays of dry sand in a cool place. In the
early spring, moisten the trays of tubers
and move them to a warm place before
planting out in late spring, in moist but
well-drained soil in partial shade.

☀ ◊   H11–10

↕ to 24in (60cm) ↔ to 18in (45cm)

Campsis x *tagliabuana* 'Madame Galen'

CLIMBER

The trumpet creeper is a vigorous,
self-clinging climber with long, divided
leaves. From the late summer to fall
it produces clusters of orange-red,
trumpet-shaped flowers. It can quickly
cover a trellis or climb through an old
tree. Keep it clear of the roof and gutters,
and hard prune in the winter to keep
it within bounds. Vulnerable to frost
damage, in colder areas grow the vine
against a sunny wall. The soil should be
fertile and moist but well drained.

☀ ◊ ◓   Z5–9 H9–5

↕ to 30ft (10m)

Canna 'Striata'

PERENNIAL

In the late summer this striking plant shoots up tall spikes of gladioluslike orange flowers. The real scene-stealer, though, is the flamboyant foliage, marked with green and yellow stripes. It makes a wonderful plant for a border among other red or orange flowers or can be grown in pots. Plant outdoors in the late spring in sun and well-drained soil. It is tender, so lift rhizomes before the first frost, place in a tray of moist compost, and overwinter under glass.

☼ ◊   Z8–11 H11–1
↕ to 5ft (1.5m) ↔ to 20in (50cm)

Crocosmia 'Star of the East'

BULBOUS PERENNIAL

With its large, orange flowers, 'Star of the East' is a particularly attractive crocosmia. A vigorous plant with erect, sword-shaped, deep green leaves, it looks wonderful planted among shrubs or with other late-flowering perennials. If the corms become overcrowded, they will lose their vigor, so dig them up in the spring, and replant them on a fresh site. Crocosmia prefer a spot in full sun in fertile, moist but well-drained soil.

☼ ◊ ◐   Z6–9 H9–6
↕ to 28in (70cm) ↔ to 3in (8cm)

Dahlia 'Hamari Gold'

PERENNIAL

Golden-yellow blooms and deeply divided, dark green leaves make this an attractive border plant. Dahlias are not hardy, so when the foliage has been blackened by the first frost, dig up the tubers and store them in dry compost over the winter. Wait until all risk of frost has past before replanting in full sun in well-drained soil. It benefits from a stake, best inserted at planting time to avoid damaging the tubers. Feed regularly in the growing season.

☼ ◊   Z9–11 H11–1

↕ to 4ft (1.2m) ↔ to 24in (60cm)

Dahlia 'Wootton Impact'

PERENNIAL

This attractive, semi-cactus dahlia is ideal for a sunny border where space is limited. Strong stems of medium-sized, bronze-colored flowers, which are good for cutting, are held well above the main bulk of the plant. They need early staking. Like all dahlias, it requires a sunny spot in fertile, well-drained soil, while in the winter the tubers need to be dug up and stored (*see* 'Hamari Gold', *above*).

☼ ◊   Z9–11 H11–1

↕ to 4ft (1.2m) ↔ to 24in (60cm)

Fuchsia 'Coralle'

DECIDUOUS SHRUB

The tubular bells of 'Coralle', which are borne in tight clusters, will appeal to those who prefer less artificial-looking fuchsias. Upright in style, this shrub has strong stems with velvety, olive-green leaves. It is excellent for growing in a container. Use a soil-based potting mix, and choose a spot in full sun or light shade. Feed regularly throughout the summer with a balanced fertilizer, and move under glass during the winter since it is not hardy.

☼ ☀ ◊ ◗   H11–9
‡ to 36in (90cm) ↔ to 24in (60cm)

Helenium 'Septemberfuchs'

PERENNIAL

Heleniums are invaluable for providing areas of warm color in the late-summer border. This particularly tall variety benefits from early staking. It has dark green leaves and burnt-orange flowers streaked with yellow. Bees find the domed centers irresistible. For best effect plant them in groups of three or more in a sunny location in moist but well-drained fertile soil. Established clumps need dividing every couple of years.

☼ ◊ ◗   Z4–8 H8–1
‡ to 5ft (1.5m) ↔ to 24in (60cm)

Helianthus annuus 'Music Box'

ANNUAL

From late summer this small sunflower produces an abundance of bright orange, yellow, or red flowers, each bloom measuring up to 5in (12cm) across. The markings on the petals subtly darken towards the black central disc. Wonderful as cut flowers and short enough to grow in a pot, they also blend well among other plants in a sunny herbaceous or annual border. Sow the seed in the same area every spring in fertile, moist but well-drained soil.

☼ ◊ ◑ H11–1

‡ to 28in (70cm) ↔ to 24in (60cm)

Kniphofia rooperi

PERENNIAL

Living up to its common name of red hot poker and torch lily, this dazzling plant is guaranteed to brighten up the herbaceous border or gravel garden. Its globe-shaped spikes of reddish-orange flowers turn a golden color as they mature. It is a very robust, clump-forming plant with shapely, pointed, evergreen leaves. Plant it in the late spring in full sun or partial shade in fertile, well-drained, preferably sandy soil. Mulch over the winter in the first year. Divide large clumps in the spring.

☼ ☀ ◊ Z6–9 H9–4

‡ to 4ft (1.2m) ↔ to 24in (60cm)

Lilium henryi

BULBOUS PERENNIAL

Vigorous and clump-forming, this tall lily has erect stems and narrow, dark green, lance-shaped leaves. In the late summer its develops clusters of ten or more delicately scented flowers with black-spotted, swept-back petals. It is happiest in partial shade in neutral or slightly alkaline, well-drained soil. Tall liliies like this one are ideal for brightening up the back of a shrub or herbaceous border.

☀ ◊ *f*   Z2–7 H7–1
‡ to 10ft (3m)

Lonicera sempervirens

CLIMBER

The beautiful trumpet honeysuckle is semi-evergreen in mild winters and in the summer produces clusters of tubular, orange-red flowers with a yellow throat. The oval, paired leaves help to frame the flowers and highlight their intense color. In the fall the plant is covered with bright red berries, giving it a long season of interest. Use it to cover a warm wall, or to brighten up a sheltered location in the garden. Plant it in full sun or partial shade in fertile, well-drained soil.

☀ ☼ ◊   Z4–9 H9–1
‡ to 12ft (4m)

Mimulus aurantiacus

EVERGREEN SHRUB

The shrubby musk is an attractive, small plant for a warm, sunny border. The dark green, sticky, lance-shaped leaves are the perfect foil for the orange, trumpet-shaped flowers, which appear from the late summer through the fall. Plant it in fertile, well-drained soil, and, since it is not completely hardy, somewhere sheltered in full sunshine. In cold areas it is best grown in a sunroom.

 ☼ ◊   Z7–11 H11–7

↔to 3ft (1m)

Xerochrysum bracteatum Monstrosum Series

ANNUAL

Everlasting flowers are erect annuals with grayish green, lance-shaped leaves. The Monstrosum Series has vibrant orange, double flowers that measure 3in (8cm) across. Other colors are available, including yellows and reds. Use it as a bedding plant, to fill spaces in an herbaceous border, or in containers. Plant in full sunshine in slightly fertile, moist but well-drained soil. Everlasting flowers dry well and retain their color for a long time.

☼ ◊ ◐   Z10–11 H12–3

to 36in (90cm) ↔to 12in (30cm)

FALL

As the days begin to shorten and night temperatures fall, many plants have completed their annual cycles and retreat underground. The end of the growing season is signalled by the brilliant colour displays of deciduous trees before they drop their leaves and enter their dormancy. The vibrance of the show varies each year but most of the maples (*Acer*) give rich, reliable autumnal tints. There is also plenty of choice for gardens that are too small to accomodate large trees: shrubs, such as *Euonymus alatus* and the stag's horn sumach (*Rhus typhina*), can provide dramatic foliage displays of crimson, scarlet and gold.

Ornamental vines *Vitis* 'Brant' and *V. coignetiae* are among the climbers with bright red foliage in the fall, and vigorous Boston ivy, *Parthenocissus tricuspidata*, transforms the appearance of walls as it turns from green and becomes a glowing sheet of scarlet.

FRUIT AND FLOWERS

Decorative fruits are much in evidence now and some of the best crops are carried on cotoneasters, rowans (*Sorbus*) and crab apples (*Malus*). And there are shrub roses, such as *Rosa rugosa*, which produce masses of shining scarlet hips.

Although the annual border has been cleared and many perennials have begun to die down, some flowering plants come into their own at this time—notably autumn crocuses and colchicums. Michaelmas daisies (*Aster*), Monkshood (*Aconitum*), and chrysanthemums of every colour will continue to flower as long as the weather permits. Do not be in too much of a hurry to clear away all remnants of summer; decorative seedheads can stay until they collapse, and allow the graceful flowerheads and foliage of ornamental grasses to stand through winter, not only so you can enjoy them, but for the protection it offers the plant.

Ageratina altissima 'Chocolate'

PERENNIAL

Formerly classified under *Eupatorium*, white snakeroot is a clump-forming perennial that is good in shade, even dry shade, and bears clusters of small white flowers in the late summer. The variety name refers to the color of the toothed leaves, which are an attractive deep brown through the spring and summer, gradually greening with age before the whole plant dies back over the winter. Plants may wilt in hot sun if not watered. Divide in the spring, as necessary.

☼ ☀ ◊ ◖   Z4–8 H8–2

↕ to 3ft (1m) ↔ to 24in (60cm)

Aralia elata 'Variegata'

DECIDUOUS TREE

The Japanese angelica tree is upright in form with stout, spreading, thorny branches arranged in tiers. In mild areas it forms a small tree but elsewhere may only be a large shrub up to 10ft (3m) tall. The leaflets, which are edged in creamy-white, turn gold in fall. Abundant clusters of small white flowers are borne in the late summer and early fall. It prefers fertile, moist but well-drained soil in sun but tolerates light, dappled shade.

☼ ☀ ◊ ◖   Z4–9 H9–1

↕↔ to 30ft (10m)

Arbutus x *andrachnoides*

EVERGREEN TREE

The Grecian strawberry tree is a shrublike, spreading evergreen with peeling, red-brown bark and oval, glossy, dark green leaves. From the fall through to the spring it bears hanging clusters of small, almost spherical, white flowers; occasionally it produces small, bright red fruits at the same time. Grow it in a site sheltered from cold winds in full sun in organic, well-drained soil. It tolerates alkaline soils as long as they are deep and rich in leafy organic matter.

☼ ◊   Z8–9 H9–8

↕↔to 25ft (8m)

Aster ericoides 'White Heather'

PERENNIAL

Asters are invaluable for fall color in herbaceous and mixed borders. This bushy perennial has wiry, upright stems smothered in tiny, long-lasting, white daisies from the late summer to late fall. The slender stems need staking. Grow in sun or partial shade in fertile, well-drained soil that does not dry out during the growing season; moisture helps reduce the risk of mildew, although this variety shows some resistance to the disease.

☼ ☀ ◊ ◑   Z5–8 H8–1

↕to 3ft (1m) ↔to 12in (30cm)

Cimicifuga simplex

PERENNIAL

The tiny, star-shaped fall flowers of this herbaceous perennial, also known as *Actea simplex*, appear brilliant white against their dark stems. The tall, arching flower spikes are seen at their best if the stems are supported by an unobtrusive, grow-through support, positioned in the spring. The leaves are glossy, finely divided, and fresh green. Good for late color in a woodland garden or shady border. Grow in moist, organic soil in light shade to prevent the sun from scorching the delicate leaves.

☼ ◑   Z4–8 H11–1

↕ to 5ft (1.5m) ↔ to 24in (60cm)

Cortaderia richardii

PERENNIAL

Commonly known as toe toe, *Cortaderia richardii* is native to New Zealand. The arching, fluffy flowerheads, up to 2ft (60cm) long, first appear in the summer, high above the tufts of long, narrow, olive-green leaves. If left on the plant, the slender, creamy-white plumes will persist through the fall and winter. They can also be cut for fresh or dried-flower arrangements. Grow in well-drained soil in sun. Cut out the dead foliage and flowerheads in the early spring—protect your hands with gloves.

☼ ◊ ◑   Z7–10 H10–7

↕ to 8ft (2.5m) ↔ to 3ft (1m)

Cortaderia selloana 'Sunningdale Silver'

PERENNIAL GRASS

Large, dense, evergreen tufts of sharp-edged, deep grayish-green leaves are topped by tall upright stems of long-lasting, silvery-white flowerheads in late summer and fall. It makes an impressive specimen plant where space is available. Leave dead foliage in place over the winter to protect the crown from frost, then, wearing stout gloves, cut and remove it in the spring. Grow in sun in well-drained soil. Cut back every two or three years in the spring to rejuvenate.

☼ ◊　　　　　　　Z7–11 H11–7

↕ to 7ft (2.1m) ↔ to 4ft (1.2m)

Crocus ochroleucus

BULBOUS PERENNIAL

This crocus bears slender, creamy-white flowers with yellow throats in the late fall when most other fall-flowering crocus are done. The leaves usually emerge with or just after the flowers, and are green with a central white stripe. It is very easy to grow in well-drained soil in sun and will naturalize if planted in drifts in short grass. Overcrowded clumps can be divided after flowering. Plant corms in the late summer.

☼ ◊　　　　　　　Z5–8 H8–4

↕ to 2in (5cm) ↔ to 1in (2.5cm)

Galanthus reginae-olgae

BULBOUS PERENNIAL

This snowdrop flowers from mid-fall to early winter with petals up to 1in (2.5cm) long. The narrow leaves appear after flowering and are dark green with a central gray stripe. Grow in sun or light dappled shade in well-drained, neutral to alkaline soil. It prefers drier soils and more sun than other snowdrops. Overcrowded clumps can be divided as the leaves start to wither. Plant bulbs in the fall.

☼ ◐ ◊   Z7–9 H9–7
‡ to 8in (20cm) ↔ to 2in (5cm)

Leucojum autumnale

BULBOUS PERENNIAL

The fall snowflake is a beautiful plant with narrow, dark green, grasslike leaves. The nodding white flowers, tinged with pink at the base, are borne on slender stems in the late summer and early fall. A native of the stony slopes of the western Mediterranean, it prefers a warm, sunny spot in light, free-draining soil. It is ideal for rock gardens, sunny banks, and patios. Plant bulbs in the late summer.

☼ ◊   Z5–9 H9–1
‡ to 6in (15cm) ↔ to 2in (5cm)

Sorbus cashmiriana
DECIDUOUS TREE

The Kashmir rowan is a spreading,
open-branched small tree. The white
or blush-pink flowers open in the late
spring or early summer. The finely
divided, rich green leaves turn gold and
russet in the fall, forming a backdrop
to the clusters of marble-sized berrylike
fruits that appear from the late summer
and early fall onward. Grow in sun or
light shade in fertile, well-drained but
moisture-retentive soil. It is most easily
propagated by seed sown as soon as it
is ripe in the fall.

☼ ☀ ◊ ◖   Z5–7 H7–5

↕ to 25ft (8m) ↔ to 22ft (7m)

Symphoricarpos albus
var. *laevigatus*
DECIDUOUS SHRUB

Snowberry is a densely upright, robust
shrub with rounded, dark green leaves.
It has tiny pink flowers in the summer,
followed by its most notable feature:
eye-catching, pure white berrylike fruits
in the fall. It grows on a range of sites,
including dry shade, but spreads by
suckers and can be invasive, so it is best
used as a boundary plant, where it could
be included in a mixed hedge. Prune out
old shoots to the base in the spring.

☼ ☀ ◊ ◖   Z3–7 H7–1

↕↔ to 6ft (2m)

Amaryllis belladonna
BULBOUS PERENNIAL

This South African bulb is grown for its late-summer and early-fall flowers. The fragrant, trumpet-shaped, pink blooms are borne in clusters on long, purple-tinted stems. The dark green, straplike leaves appear after the flowers and last until the following summer. In cold areas, protect the leaves from frost by using a cloche. Grow in a warm, sheltered, sunny site in very well-drained soil enriched with organic matter. Plant in the summer with the tip of the bulb just below the soil surface.

☼ ◊ *f*   Z7–10 H11–7
‡ to 32in (80cm) ↔ to 18in (45cm)

Camellia sasanqua
EVERGREEN SHRUB

Because most camellias bloom in spring, fall flowering *C. sasanqua* stands out. These upright shrubs or small trees are valued for their mildly fragrant flowers, which bloom in mid fall to early winter, and glossy, dark green foliage. White and pink flowered selections are available. In mild regions, *C. sasanqua* can be used as a hedge, but otherwise it will grow best in the shelter of a warm, sunny wall. Moist, humus rich, acid soil is essential. The plant will tolerate hard pruning after flowering.

☼ ☀ ◊ ◊ *f*   Z7–8 H8–7
‡ to 15ft (5m) ↔ to 8ft (2.5m)

Chrysanthemum 'Rose Yvonne Arnaud'

PERENNIAL

The fully double flowers of this florist's chrysanthemum are produced in abundance in the late summer and fall. The deep rose-pink petals are neatly backswept. The plant should be dug up in the fall after flowering and overwintered in frost-free conditions. New shoots can be planted outside after the last frost or used for basal cuttings in the early spring to produce new plants. Grow in fertile, well-drained soil in full sun.

☼ ◊　　　　　　　　Z4–9 H9–1

‡ to 4ft (1.2m) ↔ to 30in (75cm)

Clerodendrum bungei

DECIDUOUS SHRUB

This suckering shrub is not fully frost-hardy, but if the woody stems die back in cold winters, they often grow again from the base in the spring if given a deep winter mulch. The fragrant flowers are deep pink and, although tiny, are borne in large clusters throughout the late summer and early fall. The large, heart-shaped, serrated-edged leaves emit a pungent odor when brushed against. Grow in a warm, sunny, sheltered site in a organic, well-drained soil.

☼ ◊ *f*　　　　　　Z8–10 H11–8

↔ to 6ft (2m)

Colchicum x *byzantinum*

BULBOUS PERENNIAL

C. byzantinum produces up to 20 large, funnel-shaped, pale mauve-pink flowers in the fall. The broad leaves, which are ribbed or pleated, appear in the spring and last until the early summer. As they fade, they can look untidy, so hide the foliage by growing them among other plants. Plant the corms, which resemble a tiny clenched fist, in the late summer in a sunny location in soil that is moist but free draining. This colchicum establishes quickly and will spread where the conditions suit it.

☀ ◊ ◖   Z4–9 H9–1

↕ to 5in (12cm) ↔ to 4in (10cm)

Colchicum 'The Giant'

BULBOUS PERENNIAL

The flowers of this fall-flowering corm are very large. Mauve-pink with white throats, they are lightly checkered and crocuslike. This is one of the easiest colchicums to grow, and it will increase rapidly. Broad leaves appear in the winter and die back in the summer. The corms are best grown among other plants to conceal the leaves. Plant the corms in late summer in fertile, free-draining soil in sun. Plants tolerate light or partial shade.

☀ ◊   Z4–9 H9–1

↕↔ to 8in (20cm)

Crocus kotschyanus
BULBOUS PERENNIAL

In the fall this fully hardy crocus bears delicate, lilac-pink flowers with yellow centers and white stamens. The flowers open fully in sun to display the glossy surface of the petals. They are followed in the winter through to the spring by narrow, semi-erect leaves with white lines along the center. It is ideal for naturalizing in drifts in well-drained soil in a warm, sunny location. Overcrowded clumps can be divided after flowering. Plant corms in the late summer.

☼ ◊　　　　　　　　　　Z3–8 H8–1
‡ to 3in (8cm) ↔ to 2in (5cm)

Cyclamen hederifolium
PERENNIAL

This small cyclamen has ivy-shaped leaves that are intricately patterned in shades of gray-green. Appearing after the flowers in the fall, they can provide a foil for other winter-flowering bulbs until they fade by the early summer. The pink flowers appear from late summer to fall. Grow in light shade in a well-drained soil that is rich in leafy organic matter. Plant tubers in late summer about 1in (2.5cm) deep. Clumps are best left undisturbed, but self-sown seedlings can be dug up and moved.

☼ ☼ ◊　　　　　　　　　Z5–7 H9–7
‡ to 4in (10cm) ↔ to 6in (15cm)

Euonymus phellomanus

DECIDUOUS SHRUB

The corkbush is a medium-sized shrub with a reliable and wonderfully vivid display of bright pink seed capsules in the fall. Each capsule splits as it ripens to reveal bright orange seeds. The plant is named for its corklike, winged stems, which are highly unusual and particularly noticeable in the winter. It does well in sun or partial shade. The oval leaves redden in the fall before they drop. It would also be a lovely tree for a wildlife garden. Be careful of the fruit, which is toxic to humans.

☼ ◑ ◐   Z5–8 H8–5
‡ to 8ft (2.5m) ↔ to 10ft (3m)

Nerine bowdenii

BULBOUS PERENNIAL

Stout stems bear umbrellalike clusters of rose-pink flowers with wavy-edged petals from early to mid-fall. The strap-shaped leaves appear with, or just after, the flowers. Grow in sun in very free-draining soil; they are best at the foot of a warm, sunny wall and left to multiply undisturbed. Plant in the spring with the tip of the bulb at, or just below, the soil surface. In the winter in colder areas cover with a mulch of leaf mold.

☼ ◐   Z8–10 H10–8
‡ to 24in (60cm) ↔ to 6in (15cm)

Nerine bowdenii f. *alba*

BULBOUS PERENNIAL

This robust perennial is one of the best
late-flowering bulbs. In the fall it bears
open sprays of five to ten trumpet-
shaped, faintly scented, bright pink
flowers with curled, wavy-edged petals.
The straplike, fresh green leaves appear
after the flowers at the base of the plant.
Despite its exotic appearance, it will
survive winter cold with protection at
the base of a warm, sunny wall. The
flowers are good for cutting. Mulch with
leaf mold or pine needles when the bulbs
are dormant in the winter.

☼ ◊ *f*　　　　　　　　　Z8–10 H10–8

‡ to 24in (60cm) ↔ to 6in (15cm)

Schizostylis coccinea '**Sunrise**'

BULBOUS PERENNIAL

This iris family member produces tall
spikes of delicate, cup-shaped, soft pink
flowers in the late summer and fall.
The mid-green, narrow leaves are sword-
shaped, and both flowers and foliage
are excellent for indoor arrangements.
In the garden it is well-suited for sunny
borders, waterside plantings, or it can
be planted against a sunny wall. Grow
in fertile, moist, well-drained soil in full
sun. Divide regularly in the spring to
maintain the plant's vigor.

☼ ◑　　　　　　　　　　Z7–9 H9–7

‡ to 24in (60cm) ↔ to 12in (30cm)

Sedum spectabile

PERENNIAL

The ice plant is deservedly popular and flowers over long periods from the late summer to fall. It is ideal for the front of a sunny border, where its densely packed, flat heads of tiny star-shaped, soft-pink flowers will attract butterflies and bees. The leaves are fleshy and pale gray-green. Grow in any well-drained soil in full sun. The flowerheads can be cut and dried or left to stand until the winter, adding interest to the border.

☼ ◊   Z4–9 H9–1
↕↔to 18in (45cm)

Sorbus hupehensis var. *obtusa*

DECIDUOUS TREE

This rowan has a narrow, compact look. The young foliage is followed by trusses of white flowers in the late spring and early summer. Pink berries form during the late summer and become deeper pink as they mature. The leaves are divided into many leaflets that turn fiery orange and red in the fall. The berries remain long after the leaves have fallen. Grow in moisture-retentive, well-drained, neutral or slightly acidic soil in sun or light dappled shade.

☼ ◐ ◊ ◑   Z3–8 H8–1
↕ to 40ft (12m) ↔ to 25ft (8m)

Sorbus vilmorinii
DECIDUOUS TREE

The delicate-looking, fernlike leaves
of Vilmorin's rowan are dark green,
turning shades of orange to bronze-red
in the fall. This large shrub or small
tree has a rounded crown with slender,
arching branches and is suitable for
a small garden. White flowers in the
late spring are followed by fruits in
the fall, which ripen through shades
of deep red-pink to white flushed with
pink. Plant in moisture-retentive but
well-drained, neutral or slightly acidic
soil in full sun or light shade.

☼ ☀ ◊ ◊   Z6–8 H8–6
‡↔to 15ft (5m)

Zephyranthes grandiflora
BULBOUS PERENNIAL

Soft pink, funnel-shaped flowers open to
a starry shape between the late summer
and early fall above clumps of very
slender leaves. Plant bulbs 4in (10cm)
deep in the spring in a sheltered, sunny
site in well-drained, moisture-retentive
soil. In cold areas dig up after flowering,
and overwinter in a frost-free place.
It can also be grown in containers of
gritty compost and moved under glass
in the winter or grown permanently in
the greenhouse or sunroom.

☼ ◊ ◊   Z8–11 H11–9
‡ to 12in (30cm) ↔to 4in (10cm)

Acer palmatum 'Dissectum Atropurpureum'

DECIDUOUS TREE

This small tree is one of the most popular forms of Japanese maple. It has wide-spreading branches clothed with ferny, deeply divided, red-purple leaves that turn red in the fall. Grow in full sun or partial shade in fertile, moist but well-drained soil in a sheltered location; the leaves may be damaged by frosts and cold or dry winds. Grow it with other Japanese maples or in a large container of soil-based potting mix.

☼ ☀ ◊ ◖   Z6–8 H8–2

‡ to 5ft (1.5m) ↔ to 3ft (1m)

Acer palmatum 'Osakazuki'

DECIDUOUS TREE

This Japanese maple has large, bright green leaves that are divided into seven lobes, each drawn out into a finely tapered tip. In the fall they turn a vivid scarlet. Plant it in full sun or partial shade in fertile, moist but well-drained soil with shelter from hard frosts and cold, dry winds. To fully appreciate its fall foliage, it is best grown as a specimen tree.

☼ ☀ ◊ ◖   Z6–8 H8–2

‡↔ to 20ft (6m)

Acer rubrum 'October Glory'

DECIDUOUS TREE

The red maple dons its bright red fall colors early in the season and retains its leaves for several weeks, even in windy weather. The dark green summer leaves will develop their most vibrant colors if the tree is grown in acidic soil. Plant it in full sun or partial shade in fertile, moist but well-drained soil. This tree has a spreading habit.

☼ ◐ ◊ ◗　　　　　　　Z3–9 H9–1
‡ to 70ft (20m) ↔ to 30ft (10m)

Acer rubrum 'Scanlon'

DECIDUOUS TREE

There are few trees that have color as vivid in the fall as this one—the dark green leaves turn a vivid shade of deep reddish orange. Plant it in full sunshine in moist but well-drained, fertile soil. The best fall colors appear when grown in acidic soil. This tree has a narrow columnar form, making it more suitable for smaller gardens than 'October Glory'.

☼ ◊ ◗　　　　　　　　Z3–9 H9–1
‡ to 50ft (15m) ↔ to 15ft (5m)

Amelanchier lamarckii

DECIDUOUS TREE

Often shrubby, this attractive small tree has upright branches and downy young shoots. It has hanging clusters of white flowers in midspring, which are followed by edible, purplish-black fruit in the summer. The leaves are flushed bronze as they emerge in the spring, then turn dark green before becoming orange and finally red in the fall. Plant in full sun or partial shade in acidic, fertile, moist but well-drained soil. Thin out main stems if necessary to improve the appearance.

☼ ◐ ◊ ◑　　　　　　　　Z5–9 H9–5

‡ to 30ft (10m) ↔ to 40ft (12m)

Arbutus unedo

EVERGREEN TREE

The strawberry tree has a bushy, spreading style and attractive, peeling, reddish-brown bark. The oval leaves are dark green and glossy. From the late fall to spring it bears hanging sprays of small, waxy-textured white flowers that are accompanied by small, strawberrylike red fruits—these result from the previous year's flowers. Grow in full sun in a fertile, well-drained soil enriched with leafy organic matter. It is best in a sheltered spot with some protection from strong, cold winds.

☼ ◊ ◑　　　　　　　　Z8–9 H9–6

‡↔ to 25ft (8m)

Aronia x prunifolia

DECIDUOUS SHRUB

The bright green, oval leaves of this
relatively large, fan-shaped shrub turn
a rich wine red in the fall before they
drop in the winter. It is commonly
known as purple chokeberry, named
for the deep purple berries that mature
over the summer from the white
flowers in midspring. The fruits ripen
just before the fall leaves turn, making
this a fine fall plant. The plant grows
best in neutral to acid soil in full sun
or partial shade. The variety 'Brilliant'
has particularly fine leaf color.

☼ ◐ ◊ ◑　　　　　　Z5–9 H9–5

↕ to 10ft (3m) ↔ to 6ft (2m)

Berberis x ottawensis 'Superba'

DECIDUOUS SHRUB

A large shrub with gracefully arching,
thorny branches bearing red berries.
The rounded leaves open purplish-red
and turn a brilliant crimson-red in the
fall. In the spring it bears clusters of
pale yellow flowers. It is a tough shrub
that can be planted in almost any well-
drained soil and will grow happily in
full sun or partial shade. Use it in a
shrub or mixed border or as an intruder-
proof hedge. Prune hard for the best
foliage effects.

☼ ◐ ◊　　　　　　　Z4–8 H8–3

↕↔ to 8ft (2.5m)

Cercidiphyllum japonicum
DECIDUOUS TREE

The Katsura tree is pyramid-shaped when young, becoming more rounded with maturity. It has rounded, fresh green leaves that turn yellow, orange, and red in the fall with a scent like burnt sugar when they fall. It makes a beautiful specimen tree. Plant it in full sun or dappled shade in organic, moist but well-drained, neutral to acidic soil. The best fall color is obtained when it is planted in acid soil.

☼ ◑ ◊ ◐ *f*   Z4–8 H8–1
‡ to 70ft (20m) ↔ to 50ft (15m)

Chrysanthemum 'George Griffiths'
PERENNIAL

Chrysanthemums should be planted in a sheltered location in full sun. They need a fertile, moist but well-drained soil that is enriched with well-rotted manure. The flowerheads of 'George Griffiths' are heavy, and the stems should be tied in to a cane for support. Dig up the plants after flowering and overwinter in frost-free conditions. Plant out in the spring after the final frost, or raise new plants from basal cuttings. This chrysanthemum is often grown for exhibition.

☼ ◊ ◐   Z4–9 H9–1
‡ to 5ft (1.5m) ↔ to 30in (75cm)

Cotinus 'Grace'
DECIDUOUS SHRUB

This is an extremely beautiful type of smoke bush with rich purple, oval leaves. In the summer it bears plumes of small flowers that are followed by sprays of tiny, purplish-pink fruits. In the fall the leaves turn a vivid shade of scarlet. Plant it in full sun or light shade in moisture-retentive but well-drained soil. To obtain the best fall color, do not plant it in too rich a soil, and choose a sunny location; it does not color as well in the shade.

☼ ◑ ◊ ◔   Z5–8 H8–4
↕ to 20ft (6m) ↔ to 15ft (5m)

Cotoneaster 'Cornubia'
SEMI-EVERGREEN SHRUB

This vigorous shrub or small tree has arching branches clothed in dark green leaves; some of them turn bronze in the fall. It is one of the tallest of the cotoneasters. The clusters of small, white, spring flowers produce an abundance of bright red fruits in fall. Plant it in full sunshine or partial shade in moisture-retentive but well-drained soil. It can be planted as a screen, in a large shrub border, or can be trained to form a standard tree.

☼ ◑ ◊ ◔   Z6–8 H8–6
↕↔ to 30ft (10m)

Cotoneaster horizontalis

DECIDUOUS SHRUB

A low-growing shrub with flattened, wide-spreading branches covered with small, oval, dark green leaves. The branches are arranged in a distinctive herringbone pattern. Small white, pink-flushed flowers appear in the spring and are followed in the fall by bright scarlet-red fruit. The leaves also turn red in the fall, creating a breathtaking display. Grow it against a wall, or use it as ground cover. Plant it in full sun in any moderately fertile, well-drained soil.

☼ ◊   Z4–7 H7–3
‡ to 3ft (1m) ↔ to 5ft (1.5m)

Euonymus alatus

DECIDUOUS SHRUB

There are few plants that can compete with the winged spindle for dramatic fall color. It has dark green leaves that are borne on unusual, corkscrew shoots. In the fall the leaves turn a brilliant crimson-red. The purple-red fall fruits open to reveal seeds with bright orange coats. Plant it in full sun or light shade in any well-drained soil. It can be grown in a shrub border, but it also makes a beautiful specimen, planted alone so that its beauty can be fully appreciated.

☼ ☀ ◊   Z4–9 H9–1
‡ to 6ft (2m) ↔ to 10ft (3m)

Euphorbia dulcis
PERENNIAL

This spreading perennial has upright stems with oblong-shaped, green leaves. The upper part of the stem is branched and covered with triangular leaves. In the fall the stems turn purple, and the leaves take on various shades of red, yellow, and orange. Yellow-green flowerheads are produced in the early summer. It is best in a moist, organic soil in light shade, but it does tolerate drier soils. It self-seeds freely. Good for a shady border and excellent for a woodland garden.

☀ ◊ ◗   Z4–9 H9–1
↔ to 12in (30cm)

Fothergilla gardenii
DECIDUOUS SHRUB

The witch alder is a small, bushy shrub with dark green, oval leaves. In the summer it produces cylindrical spikes of small white flowers. It is mainly grown for its fall color, when the leaves become infused with intense shades of red, yellow, and orange. It should be grown in a sunny location in moisture-retentive but well-drained, organic, acidic soil. It can be grown in partial shade but the color of the fall foliage will be less vibrant.

☀ ◊ ◗ *f*   Z4–8 H9–1
↔ to 3ft (1m)

Gaultheria tasmanica

EVERGREEN SHRUB

Originating in Tasmania, this is a dwarf, mat-forming shrub with small, glossy, dark green leaves. In the spring it produces bell-shaped, white flowers that are followed in the fall by bright red fruits. It is best planted in partial shade in moist, neutral or acidic soil, but it will tolerate some sun if the soil does not dry out. It is suitable for the front of a shady border or a woodland garden. It can also be planted in containers; use acidic soil mix, and do not let it dry out.

☀ ◑   Z8–9 H9–8

↕ to 3in (7cm) ↔ to 10in (25cm)

Hakonechloa macra 'Aureola'

PERENNIAL

This clump-forming Japanese grass has arching, slender, bright yellow leaves that are narrowly striped with green. They become red tinted in the fall. In the late summer and early fall it bears spiky flowerheads. Plant it in partial shade in fertile, moist but well-drained, organic soil. It is ideal for a woodland garden or for planting at the front of a mixed or herbaceous border. It also looks good in containers.

☀ ◊ ◑   Z5–9 H9–5

↕ to 16in (40cm) ↔ to 24in (60cm)

Helenium 'Bruno'

PERENNIAL

This upright perennial forms dense clumps of mid-green leaves. From the late summer to fall it produces abundant heads of deep red-crimson, daisylike flowers with chocolate-brown centers. Although the flower stems are sturdy, they may need staking on exposed sites. Grow it in a sunny border in any moisture-retentive but well-drained, fertile soil. To keep clumps vigorous and productive, divide them every two or three years.

☀ ◊ ◖   Z4–8 H8–1

‡to 30in (75cm) ↔to 20in (50cm)

Imperata cylindrica 'Rubra'

PERENNIAL

Japanese blood grass forms clumps of narrow green leaves that turn wine-red as the season progresses. By the fall, when fluffy, silvery flowerheads appear, the leaves have become crimson-scarlet. Grow in full sun or light shade in organic, moist but well-drained soil. Protect young plants with a winter mulch. Overcrowded clumps can be divided in the early spring. It is a good plant for woodland gardens, herbaceous borders, or containers.

☀ ☀ ◊ ◖   Z5–9 H9–3

‡↔to 20in (50cm)

Liquidambar styraciflua
DECIDUOUS TREE

The distinctive, deeply lobed leaves of sweet gum trees provide excellent fall color ranging from yellow to orange, purple, and crimson. These narrowly conical deciduous trees also feature attractive bark and spiky, spherical seedpods. Because they grow quite tall, they are best suited for medium to large gardens. There are a number of selections on the market: 'Worplesdon' has intense red, orange, and yellow leaves; 'Palo Alto' also has very fine fall color; 'Rotundiloba' has rounded lobes and no seedpods.

☼ ◊ ◑　　　　　　　　　　Z7–9 H9–7

‡ to 80ft (25m) ↔ to 40ft (12m)

Lonicera periclymenum 'Belgica'
CLIMBER

Early Dutch honeysuckle is a vigorous climber with bright red berries for fall interest. It has mid-green leaves and flowers in the spring and again in the late summer. The tubular flowers, white on the inside and red outside, are highly scented. It is ideal for growing through a tree or over a trellis; if given space to ramble, it seldom needs pruning. Grow it in full sun or partial shade in organic, moist but well-drained soil.

☼ ☀ ◊ ◑ *f*　　　　　　　　Z5–9 H9–5

‡ to 22ft (7m)

Malus 'Evereste'

DECIDUOUS TREE

Crabapples are appreciated in the fall for their ornamental fruit, which often lasts right through the winter, acting as a food supply for hungry birds. 'Evereste' has cherry-sized, orange-red fruit. In the spring the whole tree is covered in white blossoms that develop from pink buds. Its neat style and year-round interest makes this a good choice for small, sunny gardens; the blossoms will also pollinate apple trees. Trim crowded and wayward branches in the late winter to keep an open, pleasing shape.

☼ ◊ ◊   Z4–8 H8–4

↨ to 12ft (4m)

Malus x *schiedeckeri* 'Red Jade'

DECIDUOUS TREE

An attractive small tree with weeping branches, 'Red Jade' has bright pink buds that open in the spring to semi-double, pink-flushed white flowers. These are followed, in the fall, by a profusion of bright red, cherry-sized fruit. The leaves are bright green and glossy. Grow it in full sun in moist but well-drained, moderately fertile soil. It makes a beautiful specimen tree that is suitable for small gardens.

☼ ◊ ◊   Z5–8 H8–5

↨ to 12ft (4m) ↔ to 20ft (6m)

Nyssa sylvatica

DECIDUOUS TREE

The tupelo is a broad, cone-shaped tree, with slightly drooping lower branches, an interesting textured bark, and exuberant fall color. The dark green leaves turn vibrant yellow, orange, and finally red-crimson shades in mid- to late fall. Plant it in a sheltered site in full sun or partial shade in neutral to slightly acidic soil that is fertile and moisture retentive but well drained. It makes a gorgeous specimen tree.

☼ ☀ ◊ ◊   Z5–9 H9–7
‡ to 70ft (20m) ↔ to 30ft (10m)

Parrotia persica

DECIDUOUS TREE

The Persian ironwood is a shrubby tree with peeling gray and brown bark. The large glossy leaves put on a glorious fall display in shades of red, orange, and yellow. In the late winter or early spring small, spidery red flowers appear on the bare branches. Plant in full sun or partial shade in a good depth of fertile, moist but well-drained soil. The best fall color occurs on acidic soil, but it also tolerates alkaline conditions. A fine specimen tree, it develops great character with age.

☼ ☀ ◊ ◊   Z4–7 H7–1
‡ to 25ft (8m) ↔ to 30ft (10m)

Parthenocissus tricuspidata

CLIMBER

Boston ivy is a vigorous, woody climber with glossy, dark green leaves that are toothed and divided into three lobes. In the fall these turn gold, brilliant red, and purple before falling. It is great for covering a large, unattractive, or featureless wall or for growing through a tall, sturdy tree. Grow it in full sun or shade in fertile, well-drained soil that is rich in humus. Provide young plants with support until they are established.

☼ ◐ ● ◊ ◊   Z4–8 H8–1
‡ to 70ft (20m)

Prunus avium

DECIDUOUS TREE

The wild cherry, or gean, is a large, spreading tree with dark green leaves that are tinted bronze in the spring and turn red and gold in the fall. In the middle of the spring it bears clusters of white flowers, followed in late summer and fall by small, dark red fruit, which the birds love to eat. Plant it in full sunshine or partial shade in fertile, moist but well-drained soil. It is a fine specimen tree and is also useful in a larger garden for attracting wildlife.

☼ ◑ ◊ ◊   Z4–8 H8–1
‡ to 70ft (20m) ↔ to 30ft (10m)

Rhus typhina 'Dissecta'

DECIDUOUS SHRUB

The staghorn sumac gets its common name from the upright, velvet-covered branch tips that resemble antlers. In the summer upright spikes of small, yellow-green flowers turn dark crimson as they fruit. The ferny leaves turn shades of brilliant red, gold, and orange in the fall. Plant in full sun in fertile, moist but well-drained soil. If its spreading suckers are a nuisance, they can be dug out over the winter when the plant is dormant.

☀ ◊ ◗ Z3–8 H8–1

↕ to 12ft (4m) ↔ to 10ft (3m)

Rosa x *odorata* 'Mutabilis'

DECIDUOUS SHRUB

This slender shrub has purple-red stems and purple flushed, dark green leaves. The single, cup-shaped flowers open pale yellow, turning first pink and then deep red; they are borne over a long period from the summer to fall and have a wonderful fragrance. Plant it in a sheltered location in fertile, organic, moist but well-drained soil. It is normally grown as a shrub rose but will climb if it is provided with some support.

☀ ◊ ◗ *f* Z7–9 H9–7

↕↔ to 6ft (2m)

Rosa rugosa

DECIDUOUS SHRUB

Easygoing and vigorous, this repeat-flowering rose has robust, prickly stems and wrinkled, bright green leaves that turn yellow in the fall. The single, fragrant, dark red flowers are borne from early summer to fall. From the late summer they are accompanied by large, spherical, orange-red hips. Tolerant of a wide range of conditions, it prefers full sun or light shade and a moist but well-drained soil. It makes an excellent, intruder-proof hedge. Trim or prune it to shape in the late winter or early spring.

☼ ☀ ◊ ◖ *f*　　　　　Z2–9 H9–1

↕↔ to 6ft (2m)

Ruscus aculeatus

EVERGREEN SHRUB

Butcher's broom is a clump-forming plant with upright stems that bear very tough, spine-tipped, leaflike modified stems. From the late summer to winter female plants produce small, round, bright red berries. Male and female or hermaphrodite plants are needed to ensure fruiting. It grows in sun or deep shade and in any but waterlogged soil; it also tolerates dry soil. The cut stems can be used in flower arrangements.

☼ ☀ ◊ ◖ ◗　　　　　Z7–9 H9–7

↕ to 30in (75cm) ↔ to 3ft (1m)

Schizostylis coccinea

PERENNIAL

From the late summer to fall this cheerful plant produces shiny, bright red flowers on strong but slender stems, which are held above green, strap-shaped, almost evergreen leaves. Remove flowers as they fade. Grow in a sunny, sheltered location in fertile, moist soil, and protect the crowns with a mulch in the winter in cold or exposed gardens. It spreads freely; divide overcrowded clumps in the spring. Plant it in an herbaceous border or beside water. It is also good for cutting.

☀ ◐   Z7–9 H9–7

↕ to 20in (50cm) ↔ to 12in (30cm)

Sorbus aucuparia

DECIDUOUS TREE

The rowan is a small or medium-sized tree with mid-green leaves divided into small leaflets. In the spring it bears clusters of creamy-white flowers that are followed by bright red berries in the fall. They are very attractive to birds. The foliage turns red or yellow in the fall. Plant in full sun or dappled shade in moderately fertile, organic, well-drained soil. It is tolerant of a wide range of conditions and will grow happily on both acidic and slightly alkaline soils.

☀ ◑ ◊   Z4–7 H7–1

↕ to 50ft (15m) ↔ to 22ft (7m)

Sorbus commixta

DECIDUOUS TREE

Slightly smaller than *Sorbus aucuparia*, this tree has dark green leaves divided into many small, lance-shaped leaflets. The fall color is outstanding because the leaves become infused with brilliant shades of vivid red, yellow, and purple. In the late spring it bears clusters of white flowers that are followed by bright orange-red or red fall fruits. It should be planted in full sunshine or dappled shade in moderately fertile, organic, moist but well-drained soil.

☼ ☀ ◊ ◊   Z6–8 H8–6

‡ to 30ft (10m) ↔ to 22ft (7m)

Sorbus sargentiana

DECIDUOUS TREE

The large leaves of this slow-growing tree are divided into lance-shaped green leaflets that take on brilliant shades of red and orange in the fall. In the winter distinctive, bright red, sticky buds form. In the early summer it produces clusters of white flowers, followed by broad sprays of small, scarlet fall fruits. Plant it in a sunny location in organic, fertile, moist but well-drained soil. It makes a beautiful specimen tree and, like other sorbus, has several seasons of interest.

☼ ◊ ◊   Z5–7 H7–5

‡↔ to 30ft (10m)

Taxus baccata 'Fastigiata'
EVERGREEN TREE

Irish yew is a dense, strongly upright conifer that becomes columnar with age, adding structure to the garden and a good visual effect during the bare winter months. The dark, needlelike leaves give it an imposing presence and make it a good specimen plant. This female variety bears fleshy, bright red fruits in the late summer—the berries are poisonous so leave them for the birds. Slow-growing, it takes many years to outgrow its location; trim back any wayward shoots in the spring. Plant in a lightly shaded site.

☀ ◊ ◊   Z7–8 H8–7
‡ to 30ft (10m) ↔ to 12ft (4m)

Viburnum opulus
DECIDUOUS SHRUB

The European cranberry bush is a vigorous deciduous shrub that bears maplelike, lobed, mid-green leaves that turn red in the fall. It grows well in a sunny or partially shaded site. Bunches of spherical, bright red berries appear from the late summer to fall, and are much-loved by birds. The berries develop from the flat heads of showy white late-spring flowers; these also have wildlife value because they attract pollinating insects. 'Compactum' is a smaller, denser variety, growing to 5ft (1.5m) tall.

☼ ☀ ◊ ◊   Z3–8 H8–1
‡ to 15ft (5m) ↔ to 12ft (4m)

Vitis 'Brant'

CLIMBER

This vigorous, woody-stemmed vine is grown for its fall color and edible, blue-black grapes that ripen in the fall. The deeply lobed leaves are green throughout the summer, but in the fall take on vibrant shades of deep red and purple with yellow veins. It can be trained against a wall on supporting wires and is excellent on a pergola. Grow it in a warm, sheltered spot in full sun in well-drained, preferably neutral to alkaline soil.

☼ ◊   Z5–9 H9–5

↕ to 22ft (7m)

Vitis coignetiae

CLIMBER

Possibly one of the best vines for fall color. This rampant climber has large, heart-shaped, green leaves that turn vivid shades of bright red and crimson in the fall. It is ideal for covering a pergola, growing through a big tree, or for disguising a large, featureless wall. Plant it in full sun or partial shade in well-drained, neutral to alkaline soil. If it gets too large, prune it back to strong buds in the winter to within 2in (5cm) of the previous year's growth.

☼ ◐ ◊   Z5–9 H9–5

↕ to 50ft (15m)

Aster 'Little Carlow'

PERENNIAL

This is an upright, clump-forming aster that has oval to heart-shaped, dark green leaves. In early to mid fall violet blue flowers with yellow centers bloom in loose clusters 6–8in (15–20cm) wide. Ideal for the outer edge of a woodland garden or in cooler regions in a sunny mixed border. Grow it in partial shade or full sun in moist but well-drained soil. In the early summer, trim off the top third of the plant with shears to encourage a more compact, bushier shape.

☼ ◐ ◊   Z4–9 H9–2

↕ to 36in (90cm) ↔ to 18in (45cm)

Aster novi-belgii 'Peace'

PERENNIAL

This vigorous New York aster produces large, mauve-purple flowerheads from the late summer to fall. It is best planted at the back or middle of the herbaceous border in full sunshine and in very fertile, moist soil. It has strong stems so supports are not necessary. It should be cut back to the ground after flowering and covered with a layer of mulch for the winter. Divide every three years in the spring.

☼ ◊   Z4–8 H8–1

↕ to 36in (90cm) ↔ to 30in (75cm)

Berberis thunbergii 'Rose Glow'

DECIDUOUS SHRUB

This is a vigorous, dense, thorny shrub with small, rounded, reddish-purple leaves. Later in the fall white and pink flecks appear on the leaves, spreading so the outer leaves become variegated. In the late spring it bears small clusters of red-tinged, yellow flowers. In the fall the leaves turn orange and red. It makes a dense hedge that grows to medium height; pruning should be delayed until after flowering. Plant in full sun or partial shade in well-drained soil.

☼ ☀ ◊   Z5–8 H8–5

↕↔ to 6ft (2m)

Billardiera longiflora

CLIMBER

The climbing blueberry has wiry stems that will climb over any suitable support. It has narrow, lance-shaped dark green leaves. The green, bell-shaped flowers of summer are followed by purplish-blue, egg-shaped fruit in the fall; some plants bear pink, red, or white fruit. Grow in a warm, sheltered site in full sun or light shade in organic, neutral to acidic soil. In very cold areas grow in a greenhouse in containers with acidic potting soil.

☼ ☀ ◊   Z8–9 H9–8

↕ to 6ft (2m)

Callicarpa bodinieri 'Profusion'

DECIDUOUS SHRUB

The beautyberry is a striking bush with upright branches and large, pale green leaves that are tinted bronze in the spring. It produces pale pink flowers in midsummer but is grown mainly for its colorful fruit that look just like clusters of shining, bright violet beads. These stay on the bare branches after leaf fall. Grow in full sunshine or light shade in well-drained, fertile soil. Planting in groups will maximize fruiting.

☼ ☀ ◊ ◖   Z5–8 H8–3
‡ to 10ft (3m) ↔ to 8ft (2.5m)

Cercidiphyllum japonicum 'Rotfuchs'

DECIDUOUS TREE

The katsura tree is a fast-growing, spreading tree with small, heart-shaped, mid-green leaves. These are bronze when young, but the tree is grown mainly for its fall color with the leaves turning to pale yellow, orange, red, or pink before they fall. At this time, the tree also exudes a "burnt-sugar" perfume. The best foliage colors are seen on neutral to acid soils. Grow in full sun or partial shade in fertile, moist but well-drained soil with plenty of depth for the roots.

☼ ☀ ◊ ◖   Z4–8 H8–1
‡ to 70ft (20m) ↔ to 50ft (15m)

Colchicum agrippinum
BULBOUS PERENNIAL

This fall-flowering colchicum has funnel-shaped, purplish-pink flowers that are marked with a conspicuous checkerboard pattern. It has upright, slightly wavy, strap-shaped leaves that appear in the early spring but disappear by summer. The corms should be planted 4in (10cm) deep in the summer or early fall. Grow in an open situation in full sun in deep, fertile, well-drained soil. It is suitable for a rock garden, a trough, or can be grown in a container.

☼ ◊　　　　　　　　　Z4–9 H9–1

↕ to 6in (15cm) ↔ to 4in (10cm)

Crocus medius
BULBOUS PERENNIAL

This is an attractive dwarf crocus with funnel-shaped, bright purple flowers in the late fall. The narrow leaves, which are green with a silvery-white line down the center, appear with or just after the flowers. It is suitable for naturalizing in grass or for planting in a rock garden. Grow it in full sunshine in gritty, very well-drained, poor to moderately fertile soil. It prefers dry conditions during the summer when it is dormant.

☼ ◊　　　　　　　　　Z3–8 H8–1

↕ to 3in (8cm) ↔ to 1in (2.5cm)

Gaultheria mucronata '**Mulberry Wine**'

EVERGREEN SHRUB

This bushy shrub has shining, spine-tipped, dark green leaves. In the late spring and summer it bears small white flowers that are followed in the fall by glossy fruits that ripen to dark purple. Grow in partial shade in acidic, organic, moist soil. Grow male and female plants together to ensure fruiting. Gaultherias associate well with heathers and are suitable for woodland gardens. There are also varieties with pink, red, or white fruits.

☀ ◐   Z8–9 H9–8

↔ to 4ft (1.2m)

Liriope muscari

PERENNIAL

Lilyturf is a densely clump-forming, evergreen perennial with narrow, strap-shaped, dark green leaves. In the late summer and early fall it produces long, slender spikes of small, violet-mauve flowers. Plant it in partial or full shade in acid to neutral, preferably moist but well-drained soil. It will tolerate dry, shady conditions. Use it as ground cover in a woodland garden or for planting toward the front of a border. Overcrowded clumps can be divided in the spring.

☀ ◐ ◐ ◐   Z6–10 H11–1

↕ to 12in (30cm) ↔ to 18in (45cm)

Sorbus reducta
DECIDUOUS SHRUB

The upright, suckering stems of this unusual shrublike rowan spread to form a dense, low thicket. The finely divided leaves turn red and purple in the fall. In the spring it bears clusters of small white flowers followed by pink-flushed white berries. Plant in an open site in full sun in organic, moderately fertile, well-drained soil. It is good for small town gardens and roadside situations because it tolerates pollution. Pull out unwanted stems when still young and soft.

☼ ◊　　　　　　Z5–8 H8–4
‡↔to 12in (30cm)

Tricyrtis formosana
PERENNIAL

This vigorous perennial spreads by means of underground stems. In the fall it produces small, pinkish-purple flowers, patterned with purple spots. It has slightly hairy, branched stems and glossy, dark green leaves. Plant it in a sheltered, shady situation in moist but well-drained, organic soil. In cold gardens it needs a deep mulch of straw or leaf mold to protect it from hard frost. It is an excellent plant for a damp woodland garden or a shady border.

☼ ☀ ◊ ◊　　　　Z6–9 H9–6
‡ to 3ft (1m) ↔to 18in (45cm)

Aconitum carmichaelii 'Arendsii'

PERENNIAL

This monkshood creates a striking display with its tall spikes of deep blue flowers that appear from early to mid-fall. An upright plant with deeply lobed, dark green leaves, it is suitable for a woodland garden and is also successful in a shaded mixed or herbaceous border. Plant in partial shade and in moist, fertile soil. It does best in a site sheltered from strong winds; support the stems with canes. All parts are toxic.

☼ ◊ ◖ ◖   Z3–8 H8–3
‡ to 5ft (1.5m) ↔ to 12in (30cm)

Aster x *frikartii* 'Wunder von Stäfa'

PERENNIAL

A superb plant for the middle of a border, this tall aster has dark green leaves and stiffly upright stems. Bright blue flowers with yellow centers are produced from the late summer until early fall. Plant in moderately fertile, well-drained, preferably alkaline soil in full sun. After flowering cut stems back to the ground and apply a layer of mulch. It can be increased quickly by division in the spring.

☼ ◊   Z5–8 H8–1
‡ to 28in (70cm) ↔ to 16in (40cm)

Ceanothus 'Autumnal Blue'

EVERGREEN SHRUB

The majority of California lilacs flower during the spring or early summer, but this one produces clusters of small, vivid blue flowers in late summer to early fall. It has broadly oval, glossy, dark green leaves. Plant it in full sun with some protection from cold winds in fertile, well-drained soil. It rarely needs pruning, but if wayward shoots spoil the symmetry of the bush, they should be removed when it has finished flowering.

☼ ◊ Z9–10 H10–9

↕↔ to 10ft (3m)

Gentiana sino-ornata

PERENNIAL

The beautiful fall gentian overwinters as a rosette of glossy, dark green leaves. Low, spreading shoots appear in the spring, each developing at its tip an upward-pointing, deep blue flower in the fall. The base of the flower's throat is greenish white, marked with distinct purplish-blue lines radiating from the center. Plant it in organic, moist but well-drained, acidic or neutral soil with some shade from strong summer sunshine. It is suitable for a rock garden or trough.

☼ ◊ ♦ Z5–7 H7–5

↕ to 2in (5cm) ↔ to 12in (30cm)

Hordeum jubatum

PERENNIAL

The squirrel-tail grass is a tufted grass with arching, narrow, green leaves. The attractive, nodding flowerheads with their long, feathery bristles appear in the summer. They are green when young, turning pale beige in the fall. Plant in full sun in well-drained, moderately fertile soil in an herbaceous border or wild garden. It is also grown for cutting, which should be done before the flowerheads have set seed.

☼ ◊　　　　　　　　　　　Z4–8 H8–1
‡ to 24in (60cm) ↔ to 12in (30cm)

Kniphofia 'Percy's Pride'

PERENNIAL

This red hot poker forms clumps of tough, slender, arching leaves and produces stout-stemmed heads of tubular flowers in the late summer and early fall. Green in bud, the flowers open greenish yellow and become cream with age. Grow in a sunny or partially shaded site in deep, fertile, moist but well-drained soil. Cover young plants with a protective mulch in their first winter, and cut back old growth in the spring.

☼ ☀ ◊ ◊　　　　　　　　　　Z6–9 H9–6
‡ to 3ft (1m) ↔ to 20in (50cm)

Miscanthus sinensis 'Silberfeder'

PERENNIAL

This tall grass forms a large clump of arching, mid-green leaves, and in early and mid-fall upright stems bearing silvery-beige flowerheads. Suitable for most soils, it grows best in full sun in moderately fertile, moist but well-drained soil. The flowerheads can be left in place during the winter but should be cut down to the ground, together with any dead growth, in the early spring. This grass is easily increased by dividing established clumps in the spring.

☼ ◊ ◐   Z6–9 H9–1

‡ to 8ft (2.5m) ↔ to 4ft (1.2m)

Miscanthus sinensis 'Zebrinus'

PERENNIAL

Zebra grass will bring drama and height to a mixed or herbaceous border or a gravel bed. It bears tall, straplike foliage marked with yellow horizontal bands. This grass forms a large clump and produces spikes of silky, maroon flowerheads in the fall. Leave the foliage and flowers to dry to a buff color during the fall and winter, and then cut them down in the spring to make way for new growth.

☼ ◑ ◊ ◐   Z6–9 H9–1

‡ to 4ft (1.2m) ↔ to 18in (45cm)

Panicum virgatum 'Heavy Metal'

PERENNIAL

This is a particularly upright-growing switch grass. In the late summer it produces beautiful, nodding spikes of small, purple-green flowers. The metallic, bluish-green leaves turn golden yellow in the late fall and finally light brown in the winter. It has a beautiful winter presence in the garden, especially when the flowerheads are left in place. Grow in a sunny site in well-drained, moderately fertile soil. Cut back before growth begins in the early spring.

☼ ◊   Z5–9 H9–1

‡ to 3ft (1m) ↔ to 30in (75cm)

Pennisetum alopecuroides 'Hameln'

PERENNIAL

Fountain grass is a clump-forming plant with flat, pointed, dark evergreen leaves. 'Hameln' is compact, and in the summer and early fall it bears long, arching spikes of pale green flowers. The leaves turn yellow before they die down, and the flowers age to a warm, pale gray-brown. Grow in full sun in moderately fertile, well-drained soil. Provide a protective winter mulch in cold areas, or grow in containers. Cut back in the spring before growth begins.

☼ ◊   Z6–9 H9–6

‡ to 5ft (1.5m) ↔ to 4ft (1.2m)

Prunus laurocerasus '**Caucasica**'

EVERGREEN SHRUB

This reliable cherry laurel is a broad-leaf shrub with dense, glossy, dark green foliage. Dependable all year-round, it is particularly nice in the fall for the small red fruits that ripen to black, and also in mid- to late spring for its abundant spikes of white flowers, which sometimes repeat in the fall. Plant as a specimen shrub or boundary hedge in a sunny or partially shaded site. It establishes quickly and will tolerate hard pruning. 'Otto Luyken' is a smaller variety, growing to 3ft (1m) tall.

☼ ☀ ◊ ◆   Z6–9 H9–6

↕↔ to 25ft (8m)

Woodwardia radicans

PERENNIAL FERN

The European chain fern is a tall, architectural plant with large and arching, dark green, feathery fronds. It is evergreen, and its leaves take on coppery tints over the winter. It makes an impressive plant for a large pot, performing best in a potting mix composed of fine pine bark, grit, and leaf mold. In the garden, place it in a damp, shady spot. It should survive outdoors easily in mild areas, otherwise mulch with straw. The arching fronds may take root at their tips, making new plants.

☀ ◆   Z8–9 H9–8

↕ to 6ft (2m) ↔ to 10ft (3m)

Ajania pacifica

PERENNIAL

Related to chrysanthemums, this low-growing, mound-forming perennial or small shrub has attractive lobed green leaves highlighted by a silver line around the outer edges. In the early fall small yellow flowers bloom in dense clusters. It spreads slowly and makes good ground cover in mixed borders or rock gardens. It thrives in well-drained soil in full sun and tolerates poor soil and drought, once established.

☀ ◊ ◊   Z5–9 H9–1
‡ to 12in (30cm) ↔ to 36in (90cm)

Betula pendula 'Tristis'

DECIDUOUS TREE

This elegant, fast-growing tree has white bark and cascading branches bearing diamond-shaped, dark green leaves that turn bright golden-yellow in the fall. It bears long, hanging, yellow catkins in the early spring. With its narrow crown it is ideal for a small garden and casts little shade. Plant it as a specimen tree or in a group in full sun or light, dappled shade. It tolerates a range of soils but prefers it moist but well-drained and moderately fertile.

☀ ☼ ◊ ◊   Z2–7 H7–1
‡ to 80ft (25m) ↔ to 30ft (10m)

Calluna vulgaris 'Robert Chapman'

EVERGREEN SHRUB

This heather has dense, golden-yellow foliage and spikes of purple-pink flowers in the late summer. In the winter the leaves take on orange and red shades, retaining the color until the new growth emerges the following spring. Plant in a group to maximize its effect; it associates well with other heathers with different foliage tints. Grow in sun in well-drained, acidic soil that is organic. Shear off flowered shoots in the spring to keep it compact.

☀ ◊   Z5–7 H7–5

‡ to 10in (25cm) ↔ to 26in (65cm)

Chrysanthemum 'Pennine Alfie'

PERENNIAL

In the early fall this chrysanthemum has bright yellow, semidouble flowers with spoon-shaped petals and bright red bases. Plant it in a sunny border in fertile, moist but well-drained soil. Support the stems with canes. Dig up plants after flowering and overwinter in frost-free conditions. Plant outside in the spring after the final frost, and raise new plants from basal cuttings.

☀ ◊ ◊   Z4–9 H9–1

‡ to 4ft (1.2m) ↔ to 30in (75cm)

Chrysanthemum 'Wendy'

PERENNIAL

A spray chrysanthemum with light bronze, double flowers in the early fall. The outer petals point downward like an umbrella. For extra large flowers remove all but four of the buds. Support stems with canes. Lift plants after flowering, and overwinter in frost-free conditions. Plant outdoors in the spring once frosts are finished, or raise new plants from basal cuttings taken in the winter. Grow in reasonably fertile, moist but well-drained soil in a sunny location.

☼ ◊ ◊   Z4–9 H9–1
↕ to 4ft (1.2m) ↔ to 30in (75cm)

Clematis 'Bill MacKenzie'

CLIMBER

In the late summer and early fall this vigorous climber produces hanging, bell-shaped flowers up to 3in (8cm) across. The blooms are yellow with red anthers and are followed by feathery, silvery seedheads. Plant in fertile, organic, moist but well-drained soil with the plant's base in shade and the upper growth in sun or light shade. Provide support. In the spring cut back the previous year's growth to a pair of strong buds about 8in (20cm) from the base.

☼ ☼ ◊ ◊   Z6–11 H9–6
↕ to 22ft (7m)

Clematis rehderiana

CLIMBER

One of the more unusual species of clematis with clusters of small, nodding, primrose yellow flowers that smell like cowslips. It flowers from the middle of the summer to fall. Plant in fertile, organic, moist but well-drained soil in full sun or partial shade but with the roots shaded and kept cool with a gravel mulch. Grow it on supports against a fence or wall, over a pergola, or into a tree. Cut back hard in the spring, and trim each shoot to a pair of strong buds 8in (20cm) from the base.

☼ ☀ ◊ ◐ *f*   Z6–9 H9–6

↕ to 22ft (7m)

Clematis tangutica

CLIMBER

This late-flowering clematis has bluish-green, divided leaves and from midsummer to fall produces large numbers of hanging, bell-shaped, bright yellow flowers. They are followed by silky seedheads that last into the winter. Grow it up a trellis, through a small tree, or allow it to scramble over a bank as ground cover. Plant in fertile, organic, moist but well-drained soil in full sun or partial shade with the roots in cool shade. Cut back hard in the spring to within 8in (20cm) of the base.

☼ ☀ ◊ ◐   Z5–11 H9–6

↕ to 20ft (6m)

Cotoneaster frigidus 'Fructu Luteo'

DECIDUOUS SHRUB

The upright stems of this shrubby or treelike cotoneaster arch gracefully as it matures. The narrow leaves are dull green but develop golden tints in the fall. In the summer the branches are wreathed with white flowers that are followed by creamy yellow fruit in the fall. Grow in sun or light dappled shade in any well-drained, moderately fertile soil. Use as an ornamental screen, for the back of a shrub border, or as a specimen.

☀ ◑ ◊   Z7–8 H8–7

↔ to 30ft (10m)

Cotoneaster 'Rothschildianus'

EVERGREEN SHRUB

This vigorous, spreading shrub has narrow, pale green leaves and clusters of white flowers along the arching branches in the early summer. In the fall it produces clusters of attractive golden yellow fruit. It is an extremely beautiful shrub for the back of a mixed or shrub border and, where there is room, makes an attractive specimen. Plant it in full sun or partial shade in any moderately fertile, well-drained soil.

☀ ◑ ◊ ◊   Z6–8 H8–6

↔ to 15ft (5m)

Ginkgo biloba
DECIDUOUS TREE

The maidenhair tree makes an elegant addition to medium to large gardens, It is valued for its unmistakable, butterfly-shaped, wavy-edged, bright green leaves, which take on lovely buttery yellow tints in autumn before they fall. Female trees produce small fruits that are messy and have an unpleasant odor, so male varieties are preferable. Tolerant of most well-drained, fertile soils. Prune out dead, diseased, crossing, or wayward shoots in late winter.

☼ ◊ ◐   Z5–9 H9–3

‡ to 100ft (30m) ↔ to 25ft (8m)

Gleditsia triacanthos '**Sunburst**'
DECIDUOUS TREE

This golden-leaf honey locust is a conical tree with open, spreading branches. The delicate, ferny leaves are golden yellow in the spring, later turning green, then brilliant yellow in the fall. 'Sunburst' is less vigorous and thorny than the species and makes a beautiful specimen for smaller gardens, especially in urban situations because it tolerates pollution. Plant it in full sun in any well-drained, fertile soil.

☼ ◊   Z3–7 H7–1

‡ to 40ft (12m) ↔ to 30ft (10m)

Hamamelis virginiana
DECIDUOUS SHRUB

Common witch hazel is an upright bush with oval green leaves that turn bright yellow in the fall. As the leaves begin to fall, small clusters of spidery yellow flowers are produced. Plant it in full sunshine or partial shade in moderately fertile, moist but well-drained, neutral to acidic soil. It prefers an open site but with some shelter from strong wind. Grow it as a specimen, at the back of a shrub border, or in a woodland garden.

☼ ◐ ◊ ◓   Z3–8 H8–1
↕↔to 12ft (4m)

Helichrysum splendidum
EVERGREEN SHRUB

This clump-forming bush has white, woolly stems and masses of tiny, silver-gray leaves. The deep yellow flowerheads appear at the tips of upright stems from the late summer to fall. They can be cut and dried for winter arrangements. It is drought tolerant and excellent for a hot, sunny bank or a mixed or herbaceous border. Grow in full sun in very well-drained, poor to moderately fertile soil. Trim each year in the spring to keep it compact. It may not survive cold, wet winters.

☼ ◊   Z9–11 H11–9
↕↔to 4ft (1.2m)

Ilex x *altaclerensis* 'Golden King'

EVERGREEN SHRUB

This variegated holly is a compact, evergreen shrub with glossy, dark green leaves edged in gold; the leaf margins may be smooth or softly toothed. The flowers are insignificant but develop into red berries in the fall. It is a wonderful shrub, ideal during the colder months when it provides for birds, which love hollies for their fruit and for the shelter they provide. Plant in full sun or partial shade. Trimmed each spring, hollies may be transformed into interesting shapes.

☼ ◐ ◑ ◊ ◊   Z7–9 H9–7

↕ to 20ft (30m) ↔ to 12ft (4m)

Kirengeshoma palmata

PERENNIAL

This is a clump-forming perennial with dark stems bearing deeply lobed, slightly hairy, pale green leaves. In the late summer and early fall it produces nodding, tubular, pale yellow flowers that have a waxy texture. Plant it in a shady situation in moist, acidic soil enriched with leaf mold. It is an elegant plant for a shady border or woodland garden and looks especially beautiful at the sides of streams or pools.

☼ ◊   Z5–8 H8–5

↕ to 3ft (1m) ↔ to 24in (60cm)

Liquidambar styraciflua 'Golden Treasure'

DECIDUOUS TREE

A slow-growing tree, this variegated sweet gum is grown mainly for its foliage. The deeply lobed, maplelike leaves have rich yellow margins, and in the late fall they take on dramatic tints as they turn red and purple with golden margins. It tolerates partial shade, but the best fall color develops in full sun. Plant in neutral to acidic, moderately fertile soil that is moist but well-drained.

☼ ☀ ◊ ◖   Z7–9 H9–7

‡ to 30ft (10m) ↔ to 20ft (6m)

Malus 'Golden Hornet'

DECIDUOUS TREE

An attractive crabapple, 'Golden Hornet' is valued for its spherical golden-yellow fruit that appears in the fall and remain on the bare branches well into the winter. In the spring it bears masses of white flowers that open from pink buds. Plant it in full sun, in fertile, moist but well-drained soil. It is best grown as a specimen tree, positioned where its pretty fruit can be fully appreciated. The slightly smaller variety, *M. calocarpa*, has bright red fruit.

☼ ◊ ◖   Z5–8 H8–5

‡ to 30ft (10m) ↔ to 25ft (8m)

Phygelius x *rectus* 'Moonraker'

EVERGREEN SHRUB

This is a long-flowering, small shrub with glossy, dark green leaves and long, upright spikes of hanging, creamy yellow flowers from midsummer to fall. Plant in full sun in fertile, moist but well-drained soil. Deadhead regularly to prolong flowering. Excellent in a mixed or herbaceous border and also good against a warm, sunny wall. In cold areas it may lose its leaves and die back, but it usually grows from the base in the spring.

☼ ◊ ◖   Z8–9 H9–8

‡ to 3ft (1m) ↔ to 4ft (1.2m)

Sambucus racemosa 'Plumosa Aurea'

DECIDUOUS SHRUB

The deeply cut, yellow leaves of this red-berried elder flush bronze when young. The creamy flowers are borne in clusters in the spring and are followed by red fruits in the summer. Plant this bushy shrub in a lightly shaded site since the foliage may scorch in bright sun. Grow in moderately fertile, moist but well-drained soil. For the best foliage effects, prune it hard in the spring to within a few buds of the base, then feed and mulch.

☼ ◊ ◖   Z3–7 H7–1

‡↔ to 10ft (3m)

Sorbus 'Joseph Rock'

DECIDUOUS TREE

Suitable for the smaller garden, 'Joseph Rock' grows quickly once established, forming a crown of upright branches. The finely divided, bright green leaves turn brilliant shades of orange, red, and purple during the fall when it also bears crops of particularly attractive, creamy-yellow berries that age to golden yellow. There are clusters of white flowers in the spring. Plant it in full sunshine or partial shade in fertile, moist but well-drained, organic soil.

☼ ☀ ◊ ▲   Z7–8 H8–7

↕ to 30ft (10m) ↔ to 22ft (7m)

Sternbergia lutea

BULBOUS PERENNIAL

Sternbergias, sometimes incorrectly called autumn daffodils, bear deep yellow, goblet-shaped flowers in fall. The narrow, dark green leaves appear with, or just after, the flowers. Plant bulbs in late summer, in a warm, sunny site, in moderately fertile, well drained soil. They are excellent plants for a rock garden or perennial border, but are also suitable for a container or a trough filled with gritty compost. If conditions are suitable, it will spread to form clumps; divide them at intervals and create new plantings.

☼ ◊   Z7–9 H9–6

↕ to 6in (15cm) ↔ to 4in (10cm)

Tricyrtis ohsumiensis

PERENNIAL

The toad lily is a clump-forming perennial with arching, slightly hairy stems and pale green leaves. In the early fall it produces star-shaped, primrose yellow flowers covered with numerous tiny brown spots. Plant in a sheltered location in deep or partial shade and in moist, leafy, organic, well-drained soil. It is excellent for a damp woodland or a shady border. In cold areas mulch with leaf mold or straw in the winter.

☼ ❂ ◊ ◐   Z6–9 H9–6

‡ to 20in (50cm) ↔ to 9in (23cm)

Ulmus glabra 'Lutescens'

DECIDUOUS TREE

With its resistance to Dutch elm disease, the golden elm is a viable garden tree. Left to grow, it becomes a large, round canopy with spreading branches, but it can easily be pollarded (cut back to a stump) every two to three years to keep it within bounds for a small garden. It responds to frequent cutting by sending out long branches clothed in its fine golden leaves, which take on lovely yellow shades in the fall before dropping. The foliage contrasts well with other trees. It is tolerant of coastal conditions.

☼ ❂ ◊   Z3–9 H8–2

‡ to 130ft (40m) ↔ to 80ft (25m)

Acer campestre
DECIDUOUS TREE

The field maple is a very underused tree that is ideal for planting in medium-sized gardens. It has a rounded crown of lobed, dark green leaves that take on fall tints of apricot yellow and, in frosty falls, shades of orange and red. It is very hardy and tolerates pollution, clay and shallow, alkaline soils. It can also be included in mixed hedges and wildlife gardens. Plant it in full sun or partial shade in any fertile, moist but well-drained soil.

☼ ☀ ◊ ◑   Z6–8 H8–4
↕ to 25ft (8m) ↔ to 12ft (4m)

Acer platanoides 'Palmatifidum'
DECIDUOUS TREE

An attractive form of Norway maple, this tree has five-lobed leaves with the lobes drawn out into fine points. In the fall the leaves turn brilliant shades of orange and red. The conspicuous clusters of small flowers emerge in the spring before the leaves. It is a large tree and needs plenty of space. Plant it in larger gardens in an open situation in full sunshine or partial shade in any fertile, moist but well-drained soil.

☼ ☀ ◊ ◑   Z3–7 H7–1
↕ to 70ft (20m) ↔ to 30ft (10m)

Chrysanthemum 'Amber Enbee Wedding'

PERENNIAL

From the late summer to mid-fall this upright chrysanthemum produces warm golden-amber flowers with yellow-green centers. It is excellent for late color in a mixed or herbaceous border. Grow in full sun in moist but well-drained, neutral to slightly acid soil that has been enriched with well-rotted organic matter. Support the stems with stakes to prevent them from falling over in wind and heavy rain.

☼ ◊ ◊   Z4–9 H9–1
‡ to 4ft (1.2m) ↔ to 30in (75cm)

Cotinus 'Flame'

DECIDUOUS SHRUB

Primarily grown for its stunning fall color, this bushy shrub or small tree has oval, light green leaves that turn a brilliant orange-red. In hot summers its sprays of tiny flowers hover like a smoky haze above the foliage. Grow in a shrub border or as a specimen in sun or light shade in moist but well-drained, moderately fertile soil. Cut back hard in the spring for the best foliage effects, and feed and mulch after pruning.

☼ ☀ ◊ ◊   Z5–8 H8–5
‡ to 20ft (6m) ↔ to 15ft (5m)

Euphorbia griffithii 'Fireglow'

PERENNIAL

The upright stems of this spurge are red when young and covered with dark green, red-veined leaves. In the early summer it produces clusters of yellow flowerheads surrounded by orange-red bracts. The leaves turn fiery orange and red in the fall. Plant in light dappled shade in moist, organic soil. It is good for woodland gardens or large shady borders. It can become invasive. The milky sap may cause an allergic skin reaction.

☼ ◐ ◖   Z4–9 H9–2

↕ to 3ft (1m) ↔ to 20in (50cm)

Hamamelis vernalis 'Sandra'

DECIDUOUS SHRUB

This vernal witch hazel has young purple leaves that gradually turn green as spring progresses, then in the fall they assume glorious shades of orange and red. The spidery yellow or reddish-yellow flowers appear on the bare shoots during the late winter and early spring. Plant it in full sun or partial shade in neutral to acidic, moist but well-drained soil. It does best in a site that is not exposed to strong winds. It will grow on deep soils over chalk.

☼ ◑ ◐ ◖   Z4–8 H9–5

↕↔ to 15ft (5m)

Hippophae rhamnoides
DECIDUOUS SHRUB

Sea buckthorn is a vigorous shrub with narrow, silvery gray-green leaves and spiny branches. Inconspicuous spring flowers are followed in the fall by clusters of shining orange fruit on female plants. Grow male and female plants together to ensure fruiting. Grow in a mixed border or as an intruder-proof hedge. Plant in full sun in moist but well-drained soil. It thrives in coastal areas and tolerates exposed sites. If it becomes too large, it can be pruned back hard in the late summer or when dormant.

☼ ◊ ◑　　　　　　　　Z3–8 H8–1

‡↔to 20ft (6m)

Malus tschonoskii
DECIDUOUS TREE

Prized for its fall color, this vigorous tree has a flame-shaped crown of rounded, glossy green leaves. It flowers in the spring, bearing pink-flushed white flowers followed by red-tinged, yellow-green fruit. In the fall, the leaves take on spectacular shades of orange, scarlet, and purple. Plant it in full sun in moderately fertile, moist but well-drained soil. It makes a beautiful specimen tree for small to medium-sized gardens.

☼ ☀ ◊ ◑　　　　　　　Z5–8 H8–5

‡ to 40ft (12m) ↔ to 22ft (7m)

Physalis alkekengi

PERENNIAL

The Chinese lantern is a vigorously spreading perennial with triangular to diamond-shaped, green leaves on upright stems. The nodding, creamy-white flowers appear in midsummer and are followed by orange-red, papery pods that enclose orange fruits. The fruit is edible when ripe. Plant it in full sun or partial shade in fertile, well-drained soil. It can be grown in a border and cut for dried arrangements. It can self-seed and become invasive in some regions.

☼ ◐ ◊   Z3–9 H8–1
↕ to 30in (75cm) ↔ to 36in (90cm)

Rosa moyesii 'Geranium'

DECIDUOUS SHRUB

'Geranium' is a more compact form of a rather vigorous species. It has strong, arching stems and delicately divided green leaves. In the summer it bears single, cup-shaped, bright red flowers, that are followed by spectacular bright orange-red, flask-shaped hips in the fall. It is good for a sunny mixed border or wild garden. Plant it in fertile, organic, moist but well-drained soil. To keep it compact, cut back the main stems by up to a third after flowering.

☼ ◊ ◐   Z6–9 H9–1
↕ to 10ft (3m) ↔ to 8ft (2.5m)

Stipa arundinacea

PERENNIAL

Pheasant's tail grass is an evergreen that forms a loose tuft of arching, leathery, dark green leaves. As the season progresses, the leaves begin to exhibit orange streaks, and by winter the whole clump has turned russet-brown. In the summer arching spikes of purplish-green flowers appear that also turn golden orange as they mature. Plant in full sun or partial shade in moderately fertile, well-drained soil. Cut back dead foliage and flowerheads in the spring.

☼ ☀ ◊   Z8–11 H11–1
‡ to 5ft (1.5m) ↔ to 4ft (1.2m)

Zelkova serrata

DECIDUOUS TREE

The Japanese zelkova is an elegant tree with wide-spreading branches that makes a fine specimen for a large garden. At maturity the gray bark peels to reveal paler orange bark underneath. The coarsely toothed, dark green leaves rustle in the breeze and have wonderful fall color in shades of yellow, orange, and red. Plant it in full sun or partial shade in deep, fertile, moist but well-drained soil. Choose a site that will lend some protection from cold, dry winds when young.

☼ ☀ ◊ ◑   Z5–9 H9–5
‡ to 100ft (30m) ↔ to 80ft (25m)

WINTER

The dark, cold months of winter need not be without cheer. Many plants flower in winter, and while few have large and exuberant blooms, several are unsurpassed for scent— the witch hazels (*Hamamelis*), wintersweet (*Chimonanthus*) and shrubby honeysuckles are among them. Mahonias produce large sprays of highly fragrant flowers in the very depths of winter and the scented white flowers of *Viburnum farreri* appear in all but the coldest spells.

Consider too the many brightly foliaged evergreens that bring living colour to the winter garden— and provide a backdrop all year round—such as the variegated hollies, *Euonymus fortunei* and skimmias bedecked with buds and berries. Some, such as the heaths and heathers (*Erica* and *Calluna*), assume the most vivid shades of orange, gold and red in winter, often prompted or enhanced by periods of very intense cold.

BARK AND SEEDHEADS

This is the best time to appreciate the branch structure of deciduous trees and enjoy the colour and texture of their bark, so often overlooked when trees are in full leaf. The snake bark maples, such as *Acer grosseri* var. *hersii*, are striped green and white and the peeling papery bark of *A. griseum* glows coppery red in low winter light. Young stems of dogwoods also look dramatic at this time: vibrant red in *Cornus sanguinea* 'Winter Beauty' and *C. alba* 'Sibirica', while those of *C. alba* 'Kesselringii' are purple.

The dried seedheads of many plants have their part to play, notably the silvery heads of pampas grass (*Cortaderia*). Leave them to stand after the autumn clear up, they look stunning when rimmed with winter frost. Any seeds will be appreciated by the birds, which will also be lured into the garden by berries lingering on pyracanthas and cotoneasters.

Abeliophyllum distichum
DECIDUOUS SHRUB

The white forsythia has spreading branches covered with oval, dark green leaves in the summer. In the late winter and early spring it carries clusters of small, white flowers on bare branches that are invaluable for bringing fragrance into the winter garden. It performs best if trained against a sunny wall in a sheltered site, but it can also be planted in a mixed border or as a freestanding shrub. Grow it in full sun in fertile, well-drained soil.

☼ ◊ *f*   Z5–9 H9–1
↔ to 5ft (1.5m)

Betula papyrifera
DECIDUOUS TREE

The paper birch has pure white bark that peels off in large sheets to expose the new, pale orange-brown bark underneath. Yellow, hanging catkins appear in the spring, and the oval, dark green leaves turn attractive shades of yellow and orange in the fall. Plant it as a specimen tree; the white bark is seen at its best against a warm red, brick wall or a dark background of evergreen shrubs. Grow in full sun or light shade in moderately fertile, moist but well-drained soil.

☼ ☀ ◊ ◑   Z2–7 H7–1
↕ to 70ft (20m) ↔ to 30ft (10m)

Galanthus elwesii
BULBOUS PERENNIAL

This is bigger than the common snowdrop in all its parts. It bears large, honey-scented, white flowers with green blotches in late winter. It is a robust plant with broad, slightly twisted, waxy, bluish-green leaves. Plant bulbs in the early fall in partial shade in organic, moist but well-drained soil. It does particularly well in alkaline soil. Grow in a woodland garden, naturalized in grass, or at the front of a mixed or herbaceous border. Divide large clumps after flowering while still in leaf.

☀ ◊ ◐ *f*　　　　　　　Z3–9 H9–1

↕ to 12in (30cm) ↔ to 3in (8cm)

Galanthus nivalis
BULBOUS PERENNIAL

The common snowdrop is a small plant with narrow, waxy leaves and hanging, sweetly scented flowers in the winter. Plant the bulbs in the early fall. It can be used beneath trees or shrubs, naturalized in grass, or in a rock garden. It grows best in partial shade in organic, moist but well-drained soil, including alkaline soil. In suitable conditions it will self-seed freely to form extensive colonies. Divide large clumps after flowering while still in leaf.

☀ ◊ ◐ *f*　　　　　　　Z3–8 H8–1

↕ to 6in (15cm) ↔ to 3in (8cm)

Helleborus niger

PERENNIAL

The Christmas rose is a clump-forming perennial with thick, leathery, dark green leaves that remain green over the winter. The large, white, saucer-shaped flowers appear in the early winter and remain until early spring; they have green centers and yellow stamens and turn pink as they age. Plant in heavy, neutral to alkaline soil in dappled or partial shade. It suits a woodland garden and can be appreciated fully in a container placed close to the house. Slugs and snails can be a problem.

☀ ◑   Z4–8 H9–1

↔ to 12in (30cm)

Lonicera fragrantissima

DECIDUOUS SHRUB

This honeysuckle is a bushy, spreading shrub. In the late winter and early spring it produces clusters of fragrant, creamy-white flowers on bare branches, followed by dull red berries. In mild gardens the oval leaves may stay attached through the winter. Plant it in full sun or partial shade in any well-drained soil. It is suitable for planting in a shrub border and can be grown as a screen or in a mixed hedge. It is also effective next to a frequently used entrance to make the most of its winter scent.

☀ ☀ ◊ *f*   Z4–8 H8–3

↕ to 6ft (2m) ↔ to 10ft (3m)

Narcissus cantabricus
BULBOUS PERENNIAL

The white hoop-petticoat is one of the earliest flowering narcissus. The blooms have a white, funnel-shaped trumpet surrounded by smaller outer petals. The leaves are narrow, dark green, and almost cylindrical. It needs sharp drainage and dry conditions for its summer dormancy. Grow it in a raised bed or rock garden in very gritty soil or in pots of one part grit to two parts soil-based potting mix, and keep it in a cold frame during the summer months.

☼ ◊　　　　　　　　　Z8–9 H9–8

↕ to 8in (20cm) ↔ to 2in (5cm)

Rubus cockburnianus
DECIDUOUS SHRUB

This is an outstanding ornamental bramble with prickly, deep purple stems that are covered with a striking, waxy white bloom. The dark green leaves are covered underneath with grayish white hairs. Plant it in full sun in well-drained, fertile soil. It can be grown in a wild garden or mixed border; the winter stems stand out best against a dark background. Cut canes to the ground each year in the spring to ensure plenty of new young stems. Feed and mulch after pruning.

☼ ◊　　　　　　　　　Z6–8 H8–6

↕↔ to 8ft (2.5m)

Sarcococca hookeriana 'Purple Stem'

EVERGREEN SHRUB

The modest white flowers tinted pink in this variety of Christmas box, emit a rich honeylike scent. The glossy, dark green leaves grow from purple shoots. The flowers are followed by blue-black fruit. It thrives in deep or partial shade in organic, moist but well-drained soil; it tolerates sun in reliably moist soil. Excellent in a woodland garden or in a sheltered niche where the fragrance intensifies in the still air.

☼ ☀ ◊ ◊ *f*   Z6–9 H9–6
↕ to 5ft (1.5m) ↔ to 6ft (2m)

Skimmia japonica 'Wakehurst White'

EVERGREEN SHRUB

An attractive shrub with oval, glossy, dark green leaves. Clusters of small, fragrant white flowers open in the spring. They are followed by spherical white fruit that persists into the winter. Grow in a mixed border or woodland garden, and plant a male plant nearby to ensure fruit, since male and female flowers are usually borne on separate plants. It prefers some shade but tolerates sun. Grow in moderately fertile, organic, moist but well-drained soil.

☼ ◊ ◊ *f*   Z7–9 H9–7
↕↔ to 20ft (6m)

Viburnum farreri
DECIDUOUS SHRUB

This upright shrub has highly fragrant, white or pink-tinged flowers, which appear on bare branches in the late fall and winter. The leaves emerge bronze-green, turn dark green as the season progresses, then color in shades of red-purple in the fall before they drop. Plant this viburnum in full sun or partial shade in fertile, moist but well-drained soil. Use it in a mixed or shrub border or as a specimen; its shape improves with age.

☼ ☀ ◊ ♦ *f*　　　　Z6–8 H8–6
↕ to 10ft (3m) ↔ to 8ft (2.5m)

Viburnum tinus 'Eve Price'
EVERGREEN SHRUB

This is a popular shrub with large, oval, dark green leaves. It has dense clusters of pink buds, deep pink in 'Eve Price', which open in the winter and early spring to white flowers. During the summer it bears small bluish-black fruit. Plant in fertile, moist but well-drained soil in sun or light shade. Use it as a flowering hedge or screen in a woodland garden or in a mixed border. Trim hedges after flowering.

☼ ☀ ◊ ♦　　　　Z8–10 H10–8
↕↔ to 10ft (3m)

Clematis cirrhosa 'Freckles'

CLIMBER

This interesting evergreen climber has deeply divided leaves that turn bronze-green during the winter. In the late winter and early spring it bears pale pink flowers that are heavily spotted and streaked with red inside. They are followed by silky seedheads. Grow in full sun with the roots in shade in organic, fertile, moist but well-drained soil. It is ideal for training over a pergola or wall or through an old tree. Cut back after flowering to keep it within bounds.

☀ ☼ ◊ ◖   Z7–11 H9–7
↕ to 10ft (3m)

Cyclamen coum Pewter Group

PERENNIAL

This tuberous perennial has dark green leaves with a pewter-silver sheen that covers almost the entire surface. The flowers appear from the late winter to early spring. They range in color from pure white to pink and crimson. Plant tubers 2in (5cm) deep in sun or partial shade in organic, rather gritty, moderately fertile, well-drained soil with added leaf mold. Excellent when grown beneath deciduous trees or shrubs.

☀ ☼ ◊   Z5–9 H9–5
↕ to 3in (8cm) ↔ to 4in (10cm)

Daphne mezereum
DECIDUOUS SHRUB

Mezereon is a compact, upright shrub,
bearing masses of small, purplish-pink,
fragrant flowers at the stem tips in
late winter and early spring before the
narrow bluish-green leaves. They are
followed by bright red, fleshy, toxic
fruits. Plant it in full sun or partial
shade in moderately fertile, organic,
neutral to alkaline soil. Mezereon
thrives in alkaline soil. Grow it in a
woodland garden, in a mixed or shrub
border, or on a sunny bank.

☼ ☀ ◊ *f*　　　　　　　Z5–8 H8–5
‡ to 4ft (1.2m) ↔ to 3ft (1m)

Daphne odora 'Aureomarginata'
EVERGREEN SHRUB

This is an extremely attractive, rounded
shrub with leathery, dark green leaves,
set off by an irregular yellow margin.
In the late winter and early spring
it produces small clusters of highly
fragrant, white flowers that are deep
pinkish-purple on the outside. It is
not completely hardy, so plant in a
site with shelter from cold winds. It
grows best in partial shade in neutral
to slightly alkaline soil that is moist but
well-drained and rich in organic matter.

☀ ◊ ◑ *f*　　　　　　　Z7–9 H9–7
‡↔ to 5ft (1.5m)

Erica carnea 'Vivellii'

EVERGREEN SHRUB

An attractive heather with dark bronze-green leaves that become completely bronzed in winter. It is very free flowering—the spikes of deep purplish-pink flowers turn magenta as they age and appear from the middle of the winter to midspring. Plant it in full sun or partial shade in peaty, well-drained soil. It will tolerate atmospheric pollution and also grows in alkaline soil. Cut back after flowering to keep it compact.

☼ ☀ ◊   Z5–7 H7–5
‡ to 6in (15cm) ↔ to 14in (35cm)

Prunus x *subhirtella* 'Autumnalis Rosea'

DECIDUOUS TREE

This is a beautiful flowering cherry for the winter garden. Clusters of delicate, semidouble, blush pink flowers appear on a skeleton of bare, spreading branches during periods of mild weather from the fall and throughout the winter until spring. The foliage is bronze-green when new in the spring and turns yellow in the fall. Plant it as a specimen tree in full sun in fertile, moist but well-drained soil.

☼ ◊ ◊   Z6–8 H8–6
‡↔ to 25ft (8m)

Rhododendron 'Christmas Cheer'

EVERGREEN SHRUB

This is a compact rhododendron with clusters of pink buds that open to pale pink flowers. It flowers in mild weather in the winter, but it will bloom in the early spring if it is cold. It is an old cultivar that was often pot-grown and forced under glass for flowers at Christmas, hence its name. Plant it in organic, acidic, moist but well-drained soil in a sheltered niche in light dappled shade. Mulch annually with leaf mold or bark chips.

☀ ◊ ◖   Z5–9 H9–5

‡↔ to 6ft (2m)

Viburnum x *bodnantense* 'Dawn'

DECIDUOUS SHRUB

This is one of the most reliable of all winter-flowering shrubs. The fragrant, deep pink flowers are produced on bare branches from the late fall to early spring. The oval, toothed leaves are bronze as they emerge in the spring, gradually turning to dark green, then red-bronze in the fall. Plant in full sun or partial shade in moderately fertile, moist but well-drained soil. It is ideal as a specimen or in a mixed border.

☀ ☀ ◊ ◖ *f*   Z7–8 H8–7

‡ to 10ft (3m) ↔ to 6ft (2m)

Acer capillipes

DECIDUOUS TREE

The snakebark maple takes on strong red tints as the fall turns to winter, first with its three-lobed leaves turning orange and red, and then as they fall, leaving the coral-red young shoots. The striated, white-veined, greenish-gray bark is also a key feature of this small tree. In the spring long, hanging clusters of yellow flowers appear that soon develop into tiny, pink-winged fruits. It does well in a sunny or lightly shaded location. Little pruning is necessary. *A. x conspicuum* 'Phoenix' is also valued for its red winter color.

☼ ◐ ◊ ◑　　　　　　　　　Z5–7 H7–5
↥↔to 30ft (10m)

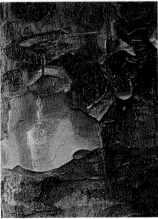

Acer griseum

DECIDUOUS TREE

The paperbark maple is an elegant tree with a spreading crown of dark green leaves that turn to vivid shades of crimson, gold, and scarlet during the fall. When leafless in the winter, it reveals the beauty of its attractive bark—a rich mahogany red, peeling away on older trees to reveal the orange-red younger bark beneath. Plant it as a specimen tree or at the back of a mixed border in full sun or partial shade in fertile, moist but well-drained soil.

☼ ◐ ◊ ◑　　　　　　　　　Z4–8 H8–1
↥↔to 30ft (10m)

Acer pensylvanicum 'Erythrocladum'

DECIDUOUS TREE

The moosewood maple is a beautiful tree with greenish, white-striped bark that becomes a vivid salmon pink in the winter; the young shoots are an especially bright reddish-pink. It has three-lobed, green leaves that turn to a warm shade of clear butter yellow in the fall. Plant it in full sun or dappled shade in fertile, moist but well-drained soil. It makes a wonderful specimen tree, and its beautiful bark is a highly distinctive winter feature.

☼ ☀ ◊ ◑   Z3–7 H7–1

‡ to 40ft (12m) ↔ to 30ft (10m)

Arbutus menziesii

EVERGREEN TREE

The madrono is a broad, spreading tree with glossy, dark green, oblong leaves. Its main attraction during the winter months is its bright reddish-brown bark, which peels away to reveal the younger, smooth, olive-green bark underneath. In the early summer it bears upright clusters of waxy, creamy-white flowers, which are sometimes followed in the fall by orange-red fruit. Plant it in full sun or dappled shade in a sheltered location on acidic, organic, moist but well-drained soil.

☼ ☀ ◊ ◑   Z7–9 H9–7

‡↔ to 50ft (15m)

Bergenia 'Ballawley'

PERENNIAL

This vigorous evergreen has large,
leathery, dark green leaves flushed with
red and bronze-purple in winter. In the
spring upright stems bearing clusters of
bright crimson flowers appear. Plant in a
sheltered site in full sun or partial shade
in organic, moist but well-drained soil.
It is an excellent ground-cover plant for
a woodland garden or for the front of
a herbaceous border. Remove ragged
leaves in the spring. Divide clumps
every 4–5 years to maintain its vigor.

☼ ◐ ◊ ◊　　　　　　　　　Z6–9 H9–6
↕↔ to 24in (60cm)

Brassica oleracea Acephala Group

BIENNIAL

The ornamental cabbages are grown
for their attractive foliage with different
combinations of green, red, pink, and
white leaves. Extremely useful as a
winter bedding plant, they attain their
deepest coloration during the cold
winter months. Plant in a sunny site,
preferably in lime-rich, fertile, well-
drained soil, or in containers. Sow
seed in the spring, or buy them as
young plants.

☼ ◊　　　　　　　　　　　Z7–11 H8–1
↕↔ to 18in (45cm)

Camellia sasanqua 'Crimson King'

EVERGREEN SHRUB

One of the earliest camellias to flower, 'Crimson King' has glossy, dark green leaves and single, crimson-red flowers from the late fall through winter; it is often in bloom at Christmas. Grow in a sheltered spot in partial shade or sun but away from early morning sun in organic, acidic, moist but well-drained soil. In cold areas, grow in containers of acidic soil mix and flower under glass.

☼ ☀ ◊ ◉   Z7–9 H9–7

↕ to 20ft (6m) ↔ to 10ft (3m)

Cornus alba 'Sibirica'

DECIDUOUS SHRUB

The red-barked dogwood is an upright shrub, usually grown for its striking red winter stems, but the dark green leaves also turn bright red before dropping in the fall. Plant it in full sun in any reasonably fertile soil. It is the new young growth that produces the brightest and longest lasting winter stem color. Cut all stems back in the early spring, just before growth begins, to within two or three buds from the ground. Feed and mulch after pruning.

☼ ◊ ◉   Z2–8 H8–1

↕↔ to 10ft (3m)

Cornus sanguinea 'Winter Beauty'

DECIDUOUS SHRUB

The oval green leaves of this vigorous shrub turn bright red in the fall, and as they drop, they reveal the vivid red and orange winter shoots. Prune hard in the early spring to stimulate new growth, which has the best color. Cut back to within 2–3 buds from the base of the plant, then feed and mulch. The color develops fully when the shrub grows in full sun. It thrives in any reasonably fertile, well-drained soil.

☼ ◊   Z4–7 H7–1

↕ to 10ft (3m) ↔ to 8ft (2.5m)

Cotoneaster cashmiriensis

EVERGREEN SHRUB

A low, mound-forming shrub with glossy, dark green leaves. Pink buds open in the summer to small, white flowers. They are followed by spherical, deep red berries that persist into the winter. It is one of the smaller prostrate cotoneasters and makes a compact ground-cover plant for a rock garden or sunny bank. Plant it in full sun or partial shade in any moderately fertile, well-drained soil, including chalk. This plant is often sold as *C. cochleatus*.

☼ ☼ ◊   Z6–8 H8–6

↕ to 12in (30cm) ↔ to 6ft (2m)

Cotoneaster conspicuus 'Decorus'

EVERGREEN SHRUB

This is an attractive, low-growing, spreading shrub with small, narrow, dark green leaves. The tiny white flowers appear in the early summer and are followed by large quantities of conspicuous, spherical, bright red berries that last for most of the winter. Plant it in full sun or partial shade in moderately fertile, well-drained soil. It is ideal for planting on a dry, sunny bank, where it will provide color throughout the winter.

☼ ☀ ◐ ◇   Z6–8 H8–6

↕ to 5ft (1.5m) ↔ to 8ft (2.5m)

Cotoneaster lacteus

EVERGREEN SHRUB

This is a substantial shrub with large, deeply veined, oval, dark green leaves with a yellowish white, woolly underside. The milky white flowers appear in large clusters in the summer and are followed in the fall by large bunches of bright red berries that last well into the winter. It makes a dense, ornamental hedge or can be grown in a mixed border. Trim lightly in the late summer to keep it in shape. Plant it in full sun or partial shade in any well-drained, moderately fertile soil.

☼ ☀ ◐ ◇   Z7–9 H9–4

↕↔ to 12ft (4m)

Gaultheria procumbens

EVERGREEN SHRUB

Wintergreen is a creeping shrub with underground stems and glossy, dark green leaves that smell strongly of wintergreen when crushed. The white or pink, urn-shaped flowers appear in the summer and are followed in the fall by bright red, aromatic fruit. It prefers partial shade but will grow in full sun if provided with soil that is reliably moist. Grow in neutral to acidic, peaty soil. It is an excellent plant for providing ground cover in a damp woodland or a shady border.

☀ ◐ *f*   Z3–8 H8–1

↕ to 6in (15cm) ↔indefinite

Hamamelis x *intermedia* 'Diane'

DECIDUOUS SHRUB

This elegant shrub is grown for its clusters of fragrant flowers that appear on bare branches in the late winter. They have threadlike, dark red petals. The rounded, bright green leaves turn red and yellow in the fall. Plant in full sun or partial shade in moderately fertile, neutral to acidic, moist but well-drained soils rich in leafy organic matter. Grow in a shrub border, or use as a specimen.

☀ ◐ ◌ ◐ *f*   Z5–9 H9–1

↕↔to 12ft (4m)

Ilex aquifolium 'J.C. van Tol'

EVERGREEN TREE

This is a form of common holly without any spiny tips. The leaves are dark green and very glossy and are carried on purple stems. It is a self-pollinating female plant that produces its bright red berries through the winter without the need for a male plant nearby. Plant it in full sun or partial shade in fertile, moist but well-drained soil. It grows happily in a woodland garden and can be used as a hedge or a specimen tree. Clip hedges in the summer.

☼ ☀ ◐ ○   Z7–9 H9–7

↕ to 20ft (6m) ↔ to 12ft (4m)

Ilex x *meserveae*
BLUE PRINCESS ('Conapri')

EVERGREEN SHRUB

An attractive hybrid holly with spiny, bluish-green leaves and tiny white or pink flowers in the late spring. It needs a male plant nearby to produce glossy red fruit in the fall and winter. Grow in a woodland garden, or use it to make an impenetrable hedge. Plant it in full sun or partial shade in fertile, organic, moist but well-drained soil. If it is grown as a hedge, it should be trimmed annually in the summer.

☼ ☀ ◐ ◑   Z5–9 H9–5

↕↔ to 10ft (3m)

Leucothoe SCARLETTA ('Zeblid')

EVERGREEN SHRUB

This small to medium-sized, upright shrub has lance-shaped, leathery leaves. They are dark red-purple in the spring, becoming dark green in the summer before finally assuming red and bronze tints in the winter. In the spring it has clusters of tiny, white, narrow, pitcher-shaped flowers. It should be grown in a shady location in acidic, organic, moist soil. It is ideal for planting in a woodland garden or shady border.

☀ ◑ ◊   Z5–8 H8–3

↕ to 6ft (2m) ↔ to 10ft (3m)

Prunus serrula

DECIDUOUS TREE

This attractive flowering cherry is grown mainly for its tactile, rich coppery-red bark. It is very shiny and particularly striking on a sunny winter's day. It has narrow, dark green leaves that turn yellow in the fall, and small, single, bowl-shaped white flowers in the spring. It should be planted in full sun in moderately fertile, moist but well-drained soil. It looks particularly dramatic when grown in a boulevard, but it also makes a handsome specimen in a smaller garden.

☀ ◊ ◊   Z6–8 H8–6

↕↔ to 30ft (10m)

Skimmia japonica 'Nymans'

EVERGREEN SHRUB

This low-spreading shrub with dark green leaves is a female plant noted for its large, red winter fruits that are borne very freely if the plant is grown with a male plant nearby. They arise from the dense clusters of white spring flowers. Grow it in partial to deep shade in moderately fertile, moist but well-drained soil. Plant in a shrub border or woodland garden. Like most skimmias, it is good in coastal and urban gardens and tolerates most soils.

☀ ☀ ◇ ◊   Z7–9 H9–7
‡ to 3ft (1m) ↔ to 6ft (2m)

Skimmia japonica 'Rubella'

EVERGREEN SHRUB

This skimmia is a compact, dome-shaped shrub with red-edged, dark green leaves. It is a male plant that produces dense clusters of deep red buds from the fall to winter. In the early spring the buds open to reveal small, fragrant white flowers. It pollinates female skimmias. Grow it in partial to deep shade in moderately fertile, moist but well-drained soil. Plant in a shrub border or woodland garden. Also good in containers.

☀ ☀ ◇ ◊ *f*   Z7–9 H9–7
‡↔ to 20ft (6m)

Bergenia cordifolia 'Purpurea'

PERENNIAL

During the late winter this evergreen perennial produces dark, stout stems of deep magenta-purple flowers. It has substantial, leathery, mid-green leaves that turn reddish-purple during the winter; the color is most intense in very cold weather. Plant it in full sun or partial shade in organic, moist but well-drained soil. It is suitable for the front of an herbaceous border or for a woodland garden. Remove tattered leaves in the spring.

☼ ☀ ◊ ◊   Z3–8 H8–1

‡↔ to 20in (50cm)

Cornus alba 'Kesselringii'

DECIDUOUS SHRUB

This striking shrub is especially valuable for its dramatic, purplish-black winter stems. Bronzed leaves open in the spring, turning green and then reddish-purple in the fall. In the spring it bears clusters of white flowers that are followed in the fall by white fruit. Cut back in the early spring to within a few buds from the ground to stimulate the growth of new, more deeply colored shoots, then feed and mulch. Plant in sun in any well-drained, reasonably fertile soil.

☼ ◊   Z2–8 H8–1

‡↔ to 10ft (3m)

Cryptomeria japonica
Elegans Group

EVERGREEN TREE

Japanese cedars are well worth planting as an alternative to other conifers. Not only are they reliable, but they are unusual since their leaf color varies with the seasons. Those of the Elegans Group take on coppery bronze-purple tints in the fall and winter. A good evergreen specimen tree for a medium to large garden, it can also be kept cut back for a smaller site or planted as a hedge—choose a sunny, sheltered site. No formal pruning is necessary.

☼ ☀ ◊ ◑   Z6–9 H9–4
‡↔ to 6ft (2m)

Iris unguicularis

PERENNIAL

A wonderful, winter-flowering iris with large, fragrant, pale lavender-purple or deep violet-blue blooms marked by a large patch of yellow on the lower petals. It has upright stems and tough, grasslike, evergreen leaves. Grow it in a rock garden, raised bed, on a terrace, or at the foot of a warm, sunny wall. Plant it in full sun in gritty, very well-drained, neutral to alkaline soil. Good for cut flowers.

☼ ◊ *f*   Z7–9 H9–7
‡ to 12in (30cm) ↔ indefinite

Acer grosseri var. *hersii*

DECIDUOUS TREE

The snakebark maple is an extremely attractive tree with upright, green-barked branches heavily marked with white striations reminiscent of snake's skin. The mid-green leaves are shallowly lobed and turn yellow and orange in the fall. Clusters of pale yellow flowers hang beneath the shoots in the spring, followed by pink-brown fall fruit. Plant it as a specimen in sun or partial shade, in fertile, moist but well-drained soil.

☼ ☀ ◊ ◑   Z5–7 H7–5
↕↔ to 50ft (15m)

Acer pensylvanicum

DECIDUOUS TREE

The moosewood maple looks equally attractive in the winter and summer. In the spring it produces long clusters of small, yellow-green flowers. The lobed, bright green leaves turn clear butter yellow in the fall, revealing the white striped, jade-green bark when they drop. Plant it in full sun or partial shade in moist but well-drained, fertile soil. Plant close to a footpath where the bark can be fully appreciated during the winter.

☼ ☀ ◊ ◑   Z3–7 H7–1
↕ to 40ft (12m) ↔ to 30ft (10m)

Arum italicum '**Marmoratum**'

PERENNIAL

The upright, dark green, arrow-shaped leaves, heavily mottled with paler green markings, last through the winter. In the early summer greenish-white hooded flowers appear, followed by spikes of bright orange-red berries. Grow in light shade or in sun with some shade from the hottest summer sunshine. Plant tubers in the spring or fall in organic, well-drained soil. It makes good ground cover beneath deciduous shrubs or in a woodland garden.

☀ ◌   Z7–9 H9–3

↕ to 10in (25cm) ↔ to 12in (30cm)

Garrya elliptica

EVERGREEN SHRUB

The silk-tassel bush is a dense shrub with wavy-edged, leathery, grayish-green leaves. Male and female flowers are borne on separate plants; the male plants are more attractive with longer, dangling, gray-green catkins measuring 8in (20cm) or more that are borne in mid-winter and early spring. Plant it in full sun or partial shade in fertile, well-drained soil. Excellent on a shady wall or shrub border and good as a specimen or as hedging in coastal gardens.

☀ ☀ ◌   Z8–11 H11–8

 ↕↔ to 12ft (4m)

Helleborus viridis

PERENNIAL

The green hellebore is a deciduous, clump-forming hellebore with very deeply divided, leathery, dark green leaves. In the late winter and early spring it produces tall stems adorned with nodding, bright green flowers. It looks best when planted against a dark background and will grow in deep shade. Plant it in a woodland garden or a shrub border. It grows best in heavy, neutral or alkaline soil in dappled shade. It often self-seeds.

☀ ☀ ◐　　　　　　　　Z6–9 H9–6
↕↔to 12in (30cm)

Ribes laurifolium

EVERGREEN SHRUB

This is a low-growing shrub with spreading branches bearing leathery, dark green leaves. In the late winter and early spring it produces substantial, hanging clusters of greenish-yellow flowers. Male and female flowers are borne on separate plants; if grown together, females produce black fruits. Plant it in a shrub border in full sun or partial shade in moderately fertile, well-drained soil. In cold areas, plant in a sheltered spot away from cold, dry winter winds.

☀ ☀ ◇　　　　　　　　Z7–9 H9–7
↕to 3ft (1m) ↔to 5ft (1.5m)

Stachyurus praecox

DECIDUOUS SHRUB

The gracefully arching branches of this spreading shrub produce hanging chains of small, pale yellow flowers in the late winter and early spring. The similar *S. chinensis* flowers about two weeks later. Plant in full sun or partial shade in fertile, organic, acidic, well-drained soil, ideally against a wall or in a woodland garden. When mature, cut out the oldest flowered shoots at the base after flowering; this ensures the production of strong, new flowering stems.

☼ ☼ ◊   Z7–9 H9–7

↕ to 12ft (4m) ↔ to 10ft (3m)

Thuja occidentalis 'Hetz Midget'

EVERGREEN SHRUB

This dwarf conifer is a slow-growing type of white cedar that forms a dense, rounded mound of golden green foliage that smells of apples when crushed. It is ideal as a specimen in a rock garden and associates particularly well with heathers. Grow in full sun in deep, moisture-retentive but well-drained, fertile soil. In cool gardens, plant in a sheltered place, away from cold, dry winds.

☼ ◊ ◗   Z2–7 H7–1

↕↔ to 20in (50cm)

Azara microphylla

EVERGREEN TREE

An upright, often shrubby small tree with oval, glossy, dark green leaves. In the late winter and early spring it bears clusters of small, vanilla-scented, yellow flowers. Plant it in full sun or partial shade in organic, well-drained, fertile soil. It can be grown in a shrub border but flowers best against a sheltered, sunny wall. When grown on a wall, train in the shoots when young to ensure good coverage. Then prune back after flowering to within 2–4 buds of the woody framework of main stems.

☼ ◐ ◊ *f*   Z8–10 H11–10

↕ to 30ft (10m) ↔ to 12ft (4m)

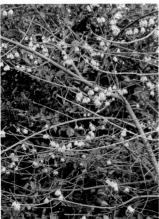

Chimonanthus praecox 'Grandiflorus'

DECIDUOUS SHRUB

The wintersweet is an upright shrub with lance-shaped, green leaves. It is especially valuable for the highly fragrant, nodding, deep yellow flowers that are stained red within. They appear on bare stems in the winter and are excellent for cutting. Plant it in full sun in fertile, well-drained soil in a warm, sheltered place. Grow as a specimen or train it against a sunny wall. If wall-trained, shorten any outward-growing shoots after flowering.

☼ ◊ *f*   Z7–9 H9–7

↕ to 12ft (4m) ↔ to 10ft (3m)

Cornus mas

DECIDUOUS SHRUB

The cornelian cherry is a vigorous shrub or small tree with spreading branches and mid-green leaves that turn red-purple in the fall. It is most dramatic in the late winter when it produces an abundance of small, yellow flowers in clusters on bare branches. Bright red fruit ripen in the late summer or early fall, often as the foliage assumes its fall tints. Grow as a specimen, in a shrub border, or in a woodland garden. Plant in full sun or partial shade in any moderately fertile, well-drained soil.

☼ ☀ ◊   Z5–8 H8–5

↔ to 15ft (5m)

Cornus sericea 'Flaviramea'

DECIDUOUS SHRUB

This vigorous dogwood forms a thicket of bright yellow stems that create a brilliant winter display. In the summer small white flowers are followed by white fruit in the fall, when the leaves turn vivid orange and red before falling. It looks beautiful at the side of pools or streams, especially if planted with the red-stemmed *C. sanguinea*. Grow in wet or moist soil in full sun. Cut back to the base each year in the early spring, and then feed and mulch.

☼ ◗   Z3–8 H8–1

↕ to 6ft (2m) ↔ to 12ft (4m)

Coronilla valentina subsp. *glauca*
EVERGREEN SHRUB

A dense, bushy plant with divided, blue-green leaves. In the late winter or early spring, and often again in the late summer, it produces clusters of bright yellow, pealike flowers. It is suitable in a shrub border or on a sheltered wall because it is not completely hardy and needs protection from cold winds. Plant it in full sun in sandy, moderately fertile, well-drained soil. In very cold areas, grow in a container as an indoor plant and move outdoors in the summer.

☼ ◊   Z8–9 H9–8
↔ to 5ft (1.5m)

Hacquetia epipactis
PERENNIAL

This is a low-growing, spreading perennial that produces tiny yellow flowers surrounded by a collar of bright emerald green, leaflike bracts in the late winter and early spring. The brilliant green leaves only develop fully after flowering. It is suitable for planting in moist, shady situations, such as by poolsides or in a damp woodland garden. Plant it in organic, moist but well-drained, acid or neutral soil. It is easily increased by dividing the clumps in the spring.

◐ ◊ ◖   Z5–7 H7–5
↕ to 2½in (6cm) ↔ to 9in (23cm)

Hamamelis x *intermedia* 'Arnold Promise'

DECIDUOUS SHRUB

This attractive, late winter-flowering shrub produces a profusion of spidery, bright yellow flowers on bare, upright branches. It is excellent in a shrub border or as a specimen because the vivid green leaves turn red and gold in the fall. Plant in full sun or partial shade in fertile, neutral to acidic, moist but well-drained soil.

☼ ☀ ◊ ◐   Z5–9 H9–1
↕↔ to 12ft (4m)

Hamamelis japonica 'Sulphurea'

DECIDUOUS SHRUB

The Japanese witch hazel is an upright, branched shrub with rounded, glossy green leaves that turn gold in the fall. In the late winter the bare branches are studded with small, sulfur-yellow flowers with very narrow petals. Plant it in full sun or partial shade in fertile, neutral to acidic, moist but well-drained soil. Plant it in groups in a woodland garden or as a specimen. It can also be grown in deep, organic soil over chalk.

☼ ☀ ◊ ◐   Z5–9 H9–5
↕↔ to 12ft (4m)

Ilex aquifolium 'Bacciflava'

EVERGREEN TREE

'Bacciflava' is a female form of common holly with spiny, glossy, dark green leaves. With a male pollinator nearby, the tiny, insignificant flowers of the spring and early summer will give rise to yellow berries that last into the winter. It is an erect, pyramidal tree that is good as a specimen and is also suitable for hedging. Trim hedges in the summer. Plant in full sun or partial shade in moist but well-drained, moderately fertile soil.

☼ ☀ ◊ ◑   Z7–9 H9–7

↕ to 70ft (20m) ↔ to 20ft (6m)

Ilex aquifolium 'Ferox Argentea'

EVERGREEN TREE

Hedgehog hollies have unusual spine-covered leaves. This variegated type is ideal for the winter: it provides excellent structure when much of the garden is bare, and the foliage is bright and pretty. It is a male plant so there are no berries, but the flowers will pollinate female hollies nearby. It is ideal in sun or partial shade as a free-standing specimen, hedging, or trimmed to shape. Remove any all-green foliage immediately because it may replace the variegaton.

☼ ☀ ◊ ◑   Z7–9 H9–7

↕ to 25ft (8m) ↔ to 12ft (4m)

Jasminum nudiflorum
DECIDUOUS SHRUB

Winter jasmine is one of the most popular winter-flowering shrubs. It has arching, scrambling, dark green stems and dark green leaves, each divided into three leaflets. It is very free flowering, bearing bright yellow flowers with six petals in the late winter. It looks best when planted against a fence or trellis but needs tying in to a support. Plant in full sun or partial shade in fertile, well-drained soil. Trim after flowering to keep it dense, cutting back to strong buds.

☼ ☽ ◌   Z6–9 H9–6

↕↔to 10ft (3m)

Mahonia japonica
EVERGREEN SHRUB

A beautiful winter-flowering shrub with upright branches covered in spiny, divided, dark green leaves. It has drooping spikes of strongly fragrant, lemon yellow flowers from the late fall to early spring. These are followed by an abundant crop of bluish-black berries. It provides a long season of interest in a shrub border or woodland garden. Plant it in a slightly shaded location in organic, moist but well-drained soil.

☽ ◌ ◊ *f*   Z7–8 H8–7

↕to 6ft (2m) ↔to 10ft (3m)

Mahonia x *media* 'Charity'

EVERGREEN SHRUB

This is one of the most attractive types of the Oregon grape. It has large, dark green leaves divided into sharply toothed leaflets. Masses of sweetly scented, bright yellow flowers are borne in dense spikes from the late fall into winter. Plant it in partial shade and moderately fertile, organic, moist but well-drained soil. It makes an architectural specimen for planting in front of a wall, in a shrub border, or in a woodland garden.

☀ ◊ ◐ *f*   Z8–9 H9–8

↕ to 15ft (5m) ↔ to 12ft (4m)

Narcissus 'Rijnveld's Early Sensation'

BULBOUS PERENNIAL

This golden-yellow daffodil flowers in the late winter, well before the other early flowering daffodils, such as 'February Gold'. It makes a valuable, long-flowering addition to the winter garden and should be planted in a bold group or naturalized in grass. Plant bulbs at one-and-a-half times their own depth in the late summer. Grow in full sun in fertile, well-drained soil. It often produces several flowers on each stem. Remove the dead flowers regularly.

☀ ◊   Z3–9 H9–1

↕ to 14in (35cm)

Pyracantha 'Soleil d'Or'

EVERGREEN SHRUB

Pyracanthas have several seasons of interest. This one has spiny red shoots and glossy green leaves. In the summer it produces sprays of small white flowers, followed by yellow fruit that last well into the winter. Plant in full sun or shade in fertile, well-drained soil. It can be trained against a wall or fence, grown as a free-standing shrub, and also makes an excellent dense, impenetrable hedge. Trim hedges in the midspring and summer.

☼ ☀ ☀ ◊   Z7–9 H9–7

↕ to 10ft (3m) ↔ to 8ft (2.5m)

Viola x *wittrockiana* Universal Series

PERENNIAL

Universal pansies are among the most prolific of all winter-flowering plants, flowering almost non-stop from the early winter to midspring. The color range includes yellow, blue, mauve, maroon, red, and white, some with darker patches at the center. Plant in sun in fertile, moist but well-drained soil. Although perennial, they are usually grown as annuals or biennials for bedding. Use in borders, containers, or hanging baskets.

☼ ◊ ◔   Z8–11 H9–1

↕↔ to 8in (20cm)

Calluna vulgaris 'Boskoop'

EVERGREEN SHRUB

This dense and compact heather bears spikes of lilac-pink flowers from the midsummer to late fall. Then the foliage, which is golden throughout the summer, begins to assume vibrant orange-red winter tints that last until the new growth emerges in the spring. Grow in full sun in organic, well-drained acid soil. Cut plants back lightly in the spring to keep them shapely. Excellent for a rock garden, it associates well with conifers and other heathers.

☼ ◊   Z5-7 H7-5
↕ to 12in (30cm) ↔ to 16in (40cm)

Ilex aquifolium 'Amber'

EVERGREEN TREE

This is one of the most attractive forms of the common holly with virtually spine-free, glossy, bright green leaves. The tiny, spring and early summer flowers give rise to profuse clusters of amber yellow fruit. The tree is female and needs a male to be planted nearby to produce fruit. Plant it in full sun in well-drained, fertile soil. It can be grown as a hedge or as an attractive specimen tree. Trim it in the summer if grown as a hedge.

☼ ◊   Z7-9 H9-7
↕ to 20ft (6m) ↔ to 8ft (2.5m)

Iris foetidissima
PERENNIAL

The stinking gladwyn is so called because the leaves have an unpleasant smell when crushed. It has clumps of evergreen leaves and in the early summer bears dull purple, yellow-tinged flowers. It really comes into its own, however, when the seed pods ripen in the fall. They split to reveal glistening orange-red seeds that remain in place until the winter. Grow in well-drained, moderately fertile, neutral to acid soil. It is one of the toughest and most useful plants for dry shade.

☀ ◐ ◌   Z4–9 H9–2

‡ to 36in (90cm) ↔ indefinite

Pyracantha 'Orange Glow'
EVERGREEN SHRUB

This is a vigorous, upright shrub with spiny stems and glossy, dark green leaves. In the late spring clusters of small white flowers are followed by masses of orange berries that last until the winter. Plant in full sun or shade in well-drained, moderately fertile soil. After flowering, shorten sideshoots back to two or three leaves to show off the berries. It can be trained against a wall but also makes an intruder-proof hedge. Trim hedges in the spring and summer.

☀ ◐ ◑ ◌   Z7–9 H9–7

‡↔ to 10ft (3m)

ALL SEASONS

It is a good idea to include a few reliable, undemanding plants that remain attractive in every season. They give the garden shape and structure, and provide a backdrop for transient seasonal displays. Use them to liven up a border, or to create focal points; shapely conifers for example, can serve as topiary—without the work. The cabbage palm (*Cordyline*) and New Zealand flax (*Phormium*) may appear as tender exotics but are tougher than they look. Their spiky shapes are portable in containers, and in borders they enhance a colourful display.

Climbers, like ivy (*Hedera*), can be used to disguise fences and sheds, to shield an unsightly compost heap by training along a trellis, or for ground cover. Evergreen ground cover plants play a valuable role in helping to suppress weeds; low-growing junipers, silvery artemisias and heathers are all good choices as, with minimal care, their foliage provides interest all year round.

More visual punctuation may be obtained using grasses and bamboos, especially if you have plenty of space. Bamboos are normally grown as an elegant, rustling screen, but some, like *Phyllostachys flexuosa*, grace the garden with the changing colour of their stems.

A STRUCTURAL BACKBONE

Evergreen hedges and screens can surround the entire garden or divide it into sections. Box (*Buxus sempervirens*) and yew (*Taxus baccata*) are traditional choices for clipped formal hedging and topiary, but hollies (*Ilex*) and pyracanthas form superb, impenetrable hedges, and may also reward you with flowers and berries. Other conifers, apart from yew, will create a tall screen, but choose with care, as some can become a nuisance if they are allowed to grow too large. Leyland cypress can reach 35m (120ft), and there many more suitable for domestic situations.

Artemisia arborescens

EVERGREEN SHRUB

This small, aromatic evergreen plant has very finely divided, silver-gray leaves that provide a foil for stronger flower colors in a sunny border or gravel garden. It also produces small yellow flowerheads in the late summer and fall. Plant it in a sunny situation in moderately fertile, well-drained soil. It can become leggy and should be pruned hard in the spring to keep it neat and compact. It dislikes cold, wet winters and in very cold areas is best grown close to a warm, sheltered wall.

☼ ◊ *f*   Z5–9 H9–5

‡ to 3ft (1m) ↔ to 5ft (1.5m)

Artemisia stelleriana 'Boughton Silver'

PERENNIAL

This attractive evergreen forms a low, spreading clump of silver-gray leaves. It looks good when planted against a background of darker foliage at the front of a border, or it can be used as path edging or in a gravel garden. The foliage looks better if the insignificant yellow flowers are removed before they open in the late summer. It prefers a position in full sun and well-drained, moderately fertile soil.

☼ ◊   Z3–7 H7–1

‡ to 6in (15cm) ↔ to 18in (45cm)

Ballota acetabulosa

EVERGREEN SHRUB

The upright, white, woolly stems of this
compact, woody plant are covered all
year with rounded, grayish-green leaves.
In the summer it produces spires of
small, purple-pink flowers. It grows
well in hot, dry sites in full sun and poor,
very well-drained soil. It may not survive
cold, wet winters, but where it does, cut it
back hard in the spring to keep it bushy.
Grow it as a backdrop for bright flower
colors in a raised bed, sunny border, or in
gravel and Mediterranean-style gardens.
Ballota pseudodictamnus is hardier.

☼ ◊ *f*   Z8–9 H9–8

↕ to 24in (60cm) ↔ to 30in (75cm)

Betula utilis
'Silver Shadow'

DECIDUOUS TREE

Birch trees are a year-round asset to
a garden. They are valued for their
graceful winter framework, attractive
bark, yellow catkins in the spring,
and leaves that color yellow in the
fall. 'Silver Shadow' has silvery bark
and makes a beautiful specimen tree,
especially against a dark background
of evergreen trees or shrubs. Plant it
in sun or dappled shade in fertile, moist,
well-drained soil.

☼ ☀ ◊ ◖   Z5–7 H7–5

↕ to 60ft (18m) ↔ to 30ft (10m)

Cortaderia selloana 'Silver Comet'

PERENNIAL GRASS

The arching clumps of tough, leathery evergreen leaves of pampas grass create an architectural presence throughout the year. The soft, silvery plumes arise in the late summer and persist through the winter. Grow it as a specimen in well-drained, fertile soil in full sun. Remove the old flowerheads and dead foliage before growth begins in the spring. The leaves are sharp-edged, so wear tough gloves to protect your hands.

☼ ◊   Z7–11 H11–7
‡ to 5ft (1.5m) ↔ to 3ft (1m)

Eucalyptus pauciflora subsp. *niphophila*

EVERGREEN TREE

The alpine snow gum is fast-growing once established and has attractive bark that peels to form a patchwork of green, gray, and cream. The leaves are blue-green and rounded in the juvenile form, lance-shaped when mature. Plant it in full sun in fertile, moist, well-drained soil. Grow it as a specimen tree, or in small gardens and borders, prune it hard every year in the spring to produce a shrub with colorful young foliage. Feed and mulch after pruning.

☼ ◊ ◖   Z9–10 H10–9
‡↔ to 20ft (6m)

Euonymus fortunei 'Silver Queen'

EVERGREEN SHRUB

Valued for its year-round foliage, this compact shrub climbs upward if given support. The oval, leathery leaves are pale yellow when young, later becoming green with an irregular white margin that flushes pink during cold weather. Excellent for brightening a dull corner, it is also very effective when grown against a wall. Plant it in full sun or light shade in any but waterlogged soil. Trim shrubs in the midspring to keep them within bounds.

☼ ☀ ◊ ◊   Z5–9 H9–2

‡ to 8ft (2.5m) ↔ to 5ft (1.5m)

Hebe pinguifolia 'Pagei'

EVERGREEN SHRUB

The purple stems of this tough hebe are covered in silvery, blue-gray leaves that remain attractive throughout the year. It produces short spikes of small white flowers over a long period from the late spring to summer. Plant it in full sun or partial shade in moderately fertile, moist, well-drained soil. Use it at the front of a mixed border, in a rock garden, or as ground cover.

☼ ☀ ◊ ◊   Z8–10 H10–8

‡ to 12in (30cm) ↔ to 24in (60cm)

Sedum spathulifolium 'Cape Blanco'

PERENNIAL

This evergreen stonecrop forms dense, low-growing mats of silvery-green foliage, comprised of rosettes of fleshy leaves covered in a waxy white bloom. The mats are sprinkled in the summer with tiny, star-shaped, yellow flowers. It is ideal for raised beds, troughs, and the tops of drystone walls. Grow it in gritty, poor to moderately fertile, very well-drained soil. The silvery foliage develops best in full sun, but the plant tolerates light shade.

☼ ◊   Z5–9 H9–5

↕ to 2in (5cm) ↔ indefinite

Sempervivum arachnoideum

PERENNIAL

The cobweb houseleek is an evergreen mat-former with rosettes of fleshy, dark green, red-tipped leaves covered with a fine web of white hairs. In the late summer it may produce sturdy stems with rose-red, star-shaped flowers at the tips. Each rosette dies after flowering, but new ones are readily formed to fill the gap. Plant it in full sun in poor to moderately fertile, very well-drained soil. Grow it in a trough, pot, rock garden, or on a drystone wall.

☼ ◊   Z5–8 H8–5

↕ to 5in (12cm) ↔ to 4in (10cm)

Senecio cineraria 'Silver Dust'

EVERGREEN SHRUB

This attractive bush has deeply divided leaves, which are covered with grayish-white felt. It produces mustard-yellow, daisylike flowers in the summer, although these should be removed before they open to maintain its foliage effect. Plant it in full sun and slightly fertile, well-drained soil. It is reasonably hardy but dislikes winter wet, and semi-ripe cuttings should be taken at the end of the summer to guarantee new plants the following year.

☼ ◊   Z8–11 H11–1

↔ to 12in (30cm)

Stachys byzantina

EVERGREEN PERENNIAL

Lambs' ears form an evergreen, soft-textured mat of bright, silvery white, woolly leaves. In the summer it produces upright, hairy stems of pinkish-purple flowers, but for the best foliage effect, remove these before the blooms open. It makes an excellent ground-cover plant beside a path, at the front of a border, or in a gravel garden. It can become straggly, and old growth should be cut back in the early spring. Grow it in a sunny situation in moderately fertile, well-drained soil.

☼ ◊   Z4–8 H8–1

↕ to 15in (38cm) ↔ to 24in (60cm)

Ajuga reptans 'Atropurpurea'

PERENNIAL

This evergreen, mat-forming perennial is grown for its glossy, bronze-purple leaves rather than the late spring spikes of blue flowers. The creeping stems root where they touch the soil, making this a superb ground-cover plant that is relatively easy to control. Grow it in a partially shaded or sunny site in moist, moderately fertile soil. It is excellent in a woodland garden or shady border. 'Multicolor' has bronze-green and white leaves, heavily suffused with purple.

☼ ◑ ◊   Z3–9 H9–1
‡to 6in (15cm) ↔to 36in (90cm)

Cordyline australis Purpurea Group

EVERGREEN TREE

The New Zealand cabbage palm is an architectural specimen with narrow, purplish-green leaves. It develops a trunk as it matures and may produce creamy-white summer flowers. It will survive outdoors in mild climates and sheltered urban gardens. Elsewhere, grow it in a container of soil-based potting mix, and move under cover in the winter. Outdoors, grow it in sun or light shade in fertile, well-drained soil, and protect it over the winter in its early years.

☼ ◑ ◊   Z10–11 H11–10
‡to 10ft (3m) ↔to 3ft (1m)

Ophiopogon planiscapus '**Nigrescens**'

PERENNIAL

The black lilyturf is a clump-forming, grasslike perennial with dark purple, almost black leaves. It looks excellent when planted as edging or in pale-colored gravel. It is also suitable for raised beds. In the summer it produces spikes of tiny, bell-shaped, purple-flushed white flowers. Plant it in full sun or partial shade in slightly acid, moist but well-drained soil.

☼ ◑ ◊ ◐   Z6–11 H11–1
‡ to 9in (23cm) ↔ to 12in (30cm)

Phormium tenax **Purpureum Group**

PERENNIAL

New Zealand flax is an evergreen with large, leathery, sword-shaped leaves in a rich copper or deep purple-red hue. In the summer tall, upright, architectural spikes of tubular, dark red flowers arise on plum-purple stems. Grow it as a specimen plant or in a border in full sun and deep, fertile, moisture-retentive soil with shelter from cold, dry winds. In cold, wet areas, provide a deep, dry mulch in the winter. Phormiums do well in coastal gardens.

☼ ◐   Z9–11 H11–2
‡ to 8ft (2.5m) ↔ to 3ft (1m)

Phyllostachys nigra

EVERGREEN BAMBOO

The black bamboo is quite well known for its darkly coloured, upright canes. It forms a gently arching clump, clothed with lance-shaped, dark green leaves. The canes emerge green and gradually turn to black in their second or third years. For the best effect, strip off some of the lower leaves to expose the canes, and occasionally remove a few of the older canes so that they remain nicely spaced. Use as a screen or as a large feature plant.

☼ ◐ ◊ ◖   Z7–11 H12–4

‡ to 25ft (8m) ↔ indefinite

Pittosporum tenuifolium 'Purpureum'

EVERGREEN SHRUB

The kohuhu is an evergreen shrub or small tree with black stems and wavy-edged, leathery, purple leaves. In the late spring it has tiny, scented, dark red, bell-shaped flowers. Plant it in full sun or partial shade in fertile, moist, well-drained soil. The leaf color is most intense in full sun, and the plant should be protected from cold winds. It is a terrific hedge for coastal gardens, and the foliage is used in floral displays. Trim hedges in the spring and early fall.

☼ ◊ ◖ *f*   Z9–11 H11–9

‡ to 30ft (10m) ↔ to 15ft (5m)

Salvia officinalis 'Purpurascens'

EVERGREEN SHRUB

Purple sage forms a shrubby mound of aromatic, red-purple leaves with spikes of purple summer flowers that are very attractive to bees. It can be grown in an herb garden for culinary use, and it is also a useful foliage foil in a sunny border or gravel garden, where it associates well with silver-leaved plants. Grow it in full sun in moderately fertile, light, well-drained soil. Cut it back in the spring and after flowering to keep it shapely.

☼ ◊ *f*　　　　Z4–10 H10–1

‡ to 32in (80cm) ↔ to 3ft (1m)

Sedum spathulifolium 'Purpureum'

EVERGREEN PERENNIAL

This low-growing evergreen forms tight, dense mats of ground-covering foliage, studded with starry yellow flowers in the summer. The rosettes of fleshy, silvery-gray leaves are flushed with purple and covered in a thick, waxy bloom. Grow it in a rock garden, a trough, on top of a drystone wall, or in a raised bed. It grows best in full sun in gritty, very well-drained, poor to moderately fertile soil. It can easily be trimmed back occasionally to restrict its spread.

☼ ◊　　　　Z5–9 H9–5

‡ to 4in (10cm) ↔ to 24in (60cm)

Festuca glauca 'Elijah Blue'

PERENNIAL GRASS

This densely tufted, evergreen grass forms a rounded clump of narrow, blue leaves with matching spikes of flowers in the early summer. It makes a valuable color foil at the front of a border or in a gravel or rock garden. The best effects are achieved by planting it in waves of 3–5 plants. Grow it in full sun in poor to slightly fertile, well-drained, rather dry soil. Divide and replant it every 2–3 years in the spring.

☼ ◊　　　　　　　　　　Z4–8 H8–1
↕ to 12in (30cm) ↔ 10in (25cm)

Juniperus squamata 'Blue Star'

EVERGREEN SHRUB

This low-growing conifer forms dense, compact mounds of sharply pointed, grayish-blue leaves that retain their color throughout the year. The older stems have attractive reddish-brown bark. It is ideal for growing as ground cover on a bank or in a gravel garden and combines well with other dwarf conifers and heathers. Plant it in full sun or dappled shade in fertile, well-drained soil. It seldom needs pruning.

☼ ☀ ◊　　　　　　　　　Z4–9 H9–1
↕ to 16in (40cm) ↔ to 3ft (1m)

Leymus arenarius

PERENNIAL GRASS

This robust, tufted grass forms loose clumps of rather stiff, bright steel blue leaves, adorned in the summer by strong-stemmed heads of blue-gray flowers that age to buff. It spreads rapidly but can be confined in a container. It will develop the best color when grown in full sun in light, well-drained, slightly fertile soil, and it is ideal for creating foliage contrasts in an herbaceous or mixed border. Cut down the faded growth in the spring, and trim back before flowering for improved foliage.

☼ ◊   Z4–10 H10–1

‡ to 5ft (1.5m) ↔ to indefinite

Ruta graveolens 'Jackman's Blue'

EVERGREEN SHRUB

This rounded shrub is grown for its deeply lobed, aromatic, blue-green leaves. In the summer it produces small yellow flowers, but these should be removed before they bloom for the best foliage effect. It will grow well in a sunny location in a gravel garden when planted in moderately fertile, well-drained soil. It can also be grown in an herb garden or in a mixed or herbaceous border. Contact with the sap can cause a severe skin reaction.

☼ ◊ *f*   Z5–9 H9–5

‡↔ to 24in (60cm)

Asplenium scolopendrium

PERENNIAL FERN

The hart's tongue fern has
shuttlecocklike clumps of emerald
green, lance-shaped fronds, which
often have wavy margins. In the
summer rust-colored spore cases are
arranged herringbone-fashion on the
undersides of the fronds. A beautiful
fern for a damp, shady wall, crevice, or
border, it is also suitable for a woodland
garden. Grow it in partial shade in a
moist, preferably alkaline, well-drained
soil. Divide large clumps in the spring.

☼ ◐ ◊ ◖   Z6–8 H8–6
‡ to 30in (75cm) ↔ to 18in (45cm)

Blechnum penna-marina

PERENNIAL FERN

A tough but delicate-looking fern, this
variety has long, slender fronds with
many small, triangular, glossy, dark
green leaflets. It spreads by means of
underground stems and can form large,
extensive colonies in ideal conditions.
It forms good year-round ground cover
in a woodland garden or a damp border,
or plant it in a shady niche by a wall.
Grow it in partial shade in moist, fertile,
slightly acid soil.

☼ ◖   Z10–11 H11–10
‡ to 12in (30cm) ↔ to 18in (45cm)

Buxus sempervirens

EVERGREEN SHRUB

The common box is a slow-growing shrub with small, dark green leaves. It is widely grown as a hedge, planted in pots, or trimmed into balls, pyramids, or other topiary shapes. If left unpruned, it eventually forms a small bushy tree. 'Suffruticosa' is best for dwarf hedges or for edging beds. Box prefers partial shade but will tolerate full sun as long the soil does not dry out. Grow it in moist, well-drained soil; it thrives on alkaline soil or in pots of soil-based potting mix. Trim once a year in the summer.

☀ ◊ ◑   Z6–8 H8–6
↕↔to 15ft (5m)

Chusquea culeou

EVERGREEN BAMBOO

This useful, slow-growing bamboo is less invasive than most and forms a fountain-shaped clump of cylindrical yellowish-green stems with whiskery sheaves of narrow leaves arising at intervals on the stems. Plant it in sun or partial shade in moist but well-drained soil. Grow it in a sheltered site, where it is protected from cold, dry winds, such as in a woodland garden or to disguise a fence. Old canes can be cut out and used for staking other plants.

☀ ☀ ◊ ◑   Z8–11 H11–10
↕ to 15ft (5m) ↔ to 8ft (2.5m)

Cupressus sempervirens

EVERGREEN TREE

The Italian cypress is unmistakable
due to its narrow, pencil-thin shape,
reminiscent of Mediterranean gardens.
Its foliage is made up of dark green
feathery fronds, and it bears attractive
round gray cones, which are a feature
of the genus. It is a valuable evergreen
structural tree, and performs best in a
sheltered location. Slow-growing, it is
tolerant of both dry soils and coastal
conditions and needs no pruning.
'Stricta' is an even narrower variety.
'Swane's Gold' has yellowish foliage.

☼ ◊ ◐   Z7–9 H9–3
‡ to 70ft (20m) ↔ to 5ft (1.5m)

Fargesia nitidia

EVERGREEN BAMBOO

The slow-growing fountain bamboo
develops clumps of erect, purplish-
green canes, topped by narrow, lance-
shaped, dark green leaves. Although it
spreads very slowly, in small gardens
its growth can be restricted by planting
it in a container or cutting back the
rootstock every few years. It makes a
good hedge or screen. Plant this bamboo
in partial or dappled shade in fertile,
moist soil, and protect it from cold,
drying winds.

☼ ◐   Z5–9 H9–5
‡ to 15ft (5m) ↔ to 5ft (1.5m)

Fatsia japonica

EVERGREEN SHRUB

A superb architectural shrub with huge, deeply lobed leaves. In the summer it produces large heads of creamy white flowers. Plant it in full sun or partial shade in fertile, moist but well-drained soil. It is hardy but needs a sheltered location away from cold drying winds, which can damage the large leaves. It also benefits from a deep mulch to give some winter protection in the early years. Tolerant of pollution, it is suitable for urban gardens and can be grown successfully by the coast, too.

☼ ◐ ◊ ◊   Z8–10 H10–8
↕↔to 12ft (4m)

Griselinia littoralis

EVERGREEN SHRUB

This vigorous shrub can become treelike in mild areas but is more often grown as a hedge, valued for its rather leathery, glossy, emerald-green leaves. Plant it in full sunshine in well-drained, fertile soil. Cold, drying winds can damage it in exposed inland gardens, but it makes a good windbreak in mild coastal areas. Clip hedges in the spring.

☼ ◊   Z7–9 H9–7
↕ to 25ft (8m) ↔ to 15ft (5m)

Hebe cupressoides **'Boughton Dome'**

EVERGREEN SHRUB

A compact, dwarf hebe, this variety forms a dense, rounded mound of bright green leaves. Mature plants may produce small spikes of white flowers. It makes a neat specimen that needs no pruning or can be used in a container, rock garden, or raised bed. Plant it in full sun or partial shade in poor to slightly fertile, moist, well-drained, neutral to alkaline soil. It is also tolerant of coastal conditions and salt spray.

☼ ◑ ◊ ◉   Z8–9 H9–8

‡ to 12in (30cm) ↔ to 24in (60cm)

Hedera colchica **'Dentata'**

CLIMBER

This Persian ivy is a vigorous climber or spreader with dark green, heart-shaped leaves that have serrated margins. The leaves are aromatic if crushed or bruised and have purplish stems. Because of its vigorous spread, this ivy is best used on a large wall or as a ground cover in an area where it can be easily contained. Grow in part to full shade in well-drained, organic-rich soil.

☼ ◑ ◊   Z6–11 H12–1

‡ to 30ft (10m) ↔ to 30ft (10m)

Hedera helix 'Erecta'

EVERGREEN SHRUB

'Erecta' is an unusual ivy in that it is a non-climbing form. It is shrublike with stiffly upright, spirelike stems covered in arrow-shaped, dark green leaves. It can be grown in a shrub border or as ground cover between trees and looks especially effective at the foot of tree stumps or boulders. Plant it in fertile, preferably alkaline, moist, well-drained soil in sun or partial shade. It needs very little pruning.

☼ ☀ ◊ ◊   Z5–11 H11–6

‡ to 3ft (1m) ↔ to 4ft (1.2m)

Juniperus communis 'Hibernica'

EVERGREEN SHRUB

This juniper forms a narrow, tapering column of dense, prickly, bluish-green foliage. It will grow happily in most well-drained soils. While many junipers tolerate some degree of shade, 'Hibernica' may become misshapen if not given a sunny location. It is a good choice for formal gardens, but can also be planted as a vertical accent in a large rock garden. It does not need regular pruning or shearing.

☼ ◊   Z2–6 H6–1

‡ to 15ft (5m) ↔ to 12in (30cm)

Juniperus procumbens

EVERGREEN SHRUB

The Bonin Island juniper is a creeping, low-growing conifer that forms a ground-hugging mound of yellowish-green, needlelike leaves. It makes a superb ground-cover plant for a bank or for the edge of a gravel garden or a patio. It associates well with heathers and more upright dwarf conifers and will grow well in full sun or partial shade in any well-drained soil; it thrives in sandy, alkaline, and dry soils. It needs no pruning and should be given space to spread.

☼ ◐ ◊   Z3–9 H9–1

‡ to 30in (75cm) ↔ to 6ft (2m)

Lonicera pileata

EVERGREEN SHRUB

The privet honeysuckle has glossy, dark green, oval- to lance-shaped leaves. In the late spring it produces clusters of creamy-white, funnel-shaped flowers, which are followed by small, violet, translucent berries in summer. Plant it in full sun or partial shade in any well-drained soil. It makes a good ground-cover plant that requires little attention and is suitable for coastal gardens since it tolerates salt spray. In cold winters it may lose some of its leaves.

☼ ◐ ◊   Z5–9 H9–5

‡ to 24in (60cm) ↔ to 8ft (2.5m)

Phyllostachys flexuosa

EVERGREEN BAMBOO

The zigzag bamboo forms clumps of slender, arching canes. The canes are bright green when they emerge, later becoming golden brown and finally almost black as they mature. Grow in a sheltered situation, such as a woodland garden, and plant it in fertile, organic, moist, well-drained soil in sun or dappled shade. In mild areas clumps will grow fast and require cutting back with a sharp spade every 2–3 years.

☼ ◑ ◊ ◊   Z6–11 H11–1

↕ to 25ft (8m) ↔ indefinite

Picea mariana 'Nana'

EVERGREEN SHRUB

This is a slow-growing, dwarf form of black spruce and bears bluish-gray leaves. It forms a neat, rounded bush that is suitable for growing in a gravel or rock garden, on a patio, or with heathers. Plant it in full sun in neutral to slightly acid, moderately fertile, well-drained soil. It occasionally produces vigorous upright shoots, which mar the appearance of the plant. Cut them back to the base as soon as they appear.

☼ ◊   Z2–6 H6–1

 ↔ to 20in (50cm)

Pinus mugo 'Mops'

EVERGREEN SHRUB

A diminutive type of the Japanese dwarf mountain pine, 'Mops' forms a small, almost spherical shrub with upright branches covered in deep green, needlelike leaves. It produces tiny, oval, dark brown cones. Very slow growing, it is suitable for planting in a rock garden or with heathers and other dwarf conifers. Choose a site in full sun with well-drained soil. It requires very little or no pruning.

☼ ◊   Z3–7 H7–1

‡ to 3ft (1m) ↔ to 6ft (2m)

Pittosporum tobira

EVERGREEN SHRUB

The Japanese mock orange forms an upright shrub or small tree that bears leathery, shiny, dark green leaves. In the late spring and early summer it produces clusters of scented, creamy-white flowers. In mild areas, grow it outdoors in a sunny, sheltered site in fertile, moist, well-drained soil, and mulch in the winter with straw. In colder gardens, grow it in a large container of soil-based potting mix, and move it to a cool sun porch or greenhouse over the winter.

☼ ◊ ◐ *f*   Z9–10 H10–9

‡ to 30ft (10m) ↔ to 10ft (3m)

Polystichum setiferum
Divisilobum Group

PERENNIAL FERN

One of the most beautiful of all hardy ferns, this variety forms a spreading, evergreen plant with soft, feathery fronds, divided several times into tiny, pale green leaflets. It will flourish when planted in full or partial shade in fertile, moist but well-drained soil. Grow it in a mixed border underneath shrubs, a dark, shady corner, or in a woodland garden.

◐ ☀ ◊ ◖   Z6–9 H9–6

‡ to 24in (60cm) ↔ to 18in (45cm)

Sasa veitchii

EVERGREEN BAMBOO

This spreading bamboo needs plenty of space. Its purple canes bear dark green leaves during the summer, but later in the year the margins dry out so that they appear variegated. Grow it in fertile, moist, well-drained soil in partial to deep shade; it tolerates sun in reliably moist soil. It is suitable for a woodland garden; elsewhere, to restrict it, plant it in a large bottomless container, plunged in the ground to the rim. Alternatively, chop back clumps with a sharp spade every couple of years.

◐ ☀ ◊ ◖   Z6–11 H11–1

‡ to 5ft (1.5m) ↔ indefinite

Stipa gigantea

PERENNIAL GRASS

Golden oats is a magnificent, evergreen grass that forms dense clumps of very narrow, dark green leaves. In the summer tall, slender but strong stems appear bearing clouds of tiny, glistening, purple-green flowers that age to gleaming gold. They make an attractive feature in the garden over the winter, so wait until early spring to cut them down, along with any dead leaves. Grow as a specimen or as a gauzy screen at the back of a border. Best in full sun in fertile, well-drained soil.

☼ ◊ Z8–11 H11–1

‡ to 8ft (2.5m) ↔ to 3ft (1m)

Taxus baccata

EVERGREEN TREE

The common yew is a large specimen tree but it is also one of the finest species for hedging and topiary. It forms a dense, dark green hedge and impenetrable barrier. Wherever possible, use plants grown from cuttings because seedlings can vary slightly in color. Plant in full sun or partial shade in fertile, moist but well-drained soil. Yew also grows well on alkaline soil. Trim hedges once a year in the late summer; refresh overgrown or misshapen hedges by cutting back hard in the late summer.

☼ ◖ ◊ ◈ Z7–8 H8–7

‡ to 70ft (20m) ↔ to 30ft (10m)

Thuja orientalis 'Aurea Nana'

EVERGREEN SHRUB

This is a dwarf, globe-shaped conifer with upright sprays of yellowish-green leaves that become bronzed in the fall and winter. It is ideal for a raised bed or rock garden, for planting with heathers, and for growing as part of a collection of dwarf conifers. Plant it in full sun in moderately fertile, moist but well-drained soil. It needs little or no pruning.

☼ ◊ ◖   Z6–9 H9–6

↕↔ to 24in (60cm)

Vinca minor

EVERGREEN SHRUB

This scrambling plant has glossy, dark green leaves and violet-blue flowers from spring to fall. A few flowers often appear in the colder months of the year. It makes an excellent ground-cover plant with spreading stems that root wherever they touch the ground—it is, however, fairly easy to control. It grows well in any moderately fertile, well-drained soil in partial or dappled shade, but it flowers most freely in sun. *V. major* is more invasive.

☼ ◊   Z4–9 H9–1

↕ to 8in (20cm) ↔ indefinite

Abies nordmanniana 'Golden Spreader'

EVERGREEN SHRUB

The Nordmann fir is a very large ornamental tree, but 'Golden Spreader' is a dwarf, slow-growing form with spreading branches. The leaves on the inner parts of the plant are green, but those on the tips are bright golden yellow, giving it a very attractive two-tone effect. It is suitable for growing in a rock or gravel garden. Plant in full sun in fertile, moist but well-drained, neutral or acidic soil.

☼ ◊ ◖   Z4–6 H6–4

‡ to 3ft (1m) ↔ to 5ft (1.5m)

Aucuba japonica 'Gold Dust'

EVERGREEN SHRUB

The spotted laurel is a rounded shrub with glossy green leaves variably spotted and splashed with golden yellow. If grown with a male plant, this female plant bears bright red berries in the fall. Aucubas are happy in most soils and tolerant of pollution and salt spray. It prefers partial shade but will tolerate deep shade and grows in any soil, except waterlogged. It can be planted as a hedge, which should be pruned with shears in the spring.

☼ ◊ ◖   Z6–10 H11–6

‡↔ to 10ft (3m)

Buxus sempervirens 'Elegantissima'

EVERGREEN SHRUB

This variegated form of the common box makes a neat, dome-shaped bush that can also be used for hedging and topiary. It grows best in dappled shade but will also tolerate full sun. Grow in any well-drained, fertile soil or as trimmed shapes in pots of soil-based potting mix. Trim hedging in the summer. If older bushes become untidy, they can be rejuvenated by hard pruning in the spring followed by an application of general-purpose fertilizer.

☀ ◐ ◊   Z6–8 H8–6

↕↔ to 5ft (1.5m)

Calluna vulgaris 'Gold Haze'

EVERGREEN SHRUB

There are several forms of Scots heather with golden-yellow foliage. 'Gold Haze' retains its brilliant color all year and in the summer produces long spikes of pure white flowers. 'Ruth Sparkes' is more compact with double white flowers. The golden leaves of 'Spitfire' turn red during the winter. All three are useful ground-cover plants. Plant in full sun in acid, moist but well-drained, fertile soil. Cut back in the spring to keep compact and bushy.

☀ ◊ ◖   Z5–7 H7–5

↕ to 18in (45cm) ↔ to 24in (60cm)

Carex oshimensis 'Evergold'

PERENNIAL

This sedge forms tufts of narrow, arching, brightly variegated leaves. The leaves are dark green with a central stripe of rich golden yellow. In mid- to late spring it also produces spikes of dark brown flowers. Plant it in full sun or partial shade in fertile, moist but well-drained soil, although it tolerates dry conditions. It looks very good in containers, near water, and toward the front of a mixed or herbaceous border.

☼ ◑ ◊ ◊　　　　　　　　Z6–9 H9–6
‡↔to 8in (20cm)

Chamaecyparis obtusa 'Crippsii'

EVERGREEN TREE

A slow-growing form of the Hinoki cypress, this lovely specimen tree forms a broad column. The rich golden-yellow color of its leaves is most strongly emphasized if it is planted against a background of darker foliage, such as a yew hedge. Plant it in full sun in fertile, moist but well-drained, neutral or slightly acid soil. It will also grow on deep alkaline soil. Pruning is unnecessary.

☼ ◊ ◊　　　　　　　　　Z4–8 H8–1
‡ to 50ft (15m) ↔to 25ft (8m)

Chamaecyparis pisifera 'Sungold'

EVERGREEN TREE

A form of Sawara cypress, this irregularly conical conifer has tiers of slightly drooping, threadlike, golden-yellow shoots. There are several other cultivars with golden-yellow foliage, but they tend to be scorched by cold winds and strong sunshine. Plant 'Sungold' in fertile, moist but well-drained, neutral to slightly acid soil. A pretty specimen tree, it looks its best when planted against the dark background of an evergreen hedge, such as yew.

☼ ☀ ◊ ◖   Z4–8 H8–1

‡ to 40ft (12m) ↔ to 15ft (5m)

Choisya ternata
SUNDANCE ('Lich')

EVERGREEN SHRUB

With its bright yellow leaves divided into three leaflets, SUNDANCE is one of the most dramatic evergreen shrubs for a mixed or shrub border. The color is more vibrant if it is planted in full sun because the leaves become yellowish green in the shade. Plant in well-drained, fertile soil and provide shelter from cold, drying winds—against a warm wall is ideal.

☼ ◊   Z8–10 H10–8

‡↔ to 8ft (2.5m)

Cordyline australis 'Torbay Dazzler'

EVERGREEN TREE

A decorative type of New Zealand cabbage palm, 'Torbay Dazzler' develops a slender trunk that bears a large cluster of creamy-white, variegated, sword-shaped leaves. In the summer it may produce creamy-white flowers. Plant it in fertile, well-drained soil in full sun or partial shade. Dry mulch for winter protection in its early years. In cold areas it is better grown as a container plant and overwintered in a frost-free sunroom or greenhouse.

☼ ◑ ◊   Z10–11 H11–10

↕ to 10ft (3m) ↔ to 3ft (1m)

Cryptomeria japonica 'Sekkan-sugi'

EVERGREEN SHRUB

This is a slow-growing type of Japanese cedar with creamy-yellow foliage that turns almost white in the winter. It is best planted in partial shade because the pale foliage is easily scorched in strong sunshine. Plant it in fertile, moist but well-drained soil. It is best planted as a specimen tree. Unusual for a conifer, if it is cut back hard it will sprout again, so it can be safely pruned if it outgrows its allotted space.

☼ ◊ ◔   Z6–9 H9–4

↕ to 25ft (8m) ↔ to 15ft (5m)

Cupressus macrocarpa 'Goldcrest'

EVERGREEN TREE

'Goldcrest' is a striking conifer that forms a narrow, column-shaped tree with bright golden-yellow leaves. Suitable for a coastal garden, plant it in full sun in any well-drained soil. Although it is fully hardy, in its early years it needs protection from severe frost. It also needs shelter from cold, drying winds, which may scorch the foliage. It makes an attractive hedge that needs only gentle trimming in the late summer—be careful not to cut back into old wood.

☼ ◊   Z7–11 H11–7

↕ to 15ft (5m) ↔ to 8ft (2.5m)

Elaeagnus pungens 'Maculata'

EVERGREEN SHRUB

This vigorous shrub has dark green, glossy, leathery leaves with a bold, central yellow blotch. In the fall it bears clusters of small white flowers. Remove any shoots that revert to plain green as soon as they appear, and in the spring trim any stray stems that spoil the shape of the plant. Suitable for hedging, it is also tolerant of coastal conditions. If grown as a hedge, trim it in the summer. Plant it in full sun or partial shade in fairly fertile, well-drained soil.

☼ ◗ ◊   Z7–9 H9–7

↕ to 12ft (4m) ↔ to 15ft (5m)

Erica carnea 'Foxhollow'

EVERGREEN SHRUB

Some heaths have especially attractive foliage, such as 'Foxhollow', which is yellow-green and has bronze-tipped young shoots. In cold winters its leaves are infused with shades of pinkish-orange and red. In the late winter and early spring it bears purple-pink flowers. Plant in full sun in moist but well-drained, fertile, acid soil. It will also tolerate slightly alkaline soil. A lovely ground-cover plant, give it a light clipping after flowering to keep it neat.

☼ ◊ ◓   Z5–7 H7–5

‡ to 6in (15cm) ↔ to 16in (40cm)

Euonymus fortunei 'Emerald 'n' Gold'

EVERGREEN SHRUB

This robust and easily grown bushy shrub has glossy green leaves with bright yellow margins; during the cold winter months they take on pinkish tints. It grows in any soil, except waterlogged, and while it will tolerate shade, the leaf color is richer and stronger in full sun. An excellent ground-cover plant, it can also be grown in containers, or as a low hedge needing only a light trim in the summer to keep it in shape.

☼ ◊ ◓   Z5–9 H9–2

‡ to 24in (60cm) ↔ to 36in (90cm)

Hebe ochracea 'James Stirling'

EVERGREEN SHRUB

The tiny, scalelike leaves of the whipcord hebe give it the appearance of a dwarf conifer. The rich, ochre-yellow leaves look particularly attractive in the winter. In the late spring and early summer it bears clusters of small white flowers. Plant it in a raised bed or in a rock garden in full sun or partial shade in moderately fertile, moist but well-drained soil. It is a tough shrub that is ideally suited to the conditions in a coastal garden.

☀ ◑ ◊ ◊   Z8–10 H10–8
‡ to 18in (45cm) ↔ to 24in (60cm)

Hedera colchica 'Sulphur Heart'

CLIMBER

Persian ivy is a vigorous, self-clinging climber with large, glossy, evergreen leaves that are marked with a central blotch of soft sulfur yellow. It provides excellent, fast-growing cover for a shady wall and can also be used as a ground-cover plant. Grow it in full sun or partial shade in fertile, moist but well-drained, preferably alkaline soil. It develops the most intense leaf color in a sunny location. Cut back at any time of year if necessary.

☀ ◑ ◊ ◊   Z6–11 H11–1
‡ to 15ft (5m)

Hedera helix 'Buttercup'

CLIMBER

An extremely attractive form of the common ivy, this self-clinging evergreen climber has large, lobed, bright butter-yellow leaves. In full sun the leaves really color up, while in shade they are a pale green. This makes for some interesting color effects since the leaves overlap each other. Grow in fertile, moist but well-drained, preferably alkaline soil. An excellent wall plant, trim it back at any time of year if it exceeds its allotted space.

☼ ☀ ◑ ◐   Z5–11 H11–6
↕ to 6ft (2m)

Ilex aquifolium 'Golden Milkboy'

EVERGREEN TREE

A dense, upright tree, this striking holly makes a fine specimen or hedge. Its spiny, dark green leaves have irregular, golden-yellow markings in the center. 'Golden Milkboy' is a male plant and does not produce berries, but it makes a good pollinator for female, berrying hollies. Plant in full sun or partial shade in fertile, moist but well-drained soil. For best leaf color, plant in full sun. Trim hedges in the summer.

☼ ☀ ◑ ◐   Z7–9 H9–7
↕ to 20ft (6m) ↔ to 12ft (4m)

Osmanthus heterophyllus 'Aureomarginatus'

EVERGREEN SHRUB

This plant has spiny, toothed leaves that resemble those on a holly bush, and in mild areas it makes a good hedging plant. 'Aureomarginatus' has glossy, bright green, mottled foliage edged in golden-yellow. In the late summer it bears small clusters of highly fragrant, small, white, tubular flowers. It is not totally hardy and should be grown in full sun or partial shade in a sheltered location and planted in fertile, well-drained soil.

☼ ◐ ◊ *f*   Z7–9 H9–7
↕↔ to 15ft (5m)

Phormium 'Yellow Wave'

PERENNIAL

The arching, sword-shaped leaves of this large, clump-forming evergreen make a bold focal point. They are a vibrant yellow-green with a broad, central green stripe. In the summer tall spikes of red-purple flowers may appear. Plant in full sun in moist but well-drained, fertile soil. During the winter in colder areas, protect the crown by covering with a thick layer of dry mulch among the leaves. Use as a specimen plant or in a mixed border. Suitable for coastal gardens.

☼ ◊ ◐   Z9–10 H10–3
↕ to 10ft (3m) ↔ to 6ft (2m)

Pinus sylvestris 'Gold Coin'

EVERGREEN SHRUB

A diminutive, slow-growing version of the Scots pine, this dwarf conifer has greenish-yellow, needlelike leaves that turn an intense shade of golden yellow in winter. A small rounded shrub, it is a good choice for an urban garden where space is limited; it is also ideally suited to a rock or gravel garden. Plant it in full sun in any moderately fertile, well-drained soil. It needs no pruning.

☼ ◊   Z3–7 H7–1
‡↔ to 6ft (2m)

Pittosporum tenuifolium 'Abbotsbury Gold'

EVERGREEN SHRUB

This kohuhu is valued for its green-margined, golden leaves. A bushy shrub or small tree, it is suitable for smaller gardens where it will thrive against a sunny wall. It can also be used for hedging, especially in coastal gardens, needing a trim only once in the spring to keep it in shape. Grow in fertile, moist but well-drained soil. Provide shelter from cold, drying winds; in areas where winters are severe, grow in containers and bring in under cover.

☼ ☀ ◊ ◌   Z9–11 H11–9
‡ to 10ft (3m) ↔ to 5ft (1.5m)

Pittosporum tenuifolium 'Irene Patterson'

EVERGREEN SHRUB

The emergent spring foliage of this attractive shrub is cream, gradually becoming marbled with dark green. Slow-growing and mound-forming, it makes an attractive specimen, but it is also suitable as a hedging plant, especially in wild and coastal gardens. Trim to shape in the spring. Plant in moist but well-drained, fertile soil in full sun or partial shade. Protect from cold, drying winds, and mulch young plants over the winter.

☼ ☼ ◊ ◐　　　　　　Z9–11 H11–9
↕ to 4ft (1.2m) ↔ to 24in (60cm)

Thuja plicata 'Stoneham Gold'

EVERGREEN SHRUB

A small, cone-shaped bush, this is a dwarf form of the Western red cedar. The irregularly arranged sprays of foliage are coppery bronze, becoming golden yellow and then green as it ages. It is slow-growing and makes a good plant for a rock garden. Plant in moist but well-drained, fertile soil in full sun. It needs to be protected from cold, drying winds to avoid foliage scorch, especially in its early years.

☼ ◊ ◐　　　　　　Z6–8 H8–6
 ↕↔ to 6ft (2m)

INDEX

PICTURE CREDITS

The publisher would like to thank the following for their kind permission to reproduce their photographs: (Key: a-above; b-below t-top)

17 Dorling Kindersley: Andrew Butler (b). **20 GAP Photos:** John Glover (b). **34 Dorling Kindersley:** Juliette Wade (t). **37 GAP Photos:** Martin Hughes-Jones (b). **39 Garden and Wildlife Matters Photo Library:** (b). **42 A-Z Botanical Collection:** Andrew Ackerley (b); Adrian Thomas (t). **43 Garden Picture Library:** Sunniva Harte (b). **56 Caroline Reed:** (t). **58 Garden Picture Library:** Brian Carter (b). **68 Garden World Images:** Trevor Sims (b). **106 Garden Picture Library:** Jacqui Hurst (b). **107 Martin Page:** (t). **109 James Young:** (t). **110 Garden and Wildlife Matters Photo Library:** (t). **118 Garden Picture Library:** Sunniva Harte (b). **119 Photolibrary:** Garden Picture Library / Michael Howes (t). **122 GAP Photos:** Neil Holmes (t). **123 Photolibrary:** Garden Picture Library / Jerry Pavia (b). **124 A-Z Botanical Collection:** Adrian Thomas (t). **125 Andrew Lawson:** (b). **127 Photos Horticultural:** (b). **128 GAP Photos:** Howard Rice (b). **130 Garden Picture Library:** Jacqui Hurst (t). **136 GAP Photos:** Martin Hughes-Jones (t). **140 The Garden Collection:** Torie Chugg (t). **143 A-Z Botanical Collection:** Jack Coulthard (t). **149 Garden World Images:** (t). **154 Marianne Majerus Garden Images:** MMGI (t). **160 Photolibrary:** JS. Sira (t). **162 Garden World Images:** (t). **164 GAP Photos:** Martin Hughes-Jones (t). **165 Garden Picture Library:** Christopher Fairweather (t). **166 Dorling Kindersley:** Andrew Butler (t). **167 GAP Photos:** Rob Whitworth (b). **168 Dorling Kindersley:** Juliette Wade (t). **173 GAP Photos:** Julie Dansereau / RHS Wisley (t). **174 Martin Page:** (b). **176 GAP Photos:** Martin Hughes-Jones (b). **187 Garden World Images:** Trevor Sims (t). **192 Martin Page:** (b). **194 Dorling Kindersley:** Roger Smith (b). **Photos Horticultural:** (t). **196 Dorling Kindersley:** Roger Smith (b). **199 Garden World Images:** (b). **Marianne Majerus Garden Images:** MMGI (t). **200 Photos Horticultural:** (b). **202 Garden World Images:** Trevor Sims (b). **204 GAP Photos:** Howard Rice (b). **205 Garden World Images:** Martin Hughes-Jones (b). **Eric Crichton Photos:** (t). **207 GAP Photos:** FhF Greenmedia (t).

ACKNOWLEDGMENTS

FIRST EDITION
Project editor: Helen Fewster
Art editor: Ann Thompson
Project art editor: Alison Donovan
Managing editor: Anna Kruger
Managing art editor: Lee Griffiths
DTP design: Louise Waller
Production: Mandy Inness
Picture research: Samantha Nunn
Picture library: Richard Dabb,
Lucy Claxton, Charlotte Oster
Index: Michèle Clarke

NEW EDITION 2011
Editors Caroline Reed, Becky
Shackleton
Editorial assistance: Rukmini Chawla
Kumar, Eva Young, Neha Pande,
Archana Ramachandran, Neha
Samuel, Suefa Lee
DTP Assistance: Tarun Sharma
Picture research: Rob Nunn
Picture library: Lucy Claxton

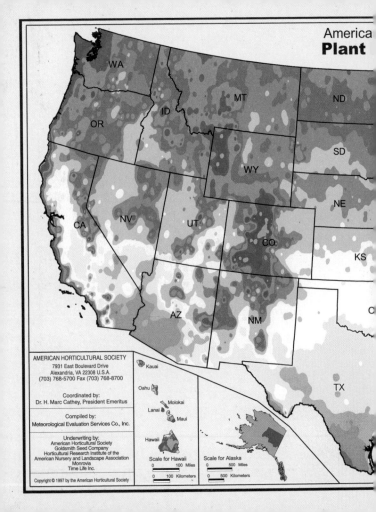

America
Plant

WA

OR

ID

MT

ND

SD

WY

NE

CA

NV

UT

CO

KS

AZ

NM

O

TX

AMERICAN HORTICULTURAL SOCIETY
7931 East Boulevard Drive
Alexandria, VA 22308 U.S.A.
(703) 768-5700 Fax (703) 768-8700

Coordinated by:
Dr. H. Marc Cathey, President Emeritus

Compiled by:
Meteorological Evaluation Services Co., Inc.

Underwriting by:
American Horticultural Society
Goldsmith Seed Company
Horticultural Research Institute of the
American Nursery and Landscape Association
Monrovia
Time Life Inc.

Copyright © 1997 by the American Horticultural Society

Kauai

Oahu

Molokai

Lanai   Maui

Hawaii

Scale for Hawaii
0   100 Miles

0   100 Kilometers

Scale for Alaska
0   500 Miles

0   500 Kilometers